The
HIGHLY SELECTIVE
THESAURUS
and
DICTIONARY
for the
EXTRAORDINARILY
LITERATE

Also by Eugene Ehrlich

Amo, Amas, Amat and More

The International Thesaurus of Quotations (with Marshall DeBruhl)

The Harper Dictionary of Foreign Terms, 3rd Edition

Veni, Vidi, Vici

Mene, Mene, Tekel (with David H. Scott)

The NBC Handbook of Pronunciation (with Raymond Hand, Jr.)

Superwordpower

Funk & Wagnalls Standard Dictionary, 2nd Edition

Oxford American Dictionary

The
HIGHLY SELECTIVE
THESAURUS
and
DICTIONARY
for the
EXTRAORDINARILY
LITERATE

EUGENE EHRLICH

Quality Paperback Book Club
New York

This edition was especially created in 2006 for Quality Paperback Book Club by arrangement with HarperCollins Publishers, Inc.

ISBN: 1-58288-212-6

Printed in the United States of America

The
HIGHLY SELECTIVE
THESAURUS
for the
EXTRAORDINARILY
LITERATE

Introduction by
Noah Adams

To my dear wife, Norma, who helped directly in the compilation of this book and continues to give unstinting support and wise counsel.

CONTENTS

ACKNOWLEDGMENTS

I wish to acknowledge my debt to my two brothers. All three of us attended the College of the City of New York and benefited from our undergraduate work at what was in our time a tuition-free institution. Leonard, Class of 1934, went on to serve generations of children as a wise and kind pediatrician until the day of his death in 1992. Albert, Class of 1938, went on to study law and to this day maintains his practice of law in New York City, putting to good use his gift for language, especially a fluency in Spanish, which he first studied in the public schools and continued to study at college.

Beyond an abiding interest in language, we shared the deep love of brothers. For this I will always be grateful.

PREFACE

When I was a City College freshman, voice as yet unchanged, I made the mistake of registering for a senior-level course in American literature. Imagine my consternation when I found myself the lone boy sitting in an enormous lecture hall with 299 other seats filled by *men*. Professor William Bradley Otis, a mythic figure to generations of CCNY students who saw Faulkner and Hemingway as their true heroes, was our lecturer.

Doc Otis tried to be nice. Whenever he noticed me he would ask, "How are you today, sonny?" Everyone else would guffaw.

I never missed a class and was rewarded by learning an important lesson, one that had nothing to do with American literature. It couldn't have been otherwise. Doc Otis never even mentioned literature during the entire term.

What I learned from Otis was the secret of success in the adult world.

It happened this way. One day, during one of the fifteen-week, three times a week digressions that constituted his enormously popular lectures, Otis used the word *indigenous*, whereupon a student sitting near me called out, "Doc, what does *indigenous* mean?"

"You don't know? I can't believe it," said Otis.

"Jack," he said, pointing to a burly student to his left, "Tell this ignorant basketball player what *indigenous* means."

The reply came back immediately: *Autochthonous*.
And Otis went on with the story he was telling.

As for me, I heard not a single word more from then
until the bell rang for the end of the lecture and I had to
run off to another class. But that brief exchange proved
more meaningful to me than any of the hundreds of literary
works I read as an English major.

It gave me one of the secrets of life—never say
indigenous when you can say *autochthonous*.

At home that fateful night, with the help of our family
dictionary, I launched a collection of uncommon
words I felt impelled to learn. My collection grew
rapidly and has never stopped growing.

I realized that I preferred to *expatiate* rather than
talk, that I engaged in *colloquies* not *discussions*, that I
partook of collations rather than *ate meals*, that I could
be *brusque* and *churlish* rather than *gruff*, and that I
preferred to *deprecate* rather than *deride*.

Of course, I rarely indulged in such lofty locutions.
In my old neighborhood—adjacent to the area in which
the play *Dead End* was set—no one got away with
speaking this way, and my college instructors for better
reasons immediately blue-penciled pretentiousness.

Nevertheless, when we wish to characterize people
who hate to part with a dollar, we can do more than call
them *stingy*. How about *avaricious, cheese-paring,
chinchy, hardfisted, ironfisted, manini, mingy, niggardly,
parsimonious,* and *penurious*? Nothing like having a
choice.

Many writers and students consider a dictionary
and a thesaurus essential elements of their reference
shelves. The dictionary enables us to make certain we
are using words precisely. The thesaurus, truly a treasury of words, has another function, and one that is
equally vital. It stands ready when we know there's a
better word to use in a sentence we are writing but cannot bring it to mind.

My goal in preparing this work for those who

already know more words than they need to know was
to help them jog their memories when they are search-
ing for a special word. I hope that readers who find
words here they do not already know will avoid embarrassment by checking such words in their dictionaries
before putting them to use.

I found it useful to arrange the terms under the relatively common headwords, arranged alphabetically, that
readers will have in mind when turning to *The Highly
Selective Thesaurus for the Extraordinarily Literate.*
Occasionally, I thought it helpful to supply some terms
under more than a single headword. For this I make no
apology.

I hope my readers will find this book useful and that
many of them will suggest additional terms for future
editions.

Eugene Ehrlich
February 1994

INTRODUCTION

The best words bounce and splash, dance and sparkle. They pucker our mouths, rumble our vocal chords and moisten our eyes. But above all, they satisfy. The correct word slips into its place in a sentence with a solid "ker-chunk," much like the sound the final stone makes when it is placed in a farmer's fence. I know that many of the writers I've admired and interviewed would have made good stonemasons.

John McPhee of *The New Yorker* has an especially good eye. As he explains, you don't look for the showy, recondite words, but you come to a place in a sentence where only the right word will do.

Many years ago, as a *Time* obituary writer, he demonstrated this theory ably when he concluded that a man who had committed suicide by jumping out of a window had died of *defenestration*. In his Princeton, N.J. office, McPhee keeps several dictionaries at hand to aid him in his search for "the right word." Sometimes, he turns to his "big one," the *OED*, such as when he needed a word meaning neat and secure. He found it. *Trig*.

A playwright once told me that he refused to fit his work into some "Procrustean bed," in order to satisfy his critics. I pretended to know the word but as soon as the interview was over, I hurried out of the studio to look it up: "Named after Procrustes, a robber in Greek legend, who fitted victims to his bed by stretching them or lopping bits off."

And then there was the retired coal miner in Virginia I once interviewed who reintroduced me to a word I took delight in. He told me that an ongoing United Mine Workers strike had him all "bumfuzzled." His ancestors, back in the Borders region of England and Scotland, used the same word when they were confused.

I once—by accident—made up a word that I admired. I was writing about a hornet's nest outside of my house, which I described as being "about the size of a basketball, the color of dry leaves, *sworls* of browns and grays and yellows." When I presented the piece to my editor, the response was: "No such word. Let's change it to *whorls*." And so we did, but to me, *sworls* still sounds useful as a word which exists in between *swirl* and *whorl*.

Over the years, we've had several "new word" contests on "All Things Considered," when we ask our listeners to help us fill some odd lexicographical gap. Our most successful endeavor brought us *osmyrrah*. I had noticed, in writing about Martha's Vineyard, trying to describe the early morning smell of the sea and the wild roses, that there isn't a word that means "a mingling of pleasant aromas." I mentioned this on the air and two hundred listeners sent in their ideas. We chose *osmyrrah*—it's from the Greek *osmee*, "to smell," and *smurna*, "to mingle with."

Our winning neologist, Thomas Cowdry of Tucson, Arizona, even imagined how John Milton could have used such a word in *Paradise Lost*: "Trapped so long beneath the surface in darkness thick with sulphur fumes he winced at the brightness as they brought him forth and gasped in the *osmyrrah* of the living earth." (Milton, in a similar passage, was stuck with *smell*.)

Eugene Ehrlich has been the official judge for the "All Things Considered" word searches and he's hon-

ored the task with enthusiasm and humor. I've always
suspected, too, that he likes the treasure-hunting aspect
of reading through hundreds of entries: to use a word
from *The Highly Selective Thesaurus*, he would find the
boxes of mail we send him *diamantiferous*.

There are certainly acres of diamonds in this thesaurus. And it's a pleasant search; don't worry about the
long (*sesquipedalian*) words, don't fret that you'll be
accused of ornamental (*churrigueresque*) usage, or of
being abstract (*noetic*) or mysterious (*sibylline*). Such
discouragement could only come from a *Pecksniff* (*person, hypocritically virtuous*).

The proper words are collected here—the ones that
can fill the empty spaces in our sentences. But once
we've built the stone fence, we can leap over it and
romp through the fields because the playful words are
waiting for us on the other side: *spillkin* and *wambly,
callathump, flittermouse, flubdub, funambulist, zugzwang*. . .

Enjoy.

Noah Adams
Host, "All Things Considered"
National Public Radio

A

abacus *n.* soroban
abandoned *adj.* cade, derelict, profligate
abate *v.* mitigate, palliate, quash
abdicate *v.* abjure, abnegate, demit
abject *adj.* craven, fawning, ignominious
able *adj.* habile
abnormal *adj.* heteroclite, preternatural
abnormality *n.* deuteropathy
abolish *v.* disestablish, extirpate
abominable *adj.* flagitious, odious
Abominable Snowman yeti
aborigine *n.* autochthon, indige-
    nous inhabitant
abound *v.* exuberate
abridge *v.* attenuate,
    epitomize
abscond *v.* decamp
absent-minded *adj.*
    distrait, distraite
absinth *n.* worm-
    wood
absolute *adj.* **1.** rank, unmitigated; **2.** assoluta, inviolable,
    peremptory
absolution, grant shrive
absorbent *adj.* bibulous
absorption *n.* immersion, prepossession
abstain *v.* eschew, forbear
abstention *n.* abstemiousness
abstract *adj.* noetic
abstract *n.* compendium, epitome
abstract *v.* prescind
abstruse *adj.* involuted, recondite
absurdity *n.* bêtise

abundance *n.* cornucopia, plenitude, profligacy
abuse *v.* calumniate, castigate, rail, revile, traduce
abuse *n.* aspersion, billingsgate, calumniation, castigation, obloquy, opprobrium, traducement
academic *adj.* moot
accept *v.* stomach
accessible *adj.* pervious
accessory *n.* ancillary, appurtenance, parergon
accident *n.* allision, fortuity
accidental *adj.* adventitious, aleatory, fortuitous, serendipitous
acclaim *n.* éclat, kudos
accomplish *v.* compass, effectuate
accomplished *adj.* compleat, consummate
accomplishments *n.* res gestae
account *n.* hexaemeron
accrue *v.* redound
accumulation *n.* alimentation, hypertrophy
accusation *n.* gravamen, impeachment
accuse *v.* impeach, implead, inculpate, recriminate
accusing *adj.* accusatory, criminative
accustom *v.* acculturate, inure, wont
achievement *n.* capstone, tour de force
acknowledge *v.* avouch, homologate
acme *n.* apogee, *ne plus ultra*
acquiescence *n.* complaisance
acquit *v.* exculpate
acronym *n.* initialism
active *adj.* volitant
actor *n.* deuteragonist, onnagata, protagonist
actress *n.* ingénue, soubrette
actual *adj.* veridical
actuality *n.* entelechy
adage *n.* aphorism, apothegm
adapt *v.* indigenize, quadrate
adaptation *n.* rifacimento
added *adj.* postiche
addition *n.* **1.** additament, adjunct, appendicle; **2.** parogoge
additional *adj.* adscititious
address *n.* allocution, apostrophe, salutatory
address *v.* apostrophize
adherent *n.* ideologue, précisian
adhesive *adj.* viscid, viscoid, viscose
adjacent *adj.* limitrophe, vicinal
adjunct *n.* appanage
adjust *v.* collimate
administer *v.* adhibit

admirer *n.* votary
admit *v.* intromit
adoring *adj.* idolatrous, seraphic
adorn *v.* bedizen, emmarble, titivate
adornment *n.* frippery, garniture
adulation *n.* blandishment, fulsomeness, sycophancy
adulterated *adj.* adulterine
adulterer *n.* Ischys
adultery *n.* cuckoldry, fornication
advance *n.* anabasis
Advent *n.* Parousia
adventure *n.* emprise
adventurer *n.* filibuster, landloper
adviser *n.* consigliere, consultor
advisory *adj.* exhortatory, hortative, hortatory
advocate *n.* paladin, paraclete
affected *adj.* minikin, missish, niminy-piminy, précieuse, précieux,
   recherché
affected speech euphuism, periphrasis
affecting *adj.* connotative, emotive
affection *n.* corazón, dotage, predilection
affirm *v.* asseverate, predicate
affix *v.* adhibit
affront *n.* lèse majesté, lese majesty
afraid *adj.* disquieted, fearsome, pavid
afresh *adv. de nouveau, de novo*
after a death *post obitum*
after a meal postprandial
after a war postbellum
aftereffect *n.* sequela
afterlife *n.* futurity
aftermath *n.* rowen
after the fact ex post facto, post factum
after the Fall postlapsarian
after the Flood postdiluvian
agent *n.* comprador, éminence grise
agile *adj.* lissome, yare
agility *n.* alacrity, celerity, legerity
aging *adj.* senescent
agitate *v.* commove, discompose
agitated *adj.* corybantic, overwrought
agitator *n.* agent provocateur, incendiarist
agnosticism *n.* nescience
agrarian *adj.* agrestic, predial
agreeable *adj.* complaisant, consensual, consonant, conversable,
   ingratiating, sapid, sipid

aggressive *adj.* assaultive, officious
agricultural *adj.* geoponic, georgic
aide *n.* coadjutant
aimlessness *n.* circuity, fecklessness
air, stale fug
air hole spiracle
airs *n.* flubdub, hauteur, superciliousness
airy *adj.* ethereal, illusory
akin *adj.* cognate, consanguineous
alarm *n.* tocsin
alarmist *n.* Jeremiah
alchemist *n.* Paracelsus
alcoholic *n.* dipsomaniac, inebriate
alcove *n.* carrel, inglenook
alibi, person providing an compurgator
alien *n.* metic
alien *adj.* heterochthonous, peregrine
alignment *n.* syzygy
allegiance *n.* fealty
allied *adj.* connate, federate
alligator *n.* caiman
alluring *adj.* sirenic, toothsome
almond-shaped *adj.* amygdaline, amygdaloid
alms *n.* maundy money
aloofness *n.* froideur
alphabet *n.* christcross-row, Glagolitic, ogham
altar boy acolyte
altar cloth pall, pallium
alter *v.* bushel, jigger, sophisticate
altogether *adv.* holus-bolus
amalgamate *v.* commingle, conjoin
amalgamation *n.* conflation
ambassador *n.* chiaus, internuncio, nuncio, plenipotentiary
ambiguity, remove disambiguate
ambiguous *adj.* Delphic, equivocal, oracular
ambitious person arriviste
ambulance chasing barratry
ambush *n./v.* ambuscade
amenities *n.* suavities
amiss *adj.* catawampus, cock-a-hoop
amity *n.* comity
among other things *inter alia*
amount *n.* quantum, scantling, spate
amplify *v.* dilate, expatiate
amuse *v.* beguile, disport
amusing *adj.* amusive, divertive

anagram *n.* logogriph
analysis *n.* explication de texte
analyze *v.* anatomize, construe, explicate, parse
ancestor *n.* primogenitor, progenitor
anchor *n.* drogue, killich
ancient *adj.* centuried, grizzled, primeval
andiron *n.* firedog
anecdote *n.* exemplar
anemic *adj.* exsanguine
angelic *adj.* beatific, cherubic, seraphic
anger *n.* choler, dander, irascibility, petulance, rancor
angled *adj.* angulate
angry *adj.* choleric, churlish, crabbed, fractious, shirty, snappish, wroth
anguish *n.* angst, calvary, katzenjammer
animal, castrated spado
animal, wild wilding
animating *adj.* proceleusmatic
anklebone *n.* talus
annex *v.* mediatize
annihilation *n.* ecocide
annointing *n.* inunction
annotation *n.* scholium
announcement *n.* annunciation, rescript
announcing *adj.* internuncial
annoy *v.* importune, nettle, roil
annoyable *adj.* nettlesome
annoying *adj.* importunate, rebarbative
annually, occurring etesian
annuity scheme tontine
annulment *n.* obrogation, rescission
anonymous *adj.* innominate
answer *n.* rescript, riposte
ant *n.* dinergate, ergate, pismire
antagonistic *adj.* oppugnant
anthology *n.* florilegium
antic *n.* dido
anticipation *n.* prelusion, prolepsis
anticipatory *adj.* prevenient
anticlimax *n.* bathos, insipidity
antidote *n.* mithridate
anti-flatulent *n.* carminative
antiperspirant *n.* antisudorific
antiquated *adj.* antediluvian, superannuated
antisocial *adj.* misanthropic
ant nest formicarium, formicary

anus *n.* fundament
anvil *n.* bick-iron, stithy
anxiety *n.* angst, swivet
apartment *n.* diaconicon, oecus, pied-à-terre, sacristy
apathy *n.* acedia, torpor
apelike *adj.* pithecoid
aphorism *n.* gnome
aphorisms, collection of sutra
aphorist *n.* gnomist
apologetic *adj.* deprecatory
apostate *n.* recreant
apparent *adj.* ostensive, patent, prima facie, semblable
apparition *n.* chimera, fetch, phantasm, wraith
appeal *n.* adjuration, conjuration, démarche, suppliance
appearance *n.* guise, facies, mien, superficies
appease *v.* assuage, dulcify, propitiate
appendix *n.* allonge
appetite *n.* appetence, edacity
appetite, lack of inappetence
applause *n.* acclamation, éclat, plaudit
apples, pertaining to pomaceous
application *n.* **1.** praxis; **2.** assiduity
apportion *v.* admeasure
apprehensive *adj.* trepid, trepidant
apprenticed *adj.* articled, bound
appropriate *adj.* apposite, condign, idoneous, meet
appropriate *v.* arrogate, sequestrate
approve *v.* approbate, homologate
approving *adj.* approbative
aptitude *n.* acumen, forte, predilection, proclivity
Arab quarter medina
arbitration *n.* arbitrament
arboreal *adj.* dendrophilous
arcade *n.* lesche
arcane *adj.* recherché, recondite
arched *adj.* arcuate, embowed
archer *n.* toxophilite
archivist *n.* chartophylax, chartulary
area, public palestra
argue *v.* expostulate, remonstrate
argument *n.* argy-bargy, contretemps, elenchus, polemic, quodlibet, sorites, syllogism
argument, fallacious paralogism, philosophism, sophism
argumentation *n.* choplogic, dialectic, pilpul
aristocracy *n.* patriciate
aristocrat *n.* effendi, eupatrid, Junker

arm, of the brachial
armor, suit of panoply
armpit *n.* axilla, oxter
aromatic *adj.* odoriferous, redolent
around *adv.* circumferentially
around, walk circumambulate
arouse *v.* inspirit, titillate
arrange *v.* collocate, concert, concinnate
arranged in series polystichous
array *n.* panoply
arrogance *n.* contumely, hauteur, hubris
arrogant *adj.* fastuous
arrow-maker *n.* fletcher
article, introductory prolusion
artificial *adj.* delusory, ersatz, factitious, faux, postiche
artisan *n.* artificer
as *adv.* qua
ascent *n.* acclivity
ascertainment *n.* constatation
ascetic *n.* dervish, Euchite, fakir, Khylist, Nirmalin, sadhu, sannyasi, stylite
asexual *adj.* agamic, agamous
ash *n.* pozzolana
ashen *adj.* cinereous, pallid
ask *v.* adjure, impetrate
askew *adj./adv.* catawampus, cock-a-hoop
aspersion *n.* animadversion, calumniation
assailable *adj.* pregnable
assassin *n.* ninja
assembly *n.* agora, coven, ecclesia, gemot, ingathering, levee, synaxis, synod
assertion *n.* asseveration, contestation, predication
assimilate *v.* coopt
associate *n.* accessory, confrere, yokefellow
association *n.* concomitance, confraternity, consortium, gemeinschaft, gesellschaft, sodality
assume *v.* endue, hypostasize, hypothecate, posit, premise
assumed *adj.* supposititious
assumptions, set of donnée
astronomical almanac ephemeris
athletic club turnverein
at home en famille
atlas *n.* portolano, rutter
atomize *v.* nebulize
atoning *adj.* expiatory, piacular, restitutive
atrociousness *n.* enormity, heinousness

attached *adj.* sessile
attack *v.* aggress, asperse, deprecate, impugn, inveigh, oppugn, revile, scathe
attendants *n.* douzepers, famuli, Haiduks, halberdiers, lictors, pursuivants, servitors, tipstaffs, tipstaves
attention-getter *n.* cynosure, lodestar, polestar
attractive person peri
attribute *v.* adduce, ascribe, impute
auction *n.* outcry, vendue
audacity *n.* effrontery, cheek, chutzpa, temerity
audience *n.* durbar, levee, majlis
aura *n.* emanation
austere *adj.* astringent, monastic, Spartan
authentic *adj.* echt
authenticity *n.* bona fides
authenticity, of doubtful apocryphal
authorial *adj.* auctorial
authoritative *adj.* ex cathedra, magisterial
authority *n.* carte blanche, diadem, potestas, seigniory
authorization *n.* exequatur, nihil obstat, procuration
autistic *adj.* dereistic
automaton *n.* android, golem
autopsy n. necropsy, necroscopy
autosuggestion *n.* Couéism
auxiliary *adj.* adjuvant, ancillary
avert *v.* parry, ward
avoidable *adj.* evitable
award *v.* premiate, vouchsafe
aware *adj.* cognizant, sentient, witting
awkwardness *n.* gaucheness, gaucherie, infelicity, maladroitness
awning *n.* velarium

B

babble *n.* backchat, galimatias, prattle
baby *v.* cosset, mollycoddle
baby talk hypocorism

backbone *n.* chine
back door postern
backing *n.* aegis, auspice, auspices
backslide *v.* recidivate
backward, directed postrorse
backwards *adv.* arsy-varsy
bacon, portion or slice of rasher
bad breath halitosis, ozostomia
bad faith, in *mala fide*
baffle *v.* discomfit
bag *n.* ballonet, bota, chagul, poke, reticule, woolsack
baggage *n.* dunnage, impedimenta
baglike *adj.* utricular
bagpipe, play the skirl
baking soda saleratus
balance *v.* countervail, equilibrate
balcony *n.* mirador
bald *adj.* alopecic, calvous, glabrous
bald-headed man pilgarlic
balding *n.* psylosis
baldness *n.* alopecia, calvities
ball *n.* boule, masque, ridotto
ballet enthusiast balletomane
balloon *n.* montgolfier, sonde
ballot *n.* ostracon
ban *n.* juju, proscription
band *n.* annulus, armlet, brassard, girth
bandage *v.* swathe
bandaging *n.* fasciation
bandit *n.* bandito, brigand, pistolero
bane *n.* bête noire, bugbear
banish *v.* ostracize, proscribe, sequestrate
banker *n.* Lombard, shroff, soucar
banner *n.* gonfalon, labarum, oriflamme
banter *n.* badinage, chaff, persiflage, raillery
baptism *n.* immersion, pedobaptism
barb *n.* barbule, fluke, spicula, spicule
barbarism *n.* vox barbara
barbarous *adj.* gothic, hunnish, tramontane
barbecue *n.* babracot
barber, of a tonsorial
barefoot *adj.* discalced
bargain *v.* chaffer, higgle, truck
barge *n.* hoy, scow, wherry
bark *v.* kyoodle

barometer *n.* statoscope
barracks *n.* casern
barrel *n.* bota
barrel-making cooperage, coopery
barren adj. fallow, infecund
barricade *n.* abatis
barrier *n.* battlement, breastwork, campshot, palisade, portcullis
barroom *n.* barrelhouse, bierstube, blind tiger, cantina, dramshop, drinkery, groggery, hofbrau, pulquería, shebeen
basically *adv.* au fond
basics *n.* accidence, bedrock
basin *n.* aspergillum, aspersorium, bidet, cirque, font, impluvium, lavabo, piscina, sacrarium, stoup
basis *n.* keystone, linchpin
basket *n.* cesta, creel, cresset, dosser, flasket, frail, kago, kalathos, pannier, skep
bat *n.* flittermouse
bath *n.* mikvah, sudatorium, sudatory, thermae, wudu
bathhouse *n.* hammam
bathtub *n.* furo, laconicum, ofuro
batten *n.* splat
battle *n.* naumachia, rencontre, rencounter, theomachy
battleship *n.* dreadnought
bay *n.* bight, embayment, fjord, laguna
bayou *n.* marais
beach *n.* littoral, plage
beach resort lido
beacon *n.* balefire, pharos
bear *v.* farrow, fawn, fructify, kindle, whelp, yean
bear, pertaining to a ursine
beasts, having the form of theriomorphic
beat *v.* belabor, buffet, cudgel, flagellate, flail, fustigate, malleate, scutch, thwack, welt
beauty *n.* comeliness, pulchritude
bed, straw *n.* pallet, palliasse
bedbug *n.* chinch, cimex
bedpan *n.* jakes
bedspread *n.* counterpane, counterpin
bedwetting *n.* enuresis
beehive *n.* skep
beer mug seidel
beetle *n.* chafer, cockchafer, longicorn, rose chafer, scarab, tumblebug, weevil
before birth *in utero*
before the Civil War antebellum

before the Fall prelapsarian
beg v. cadge, importune, obsecrate, supplicate
beggar n. almsman, almswoman, Lazarus, qalander, sannyasi
begging adj. mendicant
begging the question petitio principii
begin v. inchoate
beginner n. abecedarian, catechumen, cheechako, postulant, tyro
beginning adj. inceptive, inchoate, nascent, primeval
behead v. decollate
behold the man! ecce homo
belch v. eruct, eructate
belief n. credendum
belief, false bugbear
belittle v. decry, deprecate, derogate
bells, ringing of tintinnabulation
bell tower belfry, campanile
bellyache n. collywobbles, gastralgia
belly dance danse du ventre
belongings n. personalia
below adv. infra
belt n. baldric, cestus, cincture
bend n. flexion, sinuosity, tortuosity
bending n. flexure, retortion, retroflexion
bends n. caisson disease
beneficent adj. benefic
beneficial adj. salutary, salutiferous
beneficial interdependence symbiosis
benign adj. benignant, salutary
bent adj. arcuate, recurvate, resupinate, tortuous, uncinate
berate v. castigate, revile
beseech v. importune, obsecrate, obtest
best man paranymph
bet v. hazard, jeopardize, stake, venture
betray v. calumniate, traduce
betrayal n. perfidy
betrayer n. Iscariot, traditor
between you and me entre nous
bevel v. chamfer
beverage n. libation
bewilder v. consternate, discomfit, obfuscate
be worthwhile behoove, beseem
beyond anything human preterhuman
bias n. penchant, proclivity
biased adj. partisan, tendentious
bicker v. controvert, pettifog

bier *n.* catafalque
bilingual *adj.* diglot
bilingualism *n.* diglossia
bilious *adj.* liverish
bimonthly *adj.* bimensal, bimestrial
bin *n.* kench
bind *v.* astrict, astringe, colligate, fetter, ligate, sheave, swaddle, swathe
binding *adj.* styptic
biographical information curriculum vitae, personalia, vita
biography *n.* hagiography, hagiology
bird, mythical phoenix
birth *n.* accouchement, arrhenotoky, conceptus, deuterotoky, geniture, naissance, parthenogenesis, parturiency, parturition, thelytoky
birthmark *n.* nevus, port-wine stain
bisexual *adj.* ambisextrous, androgynous, autoicous, epicene, hermaphroditic
bishop *n.* coadjutor, diocesan, eparch, exarch, metropolitan, primate, primus, suffragan
bizarre *adj.* antic, outré
bit *n.* drib, driblet, mite, scintilla, tittle, whit
bitter *adj.* acerbic, acrimonious, caustic, sardonic, virulent, vitriolic
bitter herbs maror
black-and-blue *adj.* livid
blackened *adj.* ustulate
blackhead *n.* comedo
blackmail *n.* chantage
blacksmith *n.* farrier, ironsmith
bladder, pertaining to the vesical
blame *n.* aspersion, calumny, obloquy, remonstrance, reprehension, reproof, revilement, traducement
blameworthy *adj.* culpable, reprehensible
blank *adj.* inane, vacuous
blanket *n.* kambal, manta, serape, stroud
blasphemy *n.* impiety, profanation, sacrilege
blatherer *n.* blatherskite
bleach *v.* agenize, blanch
bleed *v.* exsanguinate, phlebotomize
blemish *n.* ulver
blend *n.* amalgam, coalescence, concinnity, conflation, inosculation
bless *v.* beatify, hallow
blessing *n.* benison, kiddush
blight *n.* canker, scourge
blindness *n.* typhlosis

blindness, night nyctalopia
blinds *n.* jalousies, Persian blinds, persiennes
blind spot scotoma
blissful *adj.* Elysian, paradisiacal
blistering, causing vesicant, vesicatory
blob *n.* bead, dollop, globule
blockhead *n.* dolt, dullard, loggerhead
blood, drawing of cruor, phlebotomy, scarification, venesection, venisection
blood, feeding on hematophagous, sanguivorous
blood, living in sanguicolous
blood, pertaining to hemal, hematic, hemic
blood clot thrombus
blood poisoning pyemia, septicemia, toxemia
blood pressure, instrument for measuring sphygmomanometer
bloodthirsty *adj.* sanguinary, sanguinous
bloody *adj.* ensanguined, sanguinary, sanguinolent
bloom *n.* efflorescence, florescence
bloom *v.* burgeon
blotch *n.* macula
blow *v.* insufflate, whiffle
blueness *n.* cyanosis
blues *n.* megrim, melancholy
bluish *adj.* adularescent, aeruginous
blunder *n.* faux pas, gaffe, solecism, spoonerism
blunt *v.* hebetate, obtund
blur *v.* mackle, obfuscate
blushing *adj.* erubescent, rubescent
bluster *n.* fanfaronade
boaster *n.* braggart, gascon
boastful *adj.* bombastic, cock-a-hoop, Falstaffian, rodomontade, spread-eagle, thrasonical, vaporing
boat-shaped *adj.* navicular, scaphoid
bobsled *n.* double-ripper
bodice *n.* angiya, choli, taille
body, human tabernacle
body of work corpus
bodysnatching *n.* exhumation, resurrectionism
body types asthenic, athletic, leptosome, pyknic
bog *n.* fen, mire, muskeg, quag, quagmire, slough, wash
boil *n.* furuncle
boiling *adj.* ebullient
boisterous *adj.* clamorous, rampageous, robustious, strepitous
bombastic *adj.* fustian, grandiloquent, magniloquent, orotund, purple
bond *n.* nexus, vinculum

bones, containing ossiferous
bone scraper xyster
bonfire *n.* balefire
bonus *n.* broadus, lagniappe
bony adj. osseous, osteal, sclerous
bookish *adj.* donnish
book section, separately bound fascicle, fasciculus
bookworm *n.* bibliophage
boorish *adj.* chuffy, churlish, loutish, vulgarian
bootlicking *adj.* oleaginous, smarmy, sycophantic, unctuous
border *n.* cincture, limes, list, orphrey, purfle
boring *adj.* mundane, prosaic, prosy, stodgy, yawnful
borrowing *adj.* eclectic
boss *n.* bwana, cacique, caporal, padrone, *patron*
bother *v.* discommode
bottle-shaped *adj.* ampullaceous
boulder *n.* einkanter
boundlessness *n.* infinitude
bounds *n.* purlieus
bow v. genuflect, lout, salaam
bowels *n.* entrails
bowl *n.* jorum, kantharos, kelebe, krater, kyathos, kylix, mazer,
   monteith, patchstand, tazza, verrière
bowlegged *adj.* valgus
bowler *n.* kegler
box *n.* artophorion, coffer, etui, inro, manger, papeterie, pyx, pyxis,
   skippet, solander, vasculum
boxing *n.* savate
bracket *n.* sconce
brag *v.* bukh, prate, rodomontade, vaporize, vaunt
braggart *n.* braggadocio, fanfaron, gascon, scaramouch
braid *n.* aiguillette, galloon, plait, plat, queue, soutache
brake *n.* sprag
branch *v.* divaricate, bifurcate, furcate, ramify, trifurcate
bravado *n.* fanfaronade, gasconade
bravery *n.* intrepidity, mettle, potvalor, valiancy
brawl *n.* bobbery, brannigan, donnybrook, shindy
bread, sacramental antidoron, azyme, eulogia, Host
bread, unleavened matzo
bread-eating *adj.* panivorous
breaded *adj.* pané
break *n.* caesura, entr'acte, hiatus, rupture
breakable *adj.* frangible
breakdown *n.* dégringolade
breakup *n.* debacle

breastplate *n.* pectoral
breath, foul halitosis, ozostomia
breathe *v.* hyperventilate, insufflate, respire, suspire
brevity *n.* concision, laconism
bribable *adj.* venal
bribe *n.* dash, douceur, *mordida*
bribe *v.* suborn
bribery, openness to venality
bric-a-brac stand étagère
bridegroom *n.* benedict
bride price lobolo
bridesmaid *n.* paranymph
bridle *n.* hackamore, headstall
brief *adj.* ephemeral, transitory
brigand *n.* klepht
bright *adj.* effulgent, lambent, lightsome, nitid, refulgent, relucent
brilliance *n.* coruscation, éclat, effulgence, reflet, refulgence
bristle *n.* acicula, seta
bristlelike *adj.* setaceous
bristling *n.* horripilation
bristly *adj.* echinate, hispid, setose
brittle *adj.* brickle
broad-minded *adj.* catholic
broker *n.* monger
bronze *adj.* aeneous
brooch *n.* morse, plaque
brook *n.* beck, quebrada, runnel
broom *n.* besom
brothel *n.* bagnio, bawdyhouse, crib, house of assignation, house of ill repute, juke house, lupanar, parlor house, sporting house, stew
brotherhood *n.* confraternity
brothers *n.* Castor and Pollux (the Dioscuri), Romulus and Remus
brought-back *adj.* réchauffé, redux
brownish-red *adj.* rubiginous
bruise *n.* contusion
brushwood *n.* chaparral
brutal *adj.* carnal, feral, insensate, remorseless
brutalize *v.* imbrute
bubble *v.* burble, effervesce
bucket *n.* scuttle
bud *n.* gemma
Buddha *n.* butsu, daibutsu, Gautama
buff *n.* devotee, votary
buffoon *n.* merry-andrew
bulb *n.* corm

bulge *v.* protuberate
bulimia *n.* hyperphagia
bull *n.* gomer, male cow, *toro*
bullet *n.* dumdum, fléchette
bullfighting, art of tauromachy
bullied *adj.* browbeaten
bully *v.* browbeat, cow, hector
bumblebee *n.* humble-bee
bump *n.* mogul, thank-you-ma'am
bundle *n.* fagot, fardel, fasces, fascine, skein
bungle *v.* boggle, foozle
burden *n.* albatross, cumbrance, encumbrance, fardel
burden of proof *onus probandi*
bureaucrat *n.* mandarin
burglar *n.* raffles
burial *n.* deposition, sepulture
burial chamber charnel, charnel house, cist, cistvaen, cromlech,
    cubiculum, hypogeum, sepulcher
burial wrapping cerecloth, cerement
burn *v.* cauterize, combust, deflagrate, immolate, sear, smolder
burnish *v.* furbish
burp *n.* eructation
burr *n.* moit
burrowing *adj.* fossorial
burst *v.* dehisce, implode, irrupt
bursting *adj.* dissilient, erumpent, eruptive
bury *v.* inearth, inhume, inurn
bus *n.* colectivo, jitney
busy *adj.* assiduous, engrossed
busybody *n.* Nosy Parker, Paul Pry, quidnunc
butcher *n.* charcutier
butler *n.* khansamah, major-domo
buttocks *n.* breech, derriere, nates
buttocks, having excessively large steatopygic
buttocks, having well-shaped callipygian
buyer *n.* emptor
buyer, compulsive oniomaniac
by the way *en passant*

C

cabdriver *n.* jehu
cabinetmaker *n.* arkwright
café *n.* bistro, estaminet, taverna, trattoria
cage *n.* aviary, mew, volary
cajole *v.* beguile, blandish, inveigle, seduce, wheedle
calamity *n.* cataclysm
calendar *n.* menology
calf *n.* dogie, freemartin, leppy, maverick
calf, pertaining to a vituline
callous *adj.* obdurate
calm *adj.* halcyon, limpid, lown, pacific
calmness *n.* aplomb, imperturbation, sang-froid
camel *n.* dromedary
camp *n.* cantonment, étape, laager
Canadian football rouge
canal *n.* fosse, klong
cancel *v.* disestablish, expunge
candid *adj.* artless, guileless, ingenuous
candidate *n.* confirmand, postulant
candle *n.* bougie, paschal candle, shammes, vigil light
candleholder *n.* candelabrum, girandole, menorah
candlesnuffer *n.* douter
candlestick *n.* pricket, taperstick, flambeau
cane *n.* ferule, supplejack, whangee
cannibals *n.* anthropophagi, Laestrygones
canoe *n.* piragua, pirogue
canonization *n.* apotheosis
canopy *n.* baldachin, celure, ciborium, *chuppah*, ombrellino, sparver, tester
canyon *n.* cañada
capital letter majuscule
caprice *n.* crotchet, megrim, vagary
care *n.* husbandry, ministration, tendance
carefree behavior rhathymia
careful *adj.* chary, punctilious, solicitous
careless *adj.* derelict, improvident, prodigal, wanton
caress *v.* dandle

caressing, given to embracive
caretaker *n.* warder
carnival *n.* raree show
carnivorous *adj.* predacious, sarcophagous, zoophagous
carousel *n.* flying jenny
carp *v.* niggle
carpenter *n.* joiner
carping *adj.* picayune, querulous
carrier, disease *n.* Typhoid Mary
carrion *n.* offal
carry *v.* portage
cart *n.* cariole, dray, telega, tumbrel, tumbril, wain
carving *n.* churinga, glyph, glyptograph, intaglio, netsuke,
    petroglyph, petrograph, scrimshaw, xoanon
carving board trencher
case *n.* etui, theca, vasculum, vitrine
cask *n.* firkin, hogshead, puncheon, rundet, tierce, tun
castle land *n.* castellany
cast out disembogue
castrate *v.* caponize, desex, eunuchize, geld, neuter, unman, unsex
castration *n.* orchectomy, orchidectomy, orchiectomy
casual *adj.* adventitious, fortuitous
cat *n.* gib, grimalkin
cataclysmic *adj.* apocalyptic
catacomb, burial recess in a loculus
catalog *n.* bibliotheca, catalogue raisonné
catapult *n.* mangonal, trebuchet, trebucket
catchword *n.* shibboleth
cat detester ailurophobe
category *n.* taxon
caterpillarlike *adj.* eruciform
cat fancier ailurophile
cathartic *n.* lapactic, purgative
cathedral *n.* duomo, Lateran, minster
cat's scream caterwaul
cattle enclosure kraal
causation *n.* etiology
caustic *adj.* **1.** escharotic; **2.** scathing, mordacious, mordant,
    trenchant, vitriolic
cautious *adj.* chary, circumspect
cavalryman *n.* dragoon, spahi
cave *n.* antre, rock-shelter, subterrane
cave drawing pictograph
cave dweller *n.* troglobiont, troglodyte
cave-dwelling *adj.* cavernicolous

cave explorer spelunker
caves, study of speleology
cavity *n.* alveolus, antrum, caldera, calix, cecum, fossa, loculus, moulin
cease *v.* intermit, surcease
celebration *n.* callathump, callithump, Maying, potlatch
celestial *adj.* superlunary, supernal, superterrestrial, translunary
celibate *n.* brahmachari
cemetery *n.* God's acre, golgotha, kurgan, necropolis, potter's field, urnfield
censor *v.* bowdlerize, expurgate
censor *n.* custos morum
censorship *n.* Comstockery
censure *v.* asperse, calumniate, castigate, criminate, dispraise, excoriate, reprobate
centaur *n.* sagittary
centerpiece *n.* epergne
centrifuge *n.* hematocrit
ceremonies *n.* encaenia, maundy, Panagia
certificate *n.* demit, dimit
chairperson *n.* prolocutor
chalklike *adj.* cretaceous
chalky *adj.* calcareous
challenge *v.* asperse, impugn
champion *n.* paladin, protagonist
chance *n.* fortuitousness, fortuity
chance *adj.* adventitious, aleatory, fortuitous
changeable *adj.* labile, mercurial, protean, tergiversatory, versicolor
change of fortune, sudden peripeteia
changes having been made, the necessary *mutatis mutandis*
chant *n.* canticle, dhikr, dithyramb
chant *v.* cantillate
chaos *n.* babel, tohubohu
chapel *n.* antiparabema, chantry, oratory, sacellum
chaperon *n.* duenna
characteristic *n.* faculty, idiocrasy, idiosyncrasy, parameter
character witness compurgator
charcoal *n.* fusain
charge *v.* criminate
charisma *n.* duende
charitable *adj.* eleemosynary
charity *n.* benignity, *caritas*
charlatan *n.* empiric, quacksalver
charm *n.* conjuration, duende, gris-gris, juju, menat, mojo, obeah, periapt, scarab

chaste *adj.* continent, vestal
chastise *v.* castigate, scourge
chat *v.* confabulate, coze
chatterer *n.* blatherer, jay, magpie, popinjay
cheap *adj.* brummagem
cheat *v.* chouse, cozen, cully, fob, gull, thimblerig
check *v.* vet
check *n.* counterfoil
checkered *adj.* tesellated
cheek, of the buccal, jugal
cheerful *adj.* blithesome, jocund, riant, rident
cheese, like caseous
cheeselike secretion smegma
cherish *v.* embosom
chess *n.* shogi
chess move fianchetto, zugzwang
chess player patzer
chestnut *n.* marron
chew *v.* masticate, Fletcherize
chicanery *n.* pettifoggery
chick *n.* pullus
chief *n.* sachem, sagamore
child *n.* bairn, bantling, chit, chrisom child, weanling
child, mischievous hellion, jackanapes
childbearing practice couvade
childbirth *n.* accouchement, eutocia, parturition
childbirth, pertaining to puerperal
childish *adj.* callow, jejune
childlike *adj.* guileless, ingenuous
chilling *adj.* frigorific
chilly *adj.* algid, gelid
children's shelter crèche, protectory
chimney corner inglenook
China *n.* Cathay
chinked *adj.* rimose
chisel-shaped *adj.* scalpriform
choice *adj.* recherché
choice, no Hobson's choice
choir *n.* schola cantorum
choirmaster *n.* Kapellmeister, precentor
choral society Liederkranz
choreography *n.* terpsichore
chorus leader choragus, coryphaeus
Christian *n.* Melchite, rayah
chronic *adj.* inveterate

chronology *n.* synchronism
church bench, part of a misericord, subsellium
church fathers, of the patristic
cigar *n.* locofoco, Londres, maduro
cigarette *n.* bidi
circle *n.* gyre, rondure, roundet
circuitous *adj.* anfractuous, tortuous
circular *adj.* orbicular
circumciser, ritual *n.* *mohel*
circumcision, female clitoridectomy
circumcision, male *Brith*
citadel *n.* acropolis
citizenry *n.* civitas
city *n.* conurbation, cosmopolis, megacity, megalopolis, megapolis
city-state *n.* polis
civility *n.* comity
claim *n.* droit
clairvoyance *n.* clairaudience, cryptesthesia, telegnosis
clamorous *adj.* vociferous
clan *n.* gens, gotra, phyle
clandestine *adj.* hugger-mugger
clarification *n.* disambiguation, *éclaircissement*, explication
clarity *n.* perspicuity
clasp *n.* agraffe, chatelaine, morse
classical source *locus classicus*
classification *n.* nosology, taxonomy
classifier *n.* nomenclator, nosologist, taxonomist
claw *n.* chela, dewclaw, pounce, unguis
clay *n.* fango, fuller's earth, grog, sagger
clay, made of fictile
clean *v.* debride, mundify, scud, swingle
cleansing *adj.* abluent, abstergent, abstersive, detersive
clean slate tabula rasa
clear *adj.* lucent, luculent, limpid, pellucid, perspicuous
clear, serving to exculpatory
cleared, capable of being vindicable
cleaver *n.* barong
cleft *n.* bergschrund, crevasse
clemency *n.* lenity
cleverness *n.* acumen, acutance, piquancy
cliché *n.* bromide, homily, platitude, tag
cliff *n.* cutbank, pali, scarp
climax *n.* apogee, catastasis
climb *v.* clamber
climber *n.* cragsman

climbing *adj.* scandent, scansorial
cling *v.* cleave
clip *v.* poll
clippings *n.* scissel
clique *v.* camarilla, coterie
clitoris *n.* phallus
cloak *n.* aba, capote, chlamys, domino, paenula
clock *n.* clepsydra, horologe
clockmaker *n.* horologist
clock tower horologium
clone *n.* ramet
close *v.* obturate, occlude
closure *n.* cloture
cloth, ceremonial antimension, bis, bisso, bissonata
clothe *v.* accouter, bedizen, endue, invest
clothing, pertaining to sartorial
cloud *v.* obfuscate, obumbrate
cloudlike *adj.* nebulose, nebulous
cloven-hoofed *adj.* bisulcate
clown *n.* gracioso, Joey, merry-andrew
cloying *adj.* fulsome
club *n.* knobkerrie, pogamoggan, truncheon
clubfoot *n.* talipes
club-shaped *adj.* clavate, claviform
clump *n.* coagulum
clumsy *adj.* ambisinister, ambisinistrous, bunglesome, inapt, lubberly, oafish
clustered *adj.* agminate, glomerate
coal, like carbonaceous
coal, producing carboniferous
coal bucket scuttle
coal dust slack
coarse *adj.* Rabelaisian, rank,
coat of arms escutcheon
coax *v.* blandish, inveigle
code *n.* Bushido, omertà
coexistent *adj.* coeval
coffeepot *n.* biggin
coffee shop konditorei
coffin *n.* pall, sarcophagus
cognate *adj.* paronymous
cognitive *adj.* gnostic
cohabitation *n.* hetaerism
coherent *adj.* sequacious
coiled *adj.* spiry, tortile

coin a word neologize, neoterize
coincident *adj.* coeval, coextensive, conterminous,
coins, pertaining to numismatic, nummary, nummular
coitus *n.* coition
cold *n.* catarrh, coryza, rheum
cold-blooded *adj.* hematocryal, poikilothermal
cold cuts charcuterie
collaborator *n.* jackal, quisling, scalawag
collage *n.* papier collé
collarbone *n.* clavicle
colleague *n.* compeer
collecting *n.* deltiology
collection *n.* chrestomathy, congeries, gnomology, nomocanon,
   omnium-gatherum, onomasticon, patrology
collective *n.* kibbutz, kolkhoz
college *n.* madrasah
collision *n.* allision, appulse
colony *n.* rookery
color, of tinctorial
color, of same isochroous
color blindness achromatopsia, daltonism
colors, of various parti-colored, versicolor
column *n.* atlas, stamba, telamon
columns, having many polystyle
comatose *adj.* torpid
comb *n.* currycomb, ripple
combat, futile sciamachy, sciomachy
combative *adj.* agonistic, truculent
combination *n.* conflation
combination, industrial zaibatsu
combined action synergism, synergy
comblike *adj.* pectinate
Comforter, the Paraclete
coming, belief in second chiliasm, millennialism
commander *n.* alcaide, centurion, chiliarch, condottiere, shogun
commando *n.* fedayee
commemorate *v.* enscroll, epitaph
commend *v.* preconize
commendation *n.* encomium, panegyric
commentary *n.* exegesis, Gemara, Masorah, midrash, talmud
commentator *n.* expositor, glossator, scholiast
committee *n.* divan
common people, the commonalty, demos
commonplace *adj.* banal, exoteric, platitudinous, plebeian,
   quotidian

commotion *n.* brouhaha, catouse, pother
communication, occult psychomancy
community *n.* kellion, khalsa, *moshav*, pantisocracy
compacted *adj.* serried
compassion *n.* aruna, rue, ruth
compassionate *adj.* ruthful
compatible *adj.* compossible
compensation *n.* redress, reparation, requital, solatium, wergild
competition *n.* bonspiel, concours, concours d'élégance
complaining *adj.* captious, carping, caviling, petulant, querulous, testy
complaint *n.* gravamen, jeremiad, plaint
complexity *n.* cat's cradle, complicacy, labyrinth
compliant *adj.* complaisant, deferential, obsequious, tractable
complicated *adj.* convoluted, involute, involuted, Rube Goldberg, tortuous, vermiculate
complication *n.* complicacy, nodus
component *n.* moiety
compose *v.* articulate, indite
composure *n.* aplomb, sang-froid
comprehension, beyond suprarational
comprehensive *adj.* compendious
compulsory *adj.* coactive, de rigueur, exigent, extortive
comrade *n.* compeer, cohort
conceal *v.* adumbrate, dissimulate, embosk, ensconce, occult
concealed *adj.* delitescent, perdu
concede *v.* truckle
conceit *n.* bovarism, vainglory
conceited *adj.* bloated, bumptious, overweening, vainglorious
conceited man cockalorum
conceivable *adj.* cogitable
conceive *v.* ideate
concentrate *v.* concenter, decoct
concentration *n.* cathexis, distillate
conception of the world *Weltanschauung*
concern, have reck
conciliatory *adj.* irenic, placative, placatory, propitiatory
conciseness *n.* concision, laconicism, laconism, sententiousness
conclude *v.* consummate, perorate
conclusion *n.* illation
concretion *n.* calculus
concubine *n.* hetaera, odalisque, sultana
concurrent *adj.* consentaneous, consentient
condemnation *n.* disapprobation, philippic, reprehension, reprobation

condensation *n.* conspectus, epitome
condescending *adj.* patronizing, supercilious, toplofty
condition *n.* fettle, fig
condition, indispensable sine qua non
conelike *adj.* strobilaceous
confection *n.* confiture
conference *n.* colloquium, colloquy, confabulation, indaba, palaver,
　　parley, *pourparler*
confess *v.* disbosom
confession *n.* peccavi
confident *adj.* sanguine, sanguineous
confidentially *adv.* entre nous, in camera, sub rosa
confine *v.* fetter, immure, pinfold, trammel
confirm *v.* homologate
confirmed *adj.* inveterate
confirming *adj.* confirmatory, corroborant
confiscation *n.* sequestration
conflict *n.* agon, Armageddon
conformity *n.* congruity
confrontation *n.* mano a mano
confused *adj.* **1.** addled, disjointed, flummoxed, nonplussed,
　　skimble-scamble; **2.** roiled, tumultary, turbid
congenial *adj.* boon, complaisant, connate, en rapport, simpatico
conglomeration *n.* cento, glomeration
congratulatory *adj.* gratulant, gratulatory
conjugation *n.* zygosis
conjunction, astronomical syzygy
connect *v.* catenate, inosculate
connecting *adj.* internuncial
connection *n.* conjunction, nexus
connector *n.* copula
connoisseur *n.* aficionada, aficionado, cognoscente, epicurean,
　　gastronome, oenophile
connote *v.* predicate
conquerable *adj.* expugnable, vincible
conscience *n.* superego
conscientious *adj.* punctilious, scrupulous
conscious *adj.* percipient, sentient, witting
consecutive *adj.* sequent
consent *n.* sufferance
conserve *v.* husband
consider *v.* cogitate, perpend, ratiocinate, ruminate
consideration *n.* extrospection, rumination
consign *v.* relegate
consistent *adj.* accordant, congruous, consonant

console *v.* condole, solace
conspicuous *adj.* ostensible, ostensive
conspiracy *n.* cabal, collusion, complot, machination
conspirator *n.* Catilinarian
conspire *v.* collude, complot
constant *adj.* assiduous, sedulous
constipation *n.* costiveness, obstipation
constituent *adj.* integrant
constrict *v.* constringe
construct *v.* facture
consuming *adj.* edacious
contact *n.* contiguity, contingence, osculation, taction
contemplation of one's navel omphaloskepsis
contemplative *adj.* cogitative, ruminant
contemporaneity *n.* isochrony
contemporary *adj.* coetaneous, coeval, contemporaneous
contempt *n.* contumacy, contumely, lese majesty, lèse majesty, misprision
contempt, object of pilgarlic
contemptible *adj.* execrable, ignoble, ignominious
contemptuous *adj.* contumelious, derisive, snide, sniffish, sniffy, snuffy, supercilious
contemptuous treatment contumely
contention *n.* fliting
contention, involve in embrangle
contentious *adj.* litigious
contentment *n.* kef
contest *n.* agon, rencontre, rencounter, velitation
contestant *n.* agonist
contingent *adj.* aleatory
continue *v.* perdure, perseverate
continuing *adj.* perdurable, sempiternal
contort *v.* squinch
contraction *n.* constriction, stricture, syncope
contradiction *n.* antilogy, denegation, oxymoron
contradictory *adj.* antithetical, contradictious, contradictive
contrary *adj.* antipathetic, oppugnant
contrast *n.* antithesis, contradistinction, contraposition
contribute *v.* conduce
contributory *adj.* accessory, ancillary
contrive *v.* excogitate
control of the seas thalassocracy
controversial *adj.* eristic, polemical
controversy *n.* contestation, logomachy, polemic
controversy, engage in polemicize

convent *n.* mother house
convention *n.* convocation
conversation *n.* chin-chin, interlocution, tête-à-tête, trialogue
conversationalist *n.* deipnosophist
conversion *n.* metanoia, proselytism, reification
convert *n.* catechumen, Marrano
convex *adj.* gibbous
convincing *adj.* luculent
convivial *adj.* anacreontic
convocation *n.* esbat
convulsion *n.* eclampsia
cooked in paper *en papillote*
cooking pit imu
cooking pot marmite
cooking stove brazier, hibachi
cooperating *adj.* coadjutant
cooperation *n.* concertation
cooperative *n.* nokyo
cooperativeness *n.* collegiality
copperlike *adj.* cupreous, cupric
copy *n.* apograph, exemplar, replication
copyist *n.* scrivener
coral-bearing *adj.* coraliferous
cordiality *n.* gemütlichkeit
corky *adj.* suberose, suberous
coroner *n.* prosector
corpulent *adj.* abdominous
correct *v.* disabuse, emendate
correctable *adj.* corrigible
correction *n.* amendation, corrigendum, emendation
correct user of words sumpsimus
correspondence *n.* consonance, homology
corridor *n.* syrinx
corrosive *adj.* erosive, mordant
corrugated *adj.* rugose
corruptible *adj.* venal
corruption *n.* malversation, venality
cosmetics *n. maquillage*
costume *n.* raiment, trappings
cough *n.* tussiculation, tussis
cough, of a tussive
council *n.* consistory, panchayat, synod
count *n.* landgrave, palsgrave
counterfeit *adj.* ersatz, factitious, postiche
counterpoint *n.* polyphony

counterstroke *n.* riposte
countrified *adj.* rusticated
country, live in the ruralize, rusticate
couple *n.* duad
courage *n. corazón*, derring-do, hardihood, mettle
courageous *adj.* dauntless, doughty, fortitudinous, indomitable, mettlesome
courier *n.* estafette
court *n.* durbar, presbytery, quarter sessions, Sanhedrin, Star Chamber
courteous *adj.* deferential, urbane
courtesan *n.* demimondaine, hetaera
courtesy *n.* amenity, comity, politesse
courtyard *n.* garth
cover *n.* cloche, mantle, pall
covered entrance porte-cochere
cowardly *adj.* craven, dastardly, lily-livered, poltroon, pusillanimous, recreant, thewless, white-livered
cowboy *n.* gaucho, paniolo, Pecos Bill, vaquero, wrangler
cowl-like *adj.* cucullate
cow stomachs abomasum, omasum, reticulum
cozy *adj.* gemütlich
crabby *adj.* cantankerous, gnarled
crabs *n.* pediculosis
cracked *adj.* rimose
crackle *v.* craze, crepitate
crackles *n.* craquelure
cracklings *n.* greaves
craft *n.* métier
craftiness *n.* Italian hand
crafty *adj.* arch, artful, disingenuous, insidious, jesuitical, Machiavellian, vulpine
cramps *n.* collywobbles
crane *n.* davit
craw *n.* maw
crayfish *n. écrivisse*
crazed *adj.* moon-stricken, moonstruck
creaking sound stridor
crease *v.* rimple, ruck
Creation, before the antemundane, premundane
Creation, six days of hexaemeron
creative *adj.* Promethean
creative force élan vital
creator *n.* demiurge
credit *v.* ascribe, impute

creek *n.* estuary, kill
creeping *adj.* repent, reptant, serpiginous
crescent-shaped *adj.* lunate, lunular, meniscus
crested *adj.* cristate, pileated
crevasse *n.* bergschrund
crevice *n.* interstice
cribber *n.* stumpsucker
crier *n.* muezzin
crime-producing *adj.* criminogenic
criminal *adj.* flagitious
criminal *n.* dacoit, malefactor
criminal, habitual recidivist
crimson *adj.* incarnadine, sanguinary
crisis *n.* conjuncture, crise, Dunkirk
criterion *n.* canon, gauge, touchstone
critic *n.* aristarch, criticaster, gadfly, hypercritic
critical *adj.* captious, carping, caviling, hypercritical, mordant
critical period climacteric
criticize *v.* animadvert, brickbat, carp, castigate, cavil, denigrate,
     deprecate, derogate, disparage, excoriate, flay, fustigate, indict,
     niggle, reprove, scourge, traduce
crooked *adj.* flexuous, involute, sinuous, tortuous, vermiculate
cross *adj.* cantankerous, churlish, crabbed, petulant
crossbow *n.* prodd
cross-eyed *adj.* strabismic, walleyed
crossroads *n.* carrefour
cross-shaped *adj.* cruciate, cruciform
crouch *v.* hunker, scrooch
crowlike *adj.* corvine
crown *n.* capstone, coronal, coronet, diadem, pschent
crucifix *n.* rood
crude *adj.* incondite, kutcha
crudeness *n.* gaucherie
cruel *adj.* draconian, fell, implacable, insensate, insensible,
     ironhearted, truculent
cruelty *n.* bestiality, brutishness, depravity, sadism
cruet *n.* caster, muffineer
crumble *v.* molder
crumbly *adj.* friable, pulverulent
crumple *v.* rimple
crush *v.* quash, quell
crushed *adj.* écrasé
cry *n.* bleat, caterwaul, cri de coeur, yawp
crypt *n.* undercroft
cryptic *adj.* elliptical, enigmatic

cube-shaped *adj.* cubiform
cubicle *n.* carrel
cuckold *n.* cornuto, wittol
cuckold *v.* cornute
cud-chewer *n.* ruminant
cult *n.* cultus, macumba
cultivation *n.* tillage, tilth
cultivator *n.* ama
culture *n.* eidos
cultured *adj.* couth
cuneiform character sphenogram
cupid *n.* amoretto, amorino
cup-shaped *adj.* poculiform, scyphate
curare *n.* woorali
curative *adj.* sanative, sanatory
curdle *v.* lopper
cure-all *n.* catholicon, elixir, panacea
curio *n.* bibelot
curiosities *n.* curiosa
curious *adj.* outré
currency dealer cambist
curse *v.* anathematize, comminate, execrate, fulminate, imprecate
curt *adj.* peremptory
curtain *n.* arras, brise-bise, lambrequin, *mehitzah*, *parokheth*,
   portiere, purdah, sparver
curvature *n.* flexure, gonycampsis, kurtosis, kyphosis, lordosis,
   scoliosis
curved *adj.* adunc, arcuate, bombé, excurved, falcate, falciform,
   incurvate, reclinate, recurved, retroussé
cushion *n.* zabuton
cushion *v.* buffer, mitigate
cushion-shaped *adj.* pulvinate
custard *n.* crème brûlée
customary *adj.* consuetudinary, quotidian, wonted
customs *n.* folkways, mores, praxes
customs union Zollverein
cut *v.* abscind, chamfer, rabbet, skive
cut *n.* kerf, scotch
cut across transect
cut off dock, exscind
cut open eviscerate, exenterate
cut out excide, exscind, exsect, resect
cuttable *adj.* sectile
cutting *n.* scission
cutting, technique of stereotomy
cutting off, a abscission, cloture

cycling arena velodrome
cylinder *n.* gabion, platen
cylindrical *adj.* terete
cynical *adj.* mordant, sardonic
cyst *n.* vesicle, wen

D

dabble *v.* dally, fiddle, smatter
dabbler *n.* dabster, dilettante
daddy-longlegs *n.* harvestman
dagger *n.* anlace, choora, creese, dirk, dudgeon, khanjar, kirpan, kris,
  main gauche, misericord, poniard, puntilla, skean, stylet
daily *adj.* circadian, diurnal, quotidian
dally *v.* coquet
dam *n.* weir
damages *n.* solatium
damaging *adj.* baneful, deleterious, pernicious
damned *adj.* dratted, infernal, reprobate
dance, manic impulse to tarantism
dance, public ridotto, Sadie Hawkins
dancer *n.* coryphée, kachina, nautch, ropedancer, ropewalker,
  terpsichorean
dancing *adj.* saltant

Just stayin' alive!

I hope we have a terpsichorean tomorrow.

dancing girl nautch
dandruff *n.* furfures, scall, scurf
dandy *n.* Beau Brummell, coxcomb, dasher, fop, macaroni, muscadin, popinjay, précieux
dangerous *adj.* jeopardous, malignant, parlous
dark *adj.* fuliginous, fuscous, Stygian, subfuscous, swart, swarth, tenebrous
darken *v.* darkle, lower, obnubilate, obumbrate
darkness, causing tenebrific
darling *n.* mavourneen
dash *v.* bolt, dartle
dash *n.* élan
dawdle *v.* finick, piddle, shilly-shally
daydreamer *n.* lotus-eater, stargazer, Walter Mitty, woolgatherer
day of wrath *dies irae*
daze *n.* torpidity
dazed *adj.* narcose
dazzling *adj.* foudroyant, fulgent
dead *adj.* exanimate
deaden *v.* obtund, petrify
deadly *adj.* fell, implacable, internecine, mortiferous, virulent
dead matter, feeding on saprophagous
dealer *n.* monger
dear *adj.* boon, bosom
death *n.* bane, decease, dissolution, Grim Reaper, necrosis, quietus, Thanatos
death, after *post obitum*
death, contemplation of thanatopsis
death, near *in extremis*
death, reminder of memento mori
death, study of thanatology
deathblow *n.* coup de grâce, quietus
debate *n.* agon
debate point quodlibet
debauchery, place of sty
debility *n.* asthenia
debris *n.* detritus
debunk *v.* excoriate, lampoon
decade *n.* decennium
decadent *adj.* effete, fin de siècle
decapitate *v.* decollate
decay *n.* desuetude, putrefaction
decay, producing saprogenic
decayed *adj.* carious, dozy
deceitful *adj.* duplicitous, false-hearted, Janus-faced, perfidious
deceive *v.* beguile, cozen, cuckold, dissemble, dissimulate, gull

decent *adj.* decorous, seemly
decentralize *v.* demassify
deception *n.* chicane, chicanery, dissimulation, duplicity, gammon, imposture, Potemkin village
deceptive appearances, series of phantasmagoria
decimal *adj.* denary
deck out bedizen
declamation *n.* recitatif, recitative
declare *v.* asseverate, aver, enunciate
declaw *v.* expeditate
decline *n.* decadence, degeneracy, degeneration, diminution, retrogradation, retrogression, turpitude
decode *v.* decrypt
decorated *adj.* pointillé
decoration *n.* bocage, cuspidation, decoupage, froufrou, racinage
decorations *n.* regalia
decrease *n.* decrement, degression
decreasing *adj.* decrescent
decree *n.* decretal, diktat, irade
dedicated *adj.* consecrated, votive
deduce *v.* educe
deduction *n.* corollary, illation, inference
deductive *adj.* a priori
deeds *n.* res gestae
deer *n.* staggard
deerlike *adj.* cervine
defamatory *adj.* calumniatory, calumnious
defame *v.* backbite, calumniate, denigrate, derogate, revile, traduce, vilipend
default *n.* dereliction
defeat *n.* dusting, pratfall, Waterloo
defeat *v.* defease, unhorse, worst
defecation *n.* encopresis, evacuation
defending *adj.* phylactic
defer *v.* prorogue
defiant *adj.* contumacious, recalcitrant, refractory
deficiency *n.* paucity
definitely *adv.* categorically, unequivocally
definition *n.* definiens, explicans
deflective *adj.* refracting, refractive, refrangible, refringent
deflower *v.* despoil
deflowering *n.* defloration
defraud *v.* bilk, cozen, mulct, rook
deft *adj.* dextrous
defy *v.* flout
degrade *v.* abase, demean, vitiate

degrading *adj.* abjective
degree *n.* aegrotat
degree holder licentiate
deification *n.* apotheosis
deign *v.* condescend, vouchsafe
dejected *adj.* chapfallen, dour, heartsore
delay *n.* cunctation, moratorium, procrastination
delay, authorizing moratory
delaying *adj.* dilatory, Fabian
delete *v.* excise, expunge
deliberate *adj.* prepense, volitional
deliberate *v.* perpend
delicious *adj.* ambrosial, savory, succulent, toothsome
delight *n.* delectation, rapture, transport
delightful *adj.* captivating, Elysian, frabjous
delineate *v.* limn
deluge *n.* cataclysm
delusion *n.* ignis fatuus, lycanthropy, mare's-nest
demagogue *n.* firebrand
demand *v.* importune, postulate
demanding *adj.* hardscrabble
demeanor *n.* mien
demented person ament, dement
demolish *v.* raze, unbuild
demon *n.* afreet, afrit, Azazel, cacodemon, Danava, duende,
    dybbuk, eudemon, incubus, Jeh, lamia, Lilith, succuba, succubus
demonstrative *adj.* effusive, ostensive
demur *v.* scruple, stickle
denial *n.* abnegation, confutation, démenti, rejoinder
denouement *n.* anagnorisis
dense *adj.* spissatus
density, of equal isopycnic
denunciation *n.* castigation, commination, contumely, excoriation,
    fulmination, impugnment, objurgation, philippic, screed
deny *v.* abjure, abnegate, gainsay, rebuff, recant
denying *adj.* negatory
depart *v.* absquatulate, debouch, decamp, fuddle-duddle
departing *adj.* apopemptic, valedictory
departure *n.* apostasy, defection, exodos, exodus
dependence *n.* vassalage
depict *v.* delineate, epitomize, limn
depiction *n.* deesis
deplete *v.* enervate
deplorable *adj.* rueful, scurvy
depopulate *v.* depeople, dispeople, unpeople

deportation *n.* deracination, expatriation
depose *v.* defrock, discrown, unfrock, unmake, unmiter
deposit *n.* argol, tartar
depraved *adj.* miscreant, nefarious
depraved act turpitude
depreciation *n.* derogation, pejoration
depressed *adj.* disconsolate, morose
depression *n.* melancholia
deprivation, causing privative
deprive *v.* disembody, disendow
depths, out of the *de profundis*
deputy *n.* exarch, locum tenens, surrogate, vicar
deride *v.* banter, chaff, decry, deprecate, flout, pillory, scout
derived externally exogenous
derived internally endogenous
derogatory *adj.* deprecatory, derogative, pejorative
dervish *n.* calender, fakir, marabout, qalandar
dervishes, group of Rifa'iya
descend *v.* abseil, rappel
descent *n.* declivity, degression, descension
describe *v.* delineate, limn
descriptive *adj.* expositive
desertion *n.* apostasy, defection, dereliction
deserved *adj.* condign
designate *v.* denominate, denote
designation *n.* appellation
desire *n.* affinity, appetence, hankering
desire, insatiable cacoëthes
desired, something desideratum
desirous *adj.* appetent, covetous, rapacious
desist *v.* surcease
desk, writing escritoire
despicable *adj.* reptilian, scurvy
despise *v.* contemn, disprize, execrate, misprize
despised person pariah
despotism *n.* autarchy
dessert table Viennese table
destiny *n.* karma, kismet
destitute *adj.* impecunious, penurious
destroy *v.* decimate, extirpate, immolate, raze, unmake
destroyer *n.* iconoclast, Luddite
destruction *n.* apocalypse, ecocide, Götterdämmerung, menticide,
    Ragnarok, spoliation
destructive *adj.* baneful, biolytic, epiphytotic, fell, internecine,
    malefic, noxious

detach *v.* disjoin, dissociate, sunder
detached *adj.* dégagé
detention *n.* demurrage
deterioration *n.* dégringolade, retrogression
determined *adj.* iron-jawed, staunch
detestable *adj.* execrable, loathsome, odious
detonate *v.* fulminate
detraction *n.* derogation, disparagement, obloquy
develop *v.* dilate, expatiate
development *n.* ontogeny, phylogeny
divert *v.* sublimate
device *n.* artifice, stratagem
devil *n.* Beelzebub, Belial, cacodemon, Old Harry, Old Scratch,
    Scratch, the Tempter
devious *adj.* circuitous, tortuous, vermiculate
devise *v.* excogitate
devour *v.* engorge, gormandize, guttle, raven
devouring *adj.* edacious
devoutness *n.* fervency, religiosity
dexterity *n.* sleight
diagnosis *n.* pathognomy
diagonal *adj.* antigodlin, cater-cornered
diagram *n.* schema
dialect *n.* joual, koine, Krio, patois, pidgin
dialogue *n.* colloquy, duologue, interlocution, stichomythia
diamonds, like diamantine
diamonds, yielding diamantiferous
diaper cover pilch
diaphragm *n.* pessary
dictator *n.* autocrat, Caesar, caudillo, duce
dictatorial *adj.* imperious, overbearing
diction *n.* hypercorrection
dictionary *n.* gradus, lexicon
die *v.* necrotize
difference *n.* dissimilitude, imparity
different names, of heteronymous
different parts, having heteromerous
differing *adj.* discrepant
difficult *adj.* arcane, esoteric, impalpable, obdurate, recondite,
    unfathomable
difficulties, cause straiten
difficulty *n.* exigency, nodus, pons asinorum, strait, trilemma
diffuse *v.* perfuse, pervade
digest *n.* pandect
digestion *n.* dyspepsia, eupepsia

digging *adj.* fossorial
dignified *adj.* august, decorous
dignity *n.* exaltation, izzat
dignity, beneath infra dig
digress *v.* divagate, expatiate
digressive *adj.* circumlocutory, excursive, periphrastic
dig up disinhume, disentomb
dilated *adj.* distended, protuberant
diligent *adj.* assiduous, indefatigable, sedulous
dillydally *v.* procrastinate, vacillate
diluting *adj.* diluent, humectant
dim *adj.* crepuscular
diminish *v.* mitigate, peter, remit, scant
diminishing *adj.* decrescent
dimple *n.* fossette
dim-sighted *adj.* gravel-blind, purblind, sand-blind, stone-blind
dining companion commensal, convive
dining hall refectory
dining room oecus, triclinium
diocese *n.* bishopric, episcopate, see
dip *v.* bail, dap, douse, immerge
diploma, holder of diplomate
diplomat *n.* chargé d'affaires, nuncio, plenipotentiary
dipper *n.* simpulum
director *n.* régisseur
dirge *n.* coronach, epicedium, Linus, pibroch, threnody
dirt *n.* scud
dirty *v.* bemire, defile, sully
disadvantage *n.* disamenity, incommodity
disagreeing *adj.* dissentient
disagreement *n.* contrariety, discordance, dissidence
disappear *v.* evanesce, evanish, immerge, molder
disappoint *v.* disenchant, disenthrall, disillusionize
disappointment *n.* Dead Sea fruit
disapproval *n.* animadversion, aspersion, reprehension,
    reprobation
disapproving *adj.* deprecative, deprecatory, dyslogistic, opprobrious
disastrous *adj.* cataclysmic, funest
discard *v.* jettison
discernment *n.* percipience, perspicacity
discharge *v.* disembogue, disgorge, egest, ejaculate, exude
disciple *n.* chela, proselyte
disciplinarian *n.* martinet
discipline *v.* castigate, chasten
disclose *v.* broadcast, unbosom, unbutton, unkennel

discoloration *n.* foxing
disconcert *v.* daunt, discomfit
disconnected *adj.* desultory, scatterbrained
discontented *adj.* alienated, disaffected
discontinue *v.* intermit
discontinuous *adj.* discrete
discordant *adj.* cacophonous, disharmonious, inconsonant
discourage *v.* daunt, discountenance, dispirit
discouraged *adj.* crestfallen, dispirited
discourager *n.* Job's comforter
discourse *v.* dissert, dissertate
discourse *n.* disquisition, dissertation, exercitation, prolegomenon, screed
discourteous *adj.* inurbane, loutish
discovery *n.* anagnorisis, secernment, serendipity
discovery, encouraging heuristic
discredit *v.* confute, controvert
discreet *adj.* circumspect, meet, politic
discrepancy *n.* contrariety
discretion *n.* sophrosyne
discriminate *v.* discern, secern
discriminating *adj.* percipient
discuss *v.* dissertate, ventilate
discussion *n.* confabulation, excursus, prolegomenon
discussion, preliminary *pourparler*
discussion topic *cheval de bataille*
disdain *n.* hauteur, superciliousness
disease *n.* epizooty, gynecopathy, morbidity
disease, causing morbific
disease, predisposition to diathesis
disembowel *v.* draw, embowel, eviscerate, exenterate
disentangle *v.* disembroil, disencumber
disgorge *v.* regorge
disgrace *n.* contumely, ignominy, obloquy, odium, opprobrium
disgusting *adj.* abominable, ad nauseam, loathsome, odious
dish *n.* bonbonnière, comport, compote, compotier, coolamon, nappy, paten, porringer, ramekin, ramequin, salver, terrine, tureen
disheveled *adj.* raggle-taggle, ragtag, tousled
dishonesty *n.* improbity, mendacity, obliquity, perfidy
dishonor *v.* desecrate, dishallow, profane
dishonorable *adj.* basehearted, ignoble, ignominious, meanspirited, reptilian
disillusion *v.* disabuse, disenamor, undeceive
disinheritance *n.* disherison

disintegrate *v.* corrade, disgregate, molder
disinter *v.* disentomb
disk *n.* planchet
dislike *n.* antipathy, disesteem, disfavor, disrelish, scunner
dislocate *v.* luxate, splay
disloyal *adj.* apostate, disaffected, perfidious, recreant, seditious
dismal *adj.* dour, funereal, lowering, lugubrious, sepulchral
dismay *v.* affright, consternate, daunt, unnerve
dismiss *v.* cashier
dismissal *n.* demission
disobedient *adj.* contumacious, refractory
disobey *v.* contravene, flout, transgress
disorder *n.* bedlam, chaos, mayhem
disorderly *adj.* recalcitrant, refractory, wayward
disorderly thinking dishabille
disown *v.* abjure, disavow
disparaging *adj.* pejorative
disparate *adj.* discordant, incongruous
dispensation *n.* indult
dispersion *n.* diaspora
displace *v.* eloign, unsphere
displacement *n.* parallax
display *n.* éclat, flourish, frippery, panoply
dispossess *v.* expropriate
disprove *v.* confute, controvert, gainsay
disputation, art of eristic
disputatious *adj.* contradictious, polemical
dispute *n.* contretemps, flite, fliting, flyte, logomachy, velitation
dispute *v.* altercate, controvert, gainsay, oppugn
disregard *v.* flout, overslaugh, pretermit
disregard *n.* preterition
disrepute *n.* obloquy, odium, opprobrium
dissection *n.* zootomy
disseminate *v.* effuse
dissension *n.* alienation, disjunction, schism
dissenter *n.* apostate, dissentient, maverick
dissenting *adj.* dissentient, dissident
dissertation *n.* disquisition, lucubration
dissimilar *adj.* disparate, divergent
dissipated *adj.* dissolute, jaded, profligate, raffish, rakish, wanton
dissolving *n.* diffluence, deliquescence, liquefaction
dissonant *adj.* cacophonous
distance *v.* decathect
distillation *n.* decoction
distinct *adj.* manifest, patent, trenchant

distinctive *adj.* diacritical
distinguish *v.* secern, signalize
distinguished *adj.* distingué, distinguée, supereminent
distinguishing *adj.* disjunctive, precisive
distress *v.* beset, harrow, lacerate, rend, rive
distressing *adj.* afflictive, agonal
distribute *v.* mete, parcel
distribution center entrepôt
district *n.* bailiwick, bishopric, canton, catholicate, deanery,
    diocese, episcopate, pale, sanjak, see, vicinage, zillah
distrustful *adj.* chary, jaundiced
disturb *v.* discommode, harrow, incommode, roil
disturbance *n.* bobbery, catouse, foofaraw, rabblement
disuse *n.* desuetude
ditch *n.* entrenchment, fosse
diver *n.* ama
divergent *adj.* divaricate, diverse
diverse *adj.* heterogeneous, multifarious
diversified *adj.* daedal, motley, variegated
divert one's energy sublimate
divide *v.* Balkanize, bifurcate, cantonize, cleave, dichotomize,
    dissever, furcate, rend, rive, section, sunder, trifurcate
divider *n.* separatrix, solidus, virgule
dividing *n.* polytomy
divination *n.* aeromancy, alectryomancy, aleuromancy,
    aphitomancy, arithmancy, astromancy, augur, augury, auspex,
    auspice, belomancy, bibliomancy, chiromancy, cleromancy,
    geomancy, haruspicy, hydromancy, *I Ching*, necromancy,
    oneiromancy, pyromancy, rhabdomancy, scapulimancy, sortes,
    sortilege, zoomancy
divination, of mantic
divine *adj.* deiform, supernal
divine and human, both theantropic
divisible *adj.* discerptible, partible, scissile
division *n.* dichotomy, diremption, disjunction, schism, scission,
    trichotomy
divisive *adj.* dissentious, factious, schismatic
divorce *n.* breach, get, decree nisi
divulge *v.* disembosom
dizzy *adj.* vertiginous
doctor *v.* adulterate, cobble
doctrine *n.* canon, credo, doxy, precept
document *n.* papyrus
doddering *adj.* anile, fribbling
dog *n.* crackie, towser

dogged *adj.* mulish, tenacious
dogmatic *adj.* arbitrary, doctrinaire, doctrinal, oracular, pontifical, thetic
dog pack kennel
dog pound pinfold
doleful *adj.* lugubrious
doll *n.* daruma, golliwogg, kachina
domain *n.* seigneury
dome *n.* cupola, dagoba
dominating woman dominatrix
domination *n.* ascendancy, heteronomy, primacy
do more than required supererogate
donation *n.* benefaction, donative, ex-voto, oblation
donkey *n.* dickey, hinny, jennet, jenny
doomed *adj.* hapless, ill-starred
doorkeeper *n.* concierge, ostiary, warder
dormant *adj.* dormient, latent, torpid
dormitory *n.* dorter, rampasture
dot *n.* tittle
dotted *adj.* punctulate
double *adj.* diploid, duple
double *v.* geminate, plait
double dagger diesis
double-dealing *adj.* duplicitous
double-talk *n.* razzmatazz, gobbledegook
doubtful *adj.* dubitable, dubitative, moot
dough *n.* masa
doughnut *n.* fasnacht, friedcake, olykoek, sinker
dovelike *adj.* columbine
dowdy *adj.* bedraggled, draggle-tailed, frumpy
downfall *n.* *dégringolade*, labefaction, nemesis, Waterloo
downright *adj.* arrant
downward sloping declivent, declivitous, declivous
downy *adj.* comose, flossy, lanuginose, lanuginous, sericeous
dowry *n.* arras, dower
dowse *v.* water-witch, witch
dowsing *n.* rhabdomancy
draft *v.* conscribe, conscript, impress
dragon *n.* firedrake
dragon-like *adj.* draconic
drain blood exsanguinate
dramatist *n.* dramaturge
draw *v.* limn
drawbridge *n.* pontlevis
draw forth educe

drawing *n.* analytique, graffito, petroglyph, petrogram, pictograph, plumbago
drawing in intussusception, invagination
dread *v.* quail
dread *n.* angst, aversion, trepidation
dreamer *n.* fantast, visionary
dream interpreter oneirocritic
dreamland *n.* cloud-cuckooland, cloudland
dreams, interpretation of oneirology
dreams, pertaining to oneiric, onomastic
dregs *n.* draff, dross, fecula, lees, vinasse
drench *v.* imbrue, ret
dress *v.* accouter, bedeck, bedizen, caparison, deck, gussy, tog
dressed *adj.* habited
dressing *n.* pledget
dried-up *adj.* wizened
drilling machine stoper
drink, farewell doch-an-dorrach, stirrup cup
drink, medicinal ptisan
drinkable *adj.* potable
drinker *n.* bibber, compotator, convive, soaker, tippler, toper
drinking, given to potatory
drinking horn rhyton
drivel *v.* balderdash, gabble, gibble-gabble, gobbledegook, pablum, pabulum, pap, razzmatazz, twaddle
driver *n.* jehu, mahout, postilion
drizzle *n.* cacimbo
droll *adj.* waggish
drool *v.* drivel, slaver, slobber
droop *v.* flag, languish
drooping *adj.* flaccid, pendent, pendulous
drop *n.* globule, gobbet, gutta
drop-like *adj.* guttiform
droppings *n.* excreta, guano
drop-shaped *adj.* stilliform
drowsiness *n.* narcosis, oscitation
drowsiness, pertaining to hypnagogic
drowsy *adj.* dozy, oscitant, soporific
drudgery *n.* moil
drum *v.* rataplan
drum exercise paradiddle
drumstick *n.* tampon
drunken *adj.* bacchic, besotted, bousy, Dionysian, fuddled, sotted, sottish
dry *adj.* insipid, jejune, vapid

dry *v.* desiccate, exsiccate
dry environment, adapted to a xerothermic
dry environment, pertaining to a xeric
drying *n.* aridification, desiccation, exsiccation
drying *adj.* siccative
dualist *n.* Manichean
dubious *adj.* louche
duct *n.* hypocaust
dueling *n.* duello
dues *n.* pewage
dull *adj.* jejune, passionless, prosy, saltless, torpid, vapid
dullness *n.* hebetude, tedium
dunce *n.* dolt, dullard, dummkopf, dunderhead, pumpkin head
dune *n.* barchan, seif
dung, of stercoraceous, stercorous
dung-eating *adj.* coprophagous, merdivorous, scatophagous
dungeon *n.* donjon, oubliette
dunghill *n.* midden
dupe *n.* cat's-paw, gudgeon
duplicate *v.* geminate, replicate
duplicated, capable of being replicable, replicative
durable *adj.* perdurable
dusk *n.* crepuscule, evenfall
dusky *adj.* fuscous, subfusc, subfuscous
dwarf *n.* homunculus, hop-o'-my-thumb, manikin
dwarfism *n.* hypermicrosoma
dying *adj.* expiring, *in extremis*, moribund
dynamite *n.* gelignite

E

eagerness *n.* alacrity, avidity, fervor, zeal
eagle *n.* alerion
ear *n.* auricle, auricular, auriculate, auriform, concha
ear, pertaining to the otic
earache *n.* otalgia
earnest *adj.* fervid, zealous

earnestness *n.* unction
earring *n.* girandole
earth, inhabitant of tellurian, tellurion
earth, living in or on terricolous
earthenware *n.* faience, majolica, raku
earthly *adj.* secular, terrene
earthquake *n.* seism, temblor
earthworm, resembling the lumbricoid
earthy *adj.* terrene
earwax *n.* cerumen
ease *v.* assuage, disburden, palliate
eat *v.* chank, gormandize, ingurgitate, raven, stodge
eater, heavy trencherman
eater of raw food omophagist
eating disorders anorexia, bulimia, polyphagia
ebb *n.* reflux
ebbing *adj.* refluent
eccentric *n.* heteroclite
eccentricity *n.* crotchet, idiosyncrasy
echoic *adj.* onomatopoeic
economy *n.* niggardliness, parsimony, providence
ecstasy *n.* nympholepsy, raptus, ravishment
eddy *v.* moil, purl
edgy *adj.* nudgy
edible *adj.* comestible, esculent
edict *n.* bull, dictum, firman, pronunciamento, rescript, ukase
edit *v.* bowdlerize, emend, emendate, expunge, redact, vet
effectiveness *n.* efficacity, efficacy
effeminate *adj.* emasculate, epicene, niminy-piminy
effeminate person chulo
effigy *n.* simulacrum
effort *n.* assiduity
effrontery *n.* cheek, churlishness
egg case ootheca
eggs, lay oviposit
egg-shaped *adj.* obovoid, ovate, oviform, ovoid
egg white albumen, glair
egg yolk vitellus
egoism *n.* narcissism, solipsism
eighth note quaver
eighty-year old person octogenarian
eject *v.* ejaculate, spume
ejection *n.* defenestration
elation *n.* euphoria, transport
elder *n.* presbyter

elect *v.* coopt
elections, study of psephology
elegance *n.* concinnity, luxe
elegance of speech atticism
elegant *adj.* Chesterfieldian, featly, la-di-da
element, indispensable linchpin, sine qua non
elephant driver mahout
elephant trap kheda
elf *n.* leprechaun, ouphe
elicit *v.* educe
eliminate *v.* extirpate, quash
elliptical *adj.* vesical
elusive *adj.* fugitive
emaciation *n.* tabes
emanate *v.* mofette
emasculate *v.* eunuchize, unman
embarrassment *n.* abashment, discomfiture, disconcertment, mortification
embellish *v.* blazon, fancify
embellishment *n.* emblazonry, paraph, parergon
embezzlement *n.* defalcation, peculation
emblem *n.* colophon, fasces, impresa, totem
emblems *n.* regalia
embodiment *n.* avatar, elixir, quintessence
embody *v.* exemplify, incarnate
embolism *n.* embolus, occlusion
emboss *v.* chase, pounce
embossed *adj.* ciselé
embossing *n.* celature
embroidery frame taboret
embroil *v.* embrangle, mire
emerge *v.* debouch, emanate
emergency *n.* exigency
emetic *adj./n.* vomitory
emit *v.* effuse, emanate, eruct, exude
emotion *n.* affect
emotional *adj.* effusive, fervid, maudlin, mawkish
emotionless *adj.* callous, phlegmatic, stoical
emperor *n.* imperator, Negus, padishah
emphatic *adj.* resounding, unequivocal
empty *adj.* banal, delusive, vacuous, vapid
enamel *n.* champlevé, cloisonné
enamelware *n.* Fabergé
encampment *n.* hutment
enchanted *adj.* fey

enchantress *n.* Circe
encircle *v.* encincture, engirdle
enclose *v.* circumscribe, embosom, enswathe, enwomb, immure
enclosure *n.* cofferdam, enceinte, kraal
encode *v.* encrypt
encompass *v.* encincture
encore *interj.* bis
encounter *v.* rencontre, rencounter
encouragement *n.* fosterage
encouraging *adj.* exhortative, exhortatory, hortative, hortatory
encumbrances *n.* impedimenta
encyclopedia *n.* pandect
end *n.* expiry, omega, surcease, terminus
end *v.* culminate, surcease
endearing *adj.* hypocoristic
ending *n.* denouement, desinence
endowment *n.* dotation, dower
endure *v.* brook, countenance, perdure, stomach
enema *n.* clyster
energetic *adj.* indefatigable, sedulous
energizing *adj.* galvanic
energy *n.* birr, élan, verve
engaging *adj.* winsome
engraver *n.* chaser
engraver's tool graver, scauper
engraving *n.* chemigraphy, siderography
enjoyment, seeking apolaustic
enjoyment of life joie de vivre
enlarge *v.* aggrandize, dilate, eke, expatiate
enlarged *adj.* ampliate, turgid, varicose
enlargement *n.* dilatation, gynecomastia, hypertrophy
enlightening *adj.* luciferous
enlightenment *n.* Aufklärung, bodhi, prajna, satori
enmity *n.* acrimony, animus, rancor, venom
enough *interj. basta*
enrapture *v.* imparadise
enraptured *adj.* transported
enslavement *n.* dulosis
entangle *v.* embrangle, embroil
enterprising *adj.* venturesome, venturous
entertainer *n.* almah, diseur, diseuse, monologist, tummler
entertainment *n.* fête champêtre, kermis, masque, revue, tamasha
enthralled *adj.* exhilarated, rapt
enthusiasm *n.* fervency, *Schwärmerei*
enthusiastic *adj.* dithyrambic, ebullient, fervid, yeasty

enticer *n.* beguiler, pied piper
entire *adj.* intact, plenary
entity *n.* ens
entomb *v.* ensepulcher, immure
entrance *n.* adit, propylaeum
entreaty, pertaining to precatory, supplicatory
entrenchment *n.* vallation
enumeration *n.* litany
enunciate *v.* articulate, syllable
envelop *v.* environ, sheathe, shroud
environment *n.* ambiance, environs, milieu
environs *n.* purlieus
envoy *n.* chargé d'affaires, legate, plenipotentiary
envy *v.* begrudge, covet
epic *n.* chanson de geste, epopee, epos, Mahabharata
epicure *n.* mycophagist
epidemic *n.* epiphytotic
epigrams, make epigrammatize
epilepsy *n.* grand mal, petit mal
epitaph *n.* hic jacet
epithet *n.* antonomasia, appellative
equal *n.* compeer, peer
equal *v.* equiponderate
equality *n.* egalitarianism, isonomy
equality, lacking in inegalitarian
equilibrium *n.* equipoise, equiponderance, stasis
equip *v.* accouter, endue, invest
equipment *n.* accouterments, armamentarium, fitment
equivalent *adj.* equipollent, tantamount
equivocate *v.* palter, tergiversate
eradicate *v.* deracinate, extirpate
erasure *n.* effacement, expunction, extirpation, rasure
erect *adj.* horrent, tumescent
erection, persistent priapism
eroding *adj.* erodent, erosive
erosion *n.* corrasion, deflation
erotic *adj.* aphrodisiac, concupiscent, erogenous, lesbian, Paphian
errand boy lobbygow
erratic *adj.* capricious, vagarious
error *n.* barney, bloomer, catachresis, erratum, faux pas, gaffe, non
 sequitur, solecism
error-free *adj.* inerrant
error-prone *adj.* peccable
errors and corrections errata
erupt *v.* recrudesce

escape *v.* abscond, decamp, exfiltrate
escort *n.* cicisbeo, gallant, gigolo
escort *v.* chaperon, squire
essay *n.* disquisition, dissertation, prolusion
essence *n.* crux, pith, quintessence
essential *adj.* constitutive, de rigueur, integral
essential parts vitals
established *adj.* apodictic, inveterate
estate *n.* bergerie, demesne, estancia, latifundium, taluk
estranged *adj.* disaffected
estuary *n.* firth
et cetera *und so weiter*
eternal *adj.* perdurable, sempiternal
ethics *n.* deontology
euphoria, inducing euphoriant, euphorigenic
evaluation *n.* epicrisis
evasion *n.* circumlocution, elusion, sophistry
evasive *adj.* circuitous, elusive, evanescent, tortuous
evening *n.* crepuscule, eventide, gloaming, vespertide
even-minded *adj.* equable
even-tempered *adj.* equanimous
everlasting *adj.* perdurable, sempiternal
evidence, one who gives deponent
evident *adj.* manifest, ostensible, ostensive, palpable
evil *adj.* baleful, baneful, iniquitous, malign, malignant, nefarious,
    pernicious
evil *n.* depravity, gangrene, iniquity
evil, averting apotropaic
evil, doing *adj.* maleficent
evil, surpass in out-Herod
evolution *n.* orthogenesis, phylogeny, polygenism
exact *adj.* punctilious, scrupulous, veracious
exacting *adj.* exigent
exaggeration *n.* hyperbole, inflation, pretension, pretentiousness
exalt *v.* deify, ennoble, ensky
examination *n.* catechism, inspectum, responsions, voir dire
examine *v.* anatomize, dissect, vet
example *n.* exemplar, exemplum, paradigm
example, furnish an epitomize, exemplify
examples, set of praxis
excavation *n.* fosse, stope
excellence *n.* beau ideal, transcendence, virtu
excellent *adj.* estimable, inimitable, sterling
exceptional *adj.* anomalous, preternatural, prodigious
excerpts *n.* analects

excessive *adj.* extortionate, fulsome, inordinate, overblown, prodigal, profligate
exchangeable *adj.* commutable, fungible
excitable *adj.* combustible, volatile
excite *v.* adrenalize, animate, galvanize, intoxicate
exciting *adj.* electric, heady, rousing, spirited
exclamation *n.* ejaculation, expletive, vociferation
exclamatory passage apostrophe
exclude *v.* ostracize, preclude, proscribe
excommunicate *v.* unchurch
excommunication *n.* excision, *herem*
excrement *n.* dejecta, dejection, egesta, excreta, fecula, frass, meconium, night soil, ordure, scat
excrement, like excrementitious
excrescence *n.* caruncle, gall, knur, wattle
excusable *adj.* venial
excuse *v.* exculpate, extenuate, gloze
excuse *n.* apologia, extenuation, mitigation
execute *v.* dispatch, gibbet
execution *n.* auto-da-fé, decapitation, noyade
exegesis *n.* hermeneutics
exemption *n.* exoneration, recusal
exercise *n.* kata
exhalation *n.* effluvium, miasma, mephitis
exhausted *adj.* debilitated, effete, enervated, jaded
exhaustive *adj.* cyclopedic, encyclopedic
exhilaration *n.* ebullience, effusiveness
exile *n.* expatriation, Galuth, proscription, sequestration
exiled *adj.* expatriate
existence *n.* inherency
exit *n.* débouché, egress
exorbitant *adj.* extortionate, inordinate
exotic *adj.* recherché
expand *v.* dilate, expatiate
expandable *adj.* expansible, expansile, extensible
expanded *adj.* patulous, protuberant
expedient *n.* *pis aller*, resort
expedient *adj.* politic
expenditure, pertaining to sumptuary
experience, based on empirical, experiential
experienced *adj.* practiced, versant
experienced through others vicarious
experiences, painful via dolorosa
expiatory *adj.* piacular
explain *v.* construe, dilate, expatiate, explicate, gloss, rationalize

explanation *n.* éclaircissement, exegesis, explication, panchreston
explanatory *adj.* exegetic, explicative, hermeneutic
explode *v.* fulminate
exploit *n.* gest
explosion *n.* camouflet, fulmination
explosive device petard
expositor *n.* exegete, explicator
exposure *n.* exposal
expound *v.* asseverate, exposit
express *v.* asseverate, indite
expressed, clearly perspicuous
expressed, well apposite
expressible *adj.* effable
expressionless *adj.* impassive, vacant, vacuous
expressive *adj.* articulate, rubber-faced
expulsion *n.* renvoi
expurgate *v.* bowdlerize
exquisite *adj.* raffiné, soigné
extemporaneously *adv.* extempore
extend *v.* ramify
extendible *adj.* extensible, extensile, protrusile
extent *n.* ambit
exterminate *v.* deratize, extirpate
externalize *v.* exteriorize, objectivize
externally derived exogenous
extract *n.* citation, pericope
extraction *n.* exodontia, exodontics, evulsion
extraneous *adj.* adventitious, intervenient
extraordinary *adj.* egregious
extravagant *adj.* immoderate, improvident, prodigal, profligate
extremism *n.* ultraism
exuberant *adj.* ebullient, effusive, rank, yeasty
exult *v.* jubilate
exultant *adj.* cock-a-hoop
exultation *n.* jubilation
eye *n.* oculus
eyebrow, of the superciliary
eye for an eye lex talionis
eyelids, of the palpebral
eyelike *adj.* ocellate, ocellated
eye movement, rapid nystagmus, saccade
eyewash *n.* collyrium

F

fable *n.* allegory, apologue, parable
fables, collection of Jataka
fabric finishing decating
façade, deceptive Potemkin village
face, pale wheyface
face-lift *n.* rhytidectomy
face-to-face vis-à-vis
facing *n.* revers, revetment
fact, accomplished fait accompli
faction *n.* bloc, coterie
factional *adj.* partisan
factual *adj.* veracious
faddist *n.* weathercock
fading *adj.* evanescent
failed *adj.* manqué, miscarried
failure *n.* debacle, fiasco, miscarriage
faint *adj.* languid
faint *n.* syncope
faint-hearted *adj.* pusillanimous
fair *adj.* disinterested
fair *n. feria*, kermis, mela
fairly *adv.* equably, *pari passu*
fairy *n.* fay, leprechaun, Queen Mab, peri
faith, abandonment of apostasy
faith, bad *mala fides*
faith, false miscreance
faith, good *bona fides*
faithful *adj.* allegiant, staunch
faithless *adj.* perfidious
fake *v.* affect, dissemble, feign
fake *adj.* faux, sham
fall *v.* prolapse, toboggan
Fall, after the postlapsarian
Fall, before the prelapsarian
fallacious *adj.* delusive, sophistic
fallacy *n.* paralogism, sophism
fallen in social position déclassé

fallow *adj.* lea, ley
false *adj.* apocryphal, disingenuous, mendacious, papier-mâché, postiche
false hair merkin
falsehood *n.* mendacity, prevarication
fan *n.* devotee, hardboot
fan *v.* winnow
fanatic *adj.* frenetic, phrenetic, zealous
fanatical *adj.* doctrinaire
fancy *adj.* haute
fanfare *n.* fanfaron, tucket
fantasy *n.* fantasia, phantasm
faraway place, any Timbuktu
farewell *n.* congé
farewell, bidding valediction
farewell address valedictory
farewell drink doch-an-dorrach, stirrup cup
farm *n.* ejido, finca, grange
farmer *n.* granger, sodbuster
farming *n.* agronomy, ecofallow, husbandry, tillage
far-out *adj.* esoteric, recondite
farsighted *adj.* perspicacious, prescient
farsightedness *n.* hypermetropia, hyperopia, presbyopia
farthest point apogee
fascinating *adj.* mesmeric, mesmerizing, orphic
fashion *n.* façon, ton
fashion, out of démodé
fashion, the latest dernier cri
fashion plate Beau Brummell
fastening *n.* infibulation
fastidiousness *n.* foppishness, preciosity
fasting *n.* dharna, sawm, xerophagia
fat *adj.* abdominous, adipose, fubsy, lardy, pinguid, pursy
fat *n.* bard, cracklings, cracknels, lardon, schmaltz
fat, grow batten
fat, smear with tallow
fatal *adj.* baneful, feral, funest, mortiferous, pernicious
fat-buttocked *adj.* steatopygic
fate *n.* karma, kismet
father *n.* anba, genitor, paterfamilias, progenitor
fatiguing *adj.* debilitating, enervating, prostrating
fatness *n.* adiposity, corpulence
fatty *adj.* adipose, lardaceous, sebaceous
faucet *n.* cock, hosecock, petcock, stopcock
fault *n.* feet of clay, frailty, foible

fault, my *mea culpa*
faultfinding *adj.* captious, carping, caviling, censorious, hypercritical
faultless *adj.* exemplary, immaculate, impeccable, indefectible, unassailable, unexceptionable
faulty *adj.* peccant
favorable *adj.* auspicious, opportune, propitious, providential
favoritism *n.* cronyism, nepotism
fawning *adj.* gnathonic, sycophantic
fawn skin nebris
fear *n.* collywobbles, funk, trepidation
fearless *adj.* dauntless, doughty, indomitable, unblinking, undaunted
fears, morbid acarophobia, acrophobia, aerophobia, agoraphobia, ailurophobia, algophobia, androphobia, anthropophobia, astraphobia, aviophobia, bacteriaphobia, batophobia, batrachophobia, bibliphobia, brontophobia, cardiophobia, chremnophobia, cibophobia, claustrophobia, coprophobia, cyberphobia, cynophobia, doraphobia, dromophobia, dysmorphobia, ergophobia, erythrophobia, felinophobia, feminophobia, gamophobia, gerontophobia, gynephobia, hemophobia, heresyphobia, homophobia, hypnophobia, logophobia, lyssophobia, monophobia, mysophobia, necrophobia, nosophobia, nyctophobia, ochlophobia, pantophobia, peccatophobia, phobophobia, photophobia, pyrophobia, scotophobia, sitophobia, stasiphobia, taphephobia, thanatophobia, taxophobia, teleophobia, thalassophobia, thanatophobia, topophobia, toxicophobia, xenophobia, zoophobia
feasible *adj.* practicable, viable
feast *n.* luau, potlatch, regale
feasting *n.* gourmandise
feather *n.* aigrette, alula, hackle, vibrissa
feather, resembling a pinnate
feathery *adj.* plumose, plumy
feature *n.* pièce de résistance
fecal matter, full of feculent
feces, pertaining to stercoraceous, stercorous
feces, resembling fecaloid
fee *n.* altarage, capitation, emolument, honorarium
feebleness *n.* decrepitude, flaccidity, impuissance, languor, lassitude
feed *v.* batten, browse, regale
feeding on grass graminivorous
feeding on leaves phyllophagous
feeding on one type of food monophagous

feeding on plants herbivorous, phytophagous
feeding on roots rhizophagous
feeding on sap phytosuccivorous
feelings, shared compathy, empathy
fellowship *n.* camaraderie, communion, esprit de corps
female *adj.* distaff
female in appearance gynecomorphous
fence *n.* brandreth, hoarding, paling, palisade, palisado, weir
fence-sitter *n.* dawk, mugwump
fencing *n.* balestra, kendo
fermentation *n.* zymosis
ferryman *n.* Charon
fertilization *n.* fecundation, superfecundation, superfetation
fertilize *v.* fructify, impregnate
fertilizer *n.* guano, marl, poudrette
fester *v.* matterate, suppurate
festoon *n.* swag
fetish *n.* amulet, juju, talisman
fetus, destruction of a feticide
fever *n.* ague, febricula, hyperpyrexia, hyperthermia, octan, pyrexia,
    quartan, quintan, quotidian
fever, producing febrifacient, febriferous, febrific
feverish *adj.* aguish, febrile
feverless *adj.* afebrile
fever preventive antipyretic
fibrous *adj.* filamentous
fickleness *n.* inconstancy, volatility
fictitious *adj.* feigned, fictive, mythic
fiddle *n.* rebab, rebec
fiddle-shaped *adj.* pandurate
fidelity *n.* fealty, troth
fidgety *adj.* restive
fiend *n.* hellhound
fierce *adj.* *farouche*, fell
fiery *adj.* choleric, fervid, irascible
fifteenth century quattrocento
fifteen years, pertaining to quindecennial
fight *n.* affray, barney, bobbery, brannigan, donnybrook, dustup
fighting with an imaginary enemy sciamachy, sciomachy
figure of speech trope
file *n.* dossier
film *n.* patina, pellicle
film fan cineast
filmy *adj.* diaphanous
filth, originating from pythogenic

filthy *adj.* Augean, dreggy
final destruction apocalypse, Götterdämmerung
financial instability Queer Street
fine *adj.* abstruse, impalpable, tenuous
fine *v.* mulct
fine point punctilio
finery *n.* fallal, frippery, furbelow, gaudery, regalia
finger-like *adj.* digitiform
fingers, condition of having extra hyperdactylia, hyperdactylism
finish *v.* planish
firecracker *n.* squib, whiz-bang
fireplace, rear of reredos
firework *n.* Catherine wheel, fizgig, girandole, petard, serpent, tourbillion
fireworks display pyrotechnics
firm *adj.* adamant, obdurate, sclerous, staunch
first among equals *prima* (or *primus*) *inter pares*
first draft prolusion
firsthand *adj.* empirical, pragmatic
first night, right of droit du seigneur
fish *n.* ichthyolite
fish *v.* dap, dib, seine, sniggle, trawl, troll
fish, pertaining to ichthyic, piscine
fish-eating *adj.* ichthyophagous, piscivorous
fishing, pertaining to piscatorial, piscatory
fishing grounds haaf
fishing spot piscary
fishlike *adj.* ichthyoid
fissure *n.* crevasse
fitting *adj.* condign, congruous, meet, seemly
five, pertaining to quinary
five-fingered *adj.* pentadactyl
five-year period lustrum, quinquennium
five years, occurring every quinquennial
flabby *adj.* flaccid, loppy, lymphatic, quaggy
flag *n.* banderole, burgee, fanion, guidon, Jolly Roger, pennon, standard, vexillum
flagging *adj.* languid
flagrant *adj.* egregious, flagitious
flags, pertaining to vexillary
flamboyance *n.* panache
flamboyant *adj.* florid, ostentatious
flannel *n.* swansdown, swanskin
flap *n.* codpiece, lappet
flash *v.* coruscate, fulgurate, fulminate

flashy *adj.* meretricious
flask *n.* alembic, costrel, fiasco, flacon
flatfoot *n.* splayfoot
flattened *adj.* oblate, planate, planiform
flatterer *n.* encomiast, lickspittle, sycophant, truckler
flattering *adj.* ingratiating, smarmy, unctuous
flattery *n.* blandishment, blarney, cajolery, pandering, puffery,
    sycophancy, toadying
flaunt *v.* brandish, flourish
flavor *n.* piquancy, sapor, savor
flavor *v.* imbue, infuse, lace, leaven
flavor, imparting saporific
flavorless *adj.* insipid, vapid
fleck *v.* freak
flee *v.* absquatulate, decamp
fleeting *adj.* ephemeral, evanescent, fugacious, fugitive
flesh, feeding on carnivorous, sarcophagous
flesh, pertaining to sarcous
flesh-bearing *adj.* carniferous
flesh-eating animal sarcophile
fleshy *adj.* carnose
fleshy fold dewlap, wattle
flickering *adj.* lambent, shimmering
flight *n.* exodus, hegira
flight, engaged in volitant
flighty *adj.* anile, capricious, mercurial, volatile
flimsy *adj.* gossamer, tenuous
flinch *v.* blanch, blench, cower, funk
flirt *n.* coquette, minx, philanderer, vamp
float *v.* waft
float *n.* bob, dobber
floater *n.* musca volitans
flood *n.* deluge, inundation, spate
Flood, after the postdiluvian
flooding *adj.* inundant
floor *n.* engawa, parquet
flooring *n.* terrazzo
flophouse *n.* doss house
florid *adj.* rubicund, ruddy
flounce *n.* falbala, furbelow
flourish *n.* paraph
flourishing *adj.* bounteous, halcyon, palmy
flow *v.* effuse, extravasate, purl, reflux
flower *v.* effloresce
flower arrangement ikebana
flower-eating *adj.* anthophagous, anthophilous

flowery *adj.* bombastic, florid, grandiloquent, magniloquent, rococo
flowing *adj.* diffluent, effluent, profluent, refluent
fluent *adj.* articulate, facile, voluble
fluid *n.* ejaculate, ichor
fluster *v.* commove, unnerve
flutist *n.* flautist
flutter *n.* dither, swivet
fly *v.* rack, scud
flyer *n.* broadside
flying *n.* volitation
foamy *adj.* frothy, spumescent, yeasty
fodder *n.* ensilage, silage, stover
fog *n.* brume, frost smoke, pogonip, sea smoke
foggy *adj.* nebulous, nubilous, turbid
foghorn *n.* diaphone
fold *n.* lappet
folded *adj.* plicate, replicate
folding *n.* plication
folk song volkslied
follow *v.* ensue, supervene
follower *n.* epigone, *fidus Achates*, galloglass, myrmidon,
  pursuivant, votary
following *adj.* sequacious, sequent
fond, overly uxorious
fondness *n.* dotage, penchant, predilection, susceptibility
font *n.* laver
food, animal mast
food, lacking appetite for anorectic, anorexic
food, supply with victual
food inspector *mashgiah*
food scrap ort
fool *n.* amadan, beetlehead, dunderhead, gommie, gowk,
  ninnyhammer, patch
fool *v.* confound, gudgeon, humbug
foolish *adj.* addlepated, anile, fatuitous, fatuous, *fou*, fribble,
  spoony, vapid
foolish person dotard, mooncalf
fool's gold pyrites
foothills, area in piedmont
footing *n.* scarcement
footlike *adj.* pediform
footstep *n.* footfall
foot support ottoman, suppedaneum
forbidden *adj.* interdicted, proscribed, verboten
forbidden, not licit
force *n.* dint, duress

forced feeding gavage
forceful *adj.* cogent
forcemeat *n.* farce, farcemeat
foreboding *n.* presage, presentiment
foreboding, having a *adj.* presentient
forecast *v.* previse
forefather *n.* primogenitor
foreign *adj.* allochthonous, heterochthonous, peregrine, tramontane
foreigner *n.* gaijin, outlander, tramontane, uitlander
foreigners, hatred of xenophobia
foreign exchange agiotage
forerunner *n.* harbinger, precursor, progenitor
foresee *v.* augur, forebode, portend, prefigure, previse, prevision
foreskin *n.* prepuce
forest *n.* selva, taiga
forestry *n.* silviculture, sylviculture
foretaste *n.* prelibation
forewarn *v.* previse
forfeit *n.* deodand, philopena
forfeiture *n.* mulct
forge *n.* stithy
forgetfulness *n.* lethe
forgetfulness, substance inducing nepenthe
forgetting *n.* oblivescence, oblivion
forgiving *adj.* clement, placable, propitious
forgo *v.* forbear
forked *adj.* furcate
form *n.* gestalt, modality, morphology
formal *adj.* punctilious, sententious, starchy
formality *n.* punctilio
former *adj.* erstwhile, quondam
formidable *adj.* daunting, onerous, redoubtable
formula *n.* mantra, precept, rubric
fort *n.* acropolis, citadel, fortalice, martello tower, presidio, redoubt
forte *n.* métier
forthcoming *adj.* proximate
fortitude *n.* mettle, stoicism
fortune, good serendipity
fortune, sudden change of peripeteia
fortune-teller *n.* chiromancer, mentalist, sibyl, warlock
fortune-telling *n.* cartomancy, chiromancy, palmistry,
    (see also **divination**)
fossil remains reliquiae
fossils, consisting of diatomaceous
foster *v.* embosom
foster child fosterling

foster mother *metapelet*
foul *adj.* feculent, fetid, turbid
foul language ordure
foul-smelling *adj.* mephitic
foundation *n.* fundament, substruction
foundling home crèche
fountain *n.* hanefiyah
fountain pen stylograph
four, group of quadriad, tetrad
four-handed *adj.* quadrumanous
fourteenth century trecento
four-year period quadrennium
four years, occurring every quadrennial
fowl *n.* poult, spatchcock
fowl, resembling *adj.* gallinaceous, rasorial
fox *n.* Reynard
fox, female vixen
fox, pertaining to a vulpecular, vulpine
fragile *adj.* frangible, friable
fragments *n.* disjecta membra, flinders, smithereens
fragrant *adj.* balmy, odoriferous, redolent
frail *adj.* slimsy
frankincense *n.* olibanum
frankness *n.* candor, guilelessness, ingenuousness, veracity
frantic *adj.* berserk, corybantic, frenetic
fraud *n.* barratry
fraudulent *adj.* barratrous, supposititious
freak *n.* anomaly, lusus naturae
freckle *n.* lentigo
freckled *adj.* lentiginous
free *adj.* allodial, gratuitous, unfettered, untrameled
freedom *n.* deliverance, manumission, *uhuru*
freezing *n.* cryonics, gelation
frenzied *adj.* corybantic, demoniac, madding
frenzy *n.* delirium, musth, nympholepsy
fret *v.* chafe, repine, smolder
fretful *adj.* petulant, querulous
friend *n.* Achates, alter ego, cater-cousin, compadre, compañera,
    compañero, confidant, confidante, convive, *fidus Achates*,
    philhellene
friendliness *n.* bonhomie, camaraderie, conviviality
friends, pairs of Achilles and Patroclus, Damon and Pythias, David
    and Jonathan, Nisus and Euryalus, Pylades and Orestes
friendship *n.* affinity, camaraderie, gemütlichkeit
frieze *n.* zophorus
frills *n.* flumadiddle, frippery, tomfoolery

frisk *v.* caper, curvet, gambol
frisky *adj.* feisty
frivolous *adj.* fribble, lunatic, mercurial, puerile, yeasty
frolicsome *adj.* rollicksome, rompish
frontier *n.* limes
frontlet *n.* phylactery
frost *n.* hoarfrost, rime
frothy *adj.* spumescent, yeasty
frown *v.* glower, lower
fruit, bear fructify
fruit, having large macrocarpous
fruit-bearing *adj.* fructiferous
fruit-eating *adj.* frugivorous
fruitless *adj.* abortive, ineffectual, inefficacious, unavailing
frustrate *v.* discombobulate, discomfit, stultify
frustrated *adj.* manqué
fry *v.* frizzle
frying pan spider
fuel *n.* bois de vache, buffalo chips
fugitive *n.* runagate
fullness *n.* plenitude, repletion, satiety
fumarole *n.* solfatara
fumigate *v.* sulfurize
functionary *n.* apparat
functionless *adj.* otiose
fundamental *adj.* basilar, primal
funeral procession cortege
funeral song dirge, epicedium, keen, threnode, threnody
funereal *adj.* defunctive, sepulchral
fungi, feeding on fungivorous
fungi, pertaining to fungal, fungous
fungus-eating organism mycophagist
funnel-shaped *adj.* infundibular, infundibuliform
Furies, the Alecto, Megaera, and Tisiphone
furnish *v.* endue, invest
furniture *n.* appointments, chattel, effects
furrow *n.* stria, sulcus, vallecula
furrowed *adj.* corrugated, striated
furry *adj.* pileous, pilose
fusion *n.* conflation
fuss *n.* foofaraw, pother
fuss *v.* prink
fussy *adj.* finical, pernickety, persnickety, picayune
futile *adj.* feckless, otiose, unavailing
futon *n.* shikibuton

G

gadget *n.* whigmaleerie, whim-wham
gain *n.* emolument, lucre, spoils
gainful *adj.* lucrative, remunerative
gall *n.* asperity, chutzpa, effrontery
gallery *n.* loggia
galley *n.* quadrireme
gallop *n.* tantivy
gallows *n.* gibbet
gang *n.* camorra
gangster *n.* yakuza
gap *n.* fissure, interstice, lacuna
gape *v.* dehisce
gape *n.* rictus
gaping *adj.* oscitant, ringent
garbage *n.* spilth
garden *n.* pleasance
garland *n.* festoon, lei, swag
garment, penitential sanbenito
garments, pertaining to vestiar
garnished *adj.* garni
gas *n.* flatus
gash *v.* score, scotch
gassy *adj.* flatulent
gastric *adj.* stomachic
gate *n.* decuman, lich gate, postern
gauche *adj.* boorish, maladroit
gaudy *adj.* meretricious
gauntlet *n.* manifer
gauze *n.* gossamer
gearshift *n.* derailleur
gem *n.* briolette, cabochon, chalcedony, chaton, chevee, cuvette,
    rhodolite, rose d'Anvers, rubellite, sard, sardine, sardius, spinel
generality *n.* banality, cliché, platitude, truism
generalize *v.* universalize
generation *n.* geniture
generous *adj.* altruistic, beneficent, bounteous, free-handed,
    munificent

geniality *n.* affability, bonhomie
genital *adj.* phallic
genitals, female clitoris, pudendum, vulva
genitals, male manhood, phallus, (see also **penis**)
gentle *adj.* clement, pacific, tractable
gentleman *n.* caballero, duniewassal
gentleness *n.* gentilesse, mansuetude
genuine *adj.* echt, pukka, unfeigned, veridical
genuine text textus receptus
geriatric *adj.* gerontic
geriatrics *n.* nostology
germinate *v.* pullulate
gesture, contemptuous snook
gesturing *adj.* gesticulant
ghost *n.* apparition, doppelganger, manifestation, phantasm,
     poltergeist, preta, revenant, shade, specter, wraith
ghosts, study of spectrology
gibberish *n.* galimatias, Jabberwocky
gift *n.* acquest, arras, benefaction, donative, dower, handsel,
     lagniappe, largess, mortuary
gigantic *adj.* Brobdingnagian, Bunyanesque, cyclopean, decuman,
     gigantean, gigantesque
gigantism *n.* hypermegasoma
gild *v.* aurify
girdle *n.* cestus, cincture
girdle *v.* ringbark
girl *n.* baggage, chola, criolla, gamine, giglet, gill, hoyden, Lolita,
     pachuca, sylph, wahine
gist *n.* crux, nub, purport
gizzard *n.* ventriculus
gladiator *n.* retiarius
gladly *adv.* fain, lief
glance *n.* eyebeam, leer, *oeillade*
glass, make into vitrify
glass, molten parison
glass, pane of quarrel, quarry
glass, pertaining to vitreous, vitric
glassworker *n.* gaffer, servitor
glaze *n.* verglas
glazed surface ciré
gleaming *adj.* coruscant, coruscating, refulgent, splendent
gleanings, literary analects
glib *adj.* facile, voluble
glide *v.* volplane
glide *n.* glissade

glimpse *n.* aperçu
glittering *adj.* clinquant, gemmy, glinting, rutilant
globe *n.* georama
globular *adj.* globate, globose, stilliform
gloomy *adj.* atrabilious, feral, Gothic, lowering, lowery, lugubrious, muzzy, saturnine, sepulchral, splenetic, Stygian, tenebrous
glorify *v.* apotheosize, canonize, venerate
glorious *adj.* halcyon, palmy
glory *n.* effulgence, refulgence
glove *n.* gage, gauntlet
glow *n.* glinn, incandescence
glowing *adj.* candent, candescent, fervid, florid, rutilant, suffused
glut *v.* pall, sate, stodge, surfeit
glut *n.* plethora, profusion, repletion, surfeit
gluttony *n.* gormandizing, gulosity
gnarled *adj.* knurled
go *v.* betake, repair, wend
goad *n.* ankus, gad
goad *v.* pique, prick
goatlike *adj.* caprine, hircine
goat underhair pashm
gobbledegook *n.* claptrap, gallimatias
goblet *n.* chalice
goblin *n.* barghest, bugbear, duende, kobold, ouphe, puca
God *n.* Adonai, Allah, Tetragrammaton, Yahweh, YHTD
godfather *n. padrino*
godlike *adj.* deiform
gods or **goddesses** daemon, demigod, demigoddess, deux ex machina, deva, faun, godling, household god, lares and penates, pantheon, yazata, zombie
God willing *Deo volente*
gold, made of chryselephantine
golden *adj.* aureate, auriferous, aurous
gold powder ormolu
gold therapy chrysotherapy
gong *n.* tam-tam
good *adj.* pukka
good, the highest *summum bonum*
good faith *bona fides*
good life, the *dolce vita*
goodness *n.* probity, rectitude
good news evangel
goose, like a anserine
goose flesh horripilation
gorge *n.* couloir, defile

gorge *v.* stodge, surfeit
gossip *n.* gabbler, quidnunc, rumormonger, tabby, tittle-tattle
gossip *v.* palaver, prate, tittle-tattle
gossipy *adj.* dishy, long-tongued
gourd *n.* calabash, cucurbit, maraca
gourmet *n.* bon vivant, epicure, *feinschmecker*, gastronome
gout *n.* podagra
governess *n.* duenna
governments, types of androcracy, diarchy, dinarchy, duarchy, dulocracy, duumvirate, ethnarchy, gerontocracy, gynarchy, gynecocracy, hagiarchy, hagiocracy, heptarchy, isocracy, kakistocracy, mediocracy, meritocracy, mobocracy, monocracy, ochlocracy, octarchy, oligarchy, pentarchy, plutocracy, polyarchy, quadrumvirate, stratocracy, thearchy, theocracy, timocracy, triarchy, triumvirate
governor *n.* bey, dey, harmost, hospoder, nomarch, satrap, sherif, subadar, tuchun, voivode
graceful *adj.* featly, lightsome, lissome
graffiti *n.* placas
grain, feeding on granivorous
grammar *n.* hypercorrection
grammar, error in solecism
grammatical subordination hypotaxis
grandmother *n.* babushka
grant *n.* demise, subvention
grape *n.* scuppernog
grape juice stum
graph *n.* nomogram
graphite *n.* plumbago
grasp *n.* intellection
grasping, adapted for prehensile
grass, clump of tussock
grass, feeding on graminivorous
grassy *adj.* gramineous, verdant
grating sound stridor
gratuity *n.* baksheesh, benefaction, broadus, cumshaw, dash, douceur, lagniappe, pilon, *pourboire*
grave *n.* cenotaph, Davy Jones's locker
grave *adj.* sobersided, staid
graveclothes *n.* cerecloths, cerements, wrappings
gravedigger *n.* fossarian, fossor
graverobber *n.* ghoul
gravy boat sauceboat
gray *adj.* griseous, grizzle, grizzly, hoary
grease *n.* schmaltz, suint

greasy *adj.* oleaginous, unctuous, unguinous
great work magnum opus
greedy *adj.* acquisitive, avaricious, covetous, esurient, mercenary,
    prehensile, rapacious, voracious
greedy person harpy
Greeks, friend of the philhellene
green *adj.* verdant, virid
greenhouse *n.* conservatory, orangery
greenness *n.* greenth, verdancy, verdure, verdurousness, viridity
grid *n.* grillage, grille, lattice
griddle *n.* comal
grief *n.* dolor
grievance *n.* gravamen
grievous *adj.* dolorous, flagitious, heinous
grill *n.* babracot
grimace *n.* mop, moue
grin *v.* fleer
grind *v.* comminute, kibble, levigate, masticate, triturate
grinding stone mano
grinding wheel skeif
gritty *adj.* sabulous
groin, of the inguinal
groove *n.* croze, flute, rabbet, regle, sulcus
grope *v.* flounder, grabble
grotesque *adj.* antic, baroque
grotesque person golliwogg
grouch *n.* crosspatch, curmudgeon
grouchiness *n.* mulligrubs
grouchy *adj.* grouty, grum, growly, morose
ground floor *rez-de-chaussée*
groundless *adj.* untenable
group *n.* aggregation, bevy, bloc, cabal, camarilla, cete, chiliad,
    clowder, collegium, cortege, coterie, coven, covey, ennead,
    galaxy, galère, gemeinschaft, gesellschaft, phylon, retinue
grove *n.* boscage, bosk, bosket, motte, shinnery
grow *v.* burgeon, wax
growing *adj.* accrescent, crescent, crescive
growl *v.* gnar, gnarl, wamble
growth *n.* accrescence, accretion, alluvion, burl, excrescence, gall,
    hypertrophy
growth hormone auxin
gruel *n.* loblolly
grumble *n.* susurration
guardianship *n.* tutelage, wardship
guerrilla fighters fedayeen, mujahedin

guess *v.* conjecture, peradventure
guidance *n.* manuduction
guide *n.* cicerone, docent, dragoman, lodestar, shikari, voyageur
guilty *adj.* culpable, felonious, nefarious
gulch *n.* coulee
gulf *n.* chasm
gullet *n.* esophagus, maw
gully *n.* arroyo, barranca, couloir, nullah, wadi
gulp *v.* englut, swizzle
gummy *adj.* mucilaginous, viscid
gurgling, intestinal borborygmus
gushing *adj.* effusive, scaturient
gut *v.* disembowel, eviscerate, exenterate
gutter *n.* cullis, kennel
gymnasium *n.* palaestra
gypsum *n.* gesso
Gypsy *n.* rye, Tzigane
gyration *n.* precession

H

habit *n.* bent, idiocracy, propensity
habitual *adj.* inveterate, wonted
habitué *n.* denizen
hackneyed *adj.* stereotyped
hag *n.* beldam, harpy, harridan, shrew, virago
haggle *v.* chaffer, higgle, palter, stickle
hail *interj.* salve
hair *n.* chignon, crine, cymotrichy, earlock, elflock, glochid, hackle,
   pile, vibrissa
hair, of pilar
hair, producing piliferous
hair, remove depilate, epilate
hair, resembling piliform
hair, study of trichology
haircutting *n.* tonsure
haired, straight lissotrichous

hairiness *n.* hypertrichosis
hairlike *adj.* capillaceous, trichoid
hair shirt cilice
hairsplitter *n.* pedant
hair tonic bandoline
hairy *adj.* comate, comose, crinite, crinose, hirsutulous, hirtellous, pileous, pilose, pilous
half *n.* moiety
half-dressed *adj. en déshabillé,* in dishabille
half-smoked pipe tobacco dottle
hall *n.* dalan, odeum, sala
hallucination *n.* formication, phantasm, phantasmagoria
halo *n.* aureole, gloriole, *Heiligenschein*
halter *n.* hackamore
ham *n.* gammon
hamlet *n.* dorp
hammer *n.* kevel, maul, Mjolnir
hammer *v.* incuse, malleate
hamper *v.* encumber, enmesh, fetter, straiten, throttle, trammel
hand, shaped like a maniform
handbag *n.* reticule
handball court sphaeristerium
handbill *n.* dodger
handbook *n.* enchiridion, vade mecum
handcuff *n.* bilboes, fetter, gyve, manacle
handkerchief *n.* pocketsquare, sudarium
handle *n.* ansa, bail, haft, helve
handlelike *adj.* ansate
handwriting, bad cacography
handwriting, beautiful calligraphy
handwriting expert graphologist
handy *adj.* dextrous
handyman *n.* factotum
hangnail *n.* agnail
hangover *n.* katzenjammer
hangover remedy hair of the dog, prairie oyster
haphazard *adj.* desultory, fitful
happen *v.* bechance, betide, eventuate
happiness *n.* beatitude, eudemonia, felicity
happiness, conducive to eudemoniac, felicific
happy *adj.* blithe, jocund
happy-go-lucky *adj.* heedless, improvident, insouciant
hara-kiri *n.* seppuku
harangue *n.* screed, tirade
harbor *n.* anchorage, port of call

hard *adj.* adamantine, flinty, petrosal, petrous, sclerous
hardened *adj.* indurate, inured, inveterate
hard-pressed *adj.* bedeviled, beleaguered, beset
hardship *n.* privation
hardtack *n.* sea biscuit, sea bread, ship biscuit
hard to please difficile
hardworking *adj.* assiduous, sedulous, zealous
hare *n.* leporide, leveret
harem *n.* seraglio
harem concubine odalisque
harem guard eunuch
harem room oda, odah
harmful *adj.* baleful, baneful, deleterious, insalubrious, malefic, maleficent, nocent, nocuous, noisome, noxious
harmless *adj.* benign, innocuous, innoxious
harmony *n.* concinnity, concord, consonance, correspondence
harness *n.* tack
harness maker lorimer
harpoon *n.* bomb lance, grains, lily iron
harsh *adj.* cacophonous, discordant, stridulous
harsh sound stridulation
harvest *n.* ingathering
hashish *n.* charas
haste *n.* celerity, hurry-scurry, precipitancy, swivet
hasten *v.* festinate, precipitate
hatchet *n.* mogo
hate *v.* abominate, execrate
hateful *adj.* execrable, flagitious, odious
hatred *n.* antipathy, malignity, obloquy, odium
haughtiness *n.* hauteur
haughty *adj.* cavalier, fastuous, orgulous
haunch *n.* huckle
having multiple meanings polysemic, polysemous
haystack *n.* cock, haycock, rick
hazardous *adj.* parlous, venturesome, venturous
hazy *adj.* nebulose, nebulous
head *n.* pate, poll, sconce
head, of the cephalic
head, shaving of the tonsure
headache *n.* cephalalgia, clavus, hemicrania, megrim, migraine
headband *n.* bandeau, diadem, snood
headcloth *n.* wimple
headdress *n.* atefcrown, chaperon, kaffiyeh, wimple
headless *adj.* acephalous
headlong *adj.* gadarene, precipitate

head of household paterfamilias
head shapes brachycephaly, dolichocephaly, mesocephaly, orthocephaly
head-to-toe *adj.* cap-a-pie, *de haut en bas*
healer *n.* curandero
healing *adj.* assuasive, emollient, palliative, sanative, sanatory
healthful *adj.* constitutional, salubrious, salutary, salutiferous, sanatory
heap *n.* congeries, cumulus
hearing *n.* audition, clairaudience
hearing, poor paracusis
hearse *n.* catafalque
heart *n.* *corazón*
heart, by memoriter
heartbeat, excessively rapid tachycardia
heartburn *n.* pyrosis, water brash
heart-shaped *adj.* cordate, cordiform
heat, final qualifying in a race repechage
heat, producing calorific
heat, sexual estrus, rut
heater *n.* latrobe, salamander
heating *adj.* calefacient, calefactory, incalescent
heat-producing *adj.* calorifacient, euthermic
heaven *n.* empyrean, firmament, Hel, Kur, New Jerusalem, Niflheim, satyaloka, Zion
heavenly *adj.* beatific, empyreal, empyrean, ethereal, seraphic, supernal
heckle *v.* badger, bait, hector
hedge *v.* equivocate, temporize, tergiversate
hedonist *n.* sensualist, sybarite, voluptuary
heir *n.* coparcener, parcener
heiress *n.* inheritrix
hell *n.* Gehenna, Hades, nether world, perdition, sheol
hell, dwelling in chthonic

Burt never did like to read the small print...

hellish *adj.* execrable, Stygian
helmet *n.* armet, barbut, basinet, puggaree, sallet, topee
helmet-shaped *adj.* galeate, galeiform
help *n.* manna, succor
helpful *adj.* adjuvant, effectual, efficacious, implemental, salutary
helpless *adj.* altricial, footless, ineffectual
helpmate *n.* helpmeet
hemispheric *adj.* semispheric
hemp *n.* dagga
hen *n.* poulard, pullet
herb *n.* potherb
herbal remedy galenical
herbarium *n.* hortus siccus
herd *n.* gam, manada, pod, press
here and there throughout *passim*
heretic *n.* heresiarch, schismatic
hermaphrodite *n.* freemartin
hermaphroditic *adj.* androgynous, autoicous
hermit *n.* anchoress, anchorite, cenobite, eremite, marabout,
    solitudinarian, troglodyte
hesitant *adj.* irresolute, vacillant
hesitate *v.* dither, hem and haw, stickle, whiffle
hesitation *n.* demur, irresolution
heterogeneous *adj.* motley, piebald
hex *n.* pishogue
hiccup *n.* singultus
hidden *adj.* delitescent, perdu, turbid
hide *n.* kip, fell
hide *v.* cache, embosk, ensconce
highest good *summum bonum*
highest point apogee, zenith
highway *n.* autobahn, autoroute, autostrada
highwayman *n.* footpad
hinder *v.* cumber, embar, stultify, trammel
hip *n.* coxa, haunch, huckle
Hiroshima survivor hibakusha
hiss *v.* sibilate
hissing *adj.* sibilant
historian *n.* griot
hives *n.* uredo, urticaria
hoarse *adj.* croaky, roupy
hoax *n.* canard, imposture, mare's nest
hobble *v.* trammel
hobby *n.* avocation
hobo *n.* knight of the road

hodgepodge *n.* ana, farrago, gallimaufry, mingle-mangle, omnium-gatherum, pasticcio, pastiche
hog *n.* razorback, shoat
hog, side of flitch
hole *n.* fenestra, foramen, fumarole, Mohole, ventage
hollow *adj.* sepulchral
hollowed *adj.* cavate
holy of holies sanctum sanctorum
holy oil oil of catechumens, oil of the sick
holy place halidom
Holy Spirit, the Paraclete
holy water, basin for stoup
homeless child street arab
homesickness *n.* *mal du pays*, nostomania
homonym *n.* homograph, homophone
honesty *n.* probity, rectitude, veracity
honey, producing melliferous
honeycombed *adj.* faveolate
honor *n.* accolade, brevet, deference, izzat, kudos
honor *v.* hallow, reverence, solemnize
honor, conveying honorific
honoree *n.* laureate
hooded garment capote, capuche, cowl
hoodlike *adj.* cucullate
hoofed *adj.* ungulate
hook *n.* agraffe, crampon, gaff
hook *v.* gaff
hook, surgeon's tenaculum
hooked *adj.* adunc, aquiline, falcate
hoot *v.* ululate
horizontal *n.* prone, recumbent, supine
horn *n.* corn, cornucopia, klaxon, *shofar*
horn, drinking rhyton
horned *adj.* corniculate
hornless *adj.* muley, polled
hornless animal pollard
horny *adj.* ceratoid, corneous, keratinous, keratoid
horror *n.* abomination, antipathy, *Schrecklichkeit*
horse *n.* cob, dobbin
horse, fresh remount
horse, worn-out jade, rosinante
horseflesh, eater of hippophagist
horse-lover *n.* hippophile
horseman *n.* centaur, charro, hazer
horsemanship *n.* equitation

horseman or **horsewoman** *n.* centaur
horses, team of three troika
horseshoe crab xiphosuran
horseshoer *n.* farrier
horse training dressage, manège
hospice *n.* imaret
hospital *n.* lazaret, lazaretto, leper house, leprosarium, pesthouse
hospital, pertaining to a nosocomial
hostility *n.* animus, hornet's nest, malevolence
hotel *n.* caravansary, hostelry
hotel manager hotelier
hothead *n.* hotspur
hotheaded *adj.* choleric, irascible, testy
hot springs thermae
hourly *adj.* horal, horary
house *n.* barabara, bastide, casita, chickee, columbary, crannog, dacha, earth lodge, galerie house, hale, hogan, hospitium, izba, jacal, palapa, pathan, pied-à-terre, ribat, wanigan, yurt
household *n.* ménage, ménage à trois
household gods lares and penates
housewife *n.* baleboste
howl *v.* caterwaul, ululate
hubbub *n.* charivari
huddle *v.* scrooch
hulk *n.* scow
hum *v.* bombinate
human being terrestrial, wight
humble *v.* abash, go to Canossa, mortify
humbug *n.* gammon
humiliating *adj.* contumelious, ignominious
humility *n.* humble pie, self-effacement
humor *n.* jocosity, pantagruelism, waggery
hump *n.* hubble
humus *n.* mor
hunchbacked *adj.* gibbous
hundredfold *n.* centuple
hundredth *adj.* centesimal
hundred-year-old *n.* centenarian
hunger, abnormal bulimia
hung-over *adj.* crapulent, crapulous
hungry *adj.* esurient, lupine, peckish
hunter *n.* chasseur, jacklighter, nimrod, pothunter
hunting, pertaining to venatic
huntress *n.* Diana
hurl *v.* jaculate

hurry *v.* festinate
hurry *n.* celerity
hurt *v.* aggrieve, scathe
hurtful *adj.* deleterious, nocuous, noxious
husband *n.* helpmate, helpmeet, sannup
husbands, having three trigamy (*n.*)
hush up hugger-mugger
hut *n.* jacal, rancho, scherm, wickiup
hymen *n.* maidenhead
hymn *n.* canticle, doxology, kontakion, laud, Magnificat
hymn book hymnal, hymnary
hypnotize *v.* gorgonize, mesmerize
hypocrite *n.* pecksniff, pharisee, Tartuffe, whited sepulcher
hypocritical *adj.* canting, crocodilian, Janus-faced, pecksniffian,
    pharisaic, pharisaical
hypothesize *v.* hypothecate
hypothetical *adj.* suppositious, supposititious

I

ice *n.* frazil, pan, sérac
ice, floating floe
ice accumulation embacle
ice ax piolet
iceberg *n.* floeberg, growler
icy *adj.* gelid, glacial
ideal *n.* archetype, eidolon, exemplar, nonesuch, nonpareil,
    paradigm, paragon, touchstone
idealist *n.* stargazer, visionary
identical *adj.* congruent, congruous, identic
identical backward and forward cancrine, palindromic
idiotic *adj.* asinine, fatuous
idle *adj.* fainéant, otiose, recumbent, slothful
idleness *n.* dolce far niente, flânerie, idlesse, sloth, torpor
idler *n.* drone, fainéant, flâneur, wastrel
idol *n.* golden calf, joss, Juggernaut, minion, teraph
idolatry *n.* apotheosis, Baalism, fornication

ignorance *n.* crassitude, nescience
ignorant *adj.* benighted, crass, nescient
illegitimate child catch-colt, mamzer, natural child, *nullius filius*,
   Sunday baby, whoreson
ill-fated *adj.* star-crossed
illness, pretend malinger
ill-tempered *adj.* atrabilious
ill-timed *adj.* inopportune
illuminate *v.* miniate
illuminating *adj.* luciferous
illusion *n.* chimera, Dead Sea fruit, déja vu, fata morgana, maya,
   phantasm, phiphenomenon
illusions, series of phantasmagoria
illusory *adj.* papier-mâché, phantasmal
illustrious *adj.* lustrous, redoubtable, refulgent, splendent
ill will malignity, rancor, spleen
image *n.* eikon, icon, idolum, ikon, persona, simulacrum, xoanon
images, worship of iconolatry
imaginary *adj.* chimerical, fabled, illusive, notional, quixotic
imaginative *adj.* visionary
imagine *v.* envisage, ideate, prefigure
imaging, vivid in eidetic
imitation *n.* parody, mimesis, travesty
imitative *adj.* apish, emulous, ersatz, mimetic
imitator *n.* ape, epigone, Gongorist
immaterial *adj.* asomatous, incorporeal
immature *adj.* callow, infantine, jejune, unfledged
immaturity *n.* minority, nonage
immediately *adv.* forthwith, instanter
immense *adj.* Brobdingnagian, Bunyanesque, Cyclopean, decuman
immensity *n.* vastitude, vastity
immerse *v.* submerse
imminent *adj.* looming, proximate
immodesty *n.* impudicity, temerity
immolation *n.* sati
immoral *adj.* concupiscent, dissolute, fescennine, libertine,
   libidinous, reprobate, scrofulous
immortality *n.* amrita, athanasia
immortalize *v.* eternize
immunization *n.* mithridatism
impair *v.* corrode, vitiate
impartially *adv.* disinterestedly, dispassionately, equably, *pari passu*
impassable *adj.* impervious, impractable
impassioned *adj.* perfervid
impassive *adj.* phlegmatic, stolid

impatient *adj.* chafing, petulant
impede *v.* fetter, stanch, stultify, trammel
imperative *adj.* peremptory
imperishable *adj.* perdurable
impermanence *n.* caducity, evanescence
impermanent *adj.* ephemeral, transitory
impertinent *adj.* forward
impervious *adj.* impermeable
implant *v.* imbue, infuse, inseminate
implication *n.* connotation, ramification
implore *v.* entreat, importune, supplicate
imply *v.* allude, connote, insinuate
importance *n.* centrality, concernment, moment
important *adj.* material, salient
impose *v.* foist
imposing *adj.* stately
impossible, make preclude
impostor *n.* Cagliostro, charlatan
impotence *n.* agenesis
impotent *adj.* impuissant
impractical *adj.* doctrinaire, quixotic
impregnation *n.* fecundation, semination, superfecundation, superfetation
impression *n.* percept
impressionable *adj.* susceptive
impressive *adj.* august, impactive, skookum
imprison *v.* immure, mure
imprisonment *n.* durance, duress
impromptu *adj./adv.* extempore
impropriety *n.* faux pas, gaffe, gaucherie, indecorum, solecism
improve *v.* ameliorate, emend, meliorate
improvised *adj.* autoschediastic, ersatz, extemporary, extempore, jury
impudent *adj.* brazen, cheeky, forward, presumptuous
impulse *n.* impulsion, nisus
inability *n.* impotence, incapacity
inaction *n.* languor, torpor
inactive *adj.* abeyant, fallow, indolent
inactivity *n.* stasis, torpidity
inadequacy *n.* dearth, inefficacy
inadequate *adj.* insubstantial, niggardly
inane *adj.* fatuous, vacuous
inanimate *adj.* insentient, quiescent
inanity *n.* vacuity
inappropriate *adj.* inapposite, inapt, malapropos

inattentive *adj.* oblivious, oscitant
inaugurate *v.* auspicate
inborn *adj.* cognate, connate, immanent, ingenerate
incantation *n.* conjuration, mantra
incarnation *n.* avatar, embodiment
incense *n.* joss stick
incense burner *n.* censer, incensory, thurible
incense burner, carrier of thurifer
incentive *n.* goad, golden handshake
incessant *adj.* stanchless, unrelenting, unremitting
inchworm *n.* looper, measuringworm
incidental *adj.* fortuitous, intervenient
incineration *n.* immolation, sati
incipient *adj.* inchoate
incisive *adj.* aculeate, trenchant
inciting *adj.* proceleusmatic
inclination *n.* conation, penchant, predilection, proclivity, velleity
include *v.* comprise, embody
inclusive *adj.* comprising, embracing
incomparable *adj.* inimitable, peerless
incompatible *adj.* antipathetic, disparate
incompetent *adj.* feckless
incompetent, harmless Throttlebottom
incongruous *adj.* discordant, dissonant
incongruity *n.* disparity
inconsequential *adj.* nugatory
inconsistency *n.* solecism
inconsistent *adj.* capricious, discrepant
inconsolable *adj.* disconsolate
inconstant *adj.* capricious, chameleonic, mercurial, protean
inconvenient *adj.* incommodious, inopportune, vexatious
incorporeal *adj.* discarnate
incorrigible child *enfant terrible*
incorruptible *adj.* imputrescible, inviolable
increase *v.* eke, irrupt, wax
increasing *adj.* accrescent, crescent, crescive, increscent, waxing
incurable *adj.* immedicable, irremediable
indecent *adj.* blue, indecorous, ithyphallic, licentious, salacious, scabrous
indecisive *adj.* irresolute, vacillant
indefinable something *je ne sais quoi*
indefinite *adj.* aoristic
indent *v.* deboss
independent *adj.* autocephalous
indescribable *adj.* ineffable, inenarrable

indicate *v.* betoken, evince, forebode, portend, presage
indication *n.* harbinger, indicium, portent
indicative *adj.* evincive, indicial, precursory
indicator *n.* indicant
indifferent *adj.* affectless, apathetic, cavalier, feckless, insouciant,
     pococurante
indignation *n.* dudgeon, pique
indirect *adj.* circuitous, meandering, oblique, tortuous
indiscretion *n.* faux pas, imprudence
indiscriminate *adj.* desultory, wholesale
indisputable *adj.* irrecusable, irrefragable
indistinct *adj.* crepuscular, nebulous
individualize *v.* individuate
indivisible *adj.* impartible, indiscerptible
indoctrinate *v.* inoculate
indolent *adj.* fainéant
induce *v.* foster, occasion
induction *n.* investiture
inductive *adj.* a posteriori
indulge to excess surfeit
industrial combination cartel, zaibatsu
industrious *adj.* assiduous, operose, sedulous
inept *adj.* gauche, maladroit
inequality *n.* disparity, imparity
inertia *n.* languor
inevitable *adj.* ineluctable, inexorable, predestined
inexorable *adj.* relentless, ruthless
inexperienced *adj.* callow, jejune, unfledged, unversed, verdant
inexperienced person gosling, naïf
inexpressible *adj.* ineffable
inexpressive *adj.* wooden
infallible *adj.* inerrant, unimpeachable
infamous *adj.* flagitious, nefarious
infamy *n.* ignominy
infant *n.* nursling, putto
infatuate *v.* besot
infectious *adj.* infective, pestilential
infer *v.* educe, surmise
inference *n.* extrapolation, illation, surmise
inference, incorrect non sequitur
inferential *adj.* conjectural, illative
inferior *adj.* abject, base, ignoble, scrubby
infernal *adj.* chthonic, nether, plutonian, plutonic
infidel *n.* kafir
infinitive *n.* supine

infinity *n.* infinitude
inflammable *adj.* combustible, piceous, tindery
inflated *adj.* distended, flatulent
inflexible *adj.* adamant, inexorable, intractable, obdurate
inflict *v.* levy, visit, wreak
influence *n.* good offices, leverage
influential *n.* consequential
influential person éminence grise, gray eminence
infolding *n.* invagination
inform *v.* apprise
informative *adj.* edifying, explicative
informer *n.* blabbermouth
infringement *n.* breach, contravention, encroachment, infraction, transgression
infuse *v.* imbue, inculcate, ingrain
ingenious *adj.* daedal
ingest *v.* incept
ingrained *adj.* inveterate
ingratiating, overly saccharine
inhabitant *n.* denizen, habitant
inhale *v.* inspire
inherent *adj.* congenital, immanent, innate, intrinsic, inveterate
inheritance *n.* hereditament, patrimony
initial *adj.* inceptive, inchoative, nascent
initiation *n.* rite of passage
injure *v.* blight, scathe, scotch
injustice *n.* tort
ink *n. sumi*
inland *adj.* epeiric
inland *adv.* mauka
inlet *n.* armlet, ria
inn *n.* auberge, caravansary, *fonda*, gasthaus, khan, posada, pousada, quinta, ryokan, serai
innate *adj.* connate, connatural, ingenerate
innermost recesses penetralia
innkeeper *n.* boniface
innocent *adj.* dewy-eyed, ingenuous, virginal
innovation *n.* neoterism
innovation, hatred of misoneism
innovative *adj.* germinal, seminal
innuendo *n.* aspersion, imputation
innumerable *adj.* myriad
in paper, cooked *en papillote*
in passing en passant
inquiry *n.* inquest, interrogatory

inroad *n.* encroachment
insatiable *adj.* ravenous, voracious
inscription *n.* chronogram, colophon, epigraph, epitaph, exergue,
    legend, ogham
insect *n.* creepy-crawly, midge
insect-eating *adj.* entomophagous, insectivorous
insect repellent insectifuge
insensitive *adj.* callous, pachydermatous
insertion *n.* intercalation, interpolation, tmesis
insider *n.* arcanist
insignia *n.* regalia
insignificance *n.* nugacity
insignificant *adj.* manini, minuscule, picayune, piffling
insincere *adj.* bathetic, crocodilian, disingenuous, faux-naïf,
    fulsome, meretricious
insincerity *n.* bunkum, claptrap, dissimulation, duplicity,
    mendacity
insinuate *v.* allude, intimate
insipid *adj.* jejune, vapid
insistent *adj.* clamant, exigent
insolent *adj.* brazen, cheeky, contumacious, contumelious
inspiration *n.* afflatus, duende
inspired *adj.* afflated, vatic
inspiring *adj.* infusive, proceleusmatic
instant *n.* trice
instead of vice
instill *v.* engender, imbue, infix, infuse
instruction *n.* tuition, tutelage
instructions *n.* indicia
instructive *adj.* edificatory, preceptive
insubordinate *adj.* contumacious, disaffected
insubstantial *adj.* illusory
in succession en suite
insufficiency *n.* dearth, penury
insult *v.* belittle, demean, denigrate, disparage, flout, mortify
insult *n.* affront, contumely, Parthian shot, parting shot
insurgent *n.* young Turk
integrity *n.* probity, rectitude
intellect *n.* citta, nous
intellectuals *n.* clerisy, intelligentsia, literati, mandarins
intelligent *adj.* intellective, intelligential
intend *v.* purport, purpose
intense *adj.* fervent, fervid, impassioned, poignant
intensify *v.* aggravate, potentiate
intent *n.* purport, tenor

intent *adj.* preoccupied, rapt
intentional *adj.* prepense, witting
interbreeding *n.* miscegenation
interceder *n.* intercessor, paraclete
interchangeable *adj.* fungible
interested *adj.* engaged, engrossed, preoccupied
interesting *adj.* affecting, engaging, engrossing
interfering *adj.* obtrusive, officious
interject *v.* intercalate
interlace *v.* wattle
interlock *v.* interdigitate
intermediate *adj.* interjacent
intermingle *v.* interlace, raddle, ruddle, wattle
intermittent *adj.* discontinuous, intermissive
internally derived endogenous
international language Esperanto, interlanguage, interlingua
interpose *v.* interlay, interpolate, interstratify
interpret *v.* construe, explicate, expound, gloss
interpretation *n.* anagoge, eisegesis, exegesis, explication, gloss
interpreter *n.* dragoman, exegete, explicator, glossarist, glossator,
    glossographer, hierophant, munshi, mystagogue
interruption *n.* anacoluthon, aposiopesis, caesura, disrupture,
    pretermission
intersect *v.* decussate
intersecting *adj.* intersectant
intersection *n.* groining
intervening *adj.* intercurrent, interjacent, intervenient
interweave *v.* pleach
intestinal *adj.* enteric, splanchnic, visceral
intestinal gurgling borborygmus
intestines *n.* entrails, viscera
intestines, of the enteric
in the first place imprimis
in the open air alfresco, *en plein air*
intimacy, sense of communitas
intimate *n.* bosom friend, confidant, familiar
intimate *v.* allude, insinuate
intimidated *adj.* browbeaten, cowed, daunted
intolerant *adj.* churchy, illiberal
intoxicated *adj.* bacchic, besotted, fuddled, inebriated
intoxicating *adj.* exhilarating, heady
intricacy *n.* cat's cradle, involution
intricate *adj.* crabbed, daedal, involute, labyrinthine
intrigue *n.* cabal, collusion, complot, knavery
intriguer *n.* intrigant, Jesuit

intriguing *adj.* piquant
introduction *n.* exordium, incipit, isagoge, manuduction, prelusion,
    proem, prolegomenon, prolusion
introductory *adj.* isagogic, precursory, prelusive, prolegomenous,
    propaedeutic
introspective *adj.* idiotropic
intrude *v.* obtrude
intrusive *adj.* officious
intuition *n.* Anschauung, prescience
invalid *n.* valetudinarian, valetudinary
invalid *adj.* nugatory
invalidate *v.* vitiate
invasion *n.* encroachment, irruption
invective *n.* philippic
inventive *adj.* daedal, pregnant
inventor *n.* artificer, Daedalus
inventory control kanban
inversion *n.* chiasmus, hysteron proteron
investigate *v.* indagate
investigator *n.* scrutator
invigorating *adj.* analeptic
invincible *adj.* indomitable, inexpugnable
inviolable *adj.* infrangible, sacrosanct
involve *v.* embroil, inculpate
involved, morally engagé
involvement *n.* immixture, involution
iota *n.* stiver
iridescence *n.* reflet
iridescent *adj.* nacreous, opalescent, opaline, pearlescent
Irish *n./adj.* Hibernian, Milesian
iron, tailor's flatiron, goose, sadiron
irony *n.* enantiosis
irrational *adj.* incommensurable, surd
irregular *adj.* anomalous, snatchy
irregularity *n.* abnormity, anomaly
irrepressible *adj.* buoyant, ebullient
irreverent *adj.* profane, sacrilegious
irritable *adj.* captious, choleric, fractious, huffish, irascible,
    nettlesome, peckish, peevish, petulant, querulous, snappish,
    snuffy, stomachy, tetchy, vexatious, waspish
irritated *adj.* shirty
irritating *adj.* chafing, rebarbative
irritation *n.* pinprick, vexation
island *n.* cay, crannog, key
isn't that so? *nicht wahr?*

isolate *v.* deracinate, sequester
isolated *adj.* insular
isolated person isolato
issue *v.* debouch
issuing *adj.* emanent
itch *n.* mange, scabies
itching *n.* pruritus
itemized *adj.* particularized
I think, therefore I am *cogito ergo sum*
itinerant *adj.* peripatetic
ivory, made of chryselephantine

J

jack-of-all-trades *n.* factotum, tinker
jackstraw *n.* spillikin
jagged *adj.* craggy, hackly, scraggly
jail *v.* immure, impound
jailer *n.* alcaide
jam *n.* conserve
jammed *adj.* chockablock
Japanese immigrants and their descendants Issei, Kibei, Nisei, Sansei
jar *n.* alabastron, albarello, amphora, aryballos, askos, cymaise, dolium, hydria, kalpis, lekythos, loutrophoros, pelike, pithos, potiche, psykter, stamnos
jar *v.* concuss
jargon *n.* argot, cant, patois, pidgin
jaundice *n.* icterus
jaunty *adj.* insouciant, rakish
javelin *n.* assegai, jereed, pilum
jaw *n.* mandible, maxilla
jawless *adj.* agnathous
jaws, of the gnathic
jealousy *n.* heartburn
jeer *v.* fleer, flout, gibe, scout
jerk *v.* flounce

jerky *adj.* saccadic
jest *n.* bon mot, jape, pleasantry, raillery, sally
jest *v.* jape
jester *n.* droll, mummer, wag, zany
jesting *adj.* jocose, jocular, sportive, waggish
jetty *n.* wing dam
jewel case minaudière
jewelry *n.* bijou, bijouterie, parure, rivière, rondelle
job *n.* billet, métier
jock itch tinea cruris
join *v.* conjoin, inosculate, rabbet, sypher, tenon
join, serving to *adj.* copulative
joint *n.* commissure
joke *n.* chestnut, jape, Joe Miller, jocosity, jocularity, raillery,
   waggery, wheeze
joker *n.* farceur, farceuse, wag
jolly *adj.* boon, convivial
jolt *v.* jounce
jostle *v.* elbow, justle
journey *n.* hegira, peregrination
jovial *adj.* blithe, buoyant, convivial
jowl *n.* dewlap, wattle
joyful *adj.* blithesome, buoyant, frabjous
judge *n.* adjudicator, archon, caid, Daniel, dayan, Deborah,
   deemster, dicast, hakim, puisne, qadi
judgment *n.* discernment, discretion
judicious *adj.* circumspect, discerning, sagacious
judo expert judoka
jug *n.* blackjack, oinochoe, puzzle jug
juicy *adj.* succulent
jumble *v.* garble, pi
jumble *n.* conglomeration, farrago, gallimaufry
jumbled *adj.* higgledy-piggledy, hodgepodge
jumping *adj.* salient, saltant
jurisdiction *n.* dominion, primacy, satrapy
jurisdiction, subject to justiciable (*adj.*)
jurist *n.* jurisconsult, mufti, mujtahid, mullah
justifiable *adj.* tenable, warrantable
justification *n.* apologia, raison d'être
justify *v.* legitimate, validate
juvenile *adj.* callow, jejune, puerile

K

karate *n.* tae kwon do
karate expert karateka
kazoo *n.* mirliton
keen *adj.* perspicacious, trenchant
kept, well kempt
kerchief *n.* fichu, rumel
key *n.* passe-partout
kidneys *n.* reins
kidneys, inflammation of the nephritis
kidneys, of the nephritic, renal
kidney-shaped *adj.* reniform
kidney stone calculus, nephrolith
kill *v.* jugulate, necrotize
killer *n.* deicide, fratricide, infanticide, matricide, patricide, regicide,
    sororicide
killing, mercy *n.* euthanasia
kind *adj.* altruistic, benignant
king, of a regius
kingdom *n.* regality
kingdom, mythical Ruritania
kinship *n.* consanguinity, phratry,
    propinquity
kiss *v.* buss, osculate
kiss *n.* osculation
kissing, pertaining to oscular
kitchen *n.* galley
kitchen servant scullion
knapsack *n.* musette bag
knead *v.* masticate
kneecap *n.* patella
knickers *n.* plus fours
knife *n.* barlow, barong,
    basilard, bistoury,
    bolo, bowie knife,
    choora, couteau, dirk,
    jambiya, kindjal, kukri, kwaiken, panga, parang, scramasax,
    skean, skean dhu, snickersnee, trivet, ulu
knight *n.* ritter

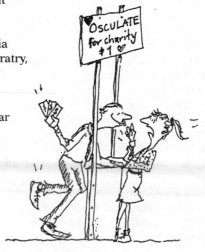

knob *n.* boss, knop, merese, nubble, pommel
knock-kneed *adj.* valgus
knoll *n.* chenier, hummock
knotty *adj.* knaggy, nodose, nodous
know *v.* apprehend, fathom, intuit
knowable *adj.* cognoscible, cognoscitive
knowing *adj.* witting
knowledgable *adj.* sciential
knowledgable people cognoscenti
knowledge *n.* cognition, gnosis, jnana, polymathy, prajna,
    precognition, privity
knowledge, hatred of misology
knowledge, pertaining to cognitive, gnostic
knowledge, pretender to sciolist
knowledge, supposed sciosophy
kowtow *v.* fawn, truckle

L

labor *n.* corvée, travail
labor *v.* drudge, slog
labor camp gulag
laborer *n.* bracero, fellah, lumper, roust, roustabout
labor-inducing *adj.* oxytocic, parturifacient
laborious *adj.* onerous, Sisyphean, toilsome
labyrinthine *adj.* Daedalean
lacerate *v.* scarify
lack *n.* dearth, paucity
lacking, something desideratum
lacrosse stick crosse
lacy *adj.* filigree, gossamer
ladylove *n.* dulcinea
laggard *adj.* dilatory
lair *n.* couch
lake *n.* nyanza, salina, tarn
lake, dry playa
lake, pertaining to a lacustrine

lake-dwelling *adj.* limnetic
lameness *n.* claudication
lament *v.* keen, ululate
lamentation *n.* coronach, jeremiad, keen, threnody
lamp *n.* glim, lampion, *Ner Tamid*, sinumbra lamp, torchiere
lampoon *n./v.* pasquinade
lamp pedestal lampadaire
land *n.* castellany, demesne, terrene
land, cleared swidden
land, promised Canaan
landed *adj.* praedial
landlord *n.* boniface, zamindar
land of plenty Goshen
landowner *n.* patroon, squireling
land reclaimed from the sea polder
language *n.* fustian, ideolect, lingua franca, lingua geral, pidgin, pidgin English, vernacular
language, of a lexical
language, use of figurative tropology
lanky *adj.* angular, gangling, rawboned
lantern *n.* luminaria
lapse *n.* faux pas, lapsus, peccadillo
large *adj.* outsize
lariat *n.* riata
lariat eye honda
larva-eating *adj.* larvivarous
last but one penult, penultimate
last but two antepenult, antepenultimate
lasting *adj.* indefectible, perdurable
last resort *pis aller*
late *adj.* dilatory
late in appearing or developing belated, serotine, tardive
latent *adj.* delitescent
late riser lie-a-bed
latticework *n.* treillage, trelliswork
laudatory *adj.* eulogistic, panegyric
laugh *v.* cachinnate, fleer, nicker, snigger
laughable *adj.* farcical, risible
laughing *adj.* riant, rident
laughter *n.* risibility
launch *v.* auspicate
lava *n.* obsidian, pahoehoe
lava fragment lapillus
lavish *adj.* churrigueresque, Lucullan, profusive
law *n.* Halachah, *lex talionis*, ordinance, ordonnance, prescript, rogation

law, relating to juridical
lawful *adj.* licit
lawgiver *n.* Draco, solon, Solon
lawn *n.* greensward
lawsuit of widespread interest cause célèbre
lawyer *n.* advocate, barrister, counsel, counselor-at-law, faqih, jurist,
     King's Counsel, Portia, Queen's Counsel, solicitor, vakeel
lawyer, rascally pettifogger, shyster
laxative *n.* aperient, aperitive, cathartic, emetic, hydragogue,
     lapactic, purgative
lay *adj.* laic, laical, secular
layer *n.* lamina, stratum
layperson *n.* secular
laziness *n.* accidie, acedia, fecklessness, oscitancy, otiosity
lazy eye amblyopia, strabismus
lead, containing plumbiferous
leaden *adj.* plumbeous
leader *n.* bellwether, cock of the walk, hegemon, pendragon
leadership *n.* dynamism, hegemony
lead poisoning saturnism
leaf *n.* folio
leaf-eating animal folivore
leaflet *n.* handbill, broadside
leaflike *adj.* foliate
leafy *adj.* foliaceous
leaning *adj.* recumbent
leaning *n.* bent, penchant, predilection, proclivity, propensity
lean-to *n.* wanigan
leap *n.* capriole, curvet, frisk, gambado, saltation
leaping *adj.* salient, saltigrade
learned person polyhistor, polymath
learning *n.* erudition, hypnopedia, pedantry, polymathy
learning disability dyslexia
leathery *adj.* coriaceous, leathern
leave *v.* decamp
leaves, feeding on phyllophagous
leaves, of foliar
leave-taking *n.* congé
leavings *n.* residua, tailings
lecher *n.* Don Juan, fornicator, libertine, pander, profligate, rake,
     rakehell, satyr, satyromaniac, sensualist, voluptuary,
     whoremaster, whoremonger
lectern *n.* altar stand, missal stand
lecture *n.* oratim
lecturer *n.* docent, lector
ledge *n.* scarcement

leech *n.* hirudinean
left behind remanent
left-handedness *n.* sinistrality
left to right, moving from sinistrodextral (*adj.*)
legal *adj.* jural, juridical
legal code pandects, Salic law
legging *n.* gambado, puttee
leggings *n.* chaps, galligaskins
legislative *adj.* nomothetic
legislator *n.* solon
legislators *n.* conscript fathers
legs, having many polyped
legs, one's own shanks' mare
lengthy *adj.* prolix
leniency *n.* lenity
lenient *adj.* compassionate, forbearing
Lenten *adj.* Quadragesimal
leper *n.* lazar
leper hospital lazaretto, leprosarium
leprosy *n.* Hansen's disease
lesbian *adj.* sapphic
lesbian *n.* sapphist, tribade
lesion *n.* chancre
lessening *n.* attenuation, diminution, extenuation, minification, mitigation, palliation, remission
lesson *n.* lection, pericope
letdown *n.* bathos
lethargy *n.* hebetude, inanition, stolidity, torpor
letter *n.* billet-doux, missive
letter-for-letter *adv.* literatim
letter of ancient alphabet rune
letters, of epistolary
lewd *adj.* Cyprian, gamy, ithyphallic, Paphian, prurient
liar *n.* Ananias, fabulist, prevaricator, romancer
libel *n.* calumniation, calumny
libel *v.* asperse, calumniate
liberal *adj.* catholic, latitudinarian
liberal arts quadrivium (arithmetic, geometry, astronomy, music); trivium (grammar, rhetoric, logic)
liberate *v.* disenthrall, manumit
library *n.* athenaeum, bibliotheca
lice *n.* crabs, pediculosis
lice, infested with pediculous
lice, pertaining to pedicular
license *n.* imprimatur, pratique

licentious *adj.* Corinthian, Cyprian, fescennine
lie *v.* dissemble, dissimulate, palter
lie *n.* canard, mendacity, prevarication
lie detector polygraph
life *n.* anima
life-extending *adj.* macrobiotic
life force élan vital
life-giving *adj.* vitalizing
life insurance tontine
lifeless *adj.* azoic, defunct, exanimate, insensate
life of self-indulgence *dolce vita*
life prolonger elixir
lifting device gantry, lewis
light *n.* Baily's beads, glim
light, pertaining to photic
light, producing luminiferous
light again relume, relumine
light and shade chiaroscuro, clair-obscure
light-emitting *adj.* luminescent, photoluminescent
light-heartedness *n.* rhathymia
lighthouse *n.* pharos
lighting *n.* balisage
lightning, resembling fulgurous
likely *adj.* disposed, prone, verisimilar
liking *n.* affinity, penchant, predilection
limited *adj.* circumscribed, constrained, one-horse, parochial, provincial
limitless *adj.* illimitable, infinite
limp *adj.* flaccid, flaggy, lank
limping *n.* claudication
line, shading hachure
lined *adj.* lineate
line of descent stirps
linguist *n.* linguistician, polyglot
liniment *n.* embrocation
lining *n.* brattice
link *n.* nexus
link *v.* catenate, concatenate, conjoin
linking verb copula, copulative verb
lintel *n.* manteltree
lionlike *adj.* leonine
lions, group of pride
lip *n.* labium, labrum
lip movement when reading mussitation
lip ornament labret

lipped *adj.* labiate
lipped, large- lippy
lipreader *n.* oralist
lips, loose *n.* flews
lips, of the labial
liquefy *v.* deliquesce
liquid, cooking blanc, court-bouillon
listening *n.* auscultation
listlessness *n.* ennui, languor, lassitude
litany *n.* synapte
literally *adv.* literatim
literary effort lucubration
literary gleanings analects
literary people republic of letters
literature *n.* belles-lettres
lithe *adj.* limber, lissome
litter *n.* dooly, palanquin
little man homunculus, manikin
live-bearing *adj.* viviparous
lively *adj.* blithe, mercurial, sprightly, yare
liver, pertaining to the hepatic
living *adj.* animate
living, capable of viable
living again redivivus (*adj.*)
lizard *n.* gecko
lizard, like a saurian
load *v.* lade
loaf *v.* lallygag, loll
loafer *n.* drone, *flâneur*, layabout, slugabed, sluggard
loan *n.* imprest
loathe *v.* abominate
loathing *n.* antipathy, scunner
lobotomy *n.* encephalotomy
lobster liver tomalley
local *adj.* vicinal
locale *n.* venue
lockjaw *n.* tetanus, trismus
lock of hair *n.* flock, forelock
locomotive *n.* barney, dinkey
lodging *n.* billet, casern
lofty *adj.* inflated, rarefied, supercilious, supernal, turgid
logger *n.* rosser
logic, employ logicize
logic, system of organon, organum
logical fallacies begging the question, ignoratio elenchi, non causa

pro causa, non sequitur, petitio principii, post hoc ergo propter hoc, undistributed middle

logician *n.* casuist, dialectician

logic terms enthymeme, episyllogism, equivocation, polysyllogism, syllogism

loin *n.* noisette

loincloth *n.* dhoti, lungi, pagne

long for desiderate

long-headed *adj.* dolichocephalic

longing *n.* desiderium

long-lived *adj.* longevous, macrobiotic

long-tailed *adj.* longicaudal, longicaudate, macrurous

long-winded *adj.* discursive, prolix

long word sesquipedalian

loop *n.* bight, dee, picot

loosen *v.* slacken, unfix

loosening *n.* laxation

lopsided *adj.* antigodlin

lord *n.* daimyo, liege, seigneur, seignior

Lord's Prayer pater, paternoster

lore, pertaining to loral

loss *n.* privation

loss of will abulia

lotion *n.* emollient, unguent

lots, drawing of sortition

lottery *n.* pakapoo

loud *adj.* blatant, clamorous, roistering, vociferous

lounge *n.* greenroom

love *n.* cupboard love, eros, grand passion

love feast agape

love letter billet-doux

love potion philter

lovers, pairs of Daphnis and Chloe, Pyramus and Thisbe, Romeo and Juliet

love song alba

loving *adj.* amative, anacreontic

lowbrow *n.* Babbitt, philistine

lower *v.* vail

lower *adj.* nether

lowest point nadir

lowly *adj.* ignoble, plebeian

low-necked *adj.* décolleté

loyalty *n.* Bushido, fealty, staunchness

lozenge *n.* cachou, jujube, pastille, troche

lucid *adj.* luculent

luck *n.* serendipity
ludicrous *adj.* risible
lukewarm *adj.* Laodicean, tepid
lullaby *n.* cradlesong
luminescence *n.* foxfire, ignis fatuus
luminous *adj.* lambent, lucent, refulgent
lump *n.* bolus, boule, dollop, gobbet, nubble
lumpy *adj.* nubby
lunar month lunation
lungs, animal lights
lure *n.* attractant, troll
lurk *v.* skulk
lush *adj.* teeming, verdant
lust *n.* concupiscence, lechery
luster *n.* iridescence, luminosity, reflet, refulgence, schiller
lustful *adj.* concupiscent, goatish, lascivious, lecherous, lubricious, ruttish
lustful thoughts, having prurient
lustrous *adj.* iridescent, nacreous, nitid
lute player lutanist, lutenist, lutist
luxuriate *v.* wallow
luxurious *adj.* Babylonian, Corinthian, Lucullan, pharaonic, Sardanapalian, sybaritic, voluptuous
lying *n.* mendacity
lying *adj.* mendacious
lying above *adj.* superjacent
lying face down *adj.* procumbent, prone, prostrate, supine
lying down *adj.* decumbent, recumbent
lying on the back *adj.* supine

machine, drilling stoper
machine gun *mitrailleuse*
machinery, destroyer of Luddite
machines, control by cybernation
madam *n.* bawd

magic *n.* black art, conjuration, diablerie, diabolism, gramarye, necromancy, occultism, sortilege, thaumaturgy, theurgy
magical broth hellbroth
magician *n.* archimage, conjurer, Dactyl, illusionist, Joukahainen, magus, necromancer, prestidigitator, Prospero, shaman, thaumaturge, thaumatrope
magistrate *n.* burgomaster, corregidor, doge, gonfalonier, gymnasiarch, podesta, praetor, praetorian, prior, quaestor, syndic
magnanimity, display of beau geste
magnet *n.* lodestone
magnetism, personal *n.* charisma, duende
magnificent *adj.* palatine, resplendent
magnifying glass loupe
maid *n.* abigail, amah, ayah
maim *v.* scotch
maintain *v.* asseverate, postulate
maintainable *adj.* tenable, viable
maintenance *n.* alimentation, sustentation
majestic *adj.* august, opulent, sublime
make *v.* actualize, confect
make disloyal disaffect, estrange
makeshift *adj.* expedient, jackleg, jury-rigged
make unnecessary obviate
makeup *n. maquillage*
malaria *n.* paludism
malcontent *n.* frondeur
male-dominated *adj.* androcentric
male relative agnate
male rule androcracy
malign *v.* asperse, calumniate
malignant *adj.* baleful, virulent
man, little homunculus, manikin
man, old gaffer
manageable *adj.* docile, regulable, wieldy
management *n.* eutaxy
manager *n.* gerent
maneuver *n.* démarche, gambit, razzle-dazzle, ruse, stratagem, wile
mangle *v.* lacerate
mania *n.* cacoëthes
manifestation *n.* avatar, epiphany
manifesto *n.* pronunciamento
mannerism *n.* affectation, preciosity
manners *n.* decorum, suavities
mantra *n.* gayatri, om, pranava

manual *n.* enchiridion, vade mecum
manufactured *adj.* factitious
manufactured item facture
manufacturer *n.* fabricant
manuscript *n.* anopisthograph, chrysograph, opisthograph, uncial, vellum
many *adj.* divers, manifold, multifarious, myriad, sundry
map *n.* planisphere, plat
map case solander
mar *v.* vitiate
marauder *n.* mosstrooper
marble *n.* brocatel, cipolin
marble, like marmoreal
marble, a playing agate, dobie, immie, taw
march *v.* debouch
march *n.* anabasis, débouché, étape, katabasis
marginal *adj.* limbic, nugatory
marginal notes marginalia
marijuana *adj.* bhang, charas, dagga, ganja, sinsemilla
marine *adj.* thalassic
marine farming mariculture
mark *v.* demarcate, hachure, hatch, obelize
mark *n.* breve, cedilla, circumflex, dagger, diacritic, dieresis, diesis, double dagger, macron, nikkud, obelus, pilcrow, tilde
marked *adj.* gyrose
marker *n.* fanion
market *n.* bazaar, *mercado*, suk
marketplace *n.* agora, maidan
marriage, of hymeneal
marriage, hatred of misogamy
marriage, types of deuterogamy, digamy, endogamy, exogamy, hypergamy, levirate, mésalliance, misalliance, monandry, monogamy, monogyny, morganatic marriage, open marriage, plural marriage, polyandry, polygamy, polygyny, sororate, trigamy
marriageable *adj.* nubile
marriage broker *shadkhan*
marriage custom levirate
marriage poem epithalamion, epithalamium, protothalamion, protothalamium
married man, newly benedict
marshy *adj.* boggy, fenny, paludal, plashy, quaggy, Serbonian
marshy region maremma
martial art tae kwon do, t'ai chi ch'uan
martyr *n.* protomartyr

marvelous to relate *mirabile dictu*
marvels *n. mirabilia*
mask *n.* loup
masked person guisard
masochism *n.* algolagnia
masquerade *n.* mummery
mass *n.* concretion, petrifaction, ruck
massacre *n.* pogrom, Sicilian Vespers
massage *n.* effleurage, reflexology, shiatsu
massage *v.* manipulate, Rolf
massage technique tapotement
masses, the hoi polloi, plebeians, proletariat, vulgus
masterly *adj.* consummate
masterpiece *n.* chef d'oeuvre
masturbation *n.* onanism, self-abuse
mat *n.* tatami
match *n.* locofoco, lucifer
match *v.* jibe, tally
matchless *adj.* consummate, inimitable
material *adj.* corporeal
materialistic *adj.* banausic
materialize *v.* reify
mating area lek
mattock *n.* twibill
mattress *n.* futon, pallet, palliasse, shikibuton
mature *adj.* fledged
mature *v.* maturate
maxim *n.* aphorism, gnome, logion, saw
maxims, some Murphy's Law, Occam's razor, Parkinson's law, Peter
  Principle
mayonnaise *n.* aioli
mayor *n.* alcalde, podesta
mazelike *adj.* labyrinthine, mazy
meadow *n.* lea
meager *adj.* exiguous, jejune
meal *n.* collation, repast
meal, after a postprandial
meal, before a anteprandial, preprandial
mean *adj.* mingy, reptile, scurvy
mean *n.* via media
meaning *n.* denotation, explicans, intendment, purport,
  signification, tenor
meaning, hidden subaudition, subtext
meaning, relating to semantic
meanings, many different polysemy

means *n.* instrumentality, wherewithal
measles *n.* rubeola
measles, German roseola, rubella
measurable *adj.* mensurable
measuring *n.* mensuration
measuringworm *n.* looper, spanworm
meat, dried pemmican
meat, slice of collop
mechanical *adj.* banausic, perfunctory
medallion *n.* encolpion, panagia
medals *n.* exonumia
meddler *n.* marplot, Nosy Parker, Paul Pry
meddlesome *adj.* intrusive, obtrusive, officious
mediate *v.* intercede, intermediate
medical *adj.* iatric
medicinal drink ptisan
medicine *n.* medicament, nostrum
medicine man angakok, curandero, kahuna, shaman
meditation *n.* abstraction, brown study, lucubration, samadhi,
    sandhya, zazen
meditation room zendo
meditative *adj.* cogitative, contemplative
medley *n.* pastiche, pasticcio
meekness *n.* mansuetude
meerschaum *n.* sepiolite
meeting *n.* assemblage, conclave, consistory, conventicle, esbat,
    sabbat, séance
meeting place exedra, thingstead
megaphone *n.* vamphorn
melancholy *adj.* atrabilious
melange *n.* cento, potpourri, varia
melodious *adj.* canorous, dulcet, mellifluous
melody *n.* descant, lied
melt *v.* deliquesce, liquefy
melted *adj.* fondue
melting *adj.* liquescent
member *n.* apparat
membrane *n.* caul, chorion, goldbeater's skin, meninx, pellicle,
    rennet
mementos, collector of memorabiliast
memorandum *n.* aide-mémoire, bordereau
memorial *n.* cenotaph, chaitya, chorten, dagoba, stupa
memory, poor forgettery
memory aid mnemonic
memory disorder paramnesia

memory trace engram
menacing *adj.* darkling, minacious, minatory
mender *n.* tinker
men's quarters selamlik
menstruation, first menarche
mental activity cerebration, mentation
mental discomfort dysphoria
mental reservation arrière-pensée
mention beforehand prenominate
mentor *n.* guru, *padrino*, preceptor
mercenary *adj.* acquisitive, avaricious, venal
merchant ship argosy, carrack
merciful *adj.* benignant, ruthful
merciless *adj.* flinty, obdurate, ruthless
mercury *n.* hydrargyrum, quicksilver
mercy *n.* clemency, lenity
mercy killing coup de grâce, euthanasia
merge *v.* conflate, intergrade
merry *adj.* jocose, jocund, sportive, waggish
merrymaker *n.* guisard, mummer
merrymaking *n.* carousal, jollification
mess *n.* kettle of fish, shambles
messenger *n.* apostle, Gabriel, herald
messiah *n.* Mahdi
metal *n.* latten
metal shavings, pile of swarf
metamorphosis *n.* transmutation
metaphor *n.* catachresis
methodical *adj.* punctilious
meticulous *adj.* fastidious, scrupulous
mica *n.* isinglass
middle *adj.* mesial, midmost
middle age middlescence
middle way, a via media
mighty *adj.* puissant
migraine *n.* megrim
migrating *adj.* peregrine, transhumant
migration *n.* transhumance
migratory *adj.* anadromous, diadromous, emigratory
mild *adj.* favonian
mildness *n.* lenity, mansuetude
milestone *n.* benchmark, watershed
military, government by the stratocracy
military leader man on horseback
military post presidio

milk *n.* beestings, bonnyclabber, clabber, clobber, colostrum, lobber, lobbered milk

milk, of lacteal, lactic

milk-producing *adj.* galactophorous, lactiferous, milch

milk production lactation

milky *adj.* adularescent, lacteal

mill *n.* quern

millennium *n.* chiliad

millennium, believer in the chiliast, millenarian

mimicry *n.* mimesis, mimetism

mincing *adj.* niminy-piminy

mind, pertaining to the noetic

mind reader mentalist

mine *n.* colliery, Golconda

mine *v.* stope

miner *n.* collier

mingle *v.* admix, commingle, commix, immingle, immix

miniature world microcosm

minimize *v.* depreciate, minify

minister of state chancellor

minister's house manse

minority *n.* nonage

minstrel *n.* gleeman, jongleur, troubadour

minute *adj.* infinitesimal, minuscule

miracles *n. mirabilia*

miracles, study of thaumatology

miracles, worker of thaumatrope, thaumaturge

miraculous *adj.* preternatural

mirage *n.* Fata Morgana, looming

mirror *n.* speculum

misappropriation *n.* defalcation

misbehavior *n.* malversation

miscellaneous *adj.* divers

miscellany *n.* ana, varia

mischievous *adj.* arch, elfin, impish

mischievous child hellion

misconduct *n.* misprision

miser *n.* chuff, churl, hunks, niggard, pinchpenny

miserable *adj.* disconsolate, forlorn, piteous, squalid, woebegone

misery *n.* dystopia

misfortune *n.* adversity, contretemps, infelicity, misadventure

misgiving *n.* compunction, demur, qualm, scruple

misjudge *v.* misapprehend

mislead *v.* coffeehouse, meacon

misleading *adj.* delusive, dissembling

misrepresent *v.* belie, traduce
missing person Enoch Arden, Judge Crater
mist *n.* bai, brume, cacimbo, pride of the morning
mistress *n.* concubine, fancy woman, hetaera, paramour, sultana
mistress of a great house chatelaine
misunderstanding *n.* imbroglio, *malentendu*, misconstruction
misuse of words malapropism
misuser of words, persistent mumpsimus, Mrs. Malaprop
mitigate *v.* extenuate
mix *v.* blunge, commingle
mixture *n.* amalgam, commixture, farrago, galimatias, gallimaufry,
    macédoine, mélange, olio, potpourri, ragbag, salmagundi
moat *n.* fossa
mob *n.* doggery, rabble
mob rule mobocracy, ochlocracy
mocking *adj.* derisive, sardonic
model *adj.* archetype, embodiment, epitome, exemplar,
    exemplification, exemplum, paradigm, paragon
moderate *adj.* centrist, temperate
moderate *v.* meliorate, mitigate, palliate
moderation *n.* continence, sophrosyne, temperance
modern *adj.* neoteric
modesty *n.* diffidence, reticence
modicum *n.* semblance
moisten *v.* sparge
moistening *adj.* humectant
molasses *n.* theriac, treacle
mold, cooking dariole
moldable *adj.* fictile
moldiness *n.* must, mustiness
molding *n.* bolection
mold inhibitor mycostat
moldy *adj.* fusty, mucedinous
mole *n.* melanism, nevus
mollifying *adj.* placative, placatory
molt *v.* exuviate
molting *n.* ecdysis
monastery *n.* abbey, cloister, friary, lamasery, laura, monkery,
    priory, stauropegion, vihara, wat
monastery room cell, misericord
monastic *adj.* austere, claustral, cloistral, monachal
monasticism *n.* monachism
money *n.* lucre, pelf, scrip, specie, sterling, tender, wherewithal,
    xenocurrency
money, expense viaticum

moneychanger *n.* cambist, shroff
moneylender *n.* Lombard, Shylock
money-lending, illegal *n.* feneration
monitor *n.* praepostor, proctor
monk *n.* bhikshu, bonze, caloyer, Carthusian, cenobite, Cistercian, Dalai Lama, Euchite, *frère*, friar, gyrovague, hegumen, hierodeacon, hieromonk, lama, marabout, monastic, rasophore, sadhu, Sesshu, votary
monkeylike *adj.* pithecoid
monogamous *adj.* monogamic, monogynous
monster *n.* afreet, basilisk, Charybdis, chimera, cockatrice, Gigantes, Gorgon, griffin, harpy, lamia, leviathan, manticore, Minotaur, opinicus
monstrosity *n.* abnormity, teratism
month, in the next proximo
monthly *adj.* mensal
monument *n.* cenotaph, chorten, Colossus of Memnon, fairy stone, gisant, henge, herm, tope, trilith, trilithon, tropaeum, tropaion, woodhenge
moody *adj.* churlish, doleful, dour, lugubrious, morose, saturnine
moon, the Cynthia
moon inhabitant lunarian
moralizing *adj.* didactic, preachy
morally involved engagé
moral virtue probity, rectitude
moreover *adv.* withal
morning, pertaining to matutinal
morning dress dishabille
mosaic, piece of tessera
mosque *n.* *masjid*
mother *n.* materfamilias
mother-of-pearl *n.* nacre
motionless *adj.* quiescent, static
motive, ulterior arrière-pensée
motiveless *adj.* gratuitous
motorboat *n.* vaporetto
mottled *adj.* dappled, piebald, parti-colored, pinto
mound *n.* agger, kitchen midden, mogul, stupa, tell, tepe
mounded *adj.* tumular, tumulous
mountain *n.* djebel
mountain, beneath a piedmont, submontane
mountain, beyond a ultramontane
mountain chain cordillera
mountain climbing alpinism
mountain peak aiguille
mountains, between intermontane

mountains, on this side of cisalpine, cismontane
mournful *adj.* dolorous, lachrymose, lugubrious, wailful
mourning *n.* shivah
mourning, sign of crepe
mourning garments sackcloth, weeds
mouth *n.* maw
mouth, of the buccal, oscular, stomatic
mouthpiece *n.* embouchure
mouthwash *n.* collutorium, collutory
move *v.* career, gangle, hurtle, jink, maunder, scud, tootle
movement *n.* peregrination, saltation, transhumance, translocation
movement by supernatural means levitation, psychokinesis,
    telekinesis
moving *adj.* ambulant, itinerant, volitant
mucus, secreting muciferous, muciparous
mud *n.* fango, sapropel
muddle *n.* farrago, fuddle, snafu
mud-dwelling *adj.* limicolous
muddy *adj.* dreggy, feculent, riley, roily, sloughy, turbid
mudhole *n.* loblolly
mug *n.* flagon, noggin, seidel, tankard, toby
mule *n.* hinny, sumpter
mule driver mule skinner, muleteer
multilingual *adj.* polyglot
munch *v.* champ
mundane *adj.* banausic
murder *v.* burke, remove
murderer *n.* Bluebeard, Cain, dacoit, femicide, filicide, fratricide,
    infanticide, Jael, matricide, parenticide, parricide, patricide,
    regicide, sororicide, tyrannicide, uxoricide, vaticide
murderous *adj.* internecine
murky *adj.* Stygian
murmur *n.* souffle, susurration, susurrus
murmuring sound sough
muscle *n.* thew
muscle pain myalgia
muscle weakness myasthenia
muse *v.* cogitate, ruminate
Muses, the *n.* Calliope, Clio, Erato, Euterpe, Melpomene,
    Polyhymnia, Terpsichore, Thalia, and Urania
mushroom fancier mycophagist
mushroom poisoning mycetism
mushy *adj.* pappy
musician *n.* Jubal, klezmer, mariachi
music-loving *adj.* philharmonic
musky *adj.* moschate

mustard plaster sinapism
musty *adj.* dank, frowsy, fusty
mutate *v.* metamorphose, transmute
muteness *n.* aglossia
mutilate *v.* grangerize
mutinous *adj.* insurrectionary, refractory, seditious
mutt *n.* feist
muttering *n.* murmuration, mussitation
mysterious *adj.* arcane, enigmatic, esoteric, numinous, occult,
    orphic, preternatural, runic, sibylline
mystery *n.* arcanum, mystique
mystic *n.* Hasid, Hesychast
mystical knowledge gnosis
myth destroyer mythoclast
myth interpretation solarism
myths, giving rise to mythopoeic *(adj.)*

N

nag *v.* badger, chivvy, harry, hector
nag *n.* harpy, scold, shrew, termagant, virago, Xanthippe
Nagasaki survivor
    hibakusha
nagging *adj.* petulant
nail-biting *n.*
    onychophagia
naive *adj.* credulous,
    dewy-eyed,
    guileless,
    ingenuous,
    unaffected
naked *adj.* au naturel,
    in puris
    naturalibus,
    undraped
name *n.* agnomen,
    allonym, anonym,
    anthroponym,

antonomasia, appellation, appellative, charactonym, cognomen, dayname, denomination, epithet, eponym, font name, forename, hypocorism, matronymic, metonym, metronymic, misnomer, nom de guerre, nom de plume, nomen, patronym, patronymic, pen name, praenomen, prenomen, sobriquet, toponym, vocable, whiteacre

name *v.* denominate

name, wrong misnomer

named *adj.* yclept

name derivation eponymy

nameless *adj.* innominate

namely *adv.* scilicet, *videlicet*, viz.

namer *n.* nomenclator

names, having several polyonymous

names, pertaining to proper onomastic

naming *n.* appellation, compellation

nanny *n.* amah

nape *n.* nucha, nuque, scruff

napkin *n.* serviette

narcotic *n.* bhang, dagga, keef, kef, stupefacient

narrate *v.* recount

narration *n.* recital, recountal, relation

narrative *n.* chronicle, iliad, recital

narrow *adj.* parochial, provincial

narrowing *n.* stenosis, stricture

narrow-minded *adj.* illiberal, insular, myopic, parochial, picayune, provincial

nasal *adj.* rhinal

nationalism *n.* chauvinism

native *adj.* aboriginal, autochthonous, endemic, indigenous

native *n.* aborigine, autochthon, indigene

natural *adj.* **1.** intuitive, unschooled; **2.** unembellished

naughty *adj.* willful

nausea *n.* wamble

nausea, experience wamble

nauseated *adj.* qualmish, queasy, squeamish, wambly

navel *n.* omphalos, umbilicus

navigate *v.* astrogate

navigation *n.* cabotage

near *adj.* juxtaposed

nearest *adj.* proximate

nearness *n.* apposition, juxtaposition, propinquity, proximity

nearsighted *adj.* myopic

neat *adj.* fastidious, kempt, natty, spruce

neatly *adv.* featly

necessarily *adv.* needs, perforce

necessary *adj.* de rigueur, exigent, imperative, requisite
necessity *n.* desideratum, requisite
neckband *n.* sautoir
necklace *n.* Brisingamen, choker, rivière
neckline *n.* décolletage
needle *n.* acus, bodkin, pinnacle
needlelike *adj.* belonoid
needless *adj.* gratuitous
needy *adj.* destitute, impoverished, indigent, necessitous
ne'er-do-well *n.* rapscallion
negate *v.* abrogate, nullify
negative *adj.* negatory
neglect *v.* pretermit, procrastinate, scant
neglect *n.* dereliction, limbo, misprision, oblivion, preterition, pretermission, remissness, slackness
neglectful *adj.* derelict, heedless, omissive, remiss
negligee *n.* wrapper
negligence *n.* laches, oscitation
negligent *adj.* heedless, offhand, remiss, watchless
negotiator *n.* negotiant
neigh *v.* whicker, whinny
neighborhood *n.* environs, purlieu, vicinage
neighboring *adj.* abutting, contiguous, juxtaposed, tangent, vicinal
nemesis *n.* Alastor, Waterloo
neophyte *n.* proselyte
nerve *n.* cheek, chutzpa, gall
nervous *adj.* restive, ruffled, timorous
nervousness *n.* fantod, nervosity, restiveness, timorousness
nest *n.* aerie, eyrie, nide, nidus, vespiary
nest, build a nidificate, nidify
nest, termite termitarium
nestling *n.* eyas
net *n.* bagwig, flew, flue, lattice, malines, seine, snood, tracery
net *v.* ensnare, seine
netlike *adj.* retiary, reticular, reticulate, reticulated, retiform
network *n.* graticule, plexus, reseau, rete, reticle, reticulation, reticulum
neutral *adj.* disinterested, dispassionate
neutral *n.* mugwump
nevertheless *adv.* withal
new *adj.* neoteric, vernal
newborn child neonate
newborn children, pertaining to neonatal
newcomer *n.* arriviste, griffin, Johnny-come-lately, malihini, outlander, parvenu

newfangled *adj.* neoteric
new-rich *n.* nouveau riche, parvenu
New Testament books homologumena
next *adj.* proximate
next to last penultimate
nicety *n.* punctilio, quiddity
nickname *n.* cognomen, sobriquet
night blindness nyctalopia
nightclub *n.* boîte
nightmare *n.* incubus, phantasmagoria
nightwalking *n.* noctambulation, noctambulism
nimble *adj.* lightsome, limber, lissome, lithe, volant
nine, consisting of nonary
ninety-year old nonagenarian
nipple *n.* dug, mammilla
nitpicker *n.* fussbox, fussbudget, fusspot
nobility, pertaining to nobiliary
nobleman *n.* boyar, grandee, hidalgo, magnifico, marchese,
     marquess, marquis, ritter, viscount
noblewoman *n.* marchesa, marchioness, marquise, viscountess
nobody *n.* cipher, mediocrity, nullity
nod *v.* nutate
nodding *n.* nutation
no further bets! *rien ne va plus!*
noise *n.* brattle, brontide, clamor, clangor, din, sonance
noisy *adj.* clamant, clamorous, obstreperous, rackety, rambunctious,
     strepitous, tin-pan, turbulent, vociferous
nominal *adj.* ostensible, putative
nominally *adv.* ostensibly, putatively
nonchalant *adj.* apathetic, debonair, dégagé, detached, insouciant,
     pococurante
nonconforming *adj.* raffish
nonconformist *n.* maverick
nonexistent *adj.* chimerical, illusory, insubstantial
non-Mormon *n.* jack Mormon
no-nonsense *adj.* resolute
nonsense *n.* amphigory, balderdash, blather, bombast, bosh,
     bunkum, bushwa, claptrap, codswallop, drivel, falderal,
     fandangle, fiddle-faddle, flimflam, flubdub, flumadiddle,
     flummery, fudge, galimatias, inanity, peddlery, poppycock,
     tomfoolery, tommyrot, trumpery, twaddle
nook *n.* cove, inglenook, recess
noose *n.* springe
nose, inflammation of the rhinitis
nosebleed *n.* epistaxis

nose job rhinoplasty
nostrils *n.* nares
notable *adj.* manifest, signal
notch *n.* crenature, crenel, crenulation, rabbet
notched *adj.* crenelated, crenulate, crenulated, emarginate, nock, serrate, serrated
note *n.* annotation, apostil, chit, scholium
notebook *n.* cahier
notes *n.* marginalia
notes, without extemporary, extempore
nothingness *n.* nullity
notice *v.* descry, espy
noticeable *adj.* manifest, salient
notify *v.* apprise
notion *n.* **1.** whigmaleerie, whim; **2.** vagary
notoriety *n.* ignominy, obloquy, odium, réclame
notorious *adj.* arrant, flagrant, infamous, patent
not wanted de trop
notwithstanding *prep./conj. non obstante*
noun *n.* bahuvrihi, substantive
nourish *v.* foster, suckle
nourishing *adj.* alimentary
nourishment *n.* aliment, manna, sustenance
nouveau riche arrivé, arriviste, parvenu
novel *adj.* singular
novice *n.* abecedarian, fledgling, novitiate, white belt, youngling
nuclear survivor hibakusha
nude *adj.* undraped (see also **naked**)
nudist *n.* naturist
nuisance *n.* bandersnatch, vexation
nullifying *adj.* defeasible, diriment
numb *adj.* anaesthetized, insensible, prostrate, stupefied, torpid
number *n.* clutch
number, large lac, legion, multitude, sea
numerous *adj.* manifold, multifarious, multifold, myriad
nun *n.* bhikshuni, Carmelite, cenobite, Cistercian, extern, votary
nurse *n.* amah, ayah
nursery *n.* crèche
nutrition, lack of innutrition
nut-shaped *adj.* nuciform
nymph *n.* dryad, hamadryad, Hyades, naiad, Nereid, Nysa, Oceanid, oread, salamander, Scylla, sylph, Syrinx, undine

O

oak, pertaining to an quercine
oar *n.* scull
oar-shaped *adj.* remiform
oath *n.* voir dire
oath, taking an juration
oatmeal *n.* flummery
obedience *n.* Bushido, deference
obedient *adj.* deferent, deferential, duteous, dutiful, malleable,
  obsequious, submissive, subservient, tractable
obituary *n.* necrology
object *v.* demur, expostulate, remonstrate, scruple
objectify *v.* **1.** externalize, rationalize; **2.** embody
objecting *adj.* exceptive
objection *n.* cavil, censure, demur, qualm, remonstrance, scruple
objectionable *adj.* noisome, odious
objective *adj.* disinterested
objects, everyday realia
obligated *adj.* beholden
obligation *n.* corvée, noblesse oblige, onus
obligatory *adj.* imperative, incumbent, irremissible, mandatory
oblige *v.* constrain
obliging *adj.* complaisant
oblique stroke solidus
oblivion *n.* lethe, limbo
oblivious *adj.* abstracted, unmindful
obnoxious *adj.* odious
obscene *adj.* blue, fescennine, ithyphallic, lascivious, prurient,
  raunchy, salacious, scurrilous
obscenity *n.* ordure, scatology, smut
obscure *adj.* abstruse, arcane, cabalistic, cryptic, Delphic, elliptical,
  enigmatic, equivocal, esoteric, fuliginous, inglorious, inscrutable,
  murky, occult, oracular, recherché, recondite, tenebrous
obscure *v.* obnubilate
obscured *adj.* perdu, turbid
obscurity *n.* obliquity
obsequious *adj.* abject, deferential, fawning, groveling, menial,
  servile, subservient, sycophantic
obsequiously, act kowtow

obsequiousness *n.* obsequence
observant *adj.* **1.** perceptive; **2.** punctilious
observation *n.* espial, introspection
observe *v.* **1.** espy, reconnoiter; **2.** introspect, opine; **3.** solemnize
obsess *v.* besot, preoccupy
obsession *n.* idée fixe
obsolete *adj.* superannuated
obsolete, make supersede
obstacle *n.* abatis, impediment, pons asinorum
obstetrician *n.* accoucheur, gynecologist
obstetrics *n.* tocology
obstinate *adj.* balky, crabbed, fractious, froward, intractable,
     mulish, obdurate, pertinacious, pervicacious, recusant,
     refractory, restive, stolid, unregenerate, willful
obstreperous *adj.* blatant, clamant, heckling, refractory, vociferous
obstruct *v.* encumber, filibuster, obturate, obviate, occlude, oppilate,
     preclude, stymie, thwart
obstruction *n.* embolism, embolization, embolus, encumbrance
obstructionist *n.* filibusterer
obtain *v.* beguile, exact, inveigle, wheedle
obtrusive *adj.* impertinent, intrusive, officious, protrusive
obtuse *adj.* insensitive, purblind
obvious *adj.* axiomatic, blatant, egregious, flagrant, manifest,
     obtrusive, palpable, patent, prima facie, transparent
occasionally *adv.* betimes
occult *adj.* cabalistic, metaphysical, supernatural
occult learning gramarye
occupant *n.* denizen
occupation *n.* métier
occupy *v.* engross, immerse
occur *v.* eventuate, materialize, supervene
occurrence *n.* contretemps, eventuality, incidence
occurring annually etesian
occurring suddenly fulminant, precipitate
ocean *n.* Davy Jones
ocean current El Niño
ocean farming mariculture
oceans, pertaining to pelagic
odds and ends flotsam, rummage
ode *n.* monody, parabasis, parodos, stasimon (see also **poems and
     poetical terms**)
odometer *n.* perambulator
odor *n.* gaminess
odorous *adj.* rammish, rank, redolent
off-color *adj.* risqué

offend *v.* affront, chafe, disoblige, incommode, nettle, pique
offense *n.* pique, umbrage
offense, apt to take umbrageous
offensive *adj.* crass, fetid, fulsome, invidious, mephitic, noisome,
    objectionable, odious, scarlet, unsavory, vexatious
offer *v.* bestow, proffer, propound, tender
offer *n.* proffer, tender
offering *n.* altarage, corban, oblation, offertory
offhand *adj.* extemporary, extempore, impromptu
office *n.* magistracy, pontificate, prelacy, prelature, priorate
officer *n.* bailiff, jemadar, justiciar, justiciary, manciple, prior,
    propraetor
officers, one of three triumvir
official *adj.* bona fide, ex officio
official *n.* bashaw, chamberlain, chiaus, dewan, Dogberry,
    functionary, gabbai, gauleiter, hayward, hierarch, induna,
    intendant, jemadar, Junker, macebearer, macer, mandarin,
    Master of the Revels, ombudsman, ombudsperson,
    ombudswoman, palatine, panjandrum, pasha, Pooh Bah,
    proconsul, procurator, prothonotary, provost, pursuivant, reeve,
    sacristan, steward, vizier, waldgrave
offset *v.* counterpoise, countervail
offspring *n.* get, issue, progeny
offspring, producing philoprogenitive
oil *n.* chrism, citronella, oil of catechumens, oil of the sick
oiliness *n.* lubricity, unctuousness
oily *adj.* lubricious, oleaginous, pinguid, unctuous, unguinous
ointment *n.* nard, pomade, pomatum, salve, unction, unguent
old *adj.* long in the tooth, patriarchal, superannuated, venerable
old, become superannuate
old age senectitude
old-fashioned *adj.* antediluvian, antiquated, archaic, fusty,
    moss-grown, obsolescent, oldfangled, passé, superannuated
old man Methuselah, patriarch, whitebeard
Old Testament Septuagint
old woman babushka, beldam, biddy, crone, dowager, Elli, matriarch
old-womanish *adj.* anile
olive, stuffed pimola
olive-shaped *adj.* olivary
omen *n.* augury, bodement, boding, foreboding, foretoken, portent,
    presage, presentiment, prognostic
ominous *adj.* bodeful, direful, fateful, inauspicious, oracular,
    portentous, sententious, unpropitious
omission apheresis, asyndeton, elision, ellipsis, haplography,
    lipography, preterition, pretermission; (see also **rhetorical terms**)

omit *v.* elide, forbear, pretermit
omnipresence *n.* ubiquity
omniscience *n.* prescience
once a day, occurring circadian
onetime *adj.* quondam
on the contrary *au contraire, per contra*
ooze *v.* exude, transude
opaque *adj.* obtuse, turbid
opaque, make opacify
open *adj.* **1.** campestral, patulous, yawning; **2.** artless, avowed, blatant, bluff, candid, flagrant, guileless, ingenuous, manifest, overt, patent, pervious, unreserved; **3.** moot, unresolved
open-air *adj.* hypaethral
open air, the plein air
open-handed *adj.* magnanimous, unstinting
opening *n.* apocope, colostomy, embrasure, fenestra, fissure, interstice, meatus, orifice, tubulure, vomitorium
opening *adj.* prefatory
openly *adv.* forthrightly, ingenuously, patently
open-minded *adj.* catholic, dispassionate
openness *n.* glasnost
open space esplanade, glade
opera *n.* opéra bouffe, opera buffa, opéra comique, opera seria, zarzuela
operating *adj.* operant
operative *adj.* efficacious, operatory
opiate *n.* anodyne, soporific
opinion *n.* **1.** conjecture, conviction, doxy, speculation, supposition, surmise; **2.** obiter dictum
opinion, express an opine
opinionated *adj.* pragmatic
opium *n.* laudanum
opium, affected by poppied
opportune *adj.* expedient, politic, providential, seasonable
oppose *v.* contravene, controvert, gainsay, recalcitrate, repugn, retroact
opposed *adj.* adverse, averse, disinclined, inimical, loath
opposite *adj.* adversative, antiphrastic, antipodal, antithetical, converse
opposite *prep.* vis-à-vis
opposition *n.* antithesis, contraposition, contrariety, contravention, recusancy
opposition, astronomical syzygy
oppress *v.* aggrieve, dragoon, Neroize, scourge
oppressed *adj.* downtrodden, overborne

oppression *n.* adversity, affliction, tribulation
optimist *n.* Dr. Pangloss, Pollyanna
optimistic *adj.* Panglossian, Pollyanna, Pollyannaish, roseate,
   sanguine
optional *adj.* facultative
oral *adj.* buccal, nuncupative, viva voce
oral historian griot
orally *adv.* buccally, viva voce
orate *v.* perorate
oration *n.* encomium, lucubration, panegyric, peroration,
   valediction, valedictory
orator *n.* rhetor, rhetorician
oratorical *adj.* rhetorical
oratory *n.* rhetoric
orchestra *n.* gamelan
ordeal *n.* gauntlet
order *n.* **1.** enjoinder, eutaxy, ukase; **2.** kilter
order *v.* enjoin
orderly *adj.* natty, trig, trim
orderly *n.* peon
ordinance *n.* prescript
ordinary *adj.* banal, exoteric, mundane, quotidian, unexceptional
organism feeding on dead matter saprophyte
organization *n.* apparat, gemeinschaft
organize *v.* codify, marshal
organs, animal offal, viscera
organs as food numbles, umbles
orgiastic *adj.* bacchanalian, Dionysian
orgy *n.* bacchanal, bacchanalia, saturnalia
orifice *n.* aperture, foramen, meatus
origin *n.* genesis, inchoation, provenance, provenience, wellspring
original *adj.* **1.** aboriginal, primal, primeval, primordial, pristine,
   Promethean; **2.** archetypal, germinal, seminal
original *n.* archetype
original text textus receptus
originate *v.* emanate
ornament *n.* fandangle, filigree, fleurette, gaud, paillette,
   skeuomorph; (see also **ornaments of many types**)
ornament *v.* bedeck, bedizen, damascene, embellish, engrail, fret,
   garnish, purfle
ornamental *adj.* churrigueresque
ornamentation *n.* drop, gadrooning, gingerbread, guilloche, gutta,
   imbrex, sgraffito, smocking
ornamented *adj.* Alhambresque, aureate, gingerbread, resplendent,
   storied

ornaments of many types adorno, aigrette, ailette, anaglyph, antefix, anthemion, appliqué, arabesque, arcade, bocage, bolection, brassard, bucranium, carcanet, chevron, chinoiserie, circlet, concha, corbeil, diamanté, encarpus, epergne, gadroon, garniture, gaud, gimcrack, gimcrackery, goffer, gorget, knosp, labret, phalera, purfle, quatrefoil, rinceau, rondelle, rosace, rosette, tchotchke

ornate *adj.* aureate, barococo, baroque, convolute, Corinthian, florid, rococo

orphaned *adj.* cade

orthodox, not heterodox

oscillate *v.* librate

oscillation *n.* libration, saltus, seiche

oscillatory eye movement nystagmus

ostentation *n.* frippery, pretentiousness

ostentatious *adj.* florid, pretentious

ostrich, like an struthious

other things being equal *ceteris paribus*

outburst *n.* ebullition, fantod, paroxysm, tantrum

outcast *n.* anathema, Ishmael, Ishmaelite, leper, pariah, reprobate

outcasts *n.* Burakumin

outcome *n.* denouement, resolution

outcry *n.* cri de coeur

outdated *adj.* fusty, neolithic, passé

outdo *v.* transcend, trump

outdoor *adj.* alfresco

outdoor entertainment fête champêtre

outdoors *adv.* alfresco, en plein air, withoutdoors

outfit *n.* equipage

outflow *n.* effluence, effluent, efflux, emanation

outgoing *adj.* expansive

outgoing person extrovert

outgrowth *n.* excrescence

outhouse *n.* see **privy**

outing *n.* jaunt

outlaw *n.* brigand, cutthroat, dacoit, malefactor, marauder, pariah

outlaw *v.* proscribe

outline *n.* contour, epitome, lineation, planform, précis

outline *v.* adumbrate

outlying district purlieu

outmoded *adj.* antediluvian, démodé, demoded, passé

out of place inapposite

outpost *n.* barbican, outsettlement, outstation

outpouring *n.* spate

outrage *n.* affront, indignity

outrage *v.* aggravate, desecrate, exasperate
outrageous *adj.* atrocious, extravagant, immoderate, monstrous, unholy, unspeakable
outright *adj.* unmitigated
outside *adv.* without
outsider *n.* carpetbagger
outspoken *adj.* forthright, vociferous
outstanding *adj.* paramount, predominant, preponderant
outstrip *v.* eclipse
outward flow effluent, efflux
outwit *v.* finesse
oven *n.* cremator, Dutch oven, lehr, salamander, tandoor
overabundance *n.* embarras de richesses, nimiety, plethora, surfeit
overbearing *adj.* despotic, haughty, imperious
overblown *adj.* recherché
overcast *adj.* lowering
overcleverness *n.* ambidexterity, duplicity
overcoat *n.* surtout, ulster
overcome *v.* overwhelm, whelm
overconfident *adj.* cocksure, overweening, presuming, presumptuous
overcritical *adj.* hypercritical
overdone *adj.* fulsome, inordinate
overdue *adj.* behindhand
overemphasize *v.* belabor
overfeed *v.* cloy, satiate, surfeit
overflow *v.* exuberate, inundate, superabound
overflow *n.* alluvion, freshet, inundation
overflowing *adj.* effusive, inundant, superabundant
overfull *adj.* plethoric, surfeited
overhang *v.* impend, loom, overlie
overhanging *adj.* superincumbent
overindulgence *n.* crapulence, crapulousness, gourmandise
overlapping *adj.* accolated, imbricated, incubous
overload *v.* overlade, surcharge
overlord *n.* suzerain
overly *adv.* immoderately, inordinately
overlying *adj.* superjacent
overpowering *adj.* steamroller
overpraise *v.* belaud
overreach *v.* overleap
overrefined *adj.* tenuous
overshadow *v.* obumbrate
overshadowing *adj.* overarching
overshoe *n.* galosh

oversight *n.* inadvertence, inadvertency
oversimplification *n.* simplism
oversimplified *adj.* simplistic
overspread *v.* suffuse, well up
overstate *v.* embroider
oversubtle *adj.* casuistic, sophistical
oversupply *n.* plethora, superabundance, superfluity, surfeit
overt *adj.* patent
overthrow *n.* labefaction
overturn *v.* overset, subvert
overuse *v.* hackney
overwhelm *v.* glut, inundate, whelm
overwhelming *adj.* inundant
ox *n.* aurochs, banteng, bullock, gayal, urus
oxcart *n.* carreta
oxygen-depleting *adj.* eutrophic
ozone, containing ozoniferous, ozonous

P

pace *n.* scuttle
pacify *v.* assuage, conciliate, disarm, mollify, pacificate, propitiate
package *n.* packet
packhorse *n.* sumpter
packing *n.* dunnage
packsack *n.* kyack
page *n.* footboy
page, left-hand verso
page, right-hand recto
paid applauder claqueur
pain *n.* angst, mittelschmerz, pang, throe, travail
pain *v.* beset, scarify
pained *adj.* lacerated
painful *adj.* algetic, poignant, torturous
painkiller *n.* acesodyne, analgesic, anodyne, antiodontalgic
painless death euthanasia
painstaking *adj.* assiduous, indefatigable, sedulous, unremitting

paint *v.* limn
painter *n.* limner
painting *n.* bambocciata, diorama, diptych, fresco, gouache, grisaille, pointillism, *sumi-e*, trompe l'oeil, ukiyo-e, *Yamato-e*
pair *n.* brace, span, Tweedledum and Tweedledee, yoke
palace *n.* Alcázar, Alhambra, chateau, palatium, palazzo, *Schloss*, seraglio
palatable *adj.* sapid, savory, toothsome
palatial *adj.* Alhambresque

My Alcázar, mini-Alhambra, dear chateau, a little palazzo, mitt Schloss, or even sweet seraglio... It's just home-sweet-home to me!

pale *adj.* cadaverous, livid, lurid, pallid, peaked, washy
pale face wheyface
paleness *n.* pallidness, pallor, pastiness
palindromic *adj.* cancrine
palm *v.* foist
palm branch lulav
palm-shaped *adj.* palmate
pamper *v.* coddle, cosher, cosset, dandle, indulge, mollycoddle
pamphlet *n.* chapbook, enchiridion, fascicle
pan *n.* pannikin, wok
panacea *n.* catholicon, elixir, nostrum
pancreas *n.* sweetbread
paneling *n.* boiserie, dado, wainscot, wainscoting
panels, connected diptych, pentaptych, polyptych, triptych
pan-fry *v.* sauté
panic *n.* consternation
panting *n.* polypnea
pantomime *n.* harlequinade
pantomimist *n.* harlequin, Pierrette, Pierrot
pantry *n.* larder
pap *n.* pablum, pabulum
papal *adj.* pontifical
paper *n.* foolscap, laid paper, Manila paper, papier-mâché, papillote, papyrus, rice paper, wove paper

paper, cooked in *en papillote*
paper-folding *n.* origami
papery *adj.* chartaceous, papyraceous
papier-mâché *n.* carton-pierre
parable *n.* allegory, apologue, fable, homily
parachute *n.* drogue
parade *n.* callathump, callithump, cavalcade, retinue
parade ground maidan
paradise *n.* Arcady, Eden, Elysian Fields, Elysium, nirvana,
    Shangri-La
paradise, like paradisal, paradisiacal
paradox *n.* antinomy
paragon *n.* phoenix
paragraph mark pilcrow
parallel *adj.* penciliform
paralysis *n.* hemiplegia, paraplegia, paresis, quadriplegia
parapet *n.* battlement
paraphernalia *n.* accouterments, appointments, appurtenances,
    trappings
parasite *n.* leech, sponge, sponger, sycophant, toady
parasitic *adj.* paratrophic
parasitism *n.* colacobiosis
parch *v.* torrefy, torrify
parchment *n.* forel, palimpsest
pardon *n.* absolution, remission
pardon *v.* absolve, condone, remit
pardon, granting a remissive
pardonable *adj.* venial
parent *n.* genitor
parish, pertaining to a parochial
parliament *n.* Folketing, Knesset, Lagting, Lok Sabha, majlis,
    Odelsting, Oireachtas, Rajya Sabha, Reichsrat, Reichstag,
    Rigsdag, Riksdag, Sejm, Storting
parlor *n.* locutorium, locutory
parochial *adj.* denominational
parody *n.* amphigory, travesty
parrot fever psittacosis
parrots, pertaining to psittacine
parry *v.* fend
part *v.* sunder
partial *adj.* partisan, tendentious
partiality *n.* predilection, predisposition, tendentiousness
participant *n.* participator
particle *n.* iota, jot, mite, moit, mote, ramentum, scintilla, tittle,
    whit

particular *adj.* fastidious, finical, finicky
particularized *adj.* pointillistic
particulars *n.* minutiae
partisan *n.* stalwart
partition *n.* brattice, bulkhead, dissepiment, septum
partition *v.* dismember
partner *n.* yokefellow
partnership *n.* consortium
party *n.* ceilidh, clambake, potlatch, Sadie Hawkins, soiree
pass *n.* Annie Oakley, *laissez-passer*
passage *n.* **1.** conduit, cryptoporticus, foramen; **2.** devolution;
    3. lection, pericope
passage, commonly cited *locus classicus*
passage, tedious longueur
passages *n.* analecta, analects
passageway *n.* adit, allure, andron, galleria, gangway
passing *adj.* fugitive
passion *n.* concupiscence, transport
passionate *adj.* ardent, fervent, fervid, fiery, impassionate,
    vehement, sultry, zealous
passive *adj.* quiescent, supine, vegetative
passive resistance satyagraha
pass over for promotion etc. overslaugh
password *n.* countersign, parole, shibboleth
pastor *n.* dominie
pastoral *adj.* bucolic, idyllic
pastry shop patisserie
pasture *n.* pasturage
pasture *v.* agist
patch *v.* cobble
patent medicine nostrum
pathetic *adj.* affecting, piteous, plaintive, poignant, woeful
pathway *n.* footway
patience *n.* composure, forbearance, longanimity, resignation,
    stoicism, sufferance
patient *n.* analysand
patina *n.* aerugo, incrustation, verdigris
patriotic *adj.* chauvinistic
patron *n.* **1.** denizen, habitué; **2.** Maecenas, padrino
patronage *n.* aegis, auspices
patronizing manner condescension
patter *n.* palaver
pattern *n.* archetype, delineator, epitome, exemplar, gestalt,
    paradigm, paragon, template, touchstone
paunch *n.* corporation

paunchy *adj.* stomachy, ventricose
pause *n.* caesura, respite
pave *v.* macadamize
pavement *n.* asarotum, macadam, pavé, pointel, telford
pavilion *n.* gazebo
paving *n.* terrazzo
paving material tarmacadam
paving stone sett
paving tool lute
pawnshop *n. mont-de-piété*
pay *v.* indemnify, recompense, requite
pay *n.* defrayal, emolument, honorarium, recompense
payment *n.* bride price, defrayal, handsel, honorarium, lobolo,
    quittance, scutage
peace *n.* concord
peace, aimed at irenic, irenical
peaceable *adj.* pacific
peace be with you *pax vobiscum, shalom aleichem*
peaceful *adj.* **1.** clement, halcyon, irenic, irenical, pacific;
    2. togated
peace of mind heartsease
peace pipe calumet
peacock, like a pavonine
peak *n.* acme, apogee, cusp, pinnacle, tor, vertex, zenith
peanut *n.* goober, groundnut, pinder
pearl *n.* baroque, cultured pearl, mabe pearl
pearl diver ama
pearly *adj.* margaritaceous, nacreous
pear-shaped *adj.* obpyriform, pyriform
peasant *n.* fellah, hind, kisan, kulak, muzhik, ryot, serf, vassal,
    villein
pea-shaped *adj.* pisiform
pebble *n.* einkanter
peculiarity *n.* anomaly, idiosyncrasy, singularity
pedantic *adj.* didactic, doctrinaire, donnish, preachy
peddle *v.* hawk
peddler *n.* arab, colporteur, hawker, higgler, packman
peddling *n.* colportage
peel *v.* desquamate, excoriate
peeper *n.* Peeping Tom, voyeur
peephole *n.* judas, judas hole, judas window
peers *n.* douzepers
peevish *adj.* bilious, fractious, pettish, petulant, splenetic
peg *n.* spile, spill
pelt *n.* fell

pelts *n.* peltry
pen *n.* hutch, kraal
pen, fountain stylograph
penance *n.* contrition, mortification, self-abasement
penance, impose shrive
pendant *n.* lavaliere
pendent *adj.* pendulous, pensile
penetrate *v.* permeate, transpierce
penetrating *adj.* poignant
peninsula *n.* chersonese
penis *n.* linga, *membrum virile*, phallus, pizzle, priapus
penitence *n.* compunction, contrition
penitent *adj.* contrite, rueful
penlike *adj.* stylar
penmanship *n.* cacography, calligraphy, chirography
pen name nom de plume
pennant *n.* ensign, guidon, jack
penniless *adj.* destitute, indigent, necessitous
penpoint *n.* nib
pension *n.* superannuation
people *n.* fry, gentry, hoi polloi, populace, rabble, vulgus
people-centered in one sense or another anthropocentric,
   anthropolatric, anthropomorphic, anthroponomical,
   anthropopathic
pep *n.* moxie
peppy *adj.* jaunty
perceive *v.* apprehend, descry, discern, divine, intuit
perceived notion percept
perceiver *n.* percipient
perceiving *adj.* **1.** palpable; **2.** percipient, sentient
perceptible *adj.* appreciable, cognizable
perceptible, barely liminal
perception *n.* Anschauung, cognition, cognizance, epiphany,
   telesthesia
perceptive *adj.* discerning, percipient, perspicacious
perching *adj.* insessorial
percolate *v.* leach
perfect *adj.* consummate, exemplary, impeccable, spheral,
   unalloyed, unmitigated
perfect *v.* consummate
perfect, tending to perfective
perfection *n.* beau ideal, consummation, fare-thee-well
perfidious *adj.* duplicitous, Machiavellian
perforated *adj.* fenestrated
perform *v.* concertize

performer *n.* artiste, geisha, vaudevillian
performers *n.* gagaku
perfume *n.* attar, frangipani, patchouli
perfume *v.* embalm
perfume, substance used in ambergris
perfume box pouncet box
perfumed *adj.* redolent
perimeter *n.* girth, periphery
perish *v.* molder
perjure *v.* forswear
permafrost *n.* pergelisol
permanence *n.* fixity, perdurability
permanent *adj.* abiding, immutable, indelible, perdurable
permeable *adj.* pervious
permeate *v.* imbrue, imbue, impregnate, inosculate, interosculate, interpenetrate, pervade, saturate, supersaturate, tincture
permeating *adj.* permeant
permission *n.* exeat, license, nihil obstat, pratique, sufferance
permissive *adj.* facultative, forbearing, indulgent
pernicious *adj.* noxious, pestiferous
perpendicular *adj.* plumb
perpetual *adj.* abiding, infinite, recurrent
perpetuate *v.* eternize
perplex *v.* nonplus
perplexed *adj.* confounded
perplexing *adj.* ambiguous, enigmatic, equivocal
persecute *v.* crucify
persecution *n.* dragonnade
perseverance *n.* pertinacity, resolution
persevere *v.* perseverate
persevering *adj.* assiduous, dauntless, endurant, pertinacious, sedulous, steadfast
persistence *n.* assiduity, incessancy, indefatigability, pertinacity
persistent *adj.* assiduous, continual, endurant, importunate, incessant, indefatigable, indomitable, pertinacious, resolute, tenacious, unremitting
persnickety *adj.* pernickety
person *n.* criollo, persona, wight
person, absurd Punchinello
person, acceptable *persona grata*
person, affected poseur
person, attractive peri
person, average everyman, everywoman
person, boorish looby, lout, lubber, philistine, yahoo
person, careless pococurante, sloven

person, clumsy gawk, lout, lummox
person, conceited coxcomb, high-muck-a-muck
person, credulous gudgeon
person, deformed lusus naturae, mooncalf
person, demented dement
person, degenerate miscreant, reprobate, wastrel
person, despicable reptile, scullion, stinkard
person, disliked bête noire, bugbear
person, dowdy frump
person, dull frump, prosaist
person, flighty flibbertigibbet, whirligig
person, foolish dotard, mooncalf
person, grasping harpy
person, grotesque golliwog
person, guilty felon, misdemeanant
person, heavy endomorph
person, honest truepenny
person, hypocritically pious tartuffe
person, hypocritically virtuous pecksniff
person, imposing magnifico
person, impotent spado
person, indispensable linchpin
person, ineffectual wimp
person, inexperienced gosling, naïf
person, influential mogul
person, insincere faux-naïf
person, intractable tartar
person, irritating gadfly
person, lazy looby, slugabed, sluggard
person, learned polyhistor, polymath
person, meddlesome kibitzer
person, naive naïf
person, objectionable rotter, wampus
person, obsequious lackey, lickspittle, toady, sycophant
person, pale wheyface
person, pompous Poo Bah
person, possessed python, pythoness
person, prominent nabob
person, quarrelsome catamaran
person, rare rara avis
person, resourceful *débrouillard*
person, retarded retardate
person, ribald ribald
person, saintly mahatma
person, savage tartar

person, scrawny scrag
person, self-seeking arriviste
person, self-taught autodidact
person, shabby tatterdemalion
person, short and muscular endomorph, pyknic
person, silly flibbertigibbet
person, slender asthenic, ectomorph, leptosome
person, stupid dolt, dunderhead, looby, lummox, noddy, noodle, oaf, simpleton
person, submissive uncle Tom, yeasayer
person, successful wunderkind
person, superfluous fifth wheel
person, terrible gorgon
person, ugly gorgon
person, ungrateful ingrate
person, unrivaled nonesuch, paragon
person, unwelcome *persona non grata*
person, vulgar vulgarian
person, wasteful wastrel
person, wealthy Croesus, Midas, nabob, nawab
person, welcome *persona grata*
person, wise Daniel, Solomon
person, young sapling, youngling
personality *n.* persona
person devoted to pleasure sybarite
person given to flaunting knowledge pedant
person given to platitudes platitudinarian
personification *n.* **1.** avatar, embodiment, lustrum; **2.** prosopopoeia
personified *adj.* incarnate
personify *v.* exemplify, personate
person eighty to eighty-nine years old octogenarian
person fifty to fifty-nine years old quinquagenarian
person forty to forty-nine years old quadragenarian
person ninety to ninety-nine years old nonagenarian
person of mixed ancestry bois brûlé, caboclo, cajan, cholo, Creole, diddikai, jackatar, mestiza, mestizo, métis, métisse, mulatto, mustee, octoroon, quadroon
person of superficial knowledge sciolist
person seventy to seventy-nine years old septuagenarian
person sixty to sixty-nine years old sexagenarian
person skilled in table talk deipnosophist
person who fears foreigners xenophobe
person who speaks many languages polyglot
perspiration *n.* diaphoresis, hidrosis

persuadable *adj.* exorable,
   persuasible
persuade *v.* wheedle
persuasion *n.* suasion
persuasive *adj.* charismatic,
   cogent, suasive
pertaining *adj.* appurtenant
pertinacious *adj.* importunate
pertinacity *n.* importunity
pertinent *adj.* apposite, germane,
   material, relevant
peruse *v.* vet
pervade *v.* interpenetrate, suffuse
perverse *adj.* refractory, willful,
   wrongheaded, wry
perversely *adv.* contrariwise
pervert *v.* **1.** sophisticate, vitiate;
   2. deprave, subvert
pervert *n.* debauchee
perverted *adj.* kinky
perverting *adj.* perversive
pesky *adj.* pestiferous, vexatious
pessimism, sentimental *Weltschmerz*
pessimist *n.* crapehanger, Jeremiah, misanthrope
pester *v.* badger, harry, hector, importune
pestle *n.* muller
pet *v.* dandle, pamper
petite *adj.* diminutive
petition *n.* entreaty, supplication
petition *v.* entreat, importune, solicit, supplicate
petitioner *n.* suppliant
pet name hypocorism
pet phrase shibboleth
petrify *v.* gorgonize
petrifying *n.* petrifaction
petty *adj.* fiddling, nickel-and-dime, niggling, pettifogging,
   picayune
petty cash imprest fund
phallic *adj.* priapean, priapic
phantom *n.* eidolon, shade, shape, specter
phantom *adj.* spectral
pharmacy *n.* apothecary
phase *n.* phasis
phenomenal *adj.* prodigious
philistine *n.* babbitt

philosopher *n.* gymnosophist, metaphysician
philosopher, inferior philosophaster, philosophe
philosophy *n.* anthroposophy, axiology, darshana, epistemology, existentialism, gymnosophy, Hegelianism, Heracliteanism, metaphysics, metempirics, Platonism
philosophy, false philosophism
phobias *n.* see **fears, morbid**
phony *n.* charlatan, dodger, mountebank, sharper
photograph *n.* balop, daguerreotype
photographer *n.* paparazzo
phrase *n.* hapax legomenon, locution
phrasemaker *n.* neologist, phrasemonger, phraseologist
phraseology *n.* locution
physical *adj.* carnal, corporal, corporeal, material, somatic
physical defect acrocephaly, acromegaly, acromicria, oxycephaly
physical love eros
physician *n.* extern, Galen, hakim, intern, locum tenens
physician, caused by a iatrogenic
physician, pertaining to a iatric; (see also **hospital, pertaining to a**)
physique *n.* somatotype
pick *n.* plectrum
picket *n.* pale
picket fence paling
pickle *n.* cornichon, gherkin
pickpocket *n.* dunnigan
picky *adj.* captious, carping, niggling
picnic *n.* burgoo
picture *v.* delineate
picture frame Lawrence frame
picture writing pictography
piddling *adj.* paltry, peddling
piece *n.* snippet
piecework *n.* taskwork
pier *n.* 1. embarcadero, jetty, quay; 2. anta, buttress, pilaster
pierce *v.* broach, gore, impale, lancinate, leister, pike, pink, riddle, transfix
pierced *adj.* abroach, cribriform
piercing *adj.* calliopean, poignant, strident
piety *n.* religiosity
piety, hypocritical sanctimony, Tartuffery
pig *n.* see **hog**
pigheaded *adj.* adamant, intransigent, obdurate, refractory
pig iron spiegeleisen
pigment *n.* colorant
pig's feet pettitoes, trotters

pile *n.* agglomeration, coacervation, cumulus
pilgrim *n.* hadji, haji, hajji, palmer, visitant
pilgrimage *n.* hadj, haji, hajj, 'umrah
pilings, group of starling
pill *n.* bolus, pilule
pillage *n.* spoliation
pillager *n.* depredator, ravager
pillar *n.* atlas, cippus, pilaster, piloti, stela, stele, telamon
pillow *n.* bolster
pilot *n.* helmsman, kamikaze
pimp *n.* bawd, chulo, fancy man, pander, procurer, procuress,
   whoremonger
pimping *n.* pandering, procuration
pimple *n.* pustule, whelk
pin *n.* bodkin
pineapple *n.* piña
pinwheel *n.* Catherine wheel
pioneer *n.* apostle
pious *adj.* rectitudinous, religiose
pious, hypocritically sanctimonious
pipe *n.* calabash, calumet, chibouk, chillum, churchwarden,
   dudeen, hookah, hubble-bubble, kalian, meerschaum, narghile,
   Oom Paul, water pipe
pipe tobacco, half-smoked dottle
pirate *n.* buccaneer, corsair, Fomorian, freebooter, picaroon, rover,
   sea dog, sea robber, sea rover, sea wolf
pit *n.* **1.** sump; **2.** alveola, faveolus, fossa, fovea, pock, variole
pitcher *n.* aquamanile, ewer, lota, oinoche, olpe, prochoos
pitcher, shaped like a urceolate
pitchman *n.* mountebank
pithy *adj.* aphoristic, sententious, succinct
pitiful *adj.* abysmal, affecting, piteous, plaintive
pitiless *adj.* callous, implacable, relentless, ruthless
pitted *adj.* alveolate, faveolate, honeycombed, variolous
pity *n.* commiseration, pathos, rue, ruth
pity, object of pilgarlic
placate *v.* conciliate, mollify
place *n.* lieu, locus, niche, stead, venue
place *v.* appose, collocate, juxtapose, repose
place, in the first imprimis
place, secluded fastness
place name toponym
plagiarism *n.* plagiary
plagiarist *n.* plagiary
plaid *n.* tartan

plain *adj.* **1.** conspicuous, manifest, patent, perspicuous, unequivocal, unvarnished; **2.** austere, frugal, homely, homespun, homey, unostentatious, unpretentious

plain *n.* bajada, campagna, campo, champaign, grassland, llano, pampa, pampas, savanna, steppe, tundra, veldt

plaintive *adj.* disconsolate, doleful, plangent, rueful

plan *n.* schema

plan *v.* **1.** envisage, purpose; **2.** premeditate, strategize

planetary system, model of orrery

plank *n.* deal

planter *n.* lavabo

plants *n.* flora

plants, feeding on herbivorous, phytophagous

plant stand jardiniere

plaster of paris *n.* gesso

plastic *adj.* ductile, labile

plate *n.* paten, platen, trivet

plate, protective escutcheon

plateau *n.* fjeld, highland, mesa, paramo, puna, tableland, upland

platelike *adj.* lamellate, lamelliform

platform *n.* almemar, bema, bimah, dais, estrade, hustings, pallet, podium, rostrum, treadle, tribunal, tribune

platitude *n.* bromide

platitudes, given to bromidic, platitudinous

platter *n.* charger

plausible *adj.* ostensible, specious

play *n.* acto, masque

playboy *n.* Corinthian

playful *adj.* arch, frolicsome, gamesome, jocose, lambent, ludic, sportive, tricksy, waggish

plaza *n.* zócalo

plea *n.* entreaty, remonstration, supplication

plead *v.* beseech, entreat, expostulate, remonstrate, sue, supplicate

pleader against beatification defender of the faith, devil's advocate

pleader for beatification postulator

pleading *n.* intercession, remonstrance

pleasant *adj.* **1.** mellifluous, sipid; **2.** affable, engaging, jocund

pleasant idleness *dolce far niente*

pleasantries *n.* facetiae

pleasantry *n.* badinage, sally

please *adv.* por favor, s'il vous plaît

please *v.* delectate

pleasing *adj.* **1.** euphonious, eurhythmic **2.** captivating, ingratiating, palatable, taking, toothsome, winning

pleasing, superficially specious

pleasure *n.* **1.** delectation, inclination; **2.** autoeroticism, hedonism, schadenfreude
pleasure, devotion to a life of hedonism, libertinism, sensualism
pleasure, of hedonic, hedonistic
pleasure-seeker *n.* bon vivant, boulevardier, hedonist, libertine, sensualist
pleat *v./n.* plait
pleated *adj.* plicate
plebeian *adj.* unwashed
pledge *n.* covenant, earnest, gage, surety, warrant
pledge *v.* covenant, hypothecate, plight, warrant
plentiful *adj.* bounteous, plenteous
plenty *n.* copiousness, luxuriance, plenteousness, profusion
pliable *adj.* **1.** amenable, docile, malleable, tractable; **2.** ductile, flexile, limber
pliant *adj.* supple, willowy
plot *n.* **1.** cabal, machination; **2.** plat
plot *v.* **1.** collude, machinate; **2.** plat
plotting *n.* collusion
plow *n.* colter, lister
pluck *v.* **1.** deplume, vellicate; **2.** thrum
plucky *adj.* feisty, gamy
plug *n.* shive, tampion, tampon
plug *v.* tampon
plum *n.* damson
plumage *n.* swansdown
plumbing fixtures sanitary ware
plume *n.* panache, pompon
plumpness *n.* corpulence, embonpoint, portliness, rotundity
plunder *v.* depredate, despoil, rape, ravage, raven, sack, spoliate
plunder *n.* rapine, ravin, spoliation
plunderer *n.* freebooter, rapparee
plundering *n.* depredation, despoliation, predation, rapine, spoliation
plunge *v.* immerge, immerse, precipitate
pocket *n.* placket
poems and poetical terms alba, Alexandrine, antiphon, antistrophe, ballade, ballata, beginning rhyme, caesura, cantar, canto, canzone, chanson de geste, cinquain, clerihew, common rhythm, crambo, dactyl, dactylic, dimeter, dithyramb, ditty, eclogue, elegiac pentameter, elegiac stanza, elegy, epitaph, epithalamion, epithalamium, epode, epopee, epos, epyllion, eye rhyme, fabliau, falling rhythm, feminine caesura, feminine ending, feminine rhyme, free verse, full rhyme, georgic, haikai, haiku, half rhyme, heptastich, heroic couplet, heroic quatrain, heroic verse, hexameter, hexastich, Horatian ode, Hudibrastic,

hypercatalectic, hypercatalexis, hypermeter, iamb, iambic, iambus, ictus, identical rhyme, idyll, iliad, imagery, imagism, imperfect rhyme, incremental repetition, initial rhyme, internal rhyme, Italian sonnet, ithyphallic, kenning, lai, lay, leonine verse, light verse, limerick, linked rhyme, linked verse, logaoedic, logaoedic verse, long measure, long meter, macaronics, madrigal, Mahabharata, masculine caesura, masculine rhyme, Mawlid, metrification, metrify, monody, monopody, monorhyme, monostich, monostrophe, mora, near rhyme, nonsense verse, octameter, open couplet, ottava rima, paeon, palinode, pantoum, pentameter, pentapody, pentastich, Petrarchan sonnet, Petrarchism, Pindaric ode, planh, poulter's measure, proceleusmatic, prothalamion, prothalamium, qasida, quatrain, redondilla, renga, rhyme royal, rhyme scheme, rime riche, rising rhythm, rocking rhythm, rondeau, rondel, rondelet, roundel, rove-over, Rubaiyat stanza, running rhythm, Sapphic ode, scansion, seguidilla, septenarius, septenary, sestet, sestina, sextain, Shakespearean sonnet, sight rhyme, single rhyme, sirvente, slant rhyme, society verse, Spenserian sonnet, spondaic, spondee, sprung rhythm, stacimon, stave, stich, strophe, syncopation, syzygy, tanka, telestich, tenson, tercet, terza rima, tetrabrach, tetrameter, tetrapody, tetrastich, tetrasyllable, tribrach, trimeter, triple rhyme, triple rhythm, triplet, tripody, trochaic, trochee, truncated, truncation, *vers de société*, verset, versicle, versification, vers libre, villanelle, virelay, waka, weak ending

poet *n.* balladmonger, bard, goliard, lyrist, metrician, metrist, minnesinger, poetaster, rhymester, rimer, rimester, scop, skald, troubadour, trouvère, versifier, vers-librist

poetry, pertaining to Parnassian, Pierian

poetry, a volume of divan

poignant *adj.* caustic, pungent

point *n.* cusp, nib, pricket, prickle, tang, tine

point, fine punctilio

pointed *adj.* **1.** acuate, aculeate, cultrate, punctiform; **2.** epigrammatic, incisive

pointed body spicule

pointer *n.* fescue

point for point *punctatim*

poise *n.* aplomb, equanimity, imperturbability, self-possession

poised *adj.* collected, self-possessed, urbane

poison *n.* antiar, bane, ratsbane, toxicant, toxin, venom, zootoxin

poison *v.* envenom

poison gas lewisite, sternutator

poisonous *adj.* baneful, malignant, mephitic, noxious, pernicious, pestilential, toxicant, venenose, venenous, venomous, virulent

poke *v.* dub
polar lights aurora australis, aurora borealis
pole *n.* manhelper, Maypole, stave, striker
polemical *adj.* agonistic
police *n.* askari, Cheka, constabulary, Gestapo, GPU, kotwal,
     NKVD
police officer constable, gendarme, peon, zaptiah
police station thana
polish *v.* burnish, furbish, levigate, schreinerize
polished *adj.* courtly, cultivated, genteel
polite *adj.* well-mannered, well-spoken
polite, overly saccharine
politeness *n.* civility, complaisance, deference, politesse
political organization polity
political rights, mutual isopolity
politician *n.* ward heeler
politics, practical realpolitik
poll tax capitation
pollute *v.* adulterate, defile, desecrate, pervert, sully, vitiate
polygamous *adj.* bigamous, trigamous, polyandrous, polygamic,
     polygynous
pomp *n.* vainglory
pomposity *n.* bombast, flatulence, magniloquence, orotundity,
     turgidity
pompous *adj.* bombastic, flatulent, high-flown, inflated,
     magniloquent, orotund, pontifical, tumescent, turgid
pompous person Poo Bah
poncho *n.* ruana
pond-dwelling *adj.* limnetic
ponder *v.* cogitate, mull, ruminate
ponderous *adj.* elephantine
pool *n.* tarn
poor *adj.* distressed, hapless, impecunious, impoverished, indigent,
     necessitous, penurious, straitened
pope, likely to become papable
populace *n.* demos
popular *adj.* demotic, exoteric
popularize *v.* vulgarize
popular opinion vox populi
population *n.* habitancy
population improvement eugenics, euthenics
porcelain *n.* Belleek, celadon, hard paste, Imari ware, Jesuit ware,
     jet-enameled ware, Kutani, nankeen, Parian ware, Sevres
porch *n.* galilee, mantapa, porte-cochere, salutatorium; (see also
     portico)

pork, salt sowbelly
porous *n.* cancellous, cavernous, leachy, poriferous
port *n.* anchorage, port of call
portable *adj.* portative
portal *n.* iwan, liwan
portend *v.* augur, forebode
portent *n.* augury, harbinger, omen, presage, presentiment
porter *n.* hamal, ostiary
portico *n.* narthex, prostoon, prostyle, stoa, xyst, xystum, xystus
portion *n.* collop, lot, modicum, quantum
portly *adj.* corpulent, plenitudinous
portray *v.* delineate, limn
pose *v.* affect, posture, posturize
poseur *n.* attitudinarian, philosophaster, philosophe
position *n.* **1.** situs; **2.** benefice
positive *adj.* categorical, peremptory, thetic
posse *n.* posse comitatus
possessed *adj.* demoniac, demoniacal, demonian, demonic
possibility *n.* contingency, prospect
possible *adj.* contingent, feasible, practicable
post *n.* benefice
poster *n.* dazibao
posterity *n.* futurity
postmortem examination autopsy, necropsy, necroscopy
postpone *v.* prorogue
postponement *n.* moratorium, prorogation
postulate *v.* hypothecate, posit
postulate *n.* axiom, conjecture
posy *n.* nosegay
pot *n.* bain-marie, cachepot, cassolette, cocotte, crock, cruse, daube, dixie, Dutch oven, gallipot, jardiniere, marmite, petite marmite, pipkin, pottle
pot, ornamental epergne
potent *adj.* puissant
potential *adj.* latent, quiescent
potential *n.* potency, puissance
pothole *n.* chuckhole
potion *n.* elixir, philter
pots, mender of tinker
pottery *n.* buccaro, delft, faience, gombroon, Mocha ware, rabat, Samarian ware, Satsuma ware, sgraffito, slipware, terra sigillata, Wedgwood, Yayoi ware
pottery, pertaining to fictile
pottery fragment ostracon, potsherd, shard
pouch *n.* alforja, burse, marsupium, sporran

pound *v.* pestle
pour *v.* decant, disembogue
pour forth effuse
pouring *n.* libation
pouring forth effusive *(adj.)*
pout *v.* glower
pout *n.* moue
poverty *n.* exigency, penury, privation, straitness
poverty-stricken *adj.* starveling
powder *n.* pounce
powder *v.* dredge, granulate, pestle, pounce, triturate
powdered *adj.* comminuted, desiccated
powdery *adj.* pulverulent
power *n.* **1.** dint, leverage, puissance; **2.** éminence grise, gray
    eminence, maya
powerful *adj.* omnificent, omnipotent, plenipotent, stentorian
powerful, make potentiate
powerful in sound stentorian
powerless *adj.* impotent, ineffectual, prostrate
powerlessness *n.* impotence, ineffectuality, inefficacy
power to evoke pity pathos
practicable *adj.* feasible, viable
practical *adj.* applicative, applicatory, banausic, pragmatic, viable
practical exercise practicum
practical person pragmatist
practical politics realpolitik
practice *n.* exercitation, externship, internship, praxis, wont
practitioner *n.* licentiate
praise *n.* doxology, encomium, eulogy, kudos, magnificat,
    panegyric, plaudit
praise *v.* eulogize, extol, panegyrize
praise, deserving laudable
praise, expressing laudatory
praise, with cum laude, magna cum laude, summa cum laude
praiseworthy *adj.* exemplary, laudable, palmary
praising *adj.* commendatory, laudatory
prance *v.* caper, cavort, flounce, gambol
prank *n.* antic, caper, caprice, dido, shenanigan
prankish *adj.* tricksy
pranks *n.* jinks
prankster *n.* scourer
prawn *n.* langoustine
pray *v.* daven, supplicate
prayer *n.* anaphora, bination, breviary, collect, commination,
    compline, Confiteor, devotion, evensong, intercession,

itinerarium, kaddish, litany, miserere, Nafi, night office, nocturn, nones, novena, office, orison, orthros, requiescat, salat, suffrage, supplication

prayer book euchologion, *mahzor*, missal, *siddur*
prayer device phylactery
prayer leader imam
prayer shawl tallith
prayer stick paho
pray for us *ora pro nobis*
preach *v.* evangelize, preachify
preacher *n.* darshan, evangelist, maggid, predicant
preaching *n.* kerygma
preaching *adj.* predicant
preaching, relating to homiletic, predicatory
preachy *adj.* didactic, sanctimonious, sententious
preamble *n.* proem
precede *v.* antecede, forgo
precedence *n.* antecedence, precession
preceding *adj.* antecedent, anterior, precursory, prevenient
precept *n.* *mitzvah*
precious *adj.* invaluable
precious-stone expert lapidary
precise *adj.* finical, punctilious, scrupulous
preconception *n.* prenotion
precook *v.* parboil
predatory *adj.* exploitive, lupine, predacious, rapacious, raptorial, vulturine
predecessor *n.* antecessor, precursor, progenitor
predestined *adj.* predestinate
predetermine *v.* foreordain, foreordinate, predestinate, predestine
predicament *n.* exigency, strait
predict *v.* augur, divine, foretell, portend, presage, prognosticate, prophesy
prediction *n.* prognostication; (see also **divination**)
predictive *adj.* prognostic
predominant *adj.* prepotent
preeminence *n.* primacy
preempt *v.* arrogate, coopt, preclude
preface *n.* proem, prolegomenon, prolusion
prefatory *adj.* prolegomenous, prolusive
preference *n.* predilection, predisposition, prepossession
pregnancy *n.* cyesis
pregnant *adj.* enceinte, gravid, hapai, impregnate, parturient
pregnant, not farrow
prejudice *n.* predilection, predisposition, prepossession

prejudice *v.* prepossess
prelate *n.* bishop
preliminary *adj.* precursory, prefatory, prolegomenous
preliminary discussion *pourparler*
prelude *n.* prelusion, proem
premature development precocity
premeditated *adj.* prepense
premise *n.* presupposition
premises, set of donnée
premonition *n.* foreboding, forewarning, harbinger, portent,
    precursor, presage, presentiment
preoccupation with bodily needs physicality
preoccupation with self solipsism
preoccupied *adj.* distrait, engrossed, immersed, rapt
preoccupy *v.* engross, immerse
preparatory *adj.* preparative
prepare *v.* preincline, unlimber
prerogative *n.* droit du seigneur, seigniorage
prescribed *adj.* prescript
prescribing *adj.* prescriptive
presence *n.* aura, carriage, charisma, mien
present *v.* proffer
present *n.* baksheesh, broadus, cumshaw, gratuity, lagniappe,
    largess
present occasion nonce
preserve *v.* ensile, husband, jerk
preserve *n.* confection, confiture
preserver *n.* conservator
press, the fourth estate
pressed *adj.* appressed
pressed together serried
pressing *adj.* clamant, exigent
prestige *n.* cachet, izzat
presumption *n.* hubris
presumptuous *adj.* forward, overweening
presuppose *v.* postulate, premise
pretend *v.* affect, dissemble, dissimulate, feign
pretended *adj.* Barmecidal, feigned, illusory, ostensible, soi-disant
pretender *n.* aspirant, claimant, poseur, seemer
pretender to knowledge of philosophy philosophaster, philosophe
pretend illness malinger
pretense *n.* artifice, charade, pretext, travesty
pretentious *adj.* affected, bombastic, flatulent, florid, grandiloquent,
    inflated, la-di-da, magniloquent, orotund, ostentatious, overblown,
    papier-mâché, recherché, tumescent, turgid

pretentiousness *n.* coxcombry, foppishness, kitsch
pretext *n.* stalking horse
pretty *adj.* dishy, mignon, well-favored
prevail *v.* predominate, preponderate
prevalent *adj.* pervasive, regnant, rife
prevent *v.* avert, forestall, forfend, obviate, occlude, parry, preclude
preventing evil apotropaic
preventive *adj.* preemptive, prophylactic
previous *adj.* antecedent, prevenient
prey *n.* quarry
priceless *adj.* inestimable
prickly *adj.* **1.** echinate, echinulate; **2.** peevish, spiky
pride *n.* hubris, vainglory
priest *n.* bacchant, bacchante, bocor, bonze, Brahman, caliph,
    canon, celebrant, confessor, curé, dastur, divine, dominie, epulo,
    flamen, haruspex, hierarch, hieromonk, honorary canon, imam,
    kahuna, lama, Magus, powwow, presbyter, protopresbyter,
    prototype, shaman, vicar
priestly *adj.* hieratic, sacerdotal
prim *adj.* missish, prissy, prudish, starched
prima donna diva
primary *adj.* primeval, primordial
primate *n.* catholicos
primer *n.* hornbook
primitive *adj.* aboriginal, antediluvian, primal, primeval,
    primordial, pristine
primp *v.* preen, prink
prince *n.* atheling, elector, Landgrave, mirza, princekin, princeling
princely *adj.* sumptuous
principle *n.* axiom, canon, principium, theorem
printers *n.* typothetae
printing *n.* boustrophedon, cuneiform
prior *adj.* antecedent, anterior
priorities, determination of triage
priority *n.* antecedence, precedence
prison *n.* Alcatraz, Attica, bagnio, barracoon, bastille, Dartmoor,
    gulag, oflag, Sing Sing
prisoner *n.* Kapo
private *adj.* auricular, esoteric
privately *adv.* sub rosa
private things, most penetralia
privilege *n.* birthright, droit du seigneur, prerogative
privy *n.* backhouse, Chic Sale, garderobe; (see also **toilet**)
prize, award a premiate
probability *n.* verisimilitude

probable *adj.* verisimilar
probe *n.* sonde
problem, insoluble tar baby
problem, intricate Gordian knot
procession *n.* cortege, precession
proclaim *v.* annunciate, blazon, emblazon, preconize
proclamation *n.* ban, banns, pronunciamento
procrastinator *n.* cunctator
procreating *adj.* procreant
procure *v.* pander
procurement *n.* procuration
prodigy *n.* portent, wunderkind
produce *v.* elucubrate, ingenerate, spawn
producer *n.* régisseur
producing *adj.* parturient, travailing
productive *adj.* fecund, generative, germinal
profane *adj.* **1.** impious, unhallowed, unpious; **2.** secular, temporal;
  3. abusive
profane *v.* blaspheme, defile, desecrate, dishallow, unhallow
profanity *n.* blasphemy, execration, malediction, obloquy, sacrilege
profess *v.* aver, consubstantiate
profitable *adj.* fructuous
profiting from trade in sacred things simony
profound *adj.* abstruse, erudite, sagacious
profuse *adj.* effuse, opulent, unsparing
progressive *adj.* avant-garde, processive
progressive *n.* progressist
prohibit *v.* debar, enjoin, interdict, preclude, proscribe
prohibition *n.* debarment, embargo, enjoinder, enjoinment,
  interdiction, ostracism, preclusion, proscription, taboo
prohibitive *adj.* exorbitant, extortionate, prohibitory
project *n.* projet
project *v.* cantilever, obtrude
projecting *adj.* erumpent, porrect, prognathous, salient
projection *n.* cantilever, crenation, crenature, planisphere,
  prominence, promontory, relief, salience, salient
proletarian *n./adj.* proletary
proliferating *adj.* proliferous
prolific *adj.* fecund, generative, philoprogenitive, rank, teeming
prolong *v.* elongate
promenade *n.* paseo, pleasance
prominence *n.* salience, saliency
prominent *adj.* erumpent, protuberant, salient
promiscuous person debauchee, debaucher, lecher
promise *v.* bode

promise *n.* sponsion, troth
promising *adj.* auspicious, propitious, roseate
promote *v.* enhance, espouse, exalt, forward, foster
promotion *n.* exaltation, furtherance, preferment
prompt *adj.* expeditious
promptness *n.* alacrity, expedition
prone *adj.* procumbent, recumbent, resupine, supine
prong *n.* tine
pronounce *v.* enounce
pronounced *adj.* unequivocal
pronouncement *n.* allocution, dictum
pronunciation *n.* articulation, elocution, hypercorrection, hyperform, hyperurbanism, inflection
pronunciation, study of orthoepy
proof, serving as probative
prop *n.* stay
propaganda *n.* agitprop
propagate *v.* engender, procreate
propagative *adj.* germinal, seminal
propel *v.* impel, scull
proper *adj. comme il faut,* decorous, *de rigueur,* meet, pukka
proper names, pertaining to onomastic
property *n.* chattel, personalty
property owner hidalgo
prophecy *n.* bodement, prevision, soothsaying, vaticination; (see also **divination**)
prophesy *v.* augur, divine, presage, previse, prognosticate, vaticinate
prophet *n.* augur, Cassandra, clairvoyant, divine, doomsayer, doomsdayer, doomster, oracle, pythoness, seer, sibyl, soothsayer
prophetic *adj.* apocalyptic, fateful, fatidic, fatidical, mantic, oracular, prescient, pythonic, sibylline, vatic
prophets *n.* Cassandra, Daniel, Deborah, Elijah, Isaiah, Jeremiah, Muhammad, Tanaquil
propitious *adj.* favonian
proponent *n.* paladin, protagonist
proportional *adj.* ratable
proportionate *adj.* accordant, commeasurable, commensurable, commensurate, consonant
proposal *n.* overture
propose *v.* proffer, propound, tender
proposition assumed as true lemma
propriety *n.* decorum, prudery, seemliness
prosaic *adj.* mundane, pedestrian, trite, vapid

prosaic expression prosaism
prosecution *n.* pursuance
prosecutor *n.* quaestor
prose narrative chantefable
prosperity *n.* opulence, weal
prosperous *adj.* bounteous, halcyon, palmy
prostitute *n.* bawd, bimbo, call girl, cocotte, concubine, courtesan,
 Cyprian, demimondaine, doxy, drab, fancy woman, *fille de joie*,
 gigolo, harlot, hetaera, lady of the evening, light-o'-love,
 magdalene, nightwalker, paphian, paramour, party girl, quean,
 roundheels, scarlet woman, slattern, slut, streetwalker, strumpet,
 succuba, succubus, tramp, trollop, trull, white slave
prostitute, pertaining to a meretricious, tarty
prostitute, reformed magdalen
prostitution *n.* harlotry
prostrate *adj.* recumbent, resupine, supine
protect *v.* forfend, harbor, husband
protecting *adj.* phylactic
protection *n.* aegis, husbandry
protective *adj.* **1.** prophylactic; **2.** tutelary
protector *n.* conservator, *padrino*
protégé *n.* ward
protest *n.* démarche, demurral, expostulation, protestation,
 remonstrance
protest *v.* asseverate, aver, demur, expostulate, inveigh, obtest,
 remonstrate, revile
Protestant *n.* Orangeman, Schwenkfelder, sectary
protocol *n.* **1.** decorum, rubric; **2.** concordat, convention
protoplasm *n.* sarcode
prototype *n.* archetype, exemplar, urtext
protracted *adj.* longsome, prolix
protrude *v.* belly, extrude, obtrude
protrusion *n.* prolapse, proptosis, protraction, protuberance
protuberance *n.* boss, gibbosity, knur, umbo
protuberant *adj.* gibbous, protrusive, ventricose
proud *adj.* disdainful, orgulous, overweening, purse-proud, pursy,
 vaunting
prove false confute
proverb *n.* adage, aphorism, apothegm, dictum, epigram, epigraph,
 maxim, saw
provide *v.* afford, fend
province *n.* eparchy, exarchate, eyalet, nomarchy, nome, oblast,
 ordinariate, presidency, satrapy, vilayet

provincial *adj.* parochial
provisional *adj.* provisory
provisioner *n.* sutler
provisions *n.* provender, sea stock, sea stores
provoke *v.* chafe, foment, nettle, pique, rile, rouse, ruffle, vex
provoker *n.* gadfly
prowess *n.* emprise, expertise
prowler *n.* mouser
proximity *n.* contiguity, propinquity, vicinage
prude *n.* bluenose, Mrs. Grundy, nice-nelly, prig
prudence *n.* discernment, discretion, providence, sophrosyne
prudent *adj.* circumspect, politic
prudish *adj.* blue, missish, priggish, puritanical, strait-laced,
    Victorian
prudishness *n.* Grundyism, nice-nellyism
prurient behavior priapism
pry *v.* prize, root
prying *adj.* inquisitorial
pseudonym *n.* anonym, nom de guerre, nom de plume
public *n.* great unwashed, hoi polloi
publicity *n.* ballyhoo, puffery, réclame
publicity, a hunger for réclame
publicize *v.* ballyhoo, puff
public square agora
public walk alameda
publish *v.* vend
pucker *v.* purse
puddle *n.* plash
Puerto Rican *puertoriqueño* (*n.*)
pugnacious *adj.* bellicose, contentious, truculent
pullet, fattened poularde
pull up extirpate
pulp *n.* pomace
pulpit *n.* bema, bimah, mimbar, rostrum, tribune
pulse *n.* sphygmus
pulverize *v.* comminute, pestle, triturate
pun *n.* double entendre, equivoque, *jeu de mots*, paronomasia
punch bowl monteith
pundit *n.* swami
pungent *adj.* caustic, piquant, poignant
punish *v.* amerce, castigate, ferule, fustigate, mulct, scourge
punishable *adj.* statutable
punishment *n.* bastinado, castigation, chastisement, cucking stool,
    ducking stool, garrote, gauntlet, *peine forte et dure*, retorsion,
    retortion, retributivism, strappado, visitation; (see also **torture**)

punishment, place in Hades for Tartarus
punitive *adj.* castigatory, retributive, vindicative, vindicatory
punk *n.* touchwood
punning *n.* paronomasia
pupil *n.* shishya
purchase *n.* acquest
pure *adj.* **1.** intemerate, inviolate, vestal, virginal; **2.** unalloyed, unqualified
purge *v.* **1.** absolve, expiate; **2.** extirpate, liquidate
purge *n.* epuration
purging *n.* catharsis, purgation
purification *n.* circumcision, depuration, elutriation, epuration, lustrum, purgation
purifier *n.* alembic
purify *v.* circumcise, depurate, elutriate, expurgate, liquate, lustrate, mundify, shrive, sublimate
purifying *adj.* depurative, lustral, purgatorial, purgatory, purificatory
puritanical *adj.* Roundheaded, strait-laced
purpose *n.* resolve
purposeful *adj.* purposive
purposeless *adj.* fatuous
purr *v.* curr
purse *n.* reticule
pursue *v.* shag
pus, discharge matterate, maturate, suppurate
push *v.* **1.** expedite, impel; **2.** jostle
push *n.* dynamism, enterprise, zeal
pushy *adj.* forward, self-assertive
puslike *adj.* pyoid
pussy *adj.* purulent, suppurative
pussyfoot *v.* sidestep, straddle
put on endue
putrid *adj.* fetid, miasmic
putrid, becoming putrescent
puzzle *n.* anomaly, conundrum, enigma, logogriph, paradox
puzzling *adj.* abstruse, enigmatic, knotty
pygmy *n.* manikin
pyorrhea *n.* Riggs' disease
Pyrrhic victory Cadmean victory

Q.E.D. *quod erat demonstrandum*
quack *n.* charlatan, empiric, humbug, mountebank, quacksalver
quackery *n.* charlatanism, empiricism
quadrivium *n.* arithmetic, geometry, astronomy, and music
quadruple *adj.* quadplex
qualification *n.* proviso
qualification, indispensable sine qua non
qualm *n.* compunction
quantity *n.* jorum, quantum, ruck
quarrel *n.* dustup, fracas, ruction
quarrel *v.* caterwaul, pettifog
quarrelsome *adj.* cantankerous, contentious, dissentious
quarrelsome person catamaran
quarter *n.* faubourg
queen *n.* regina
queen, of a regnal
queer *adj.* oddish
quell *v.* placate, subdue, tranquilize
quench *v.* allay, slake
question *n.* interrogatory, koan, mondo
question *v.* catechize, interpellate
questionable *adj.* controvertible, dubitable
question-and-answer *adj.* catechetical
question-and-answer, instruction by catechism
questioner *n.* inquisitor, querist
question mark interabang, interrobang
questionnaire *n.* questionary
quibble *n.* amphibology, amphiboly, sophism
quibble *v.* carp, cavil, equivocate, pettifog, prevaricate
quibbler *n.* casuist, pettifogger, prevaricator, sophist
quibbling *adj.* captious, carping, niggling, pettifogging
quick *adj.* expeditious, feathered, precipitate
quicken *v.* expedite, vivify
quickly *adv.* chop-chop
quick-tempered *adj.* choleric, churlish, irascible
quiet *adj.* lown, reposeful
quilt *n.* comforter, counterpane, coverlet, crazy quilt, duvet,
    eiderdown, hap, kakebuton

quilting *n.* trapunto
quintessence *n.* elixir
quip *n.* equivocation, quibble, sally
quirk *n.* crotchet, idiosyncrasy, tic, vagary
quivering *n.* fibrillation, trepidation
quivering *adj.* tremulous
quixotic conduct knight-errantry
quotation *n.* epigraph

R

rabbit *n.* lapin, leporide
rabbit fever tularemia
rabbits, breeding place for warren
rabble *n.* canaille, riffraff, the unwashed
rabies *n.* hydrophobia
race *v.* hurtle
race, endurance enduro
racehorse *n.* plater
racket *n.* crosse
racy *adj.* piquant, pungent, salty
radiance *n.* aureole, effulgence, lambency, luminosity, refulgence
radiant *adj.* effulgent, lambent, luminous, refulgent
raft *n.* kelek
ragamuffin *n.* street arab, tatterdemalion
ragged *adj.* tatty
raid *n.* forage, foray, incursion, razzia, sortie
raid *v.* maraud, ravage
raider *n.* marauder, mosstrooper, reiver
rain *n.* cacimbo, mizzle, serien
rain *v.* mizzle
rain, pertaining to hyetal, pluvial, pluvious
rainbow *n.* fogbow, mistbow, seadog, secondary rainbow, white
    rainbow
rain forest selva
rain gauge pluviometer
rain map nephanalysis
rain shower scud

rainy *adj.* pluvial, pluvious
raise *v.* broach, emboss, levitate
raisin *n.* sultana
ram, castrated wether
ramble *v.* maunder
rambling *adj.* **1.** circumlocutory, desultory, diffuse, digressive, discursive, excursive, expatiating, garrulous, maundering, periphrastic, prolix; **2.** meandering, peripatetic, skimble-scamble, tortuous
rambling *n.* circumlocution, discursion, discursiveness, garrulity, loquacity, maundering, periphrasis, prolixity
ramp *n.* gradient
rampart *n.* bastion, battlement, breastwork, bulwark, vallation
ram's horn trumpet shofar
ranch *n.* finca
random *adj.* casual, desultory, fortuitous, haphazard, stochastic
range *n.* compass, diapason, gamut, latitude, purview, spectrum, sweep
rank *n.* brevet, echelon
rape *v.* ravish, violate
rapid *n.* sault
rapids *n.* dalles
rapport *n.* affinity, empathy, freemasonry
rapture *n.* beatitude, exaltation, raptus, transport
rapturous *adj.* ecstatic
rare *adj.* recherché, tenuous, unwonted
rare book dealer bibliopole
rarefied *adj.* attenuate, tenuous
rarity *n.* curio, rara avis, tenuity
rascal *n.* blaggard, miscreant, picaro, picaroon, rapscallion, reprobate, scalawag, scapegrace, scaramouch, wastrel
rascality *n.* roguery
rascals, of picaresque
rash *adj.* brash, harum-scarum, incautious, precipitate, scatterbrain, temerarious
rash *n.* efflorescence
rashness *n.* adventurism, precipitancy, temerity
raspberry *n.* *framboise*
ratify *v.* sanction, validate
rational *adj.* lucid, sagacious
rat poison ratsbane
rattle *v.* **1.** crepitate; **2.** discompose, disconcert
rattle *n.* **1.** maraca; **2.** crepitus, rale
rattlebrain *n.* rattlehead, rattlepate
raucous *adj.* strident

ravage *v.* despoil
ravenous *adj.* lupine, predatory, rapacious, ravening
ravine *n.* arroyo, coulee, donga, flume, gulch, kloof, nullah, quebrada, rambla
ravish *v.* deflower
raw food, eating of omophagia
rawhide *n.* parfleche, thong leather, whang
razzle-dazzle *n.* razzmatazz
react *v.* retroact
reactionary *n./adj.* Bourbon
read *v.* devour, peruse
reader *n.* aliterate, bibliophage, lector
reading, variant lection
reading desk lectern
readjust *v.* redress
ready *adj.* disposed
ready-to-wear *adj.* prêt-à-porter
real *adj.* echt, praedial, veritable, viable
realism *n.* verism
realistic *adj.* pragmatic
reality *n.* Sat-cit-anan-da
realization *n.* entelechy, fruition
reappearance *n.* emersion, recrudescence
rearrange *v.* permutate, permute
reason *v.* expostulate, intellectualize, Platonize, ratiocinate, remonstrate, syllogize
reason *n.* nous
reasonable *adj.* equitable, plausible, temperate, tenable
reasonableness *n.* plausibility, rationality
reasoner, fallacious sophist, sophister
reason for being raison d'être
reasoning *n.* casuistry, choplogic, deduction, induction, inference, intellection, ijtihad, noetics, ratiocination, sophistry, syllogism
reasoning, fallacious paralogism, sophistry
reawakening *n.* Renaissance, Renascence
rebel *v.* reluct
rebel *n.* frondeur, iconoclast, seditionary
rebellion *n.* coup d'état, insurgency, insurrection, sedition
rebellious *adj.* contumacious, insubordinate, perverse, recalcitrant, refractory, seditionary, seditious
rebellious conduct rebeldom
rebelliousness *n.* contumacy, recalcitrance, seditiousness
rebirth *n.* renascence
reborn *adj.* palingenetic, renaissant, renascent
rebound *v.* resile, ricochet

rebuke *v.* censure, chide, hector, keelhaul, reproach, reprove, upbraid

rebuke *n.* admonition, censure, remonstrance, remonstration, reproach, reproof

recalcitrant *adj.* renitent

recant *v.* unswear

recantation *n.* palinode

recede *v.* retrocede, retrograde, revert

receipt *n.* chit, quittance

receivable *adj.* receptible

recent *adj.* neoteric

receptacle *n.* chrismatory, ciborium, cupel, font, hanaper, monstrance, ossuarium, ossuary, ostensorium, ostensory, phylactery, reliquary, stoup, theca

reception *n.* **1.** recipience; **2.** durbar, levee, soiree, vermissage

receptive *adj.* acceptant, amenable, susceptive

receptiveness *n.* recipience

recess *n.* **1.** alcove, ambry, armarium, oriel; **2.** closure, respite

recipient *n.* honorand

reciprocated, not unrequited

recite *v.* declaim, intone, recount

reckless *adj.* harum-scarum, heedless, imprudent, incautious, precipitate, temerarious

recklessness *n.* diablerie

reckless person kamikaze

reclining *adj.* accumbent, recumbent

recluse *n.* anchoress, anchorite, ascetic, cenobite, eremite, incluse, solitary, solitudinarian

recoil *v.* flinch, quail, resile

recollection *n.* anamnesis, anaphora

recompense *n.* quittance, solatium

recompense *v.* requite

reconcile *v.* **1.** placate, propitiate; **2.** resolve

reconciliation *n.* eirenicon, propitiation, rapprochement, syncretism

record *n.* chronicle, counterfoil, genealogy, menology, pictograph, procès-verbal

recoup *v.* indemnify, recompense

recourse *n.* resort

recover *v.* recoup, replevy

recruit *v.* conscribe, impress, proselytize

rectangular *adj.* quadrate

rectify *v.* amend

rectory *n.* presbytery

recurrent *adj.* nagging, unrelenting

red *adj.* florid, lateritious, rubicund
red, becoming rubescent (*adj.*); rubefaction (*n.*)
red, mark with rubricate
red blood cell erythrocyte
redden *v.* rubify, rubricate
reddening *adj.* erubescent
reddish *adj.* livid, rubrical, rufescent, rufous, sanguine
redemptive *adj.* salvific
red-handed *adj.* in flagrante delicto
redistrict *v.* gerrymander
redness *n.* erythrism
redness, causing rubefacient
red ochre ruddle
reduce *v.* abate, curtail, detruncate, epitomize, reduct
reduced *adj.* curtate, déclassé, epitomized
reduction *n.* ablation, decrement, detumescence, epitome
reduction to the absurd reductio ad absurdum
redundancy *n.* nimiety, pleonasm, superfluity, tautology
redundant *adj.* diffuse, excrescent, pleonastic, prolix, tautologous, verbose
reduplication *n.* dittography
reecho *v.* resound
reef *n.* atoll, cay
reestablish *v.* redintegrate
refashion *v.* recast
refer *v.* advert, allude, ascribe, impute
referee *n.* adjudicator, arbiter
reference *n.* benchmark, citation
reference book vade mecum
refine *v.* distill, hone, rarefy, subtilize
refined *adj.* courtly, cultivated, genteel, gentrified, mandarin, urbane
refined, excessively precious
refinement *n.* decorum, gentility, propriety, suavity, urbanity
refinement, affected preciosity
reflect *v.* **1.** cerebrate, cogitate, ruminate; **2.** redound
reform *v.* amend, emend, regenerate
reform, producing reformative
reformatory *n.* magdalen
refrain *n.* derry
refresh *v.* reanimate, reinvigorate
refreshment *n.* **1.** refection, regale; **2.** rejuvenation
refuge *n.* haven, oasis
refugee *n.* Marielito
refusal *n.* recusancy, repulse

refusal, expressive of declinatory
refuse *v.* balk, rebuff
refuse *n.* detritus, draff, dregs, dross, dunder, dustheap, flotsam, hards, hurds, lees, offal, rape, recrement, rejectamenta, scoria, scourings, scree, slag, spilth, strass, sullage, tailings
refuse heap midden
refutation *n.* confutation, elenchus, reductio ad absurdum, rejoinder
refute *v.* confute, rebut, repugn
regal *adj.* Junoesque, regnal
regard *v.* deem, reck
regard *n.* esteem
regeneration *n.* palingenesis
regime *n.* regimen
region *n.* oblast
register *n.* cadastre
regress *v.* backslide, recidivate, retrograde, retrogress, revert
regress *n.* declension, recidivism, regression, retrogradation, retrogression
regret *v.* bemoan, bewail, rue
regret *n.* compunction, contrition, qualm, scruple
regretful *adj.* compunctious, contrite, penitent, remorseful, rueful
regular *n.* denizen, habitué
regulatory *adj.* sumptuary
rehabilitation, road to sawdust trail
rehash *n.* réchauffé
reign *n.* dominion, sovereignty, suzerainty
reign, of a regnal
reigning *adj.* regnant
reimburse *v.* indemnify, recompense, redress, remunerate
reincarnation *n.* samsara
reintroduced *adj.* réchauffé
reiterate *v.* ingeminate
reject *v.* disavow, forswear, jettison, recuse, repudiate
rejected things rejectamenta
rejoice *v.* jubilate
rejuvenate *v.* rejuvenesce, rejuvenize
relapse *v.* recidivate, regress, retrogress, revert
relapse *n.* recidivism, regression, retrogression, reversion
relapser *n.* recidivist
relapsing *adj.* regressive, retrogressive
relate *v.* delineate, recapitulate, recount, retail
related *adj.* affined, agnate, cognate, connate, consanguineous, correlative, enate, enatic
relationship *n.* affinity, consanguinity, kinship

relationship, interdependent symbiosis
relative *n.* agnate, cognate, enate
relax *v.* abate, decompress, enervate, enfeeble, mitigate, unbrace,
   unkink, unstring
relaxation *n.* cessation, détente, diminution, remission
relaxed *adj.* slack, ungirt
relaxing *n.* laxation
release *v.* **1.** effuse, eruct; **2.** extricate, manumit, uncouple, unhand,
   unmew, unpen
release *n.* deliverance, manumission, remission
release from life quietus (*n.*)
relent *v.* abate, slacken
relentless *adj.* implacable, inexorable
relevant *adj.* ad rem, apposite, germane
relics, repository for martyrium, reliquary
relief *n.* assuagement, mitigation, succor
relieve *v.* allay, alleviate, assuage, disembarrass, mitigate, mollify,
   succor, unburden
relieving *n.* catharsis
relight *v.* reillumine, rekindle, relume, relumine
religion *n.* dharma, din, Jainism, Jansenism, monotheism,
   polytheism; (see also **worship**)
religious *adj.* conscientious, scrupulous
religious, excessively religiose
religious belief ditheism, theism
religious devotions ibada, vesper
religious instruction catechesis
relinquish *v.* abdicate, cede, forgo, forswear, renounce
reluctant *adj.* averse, disinclined, loath, reticent
remain *v.* abide
remainder *n.* dottle, fag end, overage, residuum
remaining *adj.* remanent
remains *n.* reliquiae
remark *n.* bon mot, gambit, mot, obiter dictum, Parthian shot
remarkable *adj.* bodacious, salient, singular, uncommon
remedies, various antidote, antiodontalgic, antiphlogistic,
   antipruritic, antipyretic, antipyrotic, antiscorbutic, antitoxin,
   antitussive, antivenin, arcanum, catholicon, corrective, elixir,
   febrifuge, medicament, medicant, nostrum, panacea, poultice,
   restorative, specific, vulnerary
remedy *v.* assuage, medicate, redress, succor
remember *v.* recollect, reminisce
remembrance *n.* anamnesis, recollection, reminiscence
reminder *n.* memento, memento mori, remembrancer
reminiscences *n.* personalia

reminiscent *adj.* redolent, reminiscential
remnant *n.* oddment, residuum
remodel *v.* recast
remorse *n.* compunction, contrition, penitence
remorseful *adj.* compunctious, contrite, penitent
remote *adj.* **1.** abstracted, reclusive, seclusive, sequestered;
  2. outlying
removal *n.* **1.** dislodgment, remotion; **2.** ablation, abscission,
  debridement, excision
remove *v.* **1.** dislodge, doff, eloign, expurgate, subduct;
  2. superannuate
remove hair depilate, epilate
renaming *n.* teknonymy
rendezvous *n.* assignation, tryst
renegade *n.* desperado, runagate
renegade, turn apostatize, tergiversate
renege *v.* fainaigue
renew *v.* redintegrate
renewal *n.* instauration, recrudescence, redintegration,
  rejuvenation, rejuvenescence, renascence
renounce *v.* abjure, abnegate, forswear, renege
renovate *v.* furbish, refurbish
renovation *n.* instauration, refurbishment
renowned *adj.* redoubted
renunciation *n.* abdication, abjuration, abnegation, demission,
  disavowal, disclamation, forgoing
reorganize *v.* reconstitute
repair *v.* bushel, vamp
repair *n.* instauration
repairable *adj.* remediable, reparable
reparation *n.* atonement, indemnification, redress, restitution
repay *v.* indemnify, recompense, requite
repayment *v.* amends, recompense, reparation, requital, restitution
repeal *v.* abrogate, rescind
repeat *v.* battologize, geminate, ingeminate, iterate, perseverate,
  reiterate, replicate, reprise, tautologize
repeating *adj.* iterant, reiterant
repel *v.* parry, rebuff
repellent *adj.* forbidding, rebarbative
repercussion *n.* afterclap
repetition *n.* anadiplosis, anaphora, antanaclasis, epistrophe,
  gemination, iterance, iteration, perseveration, replication,
  reprise, tautologism, tautology; (see also **rhetorical terms**)
repetitious *adj.* iterative, tautological
replace *v.* reposit, supersede, supplant

reply v. rejoin, retort, riposte
reply n. rejoinder, replication, responsum, retort, riposte
report n. chronicle, dossier, expertise, procès-verbal, roorback
report v. chronicle, recount
reporter n. intelligencer, rapporteur
repository n. charnel, chartophylacium, cimeliarch, cinerarium, columbarium, granary, reliquary, sacristy
reprehensible adj. culpable, flagrant, opprobrious
represent v. delineate, limn, prefigure, schematize
representation n. deesis, delineation, effigy, simulacrum
representative n. burgess, syndic
representative adj. exemplary
repress v. quash, quell, quench
reprimand n. castigation, remonstrance, remonstration, reprehension, reproof, reproval
reprimand v. admonish, castigate, chide, reprehend, reprove, upbraid
reproach n. castigation, opprobrium, reproval
reproachful adj. contumelious
reproduce v. manifest
reproduction n. **1.** agamogenesis, parthenogenesis; **2.** ectype
reproductive adj. germinal, progenitive, seminal
reproof n. remonstrance, reproach, reproval
reptile, flying pterodactyal, pterosaur
reptiles, study of herpetology
repudiate v. abjure, disavow
repugnance n. antipathy, aversion, contrariety, incompatibility
repulsion n. aversion
repulsive adj. fulsome, loathsome, odious, repellent, repugnant
reputed adj. putative
request v. adjure, entreat, petition, solicit, supplicate
requesting, pertaining to rogatory
requirable adj. exigible
require v. exact
required adj. de rigueur
requirement n. injunction, proviso, stipulation
rescind v. countermand, nullify, retract, unsay, unswear
rescindable adj. rescissible, rescissory
rescinding n. abrogation, nullification, rescission, retraction
rescue n. deliverance, redemption
resemblance n. semblance, similitude
resentful adj. snappish, waspish
resentment n. choler, dudgeon, huff, pique, umbrage
resentment, show bridle
reserve, lacking effusive

reserved *adj.* demure, indrawn, inobtrusive, starched, taciturn, unvocal

reservoir *n.* cenote, font, impoundment

reside *v.* sojourn, tenant

residence *n.* abode, domicile, habitation, inhabitancy, manse, prefecture, sojourn

residency *n.* inhabitancy

resident *n.* denizen, residentiary

residing *adj.* resident, residentiary

residual *adj.* remanent

residue *n. caput mortuum,* clinker, dottle, dregs, residuum, slurry, tailings, vinasse

residue, apple pomace

resign *v.* demit

resignation *n.* forbearance

resilient *adj.* buoyant

resin *n.* rumanite

resin, yielding resiniferous

resinlike *adj.* resinoid

resist *v.* rebuff, recalcitrate

resistance *n.* intransigence, renitence

resistant *adj.* recalcitrant, renitent

resolute *adj.* dauntless, doughty, purposive, stalwart, staunch, undaunted

resolution *n.* **1.** denouement, deus ex machina; **2.** resolve

resolvable *adj.* resoluble, resolutive

resonance *n.* sonority

resonant *adj.* canorous, plummy, sonorous

resonate *v.* resound

resort *n.* **1.** lido, spa, watering place; **2.** recourse, repair

resort, last *pis aller*

resounding *adj.* plangent, reboant

resource *n.* expedient, resort

resourceful *adj. débrouillard*

resourceful person *débrouillard*

respect *n.* deference, esteem, veneration

respect *v.* esteem, venerate

respect, commanding redoubtable, venerable

respect, implying honorific

respect, show genuflect

respected *adj.* redoubted

respectful *adj.* complaisant, courtly, decorous, deferent, deferential, dutiful, urbane

responding *n.* responsion

response *n.* **1.** counterblow, rejoinder; **2.** respond, responsory

responsive *adj.* **1.** amenable, forthcoming, reflex, reflexive; **2.** antiphonal
rest *v.* repose
rest *n.* hiatus
restate *v.* paraphrase
restatement *n.* paraphrase, paraphrasis
restaurant *n.* bistro, brasserie, carvery, chophouse, cookshop, rathskeller, trattoria

resting place lich stone
restitution *n.* apocatastasis
restless *adj.* restive
restlessness *n.* cabin fever, disquietude, fantod, fretfulness, inquietude, restiveness
restless person gadabout
restoration *n.* anastylosis, instauration, revanche
restore *v.* repristinate
restore courage of reman
restrain *v.* bridle, circumscribe, debar
restrained *adj.* hieratic
restraint *n.* bilbo, constraint, shackle
restrict *v.* constrain, shackle, straiten
restricting *adj.* constraining, limitative, straitening
restriction *n.* constraint, stricture
restrictive *adj.* stringent
result *n.* backwash, consequence, denouement, eventuality
result *v.* emanate, ensue, eventuate, redound
résumé *n.* curriculum vitae, dossier, vita
resurgence *n.* Renaissance, Renascence, risorgimento
retail *v.* regrate

retainers, body of retinue, suite, train
retaliate *v.* redress, requite
retaliation *n.* *lex talionis*, redress, reprisal, requital, retorsion, retortion, retributivism
retaliatory *adj.* reciprocatory, retributive
retard *v.* encumber
retarded person retardate, retardee
retch *v.* keck
reticence *n.* taciturnity
reticent *adj.* taciturn
retinue *n.* cortege, suite
retire *v.* **1.** decommission, superannuate; **2.** retrocede
retire, allow to superannuate
retired *adj.* emerita, emeritus
retiree *n.* retirant
retirement *n.* quietus, sequestration
retiring *adj.* seclusive, unassuming
retort *n.* rejoinder, riposte
retort *v.* recriminate
retract *v.* countermand, recant, rescind, unsay, unswear
retractable *adj.* retractile
retraction *n.* nullification, recantation, rescindment, revocation
retreat *n.* **1.** katabasis, regression; **2.** asylum, haven, sanctuary
retribution *n.* recompense, requital
retribution, act of nemesis
retroactively *adv.* ex post facto, retrospectively
return *v.* revert
return *n.* recession, recursion, regression, retrogression, reversion
reveal *v.* broadcast, disbosom, evince, manifest, unpack, unshroud
revealer *n.* revelator
revealing *adj.* revelatory
revel *v.* **1.** luxuriate, savor, wallow; **2.** caper, carouse, roister, rollick
revelation *n.* apocalypse, divulgation, divulgence, epiphany, eyeopener
reveler *n.* bacchant, bacchante, carouser, maenad
revelry *n.* carousal, saturnalia
revenge *n.* reprisal, requital, retribution, revanche
revenge *v.* requite
revengeful *adj.* malevolent, malignant
reverberate *v.* reverb
reverberating *adj.* reboant, resounding, reverberant
revere *v.* reverence, venerate
revered *adj.* hoary, venerated
reverence *n.* ecclesiolatry, genuflection, veneration
reverent *adj.* prayerful, reverential

reversal *n.* countermarch, chiasmus, peripeteia, reversion, volte-face

reverse *n.* affliction, misadventure

reverse *v.* countermand, rescind, unlive

reversed *adj.* retrograde

reversion *n.* atavism, recidivism, retrogression

revert *v.* recidivate, retrocede, retrograde, retrogress

revise *v.* amend, emend, redact, rescale

revision *n.* emendation, recension, redaction, revisal

revival *n.* anabiosis, metempsychosis, palingenesis, reanimation, recrudescence, renaissance, renascence, revivification, reviviscence

revive *v.* furbish, reanimate, recrudesce, regenerate, resuscitate, revivify

revived *adj.* redivivus

reviving *adj.* renascent, resurgent

revocable *adj.* ambulatory

revoke *v.* adeem, rescind, supersede

revolt *n.* intifada, jacquerie, putsch, titanism

revolutionary *n.* sans-culotte

reward *n.* desert, deserts, guerdon, palm, recompense, requital

reward *v.* recompense, remunerate, requite

rhetoric, teacher of rhetor, rhetorician

rhetorical *adj.* forensic

rhetorical terms amphibologia, anacoenosis, anacoluthon, anadiplosis, anaphora, anapodoton, anastrophe, antanaclasis, antapodosis, anthimeria, antiphrasis, antipophora, antiptosis, antithesis, antonomasia, apocope, apodioxis, apophasis, aporia, aposiopesis, apostrophe, asteimus, asyndeton, auxesis, bdelygmia, bomphiologia, bowdlerism, brachiepia, brachylogy, cacemphaton, cactolith, catachresis, chiasmus, commendatio, comparatio, concinnity, congeries, correctio, dehortatio, diacope, diastole, digressio, double entendre, ecphonesis, enantiosis, epanalepsis, epanaphora, epanodos, epanorthosis, epexegesis, epiphonema, epistrophe, epizeuxis, euphemism, gnome, gratiarum actio, hendiadys, homeoteleuton, hypallage, hyperbaton, hyperbole, hypotaxis, hypotyposis, hypozeugma, hypozeuxis, hysteron proteron, innuendo, irony, litotes, malapropism, meiosis, metabasis, metalepsis, metaphora, metastasis, metathesis, metonymy, mimesis, onomatopoeia, oxymoron, palilogy, palindromos, paralipsis, paranomasia, paregmenon, periphrasis, peroration, personification, pleonasmus, ploce, polysyndeton, preterition, prolepsis, prosopopoeia, rhetorical question, simile, syllepsis, symploce, syncope, synecdoche, tautologia, tmesis, trope, zeugma

rhinoceros *n.* pachyderm
rhyme, types of see **poems and poetical terms**
rhythm *n.* cadence, pulse; (see also **poems and poetical terms**)
ribald *adj.* irreverent, risqué, scurrilous
ribaldry *n.* scurrility
ribbed *adj.* costate
ribbon *n.* cordon, cordon bleu, ferret, festoon, lutestring, riband,
    sautoir
ribs, of the costal
rice *n.* paddy
rich *adj.* Lucullan, orotund
riches *n.* mammon
rich person see **person, wealthy**
rickets *n.* rachitis
rickety *adj.* infirm
ricksha *n.* jinrikisha, rickshaw
riddance *n.* dislodgment
riddle *n.* anomaly, conundrum, enigma, koan, paradox
ridge *n.* cordillera, cuesta, escarpment, esker, hommock, kame,
    razorback
ridgepole *n.* rooftree
ridicule *n.* badinage, chaff, derision, irony, mockery, raillery, satire
ridicule *v.* banter, burlesque, chaff, deride, haze, lampoon, parodize,
    pillory, rally, satirize, twit
ridiculous *adj.* discrepant, farcical
riffraff *n.* canaille, rabble, ragtag and bobtail, tagrag
rifle *n.* Enfield rifle, Garand rifle, Spencer, Springfield rifle
rifleman *n.* bersagliere
right *adj.* congruous, decorous, dexter, meet, seemly
right *n.* prerogative
righteousness *n.* rectitude
rightful *adj.* due, equitable
right-handedness *n.* dextrality
right of the first night droit du seigneur
right-to-left, moving from dextrosinistral
rigid *adj.* austere, stark, unresilient, unyielding
rigidity *n.* rigor mortis, turgor
rigmarole *n.* galimatias
rigor *n.* stringency
rigorous *adj.* austere, draconian, finical
rile *v.* roil
rim *n.* chime, felloe, verge
rind *n.* albedo
ring *n.* **1.** annulet, annulus, circlet, cirque, ferrule, gyre, seal ring; **2.**
    bloc, confederacy, coterie

ring *v.* resound
ringed *adj.* annulate
ringing in the ears tinnitus
ringing sound, making a tinnient
ringleader *n.* bellwether
ringlike *adj.* annular, orbicular, orbiculate
ring-shaped *adj.* circinate
ringworm *n.* tinea
riot *n.* melee
riot *v.* carouse, revel
rioter *n.* frondeur
riotous *adj.* turbulent
ripe *adj.* **1.** mature, seasoned; **2.** opportune
ripening *n.* bletting, maturation
ripple *v.* dimple, purl, ruffle, undulate
rise *v.* levitate, rear
rise again resurge
rising *adj.* ascensive
risk *n.* imprudence, uncertainty
risky *adj.* hazardous, impolitic, imprudent, jeopardous,
      venturesome, venturous
risqué *adj.* juicy, racy, ribald, titillating
rite *n.* liturgy, solemnity
rites, pertaining to sacred sacral
ritual *n.* liturgy
ritual bath mikvah
rival *n.* corrival, emulator, nemesis
rival *v.* emulate, vie
rivalry *n.* contention, emulation
river, pertaining to a fluvial, fluviatile, potamic, riverine
riverbank, pertaining to a riparian
riverbed *n.* arroyo, cañada
river inlet ria
river mouth embouchure
rivulet *n.* rigolet, rill, rillet
road *n.* causeway, corniche
roam *v.* maraud, meander
roar *v.* bluster
roast *v.* decrepitate, torrefy, torrify
rob *v.* despoil, extort, harry, rape, rifle, sack, spoliate
robber *n.* brigand, dacoit, footpad, rapparee, reiver
robbery *n.* dacoity, depredation, larceny, rapine, ravin
robot *n.* automaton, android, golem
robust *adj.* hale, robustious, stalwart
rock *n.* crag, gangue, Scylla

rocket *n.* rockoon, sonde
rocks, living among saxatile, saxicoline, saxicolous
rock salt halite
rocky *adj.* craggy
rod *n.* burin, ferule, probang
rods *n.* wattles
rods, bundle of fasces
rod-shaped *adj.* virgate, virgulate
rogue *n.* blackguard, knave, mountebank, picara, picaro, picaroon,
    scalawag, scapegrace, scaramouch
roguish *adj.* jocose, jocund, picaresque, raffish, waggish
roll *v.* **1.** gyrate, lumber, trundle; **2.** furl, swathe; **3.** billow, undulate,
    wallow, welter
roll *n.* **1.** resonance; **2.** rouleau
rolled-in *adj.* obvolute
roller *n.* platen
romantic *adj.* quixotic
Rome, near suburbicarian
romp *v.* gambol
roof *n.* catslide, French roof, mansard, rooftree
roof *v.* wattle
roofed-over *adj.* clithral
roofing tile imbrex
roofing tool zax
roofless *adj.* hypaethral
rooming house lodgment
rooms, types of alipterion, amphithalamus, andron, antehall,
    anteroom, anticum, arcosolium, atelier, atrium, bakehouse,
    boulenterion, buttery, caldarium, cella, cellule, cenacle,
    chancellery, cimeliarch, conservatory, cubicle, elaeothesium,
    epinaos, exedra, frigidarium, gallery, garde-manger, garde-robe,
    kiva, larder, locutorium, locutory, magazine, naos, nymphaeum,
    oda, odah, oecus, opisthodomos, posticum, pronaos, rotunda,
    sala, salon, saloon, salutatorium, scriptorium, serdab, solar,
    subterrane, subterranean, sudatio, sudatorium, tablinum,
    thalamus, tholos, tholus, unctuarium, undercroft
roomy *adj.* capacious, commodious, extensive
rooster *n.* chanticleer, gamecock
root out extirpate
roots, feeding on rhizophagous
rope *n.* bight, cordelle, guy, lazy guy, longe, Manila rope, mecate,
    painter, pigging string, prolonge, rode
rose garden rosarium
rosette *n.* cockade
rosin *n.* colophony

roster *n.* rota
rostrum, furnished with a rostrate *(adj.)*
rosy *adj.* roseate
rot *v.* decompose, molder, putrefy
rotate *v.* circumrotate, gyrate, pronate, supinate
rotating *adj.* rotatory, trochoid
rotation *n.* circumrotation, pronation
rotten *adj.* fetid, putrescent, rank
rottenness *n.* putrefaction, putrescence
roué *n.* bounder, lecher, libertine, rake, rakehell
rough *adj.* craggy, crenelated, hard-case, hubbly, incondite,
     scabrous, serrated
roughage *n.* stover
roughen *v.* asperate
roughness *n.* asperity
round *adj.* rotund
roundabout *adj.* ambagious, anfractuous, circuitous,
     circumlocutory, euphuistic, oblique, periphrastic, tortuous
rounded *adj.* orbicular, orbiculate
roundheaded *adj.* brachycephalic
roundness *n.* rondure
rout *v.* roust
routine *n.* regimen, rote
rove *v.* gad
roving *adj.* nomadic
row *n.* **1.** drill, hedgerow, windrow; **2.** ruckus, ruction
rowboat *n.* tag boat, wherry
rows, arranged in polystichous
royal *adj.* basilic, regnal
royal court durbar
royal rights regalia
royalty *n.* regality
rub *v.* burnish, chafe, embrocate, gall
rubber *n.* caoutchouc, caucho
rubbings, substance used for heelball
rubbish *n.* **1.** balderdash, bosh, raffle, trumpery; **2.** spilth
rub out efface, expunge, obliterate
ruby-colored *adj.* rubious
ruddy *adj.* florid, rubicund, sanguine
rude *adj.* brusque, contumelious, incult, robustious, uncivil
rudeness *n.* boorishness, contumely, incivility
rudimentary *adj.* inchoate, vestigial
ruff *n.* fraise
ruffian *n.* highbinder, myrmidon, Mohock
ruffle *n.* furbelow, goffering, jabot

rugged *adj.* craggy, ironbound
rugs, types of Aubusson, dhurrie, drugget, flokati, Ghiordes, Ispahan, kaross, Kashmir rug, kilim, Kirman, rya, Sarouk
ruin *n.* bane, debacle, despoliation, perdition, rack, spoliation, wrack
ruin *v.* spoliate
ruinous *adj.* calamitous, pernicious, wrackful
rule *n.* **1.** algorithm, axiom, canon, precept; **2.** androcracy, dominion, empery, hierocracy, raj, sway, tenure
rulers archon, ariki, ataman, autarch, bey, Caesar, caid, caliph, catholicos, caudillo, Dalai Lama, dato, decemvir, dey, duumvir, dynast, emir, eparch, ethnarch, exarch, exilarch, genearch, gerent, Gilgamesh, hakim, hetman, hierarch, imperator, interrex, Isobates, Jamshid, jarl, jefe, Jormunrek, kabaka, kaiser, khan, Laius, Lamus, landgrave, maharajah, margrave, Nizam, oligarch, pendragon, Pharaoh, potentate, primate, rajah, ranee, sachem, sagamore, seignior, sirdar, Soldan, sovereign, tetrarch, triumvir, voivode
rules *n.* sutra
ruling *adj.* hegemonic, regnant
ruling body duarchy, duumvirate, septemvirate, tetrarchate, tetrarchy, triumvirate
rumble *v.* wamble
rummage *v.* root, rout
rumor *n.* canard
rumor *v.* bruit
rump *n.* croup, nates
rumpled *adj.* disheveled, tousled
run *v.* lope, scud, scuttle, skedaddle, stot
rung *n.* rundle, stave
runner *n.* harrier, Pheidippides
running out excurrent (*adj.*)
rural *adj.* agrestic, predial, silvan, villatic
rural, make countrify, ruralize
rural life rusticity
ruse *n.* stratagem
rushing *adj.* precipitant
rustic *adj.* agrestic, Arcadian, bucolic, Doric, pastoral
rustic *n.* agrestic, country bumpkin, hind, homespun, hoosier, swain
rustling *n.* froufrou, susurration
rusty *adj.* rubiginous
ruthless *adj.* callous, fell, inexorable

S

saber *n.* yataghan
sable fur zibeline
saboteur *n.* ninja, Trojan Horse
sac *n.* follicle, vesicle
sack *n.* gunny-bag, gunnysack, poke, towsack
sack *v.* despoil, pillage
sacred *adj.* hallowed, sacrosanct, venerable
sacred objects, trade in simony
sacred objects, trader in simoniac
sacrifice *n.* corban, hecatomb, oblation, suovetaurilia, taurobolium
sacrilege *n.* profanation
sacristy *n.* diaconicon
sad *adj.* disconsolate, dispirited, dumpish, lugubrious, morose, woebegone
saddle *n.* pillion
sadism *n.* algolagnia
sadness, sentimental *Weltschmerz*
safecracker *n.* yegg, yeggman
safeguard *n.* palladium
sag *v.* flag, languish
saga *n.* *roman-fleuve*
sage *n.* graybeard, mahatma, rishi, sadhu, solon
sagging *n.* ptosis
sailor *n.* jacktar, lascar
saint, carved figure of santo
salaried workers salariat
sale *n.* vendition
salesperson, traveling drummer
saleswoman *n.* midinette
saliva *n.* drivel, slaver, spittle
salt *n.* piquancy, savor
salt, producing saliferous
salt, treat with salinize
saltworks *n.* salina, salten
salty, slightly brackish
salute *n.* obeisance, salutation
salvager *n.* salvor

salvation *n.* nirvana
salve *n.* unction
sanctimoniousness *n.* piosity
sanction *n.* imprimatur
sanction *v.* homologate
sanctuary *n.* adytum, bethel, refugium, sacrarium, sekos
sandal *n.* zori
sand bar tombolo, towhead
sand-inhabiting *adj.* arenicolous
sandy *adj.* arenaceous, arenose, sabulous
sap, feeding on phytosuccivorous
sarcasm *n.* sardonicism
sarcastic *adj.* caustic, mordant, sardonic
sash *n.* cummerbund, faja, obi
satanic *adj.* demoniac, infernal, sulfurous, sulphurous
satiation *n.* satiety, surfeit
satire *n.* burlesque, lampoon, pasquinade, travesty
satirical *adj.* mordant, sardonic
satisfaction *n.* expiation, requital, schadenfreude
satisfy *v.* assuage, palliate, requite, sate, satiate, slake
saturate *v.* imbrue, infuse
saucer-shaped *adj.* patelliform
sauciness *n.* archness
savage *adj.* fell, feral, lupine
savage *n.* boor, churl
savagery *n.* ferity, savagism
save *v.* husband
save little dissave
savor *v.* degust
savor *n.* sapor
savory *adj.* piquant, pungent
saw, surgeon's trepan, trephine
scabby *adj.* scabious
scald *v.* blanch
scale *n.* analemma
scales, come off in desquamate
scaling *n.* escalade
scaly *adj.* furfuraceous, squamate
scaly, not esquamate
scaly matter scurf
scanty *adj.* exiguous, jejune
scapegoat *n.* Azazel, whipping boy
scar *n.* cicatrix
scarcity *n.* dearth, paucity, penury
scarlet fever scarlatina

I'm not sure scaly is me...

Oh, but furfuraceous is in vogue this year Madame!

scatter *v.* broadcast, disgregate, disject, dissipate, sparge
scatterbrain *n.* featherhead
scattered *adj.* effuse
scattering *n.* Diaspora, dispersion
scavenger *n.* bhangi
scene *n.* tableau, *tableau vivant*
scenery *n.* *mise en scène*
scent *n.* spoor
scheme *n.* cabal, machination, stratagem
scholar *n.* academe, ayatollah, bluestocking, demy, savant, schoolman
school *n.* borstal, *cheder*, conservatoire, dojo, lyceum, madrasah, scholasticate, ulpan, yeshiva
schoolmaster *n.* pedagogue, scholarch
scintillating *adj.* coruscating, *diamanté*
scintillation *n.* coruscation, laurence
scold *v.* castigate, chide, excoriate, flay, objurgate, rate, reprove, vituperate
scope *n.* ambit, compass, diapason, gamut, purview
scorch *v.* torrefy, torrify, wither
scorching *n.* ustulation
scored *adj.* gyrose
scorn *n.* misprision, misprize
scorn *v.* contemn
scornful *adj.* contumelious, supercilious
scour *v.* rake, ransack
scowl *v.* glower, lower
scrap *n.* ort
scrape *v.* curette, scrabble

scraper *n.* strigil, xyster
scraping *n.* ramentum
scratch *v.* scarify, scrabble
scratching for food, given to gallinaceous, rasorial
screen *n.* abat-jour, brise-soleil, iconostasis, jalee, maksoorah,
   mehitzah, paravent, parclose, perclose, purdah, reredos, rood
   screen, scherm, shoji, tatty, transenna
scribe *n.* scrivener, sopher
scroll *n.* kakemono, makimono, orihon
sculptured figure gisant, glyph, santo
scum *n.* dross, pellicle, scoria, sloke, spume
scurrilous *adj.* fescennine
sea battle, mock naumachia
seal *n.* bull, bulla, chop, sigil, signet
seal *v.* immure, lute
seal, baby whitecoat
seals, pertaining to sphragistic
seam *n.* commissure, juncture
sea monster kraken, leviathan
seamstress *n.* midinette, sempstress
sear *v.* cauterize
search *v.* ferret, rifle
seas, dominion over thallasocracy
seas, pertaining to pelagic
seasickness *n.* *mal de mer*
sea spray spindrift, spoondrift
seat *n.* howdah, pouf, pulvinar, misericord, sedile, subsellium
seaward *adv.* makai
sea water polynya
seaweed *n.* kelp, laver, sargassum, sloke, wrack
seclusion *n.* purdah, reclusion
secondary *adj.* ancillary
Second Coming Parousia
Second Coming, belief in chiliasm, millennialism
second-rate *adj.* pedestrian
second self alter ego
second sight clairvoyance
secrecy *n.* hugger-mugger
secret *adj.* back-alley, back-channel, backdoor, backstairs,
   back-street, recondite
secret *n.* arcanum, arcanum arcanorum
secretary *n.* amanuensis, famulus, munshi
secretion *n.* colostrum, milt, smegma
secretive *adj.* diffident, reticent
secretly *adv.* in petto, privily, sub rosa

secret society camorra, Carbonari
secret things penetralia
secularize *v.* laicize, temporalize
secure *v.* stanchion, undergird
sedan chair palanquin
sedition *n.* misprision
seditious *adj.* factious
seducer *n.* Casanova, Don Juan, lothario, Romeo
seductress *n.* Delilah, femme fatale, huldre, siren, vamp
see *v. vide*
seed *n.* moit
seeming *adj.* semblable, ostensible
seer *n.* maharishi, Melampus, pythoness
seething *n.* ebullition
seize *v.* gaffle, grapple
seizure *n.* impoundment, sequestration
select *adj.* esoteric
selection *n.* pericope
selections *n.* analecta, analects, excerpta, pericopae, pericopes
self-absorption *n.* egocentricism, solipsism
self-advertisement *n.* réclame
self-assertion, empty braggadocio
self-centered *adj.* narcissistic
self-confidence *n.* aplomb, hubris
self-conscious *adj.* diffident
self-defense *n.* aikido, karate, kung fu
self-denial *n.* asceticism, self-abnegation
self-disciplne *n.* ascesis
self-esteem *n. amour-propre*
self-evident *adj.* axiomatic, prima facie
self-governed *adj.* autocephalous
self-government *n.* swaraj
self-indulgence *n. dolce vita*, hedonism, sybaritism
self-indulgent person bon vivant, epicurean, hedonist, sensualist,
    sybarite, voluptuary
selfish *adj.* avaricious, parsimonious
selflessness *n.* altruism, philanthropy
self-nourishing *adj.* autotrophic
self-produced *adj.* autogenous
self-righteous *adj.* holier-than-thou, pharisaic, pharisaical,
    rectitudinous, sanctimonious, sententious
self-sufficiency *n.* autarky
self-taught person autodidact
semantics *n.* semasiology
send back remand

senility *n.* caducity, dotage
senior person doyen, doyenne
sensation *n.* percept, esthesis
sense *n.* cogency, import, purport, sconce, significancy
sense of smell, loss of anosmia
sense of taste, abnormal parageusia
sensitive to sexual stimulation erogenous
sensitivity *n.* circumspection, esthesia
sensory apparatus sensorium
sensual *adj.* concupiscent, libidinous, Sardanapalian, sybaritic, voluptuary, voluptuous
sentimental *adj.* bathetic, cloying, maudlin, mawkish, rose-water, saccharine
sentimentality *n.* bathos, maudlinness, mawkishness, *Schwärmerei*, treacle
sentry *n.* vedette
sentry box excubitorium
separable *adj.* dissociable
separate *v.* bifurcate, compart, decathect, dialyze, disaggregate, disgregate, dissever, dissociate, sequester, sequestrate, sunder
separate *adj.* discrete, disjoined
separateness *n.* severalty
separation *n.* dieresis, diremption, disjunction, dissociation, scission
septum *n.* dissepiment
sequence *n.* consecution, continuum
serenade *n.* belling, callathump, charivari, shivaree, skimmerton
serf *n.* helot, vassal, villein
series *n.* catena, concatenation, continuum, contravallation
series, arranged in polystichous, seriate
series, in a seriatim
seriousness *n.* gravitas
sermons, collection of sutra
serpent *n.* cockatrice, hydra
serum *n.* whey
servant *n.* au pair, batman, comprador, factotum, khansamah, mozo, retainer, scullion
servile *adj.* obsequious, sequacious, sycophantic
set right disabuse
settlement *n.* mise
settler *n.* sooner
sevenfold *adj.* septuple, septuplicate
seven-sectioned *adj.* septempartite
seven-sided *adj.* septilateral
seventeenth century seicento

seventies, person in septuagenarian
sever *v.* cleave, sunder
several *adj.* divers, sundry
severe *adj.* condign, draconian, hieratic, obdurate
sewage *n.* sulcus
sewer *n.* cloaca, kennel
sexton *n.* beadle, sacristan, shammes
sexual desire aphrodisia, concupiscence, eros
sexual desire, excessive satyriasis
sexual desire, substance promoting aphrodisiac
sexual drive libido
sexual excitement estrus, heat, rut
sexuality, concerned with priapic
sexual love, of paphian
sexually developed nubile
sexually precocious girl Lolita, nymphet
sexually stimulating erogenous, erotogenic
sexual partner catamite
sexual privilege droit du seigneur
sexual repression anaphrodisia
sexual repression, substance promoting anaphrodisiac
shabby *adj.* dowdy, mangy, raggle-taggle, scroungy, scruffy, tatty
shade, casting umbriferous
shading *n.* hachure
shadow *n.* penumbra, umbra
shadows, fighting with sciamachy, sciomachy
shady *adj.* adumbral, louche, umbrageous
shaft *n.* moulin, obelisk
shaggy *adj.* hispid, thrummy, villose
shaker *n.* caster, dredger, muffineer
shaking *n.* labefaction
shaking *adj.* aguish, tremulous
shallowness *n.* inanity, superficiality
shameful *adj.* discreditable, ignominious, mortifying, opprobrious
shameless *adj.* brazen, dissolute, flagrant, impenitent, inglorious, obdurate, profligate, reprobate, unregenerate, wanton
shantytown *n.* bidonville, favela
shape *v.* brute, malleate, scabble
shapeless *adj.* amorphous, anomalous
shapely *adj.* callipygian
shaping, capable of esemplastic
share *n.* moiety, quantum, stint
shared thing philopena
sharing, spirit of communitas
sharp *adj.* caustic, trenchant

sharpen *v.* subtilize
sharpened *adj.* acuate
sharpening implement strickle, whetstone
sharp eye gimlet eye
sharp-sighted *adj.* lyncean, lynx-eyed
shattering *n.* brisance
shaving *n.* ramentum
sheath *n.* frog, scabbard
sheathe *v.* invaginate, intussuscept
sheathed *adj.* ocreate
shed *n.* pandal
shed *v.* effuse, exuviate, mew, slough
sheeplike *adj.* ovine
sheepskin *n.* mouton, woolskin
sheer *adj.* diaphanous
shelf *n.* gradin, retable
shelf for the feet suppedaneum
shell *n.* carapace, coquille, cowrie
shell game thimblerig, three-card monte
shelter *v.* embower, ensconce
shield *n.* ancile, écu, escutcheon, pavis, scutum
shield-shaped *adj.* scutiform
shiftiness *n.* lubricity
shifty *adj.* evasive, lubricous
shilly-shally *v.* vacillate, whiffle
shimmer *n.* laurence, scintillation
shinbone *n.* tibia
shingles *n.* herpes zoster, zoster
shiver *n.* frisson
shocking *adj.* egregious, flagrant, unholy
shoddy *adj.* jerry-built, ramshackle, ticky-tacky
shoeless *adj.* discalced
shoemaker *n.* crispin
shoes, wearing calced
shoot *n.* scion
shore *n.* littoral, strand
shore-inhabiting *adj.* limicoline
shortage *n.* dearth, paucity
shortened *adj.* curtate, truncated
shorthand *n.* tachygraphy
short-headed *adj.* brachycephalic
short-lived *adj.* ephemeral, ephemerous, evanescent, fugitive
short-lived phenomenon ephemeron
short-winded *adj.* pursy
shot *n.* langrage

shoulder *n.* berm, verge
shoulder, of the humeral, scapular, scapulary
shoulder blade scapula
shout *v.* vociferate
show *n.* gaudery, ostentation, pretext
show-off *n.* coxcomb
show off flaunt, vaunt
showy *adj.* brummagem, fastuous, flaunty, meretricious
shrew *n.* harridan, scold, termagant, virago, Xanthippe
shrew, qualities of a viraginity
shrewd *adj.* coony, perspicacious
shrewdness *n.* acumen, perspicacity
shrill *adj.* clarion, strident
shrill sound, make a stridulate
shrine *n.* adytum, aedicule, chaitya, delubrum, Ka'ba, lararium, martyry, qubba, reliquary, sacellum, sekos
shrink *v.* fritter, macerate
shriveled *adj.* wizened
Shrove Tuesday Quinquagesima
shudder *n.* frisson
shun *v.* eschew
shut *v.* occlude
sick *adj.* crapulent
sickly *adj.* languid, valetudinarian
sideburns *n.* dundrearies
side by side *pari passu*
sideways *adv.* askance, crabwise
sideways, moving laterigrade
sieve *n.* riddle
sievelike *adj.* cribriform, cribrous
sift *v.* bolt, winnow
sigh *n.* suspiration
sighing, sound of sough
signal *n.* annunciator, tocsin
signature flourish, a paraph
signify *v.* betoken, connote, portend, presage
signs, study of semiotics
silage *n.* haylage
silent *adj.* aphonic, reticent, saturnine, taciturn
silk *n.* habutai, Shantung, tussah
silkworm farming sericulture
silky *adj.* sericate, sericeous
silly *adj.* anserine, asinine, fatuous, inane, witless
silt *n.* sullage
silver-bearing *adj.* argentiferous

silvery *adj.* argent, argental, argenteous, argentine
simian *adj.* simious
similar *adj.* semblable
simultaneousness *n.* contemporaneity, isochrony, simultaneity, synchronism, synchrony
sin, acknowledgment of peccavi
sin, apt to peccable
sincere *adj.* heart-whole, ingenuous
sincerely *adv.* ex animo
sinful *adj.* Babylonian, flagitious, peccant, piacular, profligate
singe *v.* genappe, swinge
singer *n.* cantatrice, cantor, castrato, chansonnier, chanter, chanteur, chanteuse, chantress, chorister, comprimario, precentor
sink *v.* bemire, founder, scuttle
sinkhole *n.* cenote
sins, seven deadly pride, covetousness, lust, anger, gluttony, envy, and sloth
sinuous *adj.* flexuous, serpentine, sinuate, vermiculate
sisterly *adj.* sororal
situated above superincumbent
situation *n.* juncture
six, pertaining to the number senary
sixfold *adj.* sextuple, sextuplex
six parts, in hexamerous
sixteenth century cinquecento, cinquetist
sixteenth note semiquaver
sixty-fourth note hemidemisemiquaver
skeptic *n.* agnostic, doubting Thomas, nullifidian
skeptical *adj.* incredulous
skepticism *n.* Pyrrhonism
sketch *n.* croquis, remarque
sketcher *n.* limner
skid *n.* stillage
skier *n.* geländeläufer, kanone, langläufer, schusser
skillful *adj.* daedal, dexterous, dextrous, habile
skim *v.* skitter
skin *n.* cutis, cutis vera, integument, nebris, pellicle
skin, of the cutaneous
skin, shed exuviate
skin, through the percutaneous, transcutaneous, transdermal
skin alive flay
skinflint *n.* niggard, pinchpenny
skin graft dermoplasty
skinlike *adj.* dermatoid, dermoid

skin planing dermabrasion
skins, discarded exuviae
skin scraper strigil
skittish *adj.* skittery
skull *n.* sconce
skullcap *n.* calotte, *kipa*, pileus, yarmulke, zucchetto
sky *n.* firmament, welkin
slab *n.* stela, stele
slack *adj.* languid, ungirt
slanderous *adj.* aspersive, calumniatory, calumnious
slang *n.* argot, cant
slash mark separatrix, solidus, virgule
slat *n.* louver, spline
slate, clean tabula rasa
slaughterhouse *n.* abattoir, shambles
slave *n.* colonus, helot, hierodule, odalisque
slavery *n.* helotry, servitude, thrall, thralldom
slavery, release from manumit (*v.*), manumission (*n.*)
sleek *adj.* soigné
sleep, inducing somnifacient, somniferous, soporific
sleeplessness *n.* insomnolence
sleepwalking *n.* somnambulation, somnambulism
sleepy *adj.* somnolent, soporose
sled *n.* cariole, komatik, luge, pulka, pung, sledge
sleight of hand legerdemain, prestidigitation
slender *adj.* attenuate, tenuous
slenderness *n.* gracility, tenuity
slice *n.* collop
slime *n.* sloke
slip *n.* lapsus, *lapsus calami*, *lapsus linguae*, parapraxis, spoonerism
slipperiness *n.* lubricity
slippery *adj.* glary, lubricious
slit *n.* fissure, kerf
slob *n.* bandersnatch
sloping *adj.* acclivitous, acclivous, declivitous, declivous,
    displuviate, quaquaversal
sloth *n.* accidia, acedia, anomie
slovenly *adj.* draggle-tailed, frowsy, slatternly
slow *adj.* dilatory, glacial, indolent, languid, tardigrade
slum *n.* barriada, bidonville, bustee, cabbagetown
sly *adj.* arch
sly person slyboots
small *adj.* bantam, diminutive, exiguous, Lilliputian, manini,
    mignon, mignonne
small, make micrify

smallest creature minimus
smart *adj.* perspicacious, sapient
smear *v.* bedaub, calumniate, denigrate, smirch, traduce, vilipend
smearing *n.* inunction
smell, pertaining to sense of olfactory
smelling *n.* olfaction
smelly *adj.* fetid, frowzy, fusty, mephitic, miasmal, noisome, odoriferous, putrescent, redolent
smiling *adj.* riant, rident
smoky *adj.* fuliginous
smooth *adj.* dégagé, glabrous, lubricious
smooth *v.* levigate
smooth-talker *n.* flannelmouth
smug *adj.* priggish, unctuous
smuggler *n. pollero*
smutty *adj.* raunchy, ribald
snack *n.* gorp, nosh, tapa
snail *n.* escargot
snail fever schistosomiasis
snake *n.* ophidian
snakelike *adj.* colubrine
snake worship ophiolatry
snare *n.* springe, toils
sneer *v.* gibe
sneezing *n.* sternutation
sniff *v.* snuffle
sniffle *v.* snivel
snobbishness *n.* condescension, illiberality
snore *n.* rhonchus
snorelike sounds, making stertorous
snow *n.* firn, névé, sastruga
snowy *adj.* niveous
snuff *n.* maccaboy, parica, rappee, snoose
soak *v.* imbrue, imbue, ret
soap, make into saponify
soapy *adj.* saponaceous
so are you! *tu quoque*
sober *adj.* abstemious, temperate
so-called *adj. soi-disant*
sociability, revealing phatic
social club krewe
society *n.* confraternity, sodality
Socratic method, of the maieutic
soften *v.* assuage, intenerate
softening *adj.* demulcent, lenitive, mollescent

soil *v.* befoul, drabble, draggle, smirch
soil formation pedogenesis
soil organisms edaphon
solicit *v.* importune, supplicate
solitary *adj.* sequestered
solitary person eremite, incluse
solvent *n.* alkahest, menstruum
somber *adj.* fuscous, lugubrious
sometime *adj.* quondam
son *n.* cadet, dauphin
song, marriage epithalamion, epithalamium, prothalamion, prothalamium
songlike *adj.* antiphonic, ariose
song of lamentation threnody
soothing *adj.* anodyne, abirritant, alleviative, assuasive, demulcent, dulcet, emollient, lenitive
sooty *adj.* fuliginous
sophistry *n.* casuistry, sophism
sorcerer *n.* warlock
sorcery *n.* diablerie, diabolism, obeah, pishogue, sortilege
sorrowful *adj.* lugubrious, melancholic, rueful, ruthful
sort *v.* lemmatize, triage
soul *n.* anima, gilgul, jiva, nous, pneuma
souls *n.* manes, shades
sound, addition of a paragoge
sound, producing soniferous
sound-and-light show *son et lumière*
sour *adj.* acetous, acidulous, verjuice
sour *v.* acidulate
source *n.* fount, fountainhead, headspring, wellspring
source and origin *fons et origo*
souring *adj.* acrescent, acidulous
southern *adj.* austral, meridional
souvenirs *n.* memorabilia
sovereignty *n.* autarchy
space *n.* interstice, Lebensraum
spacious *adj.* capacious, commodious
spare *adj.* lank
sparing *adj.* penurious
spark *n.* scintilla, scintillation
sparkling *adj.* coruscant, coruscating, ignescent, scintillant, scintillating
Spartan *n./adj.* Lacedaemonian
spasm *n.* clonus, throe
spatter *v.* asperse, bedabble

spawning ground redd
spay *v.* desex, geld
speak *v.* expatiate, perorate
speaker of many languages polyglot
speaking in tongues glossolalia
speaking tube gosport
spear *n.* assegai, leister, pike
specialty *n.* forte, province
speck *n.* fleck, iota, scintilla, whit
speckled *adj.* lentiginous
spectacle *n.* tamasha
spectators *n.* dedans
specter *n.* eidolon, phantasm
speculative *adj.* conjectural, noetic
speculator *adj.* arbitrager, arbitrageur
speech *n.* lucubration, peroration, *palabra*, philippic
speech, figurative tropology
speech, meaningless psittacism
speech, sudden breaking off in aposiopesis
speed *n.* alacrity, celerity
speed *v.* career
speedily *adv.* expeditiously, posthaste
spellbind *v.* mesmerize
speller, bad cacographer
speller, correct orthographer
spelling *n.* heterography, orthography
sphere *n.* bailiwick, compass, pale, province
spherical *adj.* orbicular, spheral
spice *n.* rougail, stacte
spicy *adj.* piquant, pungent
spider *n.* arachnid, orb weaver
spidery *adj.* arachnoid
spigot *n.* spile
spike *n.* barbule, brob, piton, spicula, spicule
spillage *n.* spilth
spine, curvature of the scoliosis (see also **curvature**)
spinning *adj.* vertiginous
spinning wheel charkha
spiral *adj.* helical
spirit contact psychomancy
spirited *adj.* feisty, mettlesome
spiritless *adj.* exanimate, muzzy
spirit of the times *Zeitgeist*
spirits *n.* Lares, lares and penates, manes
spirits, low blue funk, doldrums, megrims

spiritual *adj.* incorporeal, numinous, platonic, supersensual
spiteful *adj.* malignant, spleenful, splenetic
splendor *n.* refulgence, resplendence
splash *n.* plash, splodge
splinter *n.* shive, shiver, spall
splintered *adj.* comminuted
splinters *n.* flinders
split *v.* cleave, rive, skive, spall
split *n.* breach, dichotomy, schism
split *adj.* cleft, riven
splittable *adj.* fissionable, scissile
spoil *v.* cosset, mollycoddle
spoils *n.* spolia opima
spokesperson *n.* syndic
sponge *v.* cadge
spongelike *adj.* asconoid
spooky *adj.* eldritch
spoor *n.* piste
spot *n.* lentigo, macula, maculation, macule
spotted *adj.* foxed, lentiginous, maculate
spouse *n.* consort, yokefellow, yokemate
spout *n.* gargoyle, spile
sprain *n.* subluxation
sprawl *v.* grabble, spraddle
spray *n.* spindrift, spoondrift
spread *v.* diffuse, perfuse, pervade, suffuse
spreading *adj.* serpiginous
sprightly *adj.* jaunty, jocund
spring, of primaveral, vernal
spring up pullulate
sprinkle *v.* asperse, pounce, sparge
sprout *v.* burgeon, pullulate
sprout *n.* ratoon
spunky *adj.* feisty
spur *n.* gaff
spurious *adj.* adulterine, apocryphal, factitious, meretricious, pinchbeck, supposititious
spy *n.* agent provocateur
spying *n.* comint, elint, espial, humint, sigint
squander *v.* fribble, fritter, wanton
squawk *v.* yawp
squeeze *v.* scrooch, scrooge, scrunch, squinch
squint *n.* strabismus
squire *n.* armiger
stab *v.* dirk, lancinate, transfix

stable *n.* mews
stack *v.* cock, rick
staff *n.* caduceus, crosier, mace, thyrsus, tipstaff
stagecoach *n.* diligence
stagger *v.* wamble
stagnant *adj.* moribund
stain *v.* ensanguine, imbrue
stained *adj.* foxed, maculate
stake *n.* pale, paling, pike, spile
stale *adj.* banal, bromidic, insipid
stall *v.* equivocate, temporize
stamp *n.* chop, perfin
stamp collecting philately
stand *n.* jardiniere, toddy table, torchère
standard *n.* benchmark, criterion, numeraire, touchstone
stand-in *n.* locum tenens, surrogate
stand of trees chenier, sugarbush
star *n.* hexagram, pentacle, pentagram, pentalpha, pentangle,
  Solomon's seal
starchy *adj.* farinaceous, farinose
stare *v.* gawk, gawp, glower
stars, abounding in stelliferous, stellular
star-shaped *adj.* stellate, stelliform
starving *adj.* ravening, ravenous, starveling
state *v.* asseverate, exposit, inveigh, posit, postulate
stately *adj.* Junoesque
statement *n.* allocution, ascription
statement, dogmatic *ipse dixit*
state supremacy caesaropapism
statue *n.* butsu, colossus, daibutsu, gisant, santo
steadiness *n.* equipoise
steady *adj.* equable, resolute
steal *v.* filch, peculate, rustle, snaffle
stealthy *adj.* clandestine, surreptitious
steep *adj.* abrupt, declivitous, precipitous, sheer
steep *v.* imbue, infuse, macerate, marinate
St. Elmo's fire corposant
stench *n.* fetor, funk, mephitis
stepmother, like a novercal
sterile *adj.* effete, infecund
sterilize *v.* geld, spay
stern *adj.* austere, callous, dour, obdurate
steward *n.* khansamah, major-domo, manciple, seneschal
stick *v.* cleave, cohere
stickler *n.* martinet, precisian

sticks, bundle of fagot, fascine
sticky *adj.* glairy, viscid, viscoid, viscose, viscous
stiff *adj.* constrained, mannered, starchy
stiffen *v.* congeal, starch, tauten
stiffness *n.* rigor mortis
still *adj.* quiescent, stagnant
stilted *adj.* bombastic, declamatory
stimulate *v.* fillip, innervate, innerve, titillate
stimulating *adj.* excitant, excitative, galvanic
sting *v.* nettle, urticate
stingy *adj.* avaricious, cheeseparing, chinchy, hardfisted, ironfisted,
    manini, mingy, niggardly, parsimonious, penurious
stinker *n.* stinkard
stinking *adj.* fetid, mephitic, noisome
stipend *n.* emolument, honorarium, prebend
stipend, person receiving prebend, prebendary, stipendiary
stir *v.* roil, swizzle
stock exchange bourse
stocky *adj.* blocky, stumpy
stoical *adj.* phlegmatic
stomach *n.* abomasum, gizzard, maw, omasum, psalterium,
    reticulum, rumen
stomach pain gastralgia
stone, like petrous
stone, paving sett
stone cutter lapidary
stone heap cairn
stonelike *adj.* lithoid
stones, group of peristalith
stoop *v.* deign, lout
stop *v.* belay, intermit, stanch
stoppage *n.* stagnation, stasis
stopper *n.* stopple, tampion
storeroom *n.* chandlery, lazaret, lazaretto
storm *n.* borasca, haboob, neutercane
story *n.* gest, parable
storyteller *n.* griot
stout *adj.* corpulent, plenitudinous, rotund
stoutness *n.* embonpoint
stove *n.* chauffer, salamander
straddle *v.* spraddle
strainer *n.* mazarine, strum
straining *adj.* tensive
strait *n.* euripus
strange *adj.* anomalous, fey, singular

stranger *n.* incomer, inconnu, outlander
strange to say *mirabile dictu*
strangle *v.* garrote, throttle
strap *n.* bretelle, crupper, guige, latigo
straw bed pallet
strawberry *n. fraise*
straw-colored *adj.* stramineous
stray *v.* divagate, meander
stray animal estray, waif
straying *n.* divagation, divergence
streaked *adj.* flecked, freaked
stream of fire phlegethon
street *n.* close, cul-de-sac
street cleaner whitewing
strength *n.* sthenia, thews
stretch *v.* tenter
stretching oneself pandiculation (*n.*)
strict adherent precisian
strictness *n.* punctilio, punctiliousness, rigorism
strike *v.* buffet, fillip, percuss, pommel, pummel
string of beads chaplet, rosary
strip *v.* cannibalize, denudate, denude, despoil, devoid, excoriate, flay, flense
striped *adj.* lineate, striated, vittate
stripper *n.* ecdysiast
strive *v.* moil
striving *n.* conation, conatus, nisus
stroke, oblique solidus
stroking *n.* effleurage
stroll *v.* ambulate, perambulate, saunter
strong *adj.* puissant, robustious
stronghold *n.* bastion, fastness, redoubt
structure *n.* contexture, morphology
structure, stone nuraghe
struggle *v.* reluct, scrabble
strut *v.* feist
stub *n.* counterfoil, nubbin
stubborn *adj.* fractious, froward, intractable, intransigent, mulish, obdurate, pertinacious, pervicacious, refractory
stucco *n.* albarium
student *n.* decretist, sadhaka, sadhika, scholastic, shishya, softa
studio *n.* atelier, bottega
study *v.* excogitate, expertize
study *n.* cogitation, lucubration, rumination
study, course of scholasticate
study, critical epicrisis

stuff *v.* cloy, jade, slake, steeve, stodge
stunning *adj.* foudroyant
stupefy *v.* besot, gorgonize, lethargize, narcotize, obfuscate
stupefying *adj.* stupefacient, stupefactive
stupid *adj.* asinine, blockish, doltish, fatuitous, fatuous, witless
stupidity *n.* bêtise, crassitude, fatuity
sturdy *adj.* indomitable, sthenic
stuttering *n.* psellism
sty *n.* chalazion, hordeolum
style *n.* panache
stylishness *n.* ton
suave *adj.* Chesterfieldian, silky, sleeky
subdue *v.* mitigate, quash
subject *n.* rayah, vassal
subjugation *n.* Carthaginian peace
sublimate *v.* subtilize
sublime *adj.* august, resplendent
submissive *adj.* deferential, fawning, obsequious, uxorious
submit *v.* grovel, truckle
subordinate *adj.* ancillary, subaltern
subordinate *n.* minion, understrapper
subordination, grammatical hypotaxis
subsequent *adj.* succedent
subsidence *n.* detumescence
subsidiary *adj.* succursal
subsidy *n.* subvention
substance, lacking in facile
substantiating *adj.* evidential, probative
substitute *n.* locum tenens, simulacrum, succedaneum, surrogate, vicar
subterranean *adj.* chthonian, hypogeal
subtle *adj.* elusive, finespun, subtile, tenuous
subtlety *n.* Italian hand
subtract *v.* subduct
succession *n.* consecution
successive *adj.* sequent
successor *n.* epigone
succinct *adj.* laconic, sententious
sucking, adapted for suctorial
sudden *adj.* precipitant, precipitate
sue *v.* implead
sufferer *n.* agonist
suffering *n.* calvary, gethsemane
suffering, causing tortuous
suffocation *n.* apnea, asphyxia
suffuse *v.* perfuse

sugar *n.* demerara, jaggery, muscovado, panocha, penuche
sugar, convert into saccharify, saccharize
sugarcane residue bagasse
suggest *v.* opine
suggestive *adj.* allusive, evocative, pregnant, significative
suicide *n.* felo-de-se, hara-kiri, seppuku
suitability *n.* convenance, expediency
suitable *adj.* apposite, condign, meet, propitious
suitcase *n.* gladstone
suited *adj.* accordant, consentaneous
sulfur *n.* brimstone
sulfur, containing sulfureous
sullen *adj.* beetle-browed, dour, farouche, lowering, petulant
summary *n.* catechism, compendium, conspectus, epitome,
    excerpta, précis, quintessence, summa, synaxarion, synaxarium
summer *v.* estivate
summer, appropriate to estival
summer, pertaining to late serotinal
summerhouse *n.* belvedere, bower, gazebo
summon *v.* conjure, preconize
summoner *n.* muezzin
summons *n.* azan, beck
sumptuous *adj.* Lucullan
sum up perorate
sun *n.* Phoebus
sundial *n.* horologe
sun hat topee
sunny side adret
sunstroke *n.* siriasis
sun worship heliolatry
superabundance *n.* plethora
superb *adj.* consummate
superficial *adj.* cosmetic, facile, peripheric
superfluous *adj.* excrescent, gratuitous, otiose, pleonastic
superfluous person or thing fifth wheel
superiority *n.* meliority
superman *n.* Übermensch
supernatural *adj.* fey, numinous, preternatural, supranatural
superpower *n.* imperium
supplement *n.* addendum, adjunct, codicil
supplemental *adj.* accessorial, adscititious, ancillary
supplementary matter paralipomena
supplication *n.* conjuration, entreaty, rogation
supply, inexhaustible widow's cruse
support *n.* aegis, aliment, auspices, bulwark, nurturance
support *v.* abet, bolster, buttress, inspirit, subvene, undergird

supposed *adj.* putative, supposititious
suppress *v.* burke, elide, quash
supreme *adj.* assoluta, hegemonic, paramount
supreme power imperium
surface *n.* superficies
surfeit *n.* de trop, plethora, superabundance
surging rise and fall gurgitation
surly *adj.* churlish, irascible
surmountable *adj.* superable
surname *n.* cognomen
surpassing *adj.* transcendent
surplus *n.* plethora, superabundance, surfeit
surprise *n.* peripeteia, surprisal
surrender *n.* capitulation, cession
surreptitious *adj.* subreptitious
surround *v.* circumfuse, circumscribe, encincture, engirdle, environ
surrounding *adj.* circumambient, circumjacent
surveillance *n.* invigilation
survey *n.* conspectus
survivor *n.* hibakusha, relict
suspend *v.* intermit, pretermit, prorogue
suspenders *n.* braces, galluses
suspension *n.* abeyance, hiatus
sustenance *n.* sustentation
svelte *adj.* lithe, willowy
swagger *n.* panache
swaggering *adj.* huffish, swashbuckling
swallowing *n.* aerophagia, deglutition
swamp *n.* fen, marais, quagmire
swamps, growing in uliginose, uliginous
swampy *adj.* founderous, sloughy
swan *n.* cob, cygnet, pen
swarm *v.* pullulate
swarthy *adj.* dusky, swart
swastika *n.* fylfot, hakenkreuz
sway *v.* careen
swear *v.* imprecate
sweating *n.* hidropoiesis, hidrosis, hyperhidrosis, hypohidrosis
sweating, inducing diaphoretic, sudatory, sudoriferous, sudorific, sudoriparous
sweet *adj.* cloying, doux, saccharine
sweetbread *n.* pancreas
sweeten *v.* dulcify
sweetened *adj.* mellifluous
sweetheart *n.* dulcinea, gill
sweet-sounding *adj.* dulcet, Lydian, mellifluent

swell *v.* distend, intumesce, tumefy, tumesce

swelling *n.* dilation, edema, gibbosity, hydrops, intumescence, tumescence, wheal

swift *adj.* feathered, tantivy

swiftness *n.* celerity

swimmer *n.* mermaid, merman, natator

swimming *n.* natation

swimming pool natatorium

swindle *n.* bunko game, pigeon drop, Ponzi, shell game, thimblerig

swindler *n.* blackleg, rook, sharper, thimblerigger

swine *n.* gilt

swine, pertaining to porcine

swing *v.* librate, oscillate

swollen *adj.* distended, gouty, intumescent, tumescent, tumid, turgid, ventricose

sword-shaped *adj.* ensiform, xiphoid

swordsman *n.* swashbuckler

syllogism *n.* enthymeme, episyllogism, polysyllogism

symbol *n.* device, glyph, grammalogue, ideogram, ideograph, logogram, logograph, pictogram, pictograph

symbolism *n.* iconology

symbols, set of syllabary

symposium, participant in a symposiast

symposium director symposiarch

symptom *n.* prodrome, sequela

syndrome *n.* symptomatology

synopsis *n.* conspectus, epitome, précis

synthesize *v.* synthetize

syphilis *n.* lues, treponemiasis

syphilitic *adj.* luetic

T

table linen napery

taciturn *adj.* dour, reticent, saturnine

tact *n.* circumspection, finesse, savoir-faire

tactful *adj.* politic

tactless *adj.* gauche, maladroit
tag *n.* aglet, aiguillette
tail *n.* appendage, extremity, scut
tailless *adj.* excaudate
tailor *n.* bushelman
tailors, pertaining to sartorial
tainted *adj.* scrofulous
take *v.* accroach, expropriate
take in incept, ingest
tale *n.* fabliau
talk *v.* descant, expatiate, maunder, palaver, palter, prate
talk *n.* causerie, coze, galimatias, *palabra*
talkative *adj.* garrulous, loquacious, voluble
tameness *n.* mansuetude
tangential *adj.* digressive, peripheral
tangible *adj.* palpable, tactile
tank *n.* cistern, impluvium
tape *n.* inkle
tapering *adj.* acuminate, attenuate, terete
tardy *adj.* belated, cunctatious, cunctative, cunctatory
tartar *n.* calculus
taste *v.* degust
taste, abnormal sense of parageusia
taunt *n.* raillery
tavern *n.* gasthaus, heurige
tawdry *adj.* garish, meretricious
tawny *adj.* fulvous
tax *n.* capitation, Danegeld, exaction, gabelle, impost, jizyah, octroi, Peter's pence, taille, tallage, tribute
tax collector publican, tahsildar, zamindar
taxi *n.* jitney, *público*
tea *n.* tisane
teach *v.* catechize, inculcate, inoculate
teacher *n.* catechist, darshan, guru, khoja, maharishi, *melamed*, pedagogue, pir, rabban, rhetor, sensei, sophist, starets, swami
teaching *n.* andragogy, dharma, pedagogy
tear *v.* dilacerate, rend, rive, sunder
tear *n.* rent, rift
tearful *adj.* lachrymose
tearing apart of live victims sparagmos
tears, pertaining to lachrymal, lachrymatory, lacrimal, lacrimatory
tease *v.* chaff, coquet
techniques *n.* armamentarium
tediousness *n.* operoseness, prosiness, tedium
teem *v.* abound, pullulate

teeth, grinding of bruxism
teething *n.* dentition, odontiasis
temper *n.* dander, spleen
tempered, foul splenetic
temple *n.* delubrum, Ephesus, fane, gurdwara, hieron, mandira, naos, pantheon, vihara, wat, ziggurat
temple vestibule epinaos
temporarily *adv. pro tempore*
temporary *adj.* ephemeral, fugitive, jackleg, *pro tempore*, transitory
temptation *n.* blandishment, seduction, tantalization
temptress *n.* Delilah
tenacious *adj.* pertinacious
tenant *n.* leud, socager, sokeman
tenant farmer métayer
Ten Commandments Decalogue
tendency *n.* bent, habitude, penchant, predisposition, proclivity, propensity
tenement house rookery, warren
tenfold *adj.* decimal, decuple, denary
tennis elbow epicondylitis
tension *n.* fantod
tent *n.* yurt
tenth part tithe
termination *n.* desinence, dissolution, expiry
termite nest termitarium
term of respect honorific
terrarium *n.* vivarium, Wardian case
terrestrial *adj.* tellurian, tellurion
territory *n.* nizamate, pashalik
terrorist *n.* Molly Maguire, *plastiqueur*
terse *adj.* aphoristic, epigrammatic
test *n.* assay, pons asinorum, touchstone
testes *n.* stones (see also **testis**)
testify *v.* depone, depose
testimony *n.* attestation, deposition
testis *n.* gonad, mountain oyster, prairie oyster, Rocky Mountain oyster
test word shibboleth
testy *adj.* irascible, tetchy
text, genuine textus receptus
texture *n.* woof
thanksgiving *n.* Eucharist
that is to say id est
theatrical *adj.* campy, histrionic
theorem *n.* lemma

theorist *n.* ideologue
theorist, pedantic doctrinaire
thereby *adv.* ipso facto
therefore *adv.* ergo
thicken *v.* inspissate
thicket *n.* coppice, covert, mogote
thick-skinned *adj.* pachydermatous
thief *n.* Autolycus, ladrone, nightwalker, picaroon, picklock, rustlet
thievery *n.* cleptobiosis
thighbone *n.* femur
thin *adj.* attenuated, diaphanous, tenuous
thing done fait accompli
thing given in return for another quid pro quo
thing of little value pittance, stiver
things added paralipomena
things being equal, other *ceteris paribus*
think *v.* cerebrate, cogitate, excogitate, ideate, ratiocinate,
    rationalize, ruminate
thinness *n.* tenuity
third in rank ternary
thirteen *n.* baker's dozen, long dozen
thirty-second note, a demisemiquaver
thong *n.* babiche, whang
thorny *adj.* spiniferous, spinose, spinous
thorough *adj.* cyclopedic, encyclopedic, exhaustive
though *conj.* albeit
thought *n.* intellection, lucubration
thoughtful *adj.* cogitative, contemplative, reflective
thoughtless *adj.* incogitant, indiscriminate, unreflective
thousandth *adj./n.* millesimal
thousand years millennium
thrash *v.* larrup, whale
thread *n.* babiche, cannetille, cordonnet, douppioni, inkle
thread, pertaining to a filar
thread holder looper
threadlike *adj.* filate, filiform, filose
threat *n.* commination, sword of Damocles
threatening *adj.* comminatory, fraught, lowering, lowery,
    minacious, minatory
three, set of tern, ternion
threefold *adj.* ternary
three years, period of triennial, triennium
threshing instrument flail, swingle, swipple
threshold *n.* limen
thrift *n.* husbandry

thriftless *adj.* improvident
thrifty *adj.* frugal, provident
thrill *n.* frisson
thrive *v.* batten
throne *n.* cathedra, musnud, tribune
throw *v.* jaculate
throwback *n.* atavism, reversion
thrust *v.* detrude, exsert, obtrude
thumb *n.* pollex
thumb the nose cock a snook
thunderbolt *n.* coup de foudre
thus *adv.* sic
tidal wave bore, tsunami
tidbit *n.* bonne bouche, kickshaw
tide *n.* agger
tidy *v.* redd
tie *n.* nexus, vinculum
tie *v.* ligate
tightrope walker equilibrist, funambulist
tile *n.* favus, imbrex, pantile
tile, resembling a tegular
tilled land tillage, tilth
tilt *v./n.* cant, heel
time nonexistent Greek calends
timeworn *adj.* antiquated, hackneyed
timid *adj.* diffident, fearsome, pavid, pusillanimous, thewless,
    timorous
tin *n.* stannum
tinfoil *n.* tain
tin plate latten
tinsel *n.* clinquant
tint *v.* tinct
tiny *adj.* Lilliputian, minuscule
tip *v.* cant, careen, heel
tip *n.* baksheesh, broadus, cumshaw, douceur, lagniappe
tirade *n.* philippic
tiredness *n.* debility, languor
tireless *adj.* indefatigable, resolute
tiresome *adj.* insipid, prosaic, vapid
title *n.* appellation, cognomen, rubric
toast *n.* l'chaim, prosit, prost, *salud*, *salute*, wassail
toastmaster *n.* symposiarch
tobacco *n.* caporal, cavendish, kinnikinnick, perique
toe, big hallux
toes *n.* pettitoes

toga *n.* himation, praetexta, toga virilis
toil *v.* grub, moil
toilet *n.* fontange, jakes
token *n.* earnest, jetton, vecture
tokens *n.* exonumia
tolerant *adj.* forbearing, latitudinarian
tolerate *v.* brook, stomach
tomb *n.* charnel, cistvaen, cromlech, cubiculum, marabout, mastaba, sepulcher, sepulture, tholos, tholus
tomboy *n.* hoyden
tongues, speaking in glossolalia
tongue-shaped *adj.* linguiform
too much de trop
toothless *adj.* edentulous
toothlike *adj.* dentoid, odontoid
topmost *adj.* culminant
torch *n.* flambeau, link
torture *v.* excruciate, lacerate
torture *n.* bastinado, iron maiden of Nuremberg, pilliwinks, strappado
tossing *n.* jactitation
total *v.* summate
totem pole xat
touch, of the sense of haptic, tactile
touching *adj.* abutting, contiguous, tangent
touchy *adj.* irascible, petulant
toughen *v.* anneal, inure, temper
tow *n.* cordelle
toweling *n.* huckabuck
tower *n.* bastide, broch, donjon, minah, minaret, peel, sikhara, talayot
to wit scilicet
town *n.* bastide, vill
townsman *n.* oppidan
toy top dreidel, teetotum
trace *n.* engram, scintilla, simulacrum, spoor, wrack
trace *v.* delineate
track-layer *n.* gandy dancer
trade *n.* métier
trader *n.* comanchero
traditional *adj.* consuetudinary, traditive
tragedy *n.* cothurnus
trail *n.* piste, spoor
train *v.* espalier, longe
train *n.* coffle, gotrain

traitor *n.* Judas, quisling, recreant, runagate
tranquillity *n.* ataraxia, kef
transcendence *n.* transcension
transcript *n.* apograph
transfer *n.* conveyance, devolution, translocation
transformation *n.* metamorphosis, metanoia, metastasis, sea change, transfiguration, transmogrification, transmutation
transient *adj.* ephemeral, evanescent, fugitive, volatile
transition *n.* saltation, saltus
transitional period liminality
transitory *adj.* ephemeral, evanescent
translation *n.* metaphrase, rendering
translator *n.* metaphrast
translucent *adj.* diaphanous, limpid
transmigration *n.* metempsychosis
transmission *n.* filiation
transparent *adj.* pellucid, transpicuous
transposition *n.* metathesis, paralexia, spoonerism
trap *n.* bobèche, gin, lime twig, springe, trou-de-loup
trapper *n.* coureur de bois
trappings *n.* accouterments, caparison, regalia
trash *n.* spilth
travel *v.* itinerate, peregrinate
travel *n.* jornada, odyssey, peregrination
travel allowance viaticum
traveler *n.* viator, wayfarer
travesty *n.* mockery, perversion, sham
tray *n.* salver, waiter
treacherous *adj.* insidious, perfidious, serpentine, specious
treason *n.* lese majesty, lèse majesté
treasurer *n.* bursar
treasury *n.* coffers, exchequer, fisc
treatise *n.* disquisition, lucubration, pandect, prolegomena
treaty *n.* concordat, convention, covenant, protocol
tree, sheared pollard
treelike *adj.* dendroid
tree trunk bole
trellis *n.* espalier, treillage
trembly *adj.* dithery, tremulant, tremulous
tremor *n.* temblor
trial *n.* assize, crucible
trial balloon *ballon d'essai*
triangular *adj.* cuneate, leg-of-mutton, trigonal, trigonous
triannual *adj.* triennial
tribe *n.* phyle

tribunal *n.* Sanhedrin
tribute *n.* encomium, laudation
trick *n.* artifice, imposture, stratagem, subterfuge, wile
trick *v.* bamboozle, befool, cozen, euchre, gudgeon, gull, humbug
trickery *n.* chicanery, conjuration, cozenage, dodgery, hokey-pokey, legerdemain, skulduggery, tortuosity
trickle *v.* exude
trifler *n.* fribble
trifling *adj.* niggling, picayune, piddling, piffling
trim *v.* bedeck, flounce
trimming *n.* passement, passementerie, rickrack, ruche, ruching
trinket *n.* bibelot, breloque, gaud, gimcrack, tchotchke
tripod *n.* brandreth
trite *adj.* bathetic, bromidic, platitudinal, platitudinous
triumphal column manubial column
triviality *n.* nugacity
trivialize *v.* banalize
trivium *n.* grammar, rhetoric, and logic
trouble *v.* discommode, importune, incommode
troublemaker *n.* firebrand, rabble-rouser
troublesome *adj.* pestiferous, pestilential, plaguesome, vexatious
trough *n.* manger
trounce *v.* castigate
trousers trews
truce *n.* modus vivendi, stand-down
true *adj.* apodictic, veracious
truism *n.* bromide, platitude, saw
truncate *v.* decollate
trunk *n.* wanigan
trustworthy *adj.* staunch
truthfulness *n.* veracity, veridicality
trying experiences via dolorosa
tryst *n.* assignation
tub *n.* firkin
tube *n.* pipette, tubule
tuberculosis *n.* consumption, phthisis
tuft *n.* floccus, flock, penicil
tumor *n.* myeloma, myxoma, neoplasm, neuroma, sarcoma, scirrhus
tumult *n.* bedlam, rabblement
tuneful *adj.* dulcet
tuning fork diapason
tunnel *n.* cuniculus
turban *n.* pugree
turbulent *adj.* roily, tumultuary

turf *n.* greensward, sward, swarth
turmoil *n.* moil, welter
turnabout *n.* volte-face
turn aside prescind
turned backward retrorse
turned in obvolute
turned up retroussé
turning *n.* obversion
turning point solstice, watershed
turn inside out evaginate
turn of events peripeteia
turn outward evert, extrovert
turret *n.* bartizan, mirador, tourelle
tutelage *n.* pupilage
tutor *n.* docent, mentor, preceptor
twelfth *adj.* dozenth
twentieth *adj.* vigesimal
twentieth anniversary vigentennial
twenty, pertaining to vicenary
twenty years, occurring every vicennial
twig *n.* moit, scion, withe, withy
twilight *n.* crepuscule, gloaming
twin *n.* freemartin
twin *adj.* didymous, geminate
twinkle *v.* scintillate
twins *n.* Castor and Pollux, Romulus and Remus
twisted *adj.* convoluted, intorted, tortile
twitching *n.* fibrillation, jactitation
two-faced *adj.* janiform, Janus-faced
twofold *adj.* diploid, duple
two-headed *adj.* bicephalous, bicipital, dicephalous
two parts, in dimerous, dimorphous
tying *n.* ligation, ligature
typify *v.* adumbrate
tyrannical *adj.* pharaonic
tyrannize *v.* Neronize

U

ulcer *n.* chancre
umbilicus *n.* omphalos
unalterable *adj.* immutable, inexorable
unanimous *adj.* consentaneous, consentient
unanswerable *adj.* irrecusable, irrefragable
unappeasable *adj.* implacable
unatonable *adj.* inexpiable
unattractive *adj.* rebarbative, unprepossessing
unavailing *adj.* bootless, ineffectual, inutile, nugatory, Sisyphean
unavoidably *adv.* ineluctibly, ineludibly, perforce
unaware *adj.* incognizant, unwitting
unbalance *v.* disequilibrate
unbecoming *adj.* indecorous
unbeliever *n.* infidel, kafir
unbending *adj.* adamant, flinty
unbiased *adj.* unjaundiced
unbleached *adj.* greige
unbraid *v.* unplait
unbreakable *adj.* infrangible, inviolable
unbroken *adj.* inviolate
unburden *v.* disembosom
uncanny *adj.* preternatural
uncanonical *adj.* apocryphal
uncertainty *n.* incertitude, irresolution
unchain *v.* unfetter
unchallengeable *adj.* incontrovertible, irrefragable, peremptory
unchangeable *adj.* immutable, incommutable
unchecked *adj.* arrant, rampant, unbridled
uncle-like *adj.* avuncular
unclothe *v.* denude, divest
uncomfortable *adj.* discomfited
uncommonness *n.* singularity
uncommunicative *adj.* reserved, taciturn
uncomplaining *adj.* forbearing
uncompliant *adj.* recusant
uncomplimentary *adj.* denigratory
uncomprehension *n.* anoesis

uncompromising *adj.* intractable, intransigent, steadfast
unconcealed *adj.* patent
unconcern *n.* insouciance
unconcerned *adj.* apathetic, dispassionate, impassive, insouciant
unconditional *adj.* categorical
unconquerable *adj.* indomitable, inexpugnable
unconscious *adj.* inanimate, inconscient
uncontestable *adj.* apodictic, irrefragable
uncontrolled *adj.* capricious, unbridled
unconventional *adj.* idiosyncratic, outré
uncouth *adj.* agrestic, boorish, loutish
uncover *v.* decorticate
uncultivated *adj.* fallow
undecided *adj.* moot, pendent
undecisive *adj.* irresolute, vacillating
under *adj.* nether
underground *adj.* hypogeal, subterrestrial
underhand *adj.* clandestine, surreptitious
underling *n.* henchman, spear carrier
underlying *adj.* subjacent
understand *v.* apperceive, assimilate
understandable *adj.* apprehensible, perspicuous, scrutable
understanding *n.* apprehension, discernment, intellection, prehension
understanding, lacking imperceptive, impercipient
understatement *n.* litotes, meiosis (see also **rhetorical terms**)
understood *adj.* tacit
understood, easily perspicuous
undertone, in an sotto voce
underworld *n.* antipodes
undeveloped *adj.* inchoate, incipient
undiminished *adj.* undamped
undisciplined *adj.* fractious, indocile, obstreperous
undisclosed *adj.* in petto
undisturbed *adj.* inviolate
undress *n.* disarray, dishabille
undulant fever brucellosis
undulating *adj.* fluctuant
unearth *v.* disinhume
unearthly *adj.* preternatural, spectral
uneasiness *n.* disquietude, dysphoria, inquietude
uneasy *adj.* restive
unemotional *adj.* bloodless, phlegmatic, stolid
unenthusiastic *adj.* apathetic, dispirited
unequaled *adj.* nonpareil, peerless

unerasable *adj.* inexpungible, inextirpable
unethical *adj.* meretricious
uneven *adj.* erose, hubbly
unexciting *adj.* drab, lackluster
unexpected *adj.* fortuitous
unfailing *adj.* boundless, staunch, unflagging
unfaithful *adj.* adulterous, recreant
unfathomable *adj.* inscrutable
unfavorable *adj.* inauspicious, unpropitious, untoward
unfeeling *adj.* callous, imperceptive, indurate, insensate
unflappable *adj.* imperturbable
unforceful *adj.* ineffectual, toothless
unforgiving *adj.* unrelenting, vindictive
unfortunate *adj.* hapless, inauspicious
unfriendly *adj.* disaffected, estranged, inimical
unfruitful *adj.* infecund, sterile
unfulfilled *adj.* manqué
ungenuine *adj.* fictive
ungodly *adj.* impious, profane, sacrilegious
ungrammatical *adj.* solecistic
unguarded *adj.* guileless, incautious
unhappy *adj.* dispirited, infelicitous
unhealthy *adj.* deleterious, insalubrious, noisome, noxious,
  pernicious
unify *v.* coalesce
unifying *adj.* unific
unifying, capable of esemplastic
unimportant *adj.* nugatory
uninformed *adj.* jejune
unintelligent *adj.* vacuous
unintentional *adj.* indeliberate, unwitting
uninteresting *adj.* drab, insipid, torpid, vapid
uninviting *adj.* forbidding
uninvolved *adj.* apathetic, dégagé
union *n.* Anschluss, conjuncture
unique *adj.* nonpareil, *sui generis*
unisex *adj.* androgyne, androgynous, hermaphrodite,
  pseudohermaphrodite
unite *v.* catenate, coalesce, colligate, concatenate, concorporate,
  consubstantiate, inosculate
united *adj.* conjoined, conjunct, osculant
uniting *adj.* copulative
unkempt *adj.* blowzy, tatterdemalion
unkind *adj.* incogitant, inhumane
unknowing *adj.* unwitting

unleash *v.* vent, wreak
unlikeness *n.* dissimilitude
unlucky *adj.* hapless, ill-fated, ill-starred, inauspicious, sinistrous, woebegone
unmanageable *adj.* refractory, restive
unmannerly *adj.* incondite, loutish
unmethodical *adj.* desultory
unmindful *adj.* heedless, oblivious
unmistakable *adj.* blatant, resounding
unmixable *adj.* immiscible, nonmiscible
unmixed *adj.* homogeneous, unalloyed
unnamed *adj.* innominate
unnatural *adj.* factitious, perverse
unnecessary *adj.* extrinsic, pleonastic
unnecessary, make obviate
unnerved *adj.* discomposed, unhinged, unstrung
unorthodox *adj.* avant-garde, bohemian
unparalleled *adj.* unexampled
unpartitioned *adj.* indiscrete
unperceptive *adj.* impercipient
unperforated *adj.* imperforate
unplanned *adj.* extemporary, extempore, fortuitous
unpleasant *adj.* repugnant, woeful
unpleasant, something wormwood
unpleasant word dysphemism
unpolished *adj.* incondite, incult
unpolluted *adj.* pristine
unpredictable *adj.* aleatory, fitful
unprofitable *adj.* bootless
unpublished literary works inedita
unquenchable *adj.* insatiable, insatiate
unraveling *n.* denouement
unreal *adj.* aeriform, delusive, delusory, fatuous, illusory, illusive, irreal
unrelenting *adj.* implacable, inexorable, unremitting
unreliable *adj.* perfidious
unrelieved *adj.* unmitigated
unrepentant *adj.* impenitent, obdurate, unregenerate
unrestrained *adj.* corybantic, intemperate, unbridled
unrestrained behavior, places for fleshpots
unrewarding *adj.* hardscrabble
unrivaled *adj.* inimitable, nonesuch, nonpareil
unruffled *adj.* phlegmatic
unruly *adj.* fractious, indocile, refractory, restive, wayward
unscrupulous *adj.* jackleg, meretricious, unprincipled

unselfish *adj.* altruistic, philanthropic
unsettle *v.* disconcert, nettle, unhinge
unskilled *adj.* jackleg
unsocial *adj.* dissocial
unsolvable *adj.* irresoluble
unsophisticated *adj.* guileless, ingenuous
unspeakable *adj.* execrable, heinous
unspoiled *adj.* pristine
unstable *adj.* vertiginous
unsteadiness *n.* titubation, wamble
unsteady *adj.* capricious, fluctuant, labile
unsubstantiated *adj.* tenuous
unsuccessful *adj.* bootless, ineffectual, manqué
unsuitable *adj.* unmeet
untactful *adj.* gauche, indecorous
untamed *adj.* feral
unteachable *adj.* indocile
untimely *adj.* inopportune
untiring *adj.* assiduous, indefatigable, sedulous
untruthfulness *n.* inveracity, mendacity
unusual *adj.* anomalous, singular
unutterable *adj.* ineffable
unwarranted *adj.* gratuitous
unwholesome *adj.* insalubrious, noxious
unwillingness *n.* disinclination
unwise *adj.* impolitic, injudicious
unworldly *adj.* ingenuous, provincial
unworthy *adj.* ignoble, unseemly
unwritten *adj.* nuncupative
unyielding *adj.* inductile, obdurate
upheaval *n.* cataclysm, welter
uprightness *n.* probity, rectitude
uproar *n.* bedlam, *geschrei*, hullabaloo, katzenjammer
uproot *v.* deracinate
upset *v.* discombobulate, discomfit
up-to-date *adj.* au courant
urban *adj.* oppidan
urbane *adj.* Chesterfieldian, cosmopolitan
urchin *n.* gamin, gamine, guttersnipe, street arab
urgent *adj.* clamant, compelling, exigent, importunate
urination *n.* diuresis, dysuria, emiction, enuresis, micturition, polyuria, strangury
urn *n.* samovar, situla
useful *adj.* efficacious, utile
useless *adj.* bootless, inutile, nugatory

usual *adj.* wonted
usurp *v.* arrogate
usury *n.* gombeen
utopian *adj.* idyllic
utopian community pantisocracy
utter *adj.* unqualified, veritable
utterance *n.* dixit, ejaculation

vacancy *n.* voidance
vacant *adj.* bereft, devoid
vacation *v.* estivate
vacillating *adj.* dithering, pendulous, tremulous
vagabond *n.* picara, picaro, picaroon, piepowder, runagate
vagueness *n.* nebulosity, tenuity
vain person coxcomb, popinjay
valet *n.* batman, lackey
valiant *adj.* dauntless, doughty
validity *n.* cogency, effectuality
valley *n.* bolson, coulee, dell, dingle, droke, wadi
valor *n.* arete, intrepidity
vampire *n.* lamia
vanish *v.* evanesce
vanity *n.* amour propre, narcissism, self-love, vainglory
vapor *n.* effluvium
variable *adj.* capricious, inconstant, mercurial, mutable, protean
variegated *adj.* motley, parti-colored, varicolored, versicolor
variety *n.* multiformity, multiplicity, smorgasbord
various *adj.* divers, sundry
varnish *n./v.* japan
vase *n.* amphora, lachrymatory, potiche, pseudoamphora, situla
vassal *n.* daimyo, feodary, feudatory, leud, palatine, vavasor
vat *n.* cistern, kier
vaulted *adj.* alveated, embowed
vegetable cultivation olericulture
vegetarian *n.* lactovegetarian, lacto-ovo-vegetarian, ovolactarian,
    ovolacto-vegetarian, vegan

vehement *adj.* fervid, impassioned
velvet *n.* velure
velvety *adj.* velutinous
veneration *n.* dulia, hyperdulia
vengeance *n.* requital, retribution, revanche
vengeful *adj.* vindictive
venomous *adj.* acerb, malignant, rancorous, splenetic, venenose, viperine
vent *n.* fumarole, mofette, solfatara
veranda *n.* dalan, lanai, piazza
verbatim *adv./adj.* *ipsissima verba*, letter-perfect
verbose *adj.* diffuse, pleonastic, prolix
vernacular *adj.* demotic
vernacular *n.* parlance
versatile *adj.* protean
version, revised recension
verve *n.* panache
vespers *n.* hesperinos
vessel *n.* alembic, autoclave, cuvette, gallipot, jorum, monstrance, mortar, pyx, retort, stoup
vestibule *n.* epinaos, exonarthex, galilee, mantapa, narthex, opistodomos, posticum, pronaos, propylaeum, propylon, prostas
vestments *n.* pontificals
vestry *n.* sacristy
veto *n.* liberum veto
viable *adj.* fecund, proliferous
vibrating *adj.* vibratile
viceroy *n.* nabob, nawab
vicinity *n.* environs, vicinage
victim *n.* gull
victory, costly Cadmean victory, Pyrrhic victory
vigil *n.* watch and ward
vigilant *adj.* circumspect
vigor *n.* birr, brio, verdure
vigor, drain of etiolate
vigorous *adj.* sinewy, youngblood
vigorously *adv.* roundly
vile *adj.* debased, ignominious
vilify *v.* asperse, calumniate, revile, traduce, vilipend, vituperate
villa *n.* dacha
village *n.* bustee, dorp, encomienda, kampong, kraal, *shtetl*, vill
villainy *n.* miscreancy
vindicating *adj.* exculpatory
vindictive *adj.* rancorous, splenetic
vineyard *n.* cru
vintage *n.* récolte

violate *v.* breach, infract
violated, capable of being violable
violation *n.* desecration, profanation
violent *adj.* rampageous, tempestuous, wroth
violin *n.* Cremona, Stradivarius
violin maker luthier
virtue *n.* arete, dharma
viscera *n.* offal
visceral *adj.* splanchnic
viscous *adj.* glairy, glutinous, viscose
visionary *n.* fantast
visionary *adj.* quixotic, translunary
visit *v.* interpellate
visitor *n.* habitué, interpellator, visitant
visual deception trompe l'oeil
visualize *v.* envisage, ideate
vituperation *n.* calumniation, opprobrium, vilification
vituperative *adj.* opprobrious
vivacious *adj.* buoyant, ebullient
vivacity *n.* élan
vivid *adj.* eidetic, stark
vocation *n.* métier, niche
vociferous *adj.* clamant, strident
voice of the people vox populi
voices, of many polyphonic
void *v.* abrogate, rescind
void *adj.* inoperative
volcanic ash pozzolana
volcanic glass obsidian
volcanic material tephra
volition *n.* velleity
voluptuous *adj.* Lydian, toothsome
vomit *v.* disgorge, regurgitate
vomit *n.* emesis, vomitus
vomiting, causing emetic
voodoo *n.* vodun
voracious *adj.* edacious, rapacious
vulgar *adj.* colloquial, demotic, vernacular
vulgarity *n.* billingsgate, indelicacy, invective, scurrility
vulnerable *adj.* effete, pregnable
vulnerable area underbelly
vultures, pertaining to vulturine

waffle *v.* equivocate
wag *n.* farceur, farceuse
wages *n.* emolument
wagon maker wainwright
wail *v.* caterwaul, keen, ululate
waiter *n.* garçon, mozo, steward
waive *v.* forgo, remit
wake *n.* rooster tail, train
walk *n.* ambulation, constitutional, cultus coolee, deambulation
walking *adj.* deambulatory, itinerant, peripatetic
walking on the toes digitigrade (*adj.*)
wall *n.* bailey, ballium, enceinte, revetment
wall opening gunport, hagioscope, squint
wallow *v.* welter
wampum *n.* peag, seawan, seawant, sewan, wampumpeag
wan *adj.* pallid, lurid
wander *v.* divagate, meander, traipse
wanderer *n.* drifter, itinerant, vagabond
wandering *adj.* desultory, digressive, excursive, itinerant, peripatetic, vagarious
want *n.* beggary, destitution, indigence, pauperism, penury, privation
war, an act precipitating casus belli
warden *n.* alcaide
warding off evil apotropaic (*adj.*)
warlike *adj.* bellicose, martial
warlord *n.* daimyo, tuchun
warehouse *n.* entrepôt, godown
warm-blooded *adj.* hematothermal, homoiothermal
warmed-over *adj.* réchauffé
warming *adj.* calefacient, calefactory, calescent
warmth *n.* affability
warmth, producing calefacient, calefactory
warn *v.* chide, monish, premonish
warning *n.* admonition, augury, caveat, injunction, monition, portent, premonition
warning *adj.* admonitory, auguring, exemplary, monitory, premonitory, presaging

war of words, literary fliting
wart *n.* furuncle, pustule, verruca
warty *adj.* verrucose, verrucous
wash *v.* deterge, lave
washbowl *n.* lavabo, laver
washing *n.* ablution, lavage, lavation, maundy
wasps, of vespine
wasp's nest vespiary
waste *v.* fribble, macerate
wasteful *adj.* improvident, prodigal
waste matter dejecta, dejection, dockage, excreta, rejectamenta
wasting *n.* cachexia, marasmus, tabescence
watch, keep vigilate
watchdog *n.* hellhound
watchful *adj.* Argus-eyed, circumspect, wary
watchfulness *n.* weather eye
watchword *n.* countersign, shibboleth
water, search for dowse (*v.*), water-witch (*v.*)
water, stagnant pokelogan
water carrier bheesty
waterfall *n.* cascade, cataract, sault
water hole charco
water jar hydria, kalpius
water on the brain hydrocephalus
water pipe hookah, narghile
water sprite ondine, undine
waterwheel *n.* noria
watery *adj.* serous, sodden
wattle *n.* caruncle
wavy *adj.* repand, undulate, undulating, undulatory
wavy-haired *adj.* cymotrichous
wax *n.* cerumen, cutin, klister
waxed *adj.* cerated
wax-trap *n.* bobèche
waxy *adj.* ceraceous
way, by the *en passant*
way, the middle via media
wayfarer *n.* viator
weaken *v.* attenuate, disempower, emasculate, enervate, etiolate,
    flag, mitigate, sap, unbrace, vitiate
weakening *n.* labefaction
weakness *n.* Achilles' heel, adynamia, asthenia, claudication, foible,
    hypodynamia, hyposthenia, impuissance
wealth *n.* chattels, mammon, pelf
wealthy person Croesus, Dives, Midas, nabob, nawab

wean *v.* ablactate
weaponry *n.* matériel, ordnance
weariness *n.* languor, lassitude
wearing away detrition
wearisome *adj.* operose
weary *v.* enervate, fag, jade, sap
weather vane weathercock, wind tee, wind vane
webbing *n.* macramé
web-making *adj.* retiary
wedding *n.* confarreation
wedge-shaped *adj.* cuneate, cuneiform, sphenoid
weekly *adj.* hebdomadal
weep *v.* snivel, snuffle
weepy *adj.* lachrymose
weighty *adj.* magisterial
weird *adj.* eldritch, preternatural
welcome *v.* espouse
welcome *adj.* opportune, propitious
welcoming address salutatory
well *n.* cenote
well *adj.* asymptomatic
well-being *n.* eudemonia, weal
well-deserved *adj.* condign
well-groomed *adj.* soigné
well-informed *adj.* au courant
well-wisher *n.* congratulant
werewolf *n.* lycanthrope
wet nurse amah
whale *n.* cachalot, cetacean
whalebone *n.* baleen
whales, of cetacean, cetaceous
wheat field trigo
wheel *n.* roulette, rundle
wheel-shaped *adj.* rotate, rotiform
wheeze *n.* rhonchus
whimper *v.* pule
whimsical *adj.* baroque, capricious, fey
whining *adj.* puling, querulous, sniveling
whip *n.* chabouk, flail, knout, kurbash, pizzle, quirt, scorpion, scourge, sjambok
whirling *adj.* gyral, gyratory, vertiginous, vortical, vorticose, vortiginous
whirlpool *n.* Charybdis, gurge, maelstrom
whirlwind *n.* tourbillion
whiskers *n.* burnsides, dundrearies, muttonchops, vibrissae

whiskey *n.* poteen, spiritus frumenti, usquebaugh
whisper *n.* sussuration, sussurrus
whispering *adj.* susurrant
white *adj.* alabastrine, hoary
white-hot *adj.* candent, candescent
whiten *v.* blanch, etiolate
whitening *adj.* albescent
whitewash *v.* extenuate, palliate
whitish *adj.* albescent
whole *adj.* integral
wholesale *adv.* en bloc
wholesome *adj.* salubrious, salutary, salutiferous
whooping cough pertussis
whorish *adj.* meretricious
wickedness *n.* dissoluteness, execrableness, flagitiousness, improbity, iniquity, profligacy, turpidity
wicked place Bablyon, Gomorrah, Sodom
wide-eyed *adj.* moon-eyed
widened *adj.* évasé
widespread *adj.* pandemic, pervasive
widow *n.* dowager, relict, sati
widowhood *n.* viduity
wife *n.* helpmate, helpmeet
wife, ill-tempered Xanthippe
wife, submissive toward one's uxorious
wife, typical of a uxorial
wig *n.* bagwig, buzzwig, periwig, peruke, postiche
wig stand demoiselle
wild *adj.* dissolute, prodigal, profligate
wild animal wilding
wildness *n.* ferity
wile *n.* artifice, stratagem
will *v.* bequeath, devise
willful *adj.* perverse, refractory
willingly *adv.* ad libitum, fain, lief
will-o'-the-wisp *n.* friar's lantern, ignis fatuus
willpower, loss of abulia
willy-nilly *adv.* nolens volens
wimp *n.* milksop, milquetoast
wince *v.* blench, quail
wind-blown *adj.* aeolian
windfall *n.* godsend, bonanza
wind gauge anemometer
winding *n.* convolution, copping, quilling, sinuosity, whorl
windowed *adj.* fenestrated

windowpane *n.* windowlight
windpipe *n.* trachea
winds *n.* bore, chinook, flaw, foehn, gale, ghibli, grégal, gregale, gregau, harmattan, khamsin, kona, levanter, libeccio, mistral, pampero, puna, scirocco, simoom, simoon, sirocco, tramontana, williwaw
wine, pertaining to vinaceous, vineal, vinic, vinous
wine bag bota
wine bottle balthazar, jereboam, magnum, methuselah, nebuchadnezzar, rehoboam, salmanazar
wine connoisseur oenophile
wine cooler psykter
wineglass *n.* roemer
winemaker *n. vigneron*, vintner
winemaking *n.* viniculture, vinification, vintage
wine steward sommelier
wing *n.* airfoil, ala, alette, pennon
winged *adj.* alate, pennate
wingless *adj.* apterous
winglike *adj.* alar, aliform
wink *v.* nictitate
winning *adj.* disarming, winsome
winterly *adj.* hibernal
winter quarters hibernaculum
wintry *adj.* brumal, hibernal, hiemal
wisdom *n.* acuity, acumen, discernment, enlightenment, perspicacity, perspicuity, sagacity, sapience
wise *adj.* erudite, perspicacious, perspicuous, prescient, sagacious, sapient, sapiential
wise person hakim, magus, pandit, pundit
wish *n.* velleity
wish, expressing a volitive
wit *n.* Attic salt, badinage, coruscation, raillery, repartee
witch *n.* enchantress, hex, pythoness, sibyl, siren, sorceress
witchcraft *n.* diablerie, diabolism, pishogue
witch doctor *n.* conjure man, conjurer
witches, assembly of coven, sabbat
withdrawal *n.* decathexis, exodus, extraction, recession, subduction
withdrawn *adj.* aloof, introverted
withdraw savings dissave
withered *adj.* sapless, sere, wizen, wizened
withhold *v.* forbear, scant
without *prep.* sans
without preamble in medias res
witticism *n.* bon mot, epigram, mot

witticisms *n.* facetiae
witty *adj.* epigrammatic, piquant, salty, scintillating
wizard *n.* conjurer, necromancer, thaumaturge
wobble *v.* vacillate
woe *n.* tribulation
wolf, resembling a lupine
wolf-hunter *n.* wolver
wolfish *adj.* rapacious
woman-hater *n.* misogynist
wonder *n.* veneration
wonderful *adj.* prodigious, wondrous
wonderful to relate *mirabile dictu*
wood *n.* coppice, copse, thicket
wood, boring into xylotomous
wood, feeding on xylophagous
wood, living on xylophilous
wood, made of treen
wood-eating *adj.* dendrophagous, lignivorous, xylophagous
wooded *adj.* arboreous, bosky, sylvan, sylvatic
wooden *adj.* impassive, inexpressive, stolid
woodlands, growing in silvicolous
woodlike *adj.* ligniform
woodpile *n.* rick
woods, inhabiting the silvicolous, sylvan, sylvatic
woodsman *n.* voyageur
woodworking *n.* joinery
woody *adj.* ligneous, suffrutescent
wool-bearing *adj.* laniferous
wool fibers gare
woolly *adj.* lanate, lanose
word, alteration of a Hobson-Jobson, spoonerism
word, the last dernier cri
word blindness alexia, dyslexia
word formation, of rhematic
word lover logophile
word reading the same backward and forward, a palindrome
word-related *adj.* lexical
words abraxas, dysphemism, etymon, gayatri, ghost word, heteronym, holophrase, homograph, homophone, inkhorn term, jussive, mantra, metonym, neologism, neology, neoterism, nonce word, *palabra*, portmanteau word, sesquipedalian, vocable, vox barbara
words, debate over logomachy
words, expert user of wordsmith
words, misuse of catachresis, malapropism

words, study of lexicology
words, war of fliting
word to the wise is sufficient, a verbum sap
wordy *adj.* bombastic, circumlocutory, discursive, effusive, fustian, inflated, loquacious, maundering, mouthy, pleonastic, prolegomenous, prolix, turgid, voluble
work *n.* chef d'oeuvre, magnum opus, oeuvre, opus, opuscule, opusculum
work *v.* grub, elucubrate, lucubrate, moil
work, additional parergon
work, body of corpus
workable *adj.* practicable, viable
worker *n.* artisan, wright
worker, servile drudge, jackal
workers, unskilled lumpenproletariat
working together synergetic
workmanlike *adj.* yeoman
workshop *n.* atelier
work stoppage hartal
world in miniature microcosm
worldly *adj.* blasé, cosmopolitan, urbane
worldwide *adj.* ecumenical
worm *n.* annelid, helminth, trichna
worm-eaten *adj.* vermiculate
wormlike *adj.* helminthoid, vermian, vermicular, vermiculate, vermiform
worms, substance that expels anthelmintic, vermifuge
worms, substance that kills vermicide
worn *adj.* abraded, attrite, attrited
worn down detrited
worn-out *adj.* effete, enervated
worried *adj.* distraught, hagridden
worry *n.* apprehension, disquiet, presentiment, solicitude
worse, so much the *tant pis*
worsen *v.* exacerbate, retrogress
worsening *adj.* ingravescent
worship *v.* adulate, venerate
worship, house of tabernacle
worshiper *n.* congregant, votary
worthless *adj.* brummagem, drossy, fustian, nugatory
worthless, act of estimating as floccinaucinihilipilication
worthy *adj.* estimable, exemplary
wound *v.* lacerate, mortify, pike, transfix
woven fabric weft
wrap *v.* swaddle, swathe

wreath *n.* chaplet
wreck *v.* wrack
wreckage *n.* flotsam, wrack
wrench *v.* wrest, wrick
wrestling, pertaining to palestrian
wretched *adj.* calamitous, hapless, scurvy, whoreson, woebegone, woeful
wring *v.* wrest
wrinkled *adj.* rugate, rugged, rugose
write *v.* expatiate, indite, lucubrate, prose
writhe *v.* welter
writing *n.* glyph, hieroglyph, lipogram, pictogram, pictograph, uncial
writing, unit of grapheme
writing desk escritoire, scrutoire
writing material, erased palimpsest
writing systems, study of grammatology
writing tablet diptych, triptych
writings of doubtful authenticity apocrypha, pseudepigrapha
written on one side of a page anopisthographic
wrong *adj.* agley, awry
wrongdoer *n.* malefactor, miscreant, transgressor

Y

yachtsman *n.* Corinthian
yap *v.* kyoodle
yarn *n.* cordonnet, crewel, hank, poil, skein
yawning *n.* oscitation
yaws *n.* frambesia
yearn *v.* hanker, pine
year of travel *Wanderjahr*
yellow *adj.* vitelline, xanthous
yellowish *adj.* flavescent, flaxen, stramineous, xanthic
yielding *adj.* cringing, obsequious, submissive
yoke *n.* clevis
yokel *n.* hayseed, rustic, yahoo

yolk *n.* vitellus
young *adj.* juvenescent
young, animal whelp, yeanling, youngster
young again, becoming rejuvenescent (*adj.*)
young man ephebe, ephebus
you're one too! *tu quoque*
youth *n.* minority, viridity
youth, gilded *jeunesse dorée*
youthful *adj.* vernal, yeasty, youngblood, youngling
youthful inexperience, a time of salad days
youthfulness *n.* juvenescence

Z

zeal *n.* ardor, fervor
zealous *adj.* fervid
zero *n.* aught, cipher, naught, null
zest *n.* brio, gusto, panache, piquancy, tang, verve
zone, small zonule
zones, marked with zonate

The
HIGHLY SELECTIVE
DICTIONARY
for the
EXTRAORDINARILY
LITERATE

Introduction by
Richard Lederer

Illustrations by
Amy Nicole Shimm

To Norma

CONTENTS

ACKNOWLEDGMENT

Rob Amell, of HarperCollins, by his never-failing courtesy, encouragement, and cooperation, helped the editor of this dictionary accomplish his work and earned his gratitude.

PREFACE

The Highly Selective Dictionary can be thought of as an antidote to the ongoing, poisonous effects wrought by the forces of linguistic darkness—aided by permissive lexicographers who blithely acquiesce to the depredations of unrestrained language butchers.

When these permissive lexicographers perceive that journalists and other voracious consumers of Canadian wood pulp are using an existing English word in a new sense, bingo! A new definition is added to an existing dictionary entry. And—you can count on it—the addition is noticed by the lexicographic competition and is copied widely.

With what result? The functionally illiterate take this new sense as acceptable, giving them license to say, "Well, it's in the dictionary, so it's OK to use."

By contrast, *The Highly Selective Dictionary* is prescriptive, suggesting that its principal task is to define words carefully and conservatively, paying special attention to what the entry words usually mean and counseling readers not to fall for new meanings of entry words that have resulted from blunders by writers and the cooperation of permissive lexicographers.

This is not to say that new words cannot be used in writing and speaking. In fact, the English language has grown healthily over the years and is still growing at an ever-increasing rate. This is one of the reasons why English will continue to be the language of the entire world.

The Highly Selective Dictionary supplies spellings, pronunciations, and definitions for interesting words that make life rewarding for readers, writers, and public speakers. It enables users to learn the correct meanings of words they may not already know. It wastes no space on useless entries, offers a single pronunciation for most entries, and bites the bullet in pointing out confusions in the use of words.

A word must be said about the great amount of time lexicographers spend on defining common words—words whose meanings are widely known—time that could better be spent on selecting and defining entry words that readers genuinely need. While definitions supplied for common words are often admirably and ingeniously constructed, the products of this enormous effort are hundreds, if not thousands, of useless entries that do nothing for most dictionary users.

A single example of a useless entry will make clear my impatience with lexicographers. Consider the noun *door*—and who does not know what a door is? Here are the first two definitions of *door* in the great *Webster's New International Dictionary* of 1934:

1. The movable frame or barrier of boards, or other material, usually turning on hinges or pivots or sliding, by which an entrance-way into a house or apartment is closed and opened; also, a similar part of a piece of furniture, as in a cabinet or bookcase.
2. An opening in the wall of a house or of an apartment, by which to go in and out; an entranceway; a doorway.

Who does not admire the scholarship and thoroughness of the lexicographer who produced these definitions? And who does not admire the latest generation of lexicographers who go on producing such definitions to this day? But who can fail to wonder why so much effort should be expended to produce them?

Finally, who are the children, women, and men who do not know what a door is and would consult a dictionary to find out?

And would the definitions given above do them any good?

The Highly Selective Dictionary for the Extraordinarily Literate, by choosing to forgo such useless entries, facilitates the reader's search for useful entries. Gone is the clutter of never-consulted entries defining words everybody knows well. Consider, for example, the paper and ink and the countless hours of word processor time and human effort devoted to defining *a, an, and, daughter, exit, promise, sky, son, sun, trouble, unfit,* and *zoo.*

Most dictionaries produced by permissive lexicographers also are willing to countenance poor pronunciations that arise from mistakes made by ill-educated radio hosts, so-called television anchorpersons, and public figures—all of them unequipped to read aloud correctly.

One example will suffice to illustrate this problem. Consider the word *nuclear,* which is not included as an entry word in the present book because it is commonly understood. We have all heard it mistakenly pronounced as NOO-kyə-lər instead of correctly as NOO-klee-ər or NYOO-klee-ər. Yet, following the principle of permissiveness, leading dictionaries sanction the mispronunciation, thereby giving solace to the bumblers—among them every member of our "nucyular navy" and most members of the U.S. Congress—who never fail to mispronounce *nuclear.*

We may have snickered when Dwight D. Eisenhower regularly mispronounced this word, and marveled at Jimmy Carter's struggles to pronounce the word correctly. Though most speakers do not aspire to high office, they can learn to speak better than most politicians.

Unfortunately, many people regard their favorite dictionary as a linguistic bible, to be accepted unquestioningly and used—along with the *Guinness Book of World Records*—in settling barroom bets. With this awesome responsibility implicitly bestowed on lexicographers, dictionaries will in time take more courageous stands on what they will sanction and what they will not.

And they may begin to overcome those who combine daily to beat our language down to a state of complete mush. Until they do, we will continue to lose good word after good word to the forces of darkness, ultimately bowing to the dictum of Lewis Carroll's Humpty Dumpty: "When *I* use a word, it means just what I choose it to mean—neither more nor less."

Eugene Ehrlich

PRONUNCIATION NOTES

The pronunciation of American English words follows few hard-and-fast rules and varies from region to region. In pronouncing the entry words of this highly selective dictionary, the editor has considered all the pronunciations given in standard sources and then tried to select the most common pronunciations. Notwithstanding, some of the pronunciations supplied indulge the editor's own preferences.

Each pronunciation is shown in parentheses just after the entry word, and the pronunciation is followed by the part of speech of the entry word. In almost all cases, only one pronunciation is given, although one of the entry words, **joust**, is given three pronunciations. When two pronunciations are considered to be equally desirable, they are connected by *or*.

For the convenience of the reader, pronunciations of the entry words employ a respelling scheme that is readily interpretable rather than the International Phonetic Alphabet, which many people find difficult to interpret.

Fully stressed syllables are shown in capital letters. Syllables that receive secondary stress are shown in small capital letters. Unstressed syllables are shown in lower case letters, as are pronunciations of words of one syllable. Three examples will suffice:

hangnail (HANG-NAYL) *noun*
infer (in-FUR) *verb*
stick (stik) *noun*

One exception to respelling is the use of the schwa (ə), which is defined as an indistinct vowel sound, as in the second syllable of **single** (SING-gəl) or in the last two syllables of **incredible** (in-KRED-ə-bəl).

Another exception to respelling is the use of ī, ī, and Ī to indicate a long vowel sound, as in **my** (mī), **finite** (FĪ-nīt), and **diagnostic** (DĪ-əg-NOS-tik).

A few additional examples will suffice to show the ease with which the supplied pronunciations can be interpreted:

> **abstemious** (ab-STEE-mee-əs) *adjective*
> **accede** (ak-SEED) *verb*
> **adduce** (ə-DOOS) *verb*
> **adscititious** (AD-si-TISH-əs) *adjective*

Two other representations of sounds depart from straightforward respelling.

As will be seen in the chart supplied below, *n* indicates an n that is only partially pronounced, as in many words of French origin.

Again, *th* is used to make the initial sound of the word "this," which is given as *th*is, and to pronounce "rather," which is given as RA*TH*-ər. In pronouncing "thin" and "both," the sound of th is not italicized.

PRONUNCIATION KEY

a *as in* act, hat, carry

ah *as in* balm, calm, father

ahr *as in* far, jar, darling

air *as in* fairy, scare, declare

aw *as in* audit, walk, gawk, saw

ay *as in* age, bay, heinous

b *as in* bake, babble, boob

ch *as in* choose, church, preach

d *as in* dare, fuddled, mud

e *as in* empty, led, berry

ee *as in* ease, either, meat, see

eer *as in* ear, eerie, pier, sneer

f *as in* fin, daffy, belief

g *as in* gust, bargain, hog

h *as in* hairy, hot, huddle

hw *as in* where, whet, anywhere

i *as in* in, hit, women, twist

ī *as in* bite, light, pie, spy

ī *as in* colonize, synchronize

ī *as in* mighty, lightning, surprise

j *as in* gin, just, judge, garbage

k *as in* kerchief, spoken, rack

l *as in* lag, ladle, sell

m *as in* many, common, madam

n *as in* note, knee, manner, napkin

n *as in* dénouement, frisson, soupçon

ng *as in* hunger, swinging, bring

o *as in* opportune, hot, crop

oh *as in* oppose, most, toast, sew

oo *as in* oodles, pool, ruler

oor *as in* poor, tour, sure

or *as in* aural, border, mortal

ow *as in* owl, oust, house, allow

oy *as in* oil, join, boy

p *as in* print, paper, sleep

r *as in* rash, tarry, poor

s *as in* cent, scent, lessen

sh *as in* sugar, shush, cash

t *as in* talk, utter, heat

th *as in* think, wrath, loath

th as in then, bother, loathe

u *as in* ugly, mutter, come

ur *as in* urge, her, fir, saboteur

uu *as in* brook, full, woman

v *as in* very, every, brave

w *as in* well, awash, allow

y *as in* yet, abeyance, useful

z *as in* zap, gazebo, tease

zh *as in* pleasure, vision, persiflage

Note: Headwords that are considered still to be foreign terms are given in italics.

INTRODUCTION

During the early years of space exploration, NASA scientist Wernher von Braun gave many speeches on the wonders and promises of rocketry and spaceflight. After one of his luncheon talks, von Braun found himself clinking cocktail glasses with an adoring woman from the audience.

"Dr. von Braun," the woman gushed, "I just loved your speech, and I found it of absolutely infinitesimal value!"

"Well then," von Braun gulped, "I guess I'll have to publish the text posthumously."

"Oh yes!" the woman came right back. "And the sooner the better!"

Now there was someone who needed to gain greater control over her word choices. But, given the power that words confer on our lives, don't we all wish to acquire a richer vocabulary? Justice Oliver Wendell Holmes once declared, "Language is the skin of living thought." Just as your skin encloses your body, so does your vocabulary bound your mental life.

It's a matter of simple mathematics: The more words you know, the more choices you can make; the more choices you can make, the more accurate, vivid, and varied your speaking and writing will be. "All words," observed Henry Ward Beecher, "are pegs to hang ideas on." Other things being equal, the larger your stock of word pegs, the closer you will come to finding the exact word that fits precisely the thought you want to express in speech or writing.

Ever since Adam assigned names to all the animals, we human beings have managed to come up with labels for almost everything on this planet—and beyond. The more of these names you acquire (and all of the italicized words that follow repose in this book), the more concise will be your expression. Why should you wheeze through a dozen words—"the act of throwing a thing or person out of a window"—when you can capture the act in a single noun: *defenestration*? Why scrawl out "a place real or imaginary where living conditions are considered to be as bad as possible," when you can capture the concept with eight little letters: *dystopia*? Wouldn't it be convenient if our language possessed a *discrete* and *discreet* word to denote the excessive development of fat on the buttocks? It does: *steatopygia*. Doesn't your heart leap up when it beholds the *effulgent* word *lambent*, at your service to describe the soft radiance of light or flame playing on a surface?

English is the most cheerfully democratic and hospitable language in the history of humankind. English has acquired the most abundant of all word stocks—616,500 entries officially enshrined in the Oxford English Dictionary, our fattest unabridged lexicon. That's an extraordinary number, considering that German owns about 185,000, so our English language boasts almost four times the number of words as the second-place language. Then come Russian at 130,000 and French at 100,000.

While there are more English words, Horatio, than are dreamt of in your philosophy, relatively few are in actual circulation. The average English speaker possesses a vocabulary of 10,000 to 20,000 words but actively uses only a small fraction, the others being recognition or recall vocabulary. A literate adult may recognize 60,000 or more words, the most learned among us 100,000. Just as we human beings use only one-tenth of our brain power, the most articulate verbivore interacts with only one-sixth of our English word hoard and actually employs only one-sixth of that.

Sadly then, many of us miss out on the sheer euphony and sesquipedalian playfulness of thousands of English words. Simply read aloud and listen to the tintinnabulation of the more ear-rinsing entries you are about to encounter: *absquatulate, anthrophagous, bumptious, concatenation, crapulous, dipsomaniac, eleemosynary, gallimaufry, glossolalia, ineluctable, legerdemain, lubricious, nugatory, peccadillo, persiflage, pinguid, plangent, pusillanimous, redolent, soporific, ululate.*

One of the happiest features of possessing a capacious vocabulary is the opportunity to insult your enemies with impunity. While the madding crowd gets mad with exhausted epithets such as "You rotten pig" and "You dirty bum," you can *acerbate, deprecate, derogate,* and *excoriate* your *nemesis* with a battalion of laser-precise *pejoratives.* You can brand him or her a *grandiloquent popinjay, venal pettifogger, nefarious miscreant, flagitious recidivist, sententious blatherskite, mawk-ish ditherer, arrant peculator, irascible misanthrope, hubristic narcissist, feckless sycophant, vituperative virago, vapid yahoo, eructative panjan-drum, saturnine misanthrope, antediluvian troglodyte, maudlin poet-aster, splenetic termagant, pernicious quidnunc, rancorous anchorite, perfidious mountebank,* or *irascible curmudgeon.*

When you were a child learning to speak, you seized each new word as if it were a shiny toy. This is how you learned your language, and this is how you can expand your vocabulary. As you keep com-pany and build friendships with the words in *The Highly Selective Dic-tionary,* start using them in conversation. Encourage your children to be *beneficent* and *empathic* in their relationships. Explain to Tabby that she shouldn't be so *obdurate* about trying the latest feline cuisine. Remind yourself what an *exemplary nonpareil, indefatigable autodi-dact,* and *benignant thaumaturge* you are for expanding your word hoard so *perspicaciously.* Make vocabulary growth a lifelong pursuit. In the process, you will expand your thoughts and your feelings, your speaking, your reading, and your writing—everything that makes up you.

RICHARD LEDERER,
author of *Fractured English*

THE
HIGHLY SELECTIVE
DICTIONARY
FOR THE
EXTRAORDINARILY
LITERATE

A

abecedarian (AY-bee-see-DAIR-ee-ən) *noun*

    1. a beginner in any field of learning.

    2. a person who is learning the letters of the alphabet.

abjure (ab-JUUR) *verb*

    1. repudiate, profess to abandon.

    2. renounce under oath or with great solemnity.

> Some speakers and writers confuse the verbs **abjure** and **adjure**. While such confusion can readily be seen to stem from the close similarity of the spellings of the two words, it may also be related to the fact that both words are relatively uncommon. Notwithstanding, careful writers and speakers use the words correctly: **abjure** means *repudiate, renounce,* and **adjure** means *request earnestly* and *charge or command under oath or threat of penalty.* Two examples of their proper use may help: (1) "My attorney advised me to **abjure** any further action that could be construed as harassment of my ex-wife." (2) "The judge testily **adjured** the witness to speak before the jury only in response to questions put to her by the attorneys." Clear enough?

> Related words: **abjuration** (AB-jə-RAY-shən) and **abjurer** (ab-JUUR-ər) *both nouns,* **abjuratory** (ab-JUUR-ə-TOR-ee) *adjective.*

abnegate (AB-ni-gayt) *verb*

    renounce, relinquish, surrender, or deny oneself (a convenience, a right, etc.).

> Related words: **abnegation** (AB-ni-GAY-shən) and **self-abnegation**, meaning self-denial, *both nouns.*

abominate (ə-BOM-ə-NAYT) *verb*
1. abhor; regard with loathing.
2. dislike strongly.

> Related words: **abomination** (ə-BOM-i-NAY-shən) *noun*, **abominable** (ə-BOM-ə-nə-bəl) *adjective*, **abominably** *adverb*.

abortive (ə-BOR-tiv) *adjective*
unsuccessful, fruitless.

> Related words: **abortively** *adverb*, **abortiveness** *noun*.

absquatulate (ab-SKWOCH-ə-layt) *verb*
1. flee; make off.
2. abscond.

> Related words: **absquatulater** (ab-SKWOCH-ə-LAY-tər) and **absquatulation** (ab-SKWOCH-ə-LAY-shən) *nouns*.

abstemious (ab-STEE-mee-əs) *adjective*
moderate, sparing, not self-indulgent in food and drink.

> Related words: **abstemiously** *adverb*, **abstemiousness** *noun*.

accede (ak-SEED) *verb*
1. agree, give assent, conform.
2. enter upon an office.

> Related words: **accedence** and **acceder** *both nouns*.

accouter (ə-KOO-tər) *verb*
attire, equip, outfit; generally seen as **accoutered**, its past participle.

> Related word: **accouterment** (ə-KOO-tər-mənt) *noun*.

accumbent (ə-KUM-bənt) *adjective*
reclining, recumbent.

> Related word: **accumbency** *noun*.

acerbity (ə-SUR-bi-tee) *noun*
sharpness of speech or manner.

> Related words: **acerb** (ə-SURB) and **acerbic** *both adjectives*, **acerbate** (AS-ər-BAYT) *verb*.

Achates (ə-KAY-teez) *noun*
a faithful companion, bosom friend; in the *Aeneid*, Achates was the faithful companion of Aeneas.

Acheron (AK-ə-ron) *noun*

the river in Hades over which Charon (KAIR-ən) ferried the souls of the dead, thus hell—called the infernal regions—itself.

adduce (ə-DOOS) *verb*

allege or cite as evidence or proof in argument.

Related words: **adduceable** and **adducible** *adjectives*, **adducer** *noun*.

adjure (ə-JUUR) *verb*

See **abjure**.

Adonis (ə-DON-is) *noun*

1. a handsome young man.
2. in classical mythology, a beautiful youth beloved by Aphrodite and killed by a boar while hunting.

adoptive (ə-DOP-tiv) *adjective*

acquired or related through adoption.

Some speakers and writers use **adopted** as a synonym for **adoptive**, thus producing incongruous phrases such as "My adopted parents," implying that *I adopted my parents*. It is preferable to use the phrase "My adoptive parents," which makes it clear that *my natural parents had given me up for adoption*.

Related word: **adoptively** *adverb*.

adscititious (AD-si-TISH-əs) *adjective*

1. supplemental, additional.
2. derived or added from an external source.

Related word: **adscititiously** *adverb*.

adumbrate (a-DUM-brayt) *verb*

1. foreshadow, prefigure.
2. overshadow.
3. shade, obscure.

Related words: **adumbrative** (a-DUM-brə-tiv) *adjective*, **adumbratively** *adverb*.

adverse (ad-VURS *or* AD-vurs) *adjective*

1. antagonistic in effect or purpose; hostile.
2. opposite, opposing, unfavorable.

Many speakers and writers confuse the adjectives **adverse** and **averse**. **Averse** means *feeling disinclined or opposed*, as in "I soon found she was **averse** to my every suggestion, and I knew I would soon be looking for a new job." Thus, resolve to be **averse** to the mistake of shielding young children from every **adverse** experience they may possibly encounter.

Related words: **adversely** (ad-VURS-lee) *adverb*, **adversity** (ad-VUR-si-tee) and **adverseness** (ad-VURS-nis) *both nouns.*

advert (ad-VURT) *verb*
1. refer to in speech or writing.
2. comment.

aegis (EE-jis) *noun*
sponsorship or protection.

affect (AF-ekt) *noun*
in psychiatry, an observed or expressed emotional response.

This noun, which has made its way into the general vocabulary of many educated people, is included here for two reasons. By far the more important reason is that the noun **affect**, when seen in print, may confuse some readers, who are familiar primarily with the verb **affect**, which is pronounced ə-FEKT and has such meanings as *produce an effect in, impress the mind, touch or move*, and *pretend or assume artificially*. In addition, the verbs **affect** and **effect**—the latter word is primarily used as a noun—are often confused by careless speakers and writers. If you doubt that any published writers fall victim to this confusion, consider that many current books, as well as a great number of today's newspapers, go to press with little, if any, editing. So you must take special care to use **affect** and **effect** correctly in your writing.

affinity (ə-FIN-i-tee) *noun, plural* **affinities**
1. a resemblance, connection, inherent agreement.
2. a natural or instinctive mutual attraction.

afflatus (ə-FLAY-təs) *noun*
1. inspiration.
2. divine impulse.

agape (AH-gah-pay) *noun, plural* **agapae** or **agapai** both pronounced AH-gah-pī
brotherly, unselfish love (contrasted with erotic love).

agent provocateur (AY-jənt prə-VOK-ə-TUR), *plural* **agents provoca-teurs** (AY-jənts prə-VOK-ə-TUR)

  an agent hired to detect suspected persons by inciting them to commit self-incriminating acts.

aggravate (AG-rə-VAYT) *verb*

  increase the gravity of (an offense, illness, problem, and the like); worsen.

  Many speakers and writers use **aggravate** to mean *annoy* or *irritate*, as in "The child's incessant questioning aggravated his grandmother" and in "Don't aggravate me." They also use **aggravation** to mean *annoyance*, as in "I've had all the aggravation I can take." So prevalent have these two meanings become that most dictionaries now show them as acceptable, but usually mark these usages as colloquial. The signal for good writers is clear: If you wish to speak and write well, stay away from **aggravate** meaning *irritate* and **aggravation** meaning *annoyance*. Reserve **aggravate** for *worsen*, **aggravation** for *worsening*.

  Related words: **aggravative** (AG-rə-VAY-tiv) *adjective*, **aggravator** *noun*.

agrestic (ə-GRES-tik) *adjective*

  1. unpolished, awkward, uncouth.
  2. rustic, rural.

aide-mémoire (AYD-mem-WAHR) *noun*, *plural* **aides-mémoire** (AYDZ-mem-WAHR)

  a document, usually a memorandum, written as an aid to the memory, especially in diplomacy.

akimbo (ə-KIM-boh) *adverb*

  of the arms, with hands on hips and elbows bent outward.

aleatory (AY-lee-ə-TOR-ee) *adjective*

  1. depending on luck or chance.
  2. especially in law, dependent on uncertain contingencies.
  3. done at random, unpredictable.

  Related word: **aleatoric** (AY-lee-ə-TOR-ik) *adjective*.

allocution (AL-ə-KYOO-shən) *noun*

  a formal address, especially one that is hortatory in nature.

allude (ə-LOOD) *verb*
 refer indirectly, covertly, or casually (to something assumed to be known).

 So many speakers and writers use **allude** when they should use **refer,** which means *direct attention to by naming,* that **allude** is on the list of endangered words. For anyone who wishes to use the language carefully, **allude** for **refer** is a no-no. Example: "She **alluded** to her husband's obesity by loudly asking all the physicians at dinner whether they thought overeating was really bad for one's health." "'If you intend to **refer** to your husband's proclivities,' replied the host, 'I think you ought to pay for a consultation.'" Why abandon a word that has a useful, distinctive meaning? (See also **refer.**)

 Related words: **allusion** (ə-LOO-zhən) *noun,* **allusive** (ə-LOO-siv) *adjective,* **allusively** *adverb.*

alopecia (AL-ə-PEE-shə) *noun*
 baldness, whether partial or complete.

ambagious (am-BAY-jəs) *adjective*
 1. circumlocutory, circuitous, roundabout.
 2. tortuous.

 Related words: **ambagiously** *adverb,* **ambagiousness** *noun.*

ambiguous (am-BIG-yoo-əs) *adjective*
 1. open to various interpretations.
 2. obscure, indistinct.

 Do not confuse **ambiguous** and **ambiguity** with **ambivalent** and **ambivalence,** which see.

 Related words: **ambiguously** *adverb,* **ambiguousness** and **ambiguity** (AM-bi-GYOO-i-tee) *both nouns.*

ambit (AM-bit) *noun*
 1. a sphere of operation or influence.
 2. precincts, bounds, scope, extent.

ambivalence (am-BIV-ə-ləns) *noun,* also given as **ambivalency**
 1. uncertainty, especially when caused by inability to make up one's mind.
 2. coexistence within a person of contrary tendencies or feelings.

There is a difference in the uses of **ambivalence** and **ambiguity** and the uses of their adjectival forms that is worth pointing out. **Ambivalent** is generally used to characterize the state of one's mind, while **ambiguous** is used to characterize something external to the mind. One may say, then, that people may often be **ambivalent**, but their writings should never be **ambiguous**. Again, the wording of a letter may be intentionally or unintentionally **ambiguous**, but the recipient of the letter may feel **ambivalent** toward its contents regardless of whether the letter is **ambiguous** or entirely clear, that is, **unambiguous**.

Related words: **ambivalent** *adjective*, **ambivalently** *adverb*.

amoretto (AM-ə-RET-oh) *noun, plural* **amoretti** (AM-ə-RET-ee)
a little cupid.

amphibology (AM-fə-BOL-ə-jee) and **amphiboly** (am-FIB-ə-lee) *both nouns, plurals* **amphibologies** and **amphibolies**
ambiguous speech or wording, quibble.

amphigory (AM-fi-GOR-ee) *noun, plural* **amphigories**
a nonsensical piece of verse or other writing, especially one intended as a parody.

Related word: **amphigoric** (AM-fə-GOR-ik) *adjective*.

amphora (AM-fər-ə) *noun, plural* **amphorae** (AM-fə-ree) and **amphoras**
in antiquity a two-handled Greek or Roman storage jar for oil, wine, and the like.

Related word: **amphoral** *adjective*.

anabasis (ə-NAB-ə-sis) *noun, plural* **anabases** (ə-NAB-ə-SEEZ)
a military advance, especially that of Cyrus the Younger into Asia in 401 B.C. against the forces of Artaxerxes II, as narrated by Xenophon.

anadromous (ə-NAD-rə-məs) *adjective*
of fish, migrating up rivers from the sea to spawn in fresh water.

analects (AN-əl-EKTS) and **analecta** (AN-ə-LEK-tə) *both plural nouns*
collections of literary fragments or extracts.

analogy (ə-NAL-ə-jee) *noun, plural* **analogies** (ə-NAL-ə-jeez)
a similarity between like features of two unlike things, enabling a comparison to be drawn.

Many speakers and writers, apparently perceiving **analogy** as somehow a more attractive word than **comparison**, have taken to using **analogy** as a direct synonym for **comparison**, thus thrusting **analogy** onto the precipitous path to extinction as a useful word with its own meaning. Properly, a **comparison**, not an **analogy**, is drawn between like things or persons, for example, a **comparison** of the paintings of Renoir and Degas, the baseball achievements of Roger Maris and Mickey Mantle. One may, however, draw an **analogy** between the careers of a failed artist and an unsuccessful football player, since their careers are intrinsically different.

Related words: **analogize** (ə-NAL-ə-JĪZ) *verb*; **analog** (AN-ə-LOG), **analogue**, **analogism** (ə-NAL-ə-JIZ-əm), **analogist** (ə-NAL-ə-jist), and **analogousness** (ə-NAL-ə-gəs-nis) *all nouns*; **analogous** *adjective*, **analogously** *adverb*.

Ananias (AN-ə-NĪ-əs) *noun*
1. a habitual liar.
2. in the New Testament the man who "with Sapphira his wife, sold a possession and kept back part of the price" (that is, did not give all of the proceeds to the community's common fund) and was struck dead for this act.

anaphrodisiac (an-AF-rə-DEE-zee-AK) *noun*
a drug that reduces sexual desire.

Related words: **anaphrodisia** (an-AF-rə-DEE-zhə) *noun*, **anaphrodisiac** (an-AF-rə-DEE-zee-AK) *adjective*.

anchorite (ANG-kə-RĪT) *noun*
a hermit or recluse, especially a person who has retired to a solitary place for a life of religious seclusion.

ancilla (an-SIL-ə) *noun*, *plural* **ancillas**
an accessory or adjunct.

ancillary (AN-sə-LER-ee) *adjective*
1. subsidiary, subordinate, subservient.
2. *(noun)* an ancilla.
3. something that serves in an ancillary capacity.

androgynous (an-DROJ-ə-nəs) *adjective*
1. hermaphroditic.

2. exhibiting both masculine and feminine characteristics.

3. neither clearly masculine nor clearly feminine.

Related word: **androgyny** (an-DROJ-ə-nee) *noun*.

anile (AN-īl) *adjective*

1. like a doddering, foolish old woman.

2. imbecilic.

Related word: **anility** (ə-NIL-i-tee) *noun*.

animadversion (AN-ə-mad-VUR-zhən) *noun*

1. the act of criticizing or censuring.

2. blame, censure, reproof.

Related words: **animdaversional** *adjective*, **animadvert** (AN-ə-mad-VURT) *verb*.

animus (AN-ə-məs) *noun*

1. strong dislike or enmity; hostility.

2. animating spirit, purpose.

3. animosity shown in action or speech.

anomalous (ə-NOM-ə-ləs) *adjective*

1. irregular.

2. abnormal.

3. not fitting into a familiar pattern of behavior; unusual.

Related word: **anomaly** (ə-NOM-ə-lee) and **anomalousness** *both nouns*.

anorexia nervosa (AN-ə-REK-see-ə nur-VOH-sə)

a symptom of emotional disturbance characterized by pathological fear of becoming fat and leading to excessive dieting.

See **bulimia**.

anserine (AN-sə-RĪN) *adjective*, also given as **anserous** (AN-sə-rəs)

1. gooselike.

2. silly, foolish; stupid.

antediluvian (AN-tee-di-LOO-vee-ən) *adjective*

old-fashioned, utterly out of date; belonging to the period before the Flood.

antepenultimate (AN-tee-pi-NUL-tə-mit) *adjective*

last but two; third from the end, especially said of a syllable.

Related word: **antepenult** (AN-tee-PEE-nult) *noun*.

anteprandial (AN-tee-PRAN-dee-əl) *adjective,* also given as **preprandial** (pree-PRAN-dee-əl)

before a meal.

anthropomorphism (AN-thrə-pə-MOR-fiz-əm) *noun*

an attribution of human form or personality to God, an animal, etc.

Related words: **anthropomorphic** *adjective,* **anthropomorphize** *verb,* **anthropomorphosis** (AN-thrə-pə-MOR-fə-sis) *noun.*

anthropophagy (AN-thrə-POF-ə-jee) *noun*

the eating of human flesh; cannibalism.

Related words: **anthropophagite** (AN-thrə-POF-ə-jīт) *noun;* **anthropophagic** (AN-thrə-pə-FAJ-ik), **anthropophagical**, and **anthropophagous** (AN-thrə-POF-ə-gəs) *all adjectives;* **anthropophagously** *adverb.*

antipathy (an-TIP-ə-thee) *noun, plural* **antipathies**

a natural or habitual aversion.

Related words: **antipathetic** (AN-ti-pə-THET-ik) *adjective,* **antipathetically** *adverb,* **antipatheticalness** and **antipathist** (an-TIP-ə-thist) *both nouns.*

antonomasia (AN-tə-nə-MAY-zhə) *noun*

1. use of an epithet or other name in place of a proper name.
2. use of a proper name out of its original application.

Related words: **antonomastic** (AN-tə-noh-MAS-tik) and **antonomastical** *both adjectives,* **antonomastically** *adverb.*

anxious (ANGK-shəs) *adjective*

troubled, uneasy in mind; greatly worried.

Many dictionaries give **eager** as one of the meanings of **anxious**, therefore implicitly advising that the two adjectives may be used interchangeably. There is, however, good reason for keeping the two words separate, thus maintaining for **anxious** exclusive rights to *troubled, uneasy in mind* etc., while giving full privileges to **eager** in the sense of *extremely desirous.* The mingling of the two words may stem from the fact that, in sentence after sentence, a narrow difference in meaning may separate them. Think about it. Are we always sure that in a construction such as "We are anxious to see the matter settled," the state of mind of the person saying this may be construed either as *eager* or as *uneasy in mind?* Well, that depends, doesn't it? Yet, when we say we are **eager**, no reader would misconstrue the thought as expressing *anxiety*. To avoid conveying the wrong impression in your own speech and writing, therefore, choose between the two words deliberately and consistently. Remember that a homeowner who is **eager** to sell the family home may be **anxious** that potential buyers will notice the unmistakable evidence of a basement that floods after every heavy rain.

Related words: **anxiety** (ang-ZĪ-i-tee) and **anxiousness** *both nouns,* **anxiously** *adverb.*

apiarist (AY-pee-ə-rist) *noun*
a beekeeper.

Related words: **apiary** (AY-pee-ER-ee) *noun,* **apiarian** (AY-pee-AIR-ee-ən) *adjective.*

aplomb (ə-PLOM) *noun*
imperturbable self-possession, assurance; poise.

Apocrypha (ə-POK-rə-fə) *plural noun*
books of the Old Testament and New Testament considered not to be of inspired authorship and therefore usually omitted from Protestant editions of the Bible.

apocrypha (ə-POK-rə-fə) *plural noun*
any writings or statements of doubtful authenticity.

apocryphal (ə-POK-rə-fəl) *adjective*
1. of doubtful authenticity.
2. spurious.

Related words: **apocryphally** *adverb,* **apocryphalness** *noun.*

apodictic (AP-ə-DIK-tik) *adjective*
incontestable because clearly established or proved to be demonstrable.

Related words: **apodictical** *adjective,* **apodictically** *adverb.*

apolaustic (AP-ə-LAWS-tik) *adjective*
wholly devoted to enjoyment, seeking enjoyment.

apologia (AP-ə-LOH-jee-ə) *noun*
a written defense by a writer of his opinions or conduct.

apologue (AP-ə-LAWG) *noun*
1. a moral fable.
2. an allegorical story.

aposiopesis (AP-ə-SĪ-ə-PEE-sis) *noun, plural* **aposiopeses** (AP-ə-SĪ-ə-PEE-seez)
in rhetoric, a sudden breaking off in speech, as if from inability or unwillingness to proceed.
Related word: **aposiopetic** *adjective* (AP-ə-SĪ-ə-PET-ik).

apostasy (ə-POS-tə-see) *noun, plural* **apostasies**
a total abandonment of one's religion, party, principles or the like.

apostate (ə-POS-tayt) *noun*
a person who abandons his religion, party, cause or the like.

apothegm (AP-ə-THEM) *noun*, also given as **apophthegm**, pronounced identically
a short, pithy, instructive statement.
Related words: **apothegmatic** (AP-ə-theg-MAT-ik) and **apothegmatical** *both adjectives*, **apothegmatically** *adverb*.

apotheosis (ə-POTH-ee-OH-sis) *noun, plural* **apotheoses** (ə-POTH-ee-OH-seez)
1. epitome, quintessence.
2. the highest development.
3. deification, the exaltation of a person to the rank of a god.
Related word: **apotheosize** (ə-POTH-ee-ə-SĪZ) *verb.*

apposite (AP-ə-zit) *adjective*
1. suitable.
2. well expressed.
3. pertinent.
Related words: **appositely** *adverb*, **appositeness** *noun.*

appraise (ə-PRAYZ) *verb*
See **apprise.**

apprise (ə-PRĪZ) *verb*
inform, notify.

Do not confuse **apprise** with **appraise**, which means *determine the worth of* or *put a price on* or with **appraisal**, which means *evaluation*. **Apprise** is properly used in such sentences as "Be sure to **apprise** your clients immediately when we decide to downgrade our **appraisal** of any stock."

aquiline (AK-wə-LĪN) *adjective*
1. of or like an eagle.
2. of a nose, curved like an eagle's beak; hooked.

Related word: **aquilinity** (AK-wə-LIN-i-tee) *noun*.

arcane (ahr-KAYN) *adjective*
1. mysterious, secret.
2. obscure, esoteric.

Related words: **arcanely** *adverb*, **arcaneness** *noun*.

archetype (AHR-ki-TĪP) *noun*
1. a prototype.
2. an original pattern from which copies are made.

Related words: **archetypal** (AHR-ki-TĪ-pəl), **archetypic** (AHR-ki-TĪP-ik), **archetypical** (AHR-ki-TIP-i-kəl) *all adjectives*; **archetypally** (AHR-ki-TĪP-ə-lee) and **archetypically** (AHR-ki-TIP-ik-lee) *both adverbs*.

argot (AHR-goh) *noun*
1. the jargon of a group or class.
2. slang.

Related word: **argotic** (ahr-GOT-ik) *adjective*.

Armageddon (AHR-mə-GED-ən) *noun*
1. any great and crucial conflict.
2. the final and completely destructive battle expected by some to be fought between nations.
3. in the New Testament, the site of the final battle that will be fought between the forces of good and evil.

armamentarium (AHR-mə-mən-TAIR-ee-əm) *noun, plural* **armamentaria** (AHR-mə-mən-TAIR-ee-ə)
the aggregate of equipment, techniques, and other resources available to physicians and others.

arrant (AR-ənt) *adjective*
1. complete, unmitigated.
2. notorious.

Related word: **arrantly** *adverb*.

asperity (ə-SPER-i-tee) *noun, plural* **asperities**
1. of a disposition or manner, harshness; sharpness.
2. difficulty, hardship.
3. unevenness or roughness of a surface.

asperse (ə-SPURS) *verb*
attack reputation of (a person) with damaging insinuations or charges.
Related words: **asperser** *noun,* **aspersive** *adjective,* **aspersively** *adverb.*

aspersion (ə-SPUR-zhən) *noun*
1. derogatory or defamatory criticism.
2. a damaging imputation.
3. the act of defamation or slandering.

asseverate (ə-SEV-ə-RAYT) *verb*
declare or assert earnestly or solemnly.

Related words: **asseveration** (ə-SEV-ə-RAY-shən) *noun,* **asseverative** (ə-SEV-ə-RAY-tiv) and **asseveratory** (ə-SEV-ə-rə-TOR-ee) *both adjectives,* **asseveratively** (ə-SEV-ə-RAY-tiv-lee) *adverb.*

assiduity (AS-i-DOO-i-tee) *noun, plural* **assiduities** (AS-i-DOO-i-teez)
1. diligence, industry.
2. the continuing application of attention.
Related words: **assiduous** (ə-SIJ-oo-əs) *adjective,* **assiduously** *adverb,* **assiduousness** *noun.*

assignation (AS-ig-NAY-shən) *noun*
1. an appointment, especially a lovers' secret rendezvous.
2. the act of assigning; an assignment.

assuage (ə-SWAYJ) *verb*
1. make less severe.
2. satisfy, appease.
3. soothe, mollify.
Related words: **assuagement** and **assuager** *both nouns.*

atavism (AT-ə-VIZ-əm) *noun*
1. reversion to an earlier type.
2. a reappearance of characteristics resembling those of one's grandparents or even more remote ancestors of one's parents.

Related words: **atavistic** (AT-ə-VIS-tik) *adjective,* **atavistically** *adverb.*

athanasia (ATH-ə-NAY-zhə) *noun,* also given as **athanasy** (ə-THAN-ə-see) immortality; deathlessness.

atrabilious (A-trə-BIL-yəs) *adjective,* also given as **atrabiliar** (A-trə-BIL-yər)
1. melancholy.
2. morbid.

Related word: **atrabiliousness** *noun.*

augur (AW-gər) *verb*
predict; portend.

Do not confuse **augur** with **auger,** a noun that means *a tool used in boring.* Perhaps a sentence will help you remember the difference: "The carpenter's discovery that all his **augers** had been stolen did not **augur** well for the day's work that lay before him."

auspicious (aw-SPISH-əs) *adjective*
1. propitious, favorable.
2. of good omen, promising success.

Do not confuse **auspicious** with **inauspicious,** which means *unfavorable, not of good omen.* Perhaps a sentence will help you use the two words correctly: "Morning sunshine was taken as an **auspicious** sign that the game would go well for the Yankees, but soon enough there came the **inauspicious** report that their star pitcher had a lame arm."

Related words: **auspiciously** *adverb,* **auspiciousness** *noun.*

autarchy (AW-tahr-kee) *noun,* also given as **autarky,** *plural* **autarchies** and **autarkies**
1. despotism; absolute sovereignty.
2. self-government.
3. a national policy of economic independence or self-sufficiency.

Related words: **autarchic** (aw-TAHR-kik) and **autarchical** (aw-TAHR-kə-kəl) *both adjectives,* **autarchically** *adverb,* **autarchist** (AW-tahr-kist) *noun.*

autochthon (aw-TOK-thən) *noun, plural* **autochthons** or **autochthones** (aw-TOK-thə-NEEZ)

an aboriginal inhabitant of a place; an earliest known inhabitant of a place.

autochthonous (aw-TOK-thə-nəs) *adjective,* also given as **autochthonal** (aw-TOK-thə-nəl) and **autochthonic** (AW-tok-THON-ik)

aboriginal, indigenous

Related words: **autochthonously** (aw-TOK-thə-nəs-lee) *adverb,* **autochthonism, autochthony,** and **autochthonousness** *all nouns.*

auto-da-fé (AW-toh-də-FAY) *noun, plural* **autos-da-fé** (AW-tohz-də-FAY)

1. the public declaration of judgment passed on persons tried in the courts of the Spanish Inquisition.
2. the execution by civil authorities of the sentences imposed by the courts of the Inquisition.

autodidact (AW-toh-DĪ-dakt) *noun*

a self-taught person, especially one who has mastered a subject without benefit of formal education.

Related words: **autodidactic** (AW-toh-dī-DAK-tik) *adjective,* **autodidactically** (AW-toh-dī-DAK-ti-klee) *adverb.*

avarice (AV-ər-is) *noun*

inordinate desire to acquire and hoard wealth.

Related words: **avaricious** (AV-ə-RISH-əs) *adjective,* **avariciously** *adverb,* **avariciousness** *noun.*

avatar (AV-ə-TAHR) *noun*

1. an embodiment, incarnation, or personification, as of a principle or view of life.
2. in Hindu mythology, the descent of a deity to earth in bodily form.

averse (ə-VURS) *adjective*

See **adverse.**

aversion (ə-VUR-zhən) *noun*

1. a strong feeling of dislike or antipathy.
2. an object or cause of strong dislike.

3. a person strongly disliked.

Related words: **aversive** (ə-VUR-siv) *adjective*, **aversively** *adverb*, **aversiveness** *noun*.

avidity (ə-VID-i-tee) *noun*

1. eagerness, dedication, enthusiasm.
2. greediness.

Related words: **avid** (AV-id) *adjective*, **avidly** *adverb*, **avidness** *noun*.

avuncular (ə-VUNG-kyə-lər) *adjective*
of or pertaining to an uncle.

Related words: **avuncularity** (ə-VUNG-kyə-LAR-ə-tee) *noun*, **avuncularly** (ə-VUNG-kyə-lər-lee) *adverb*.

B

badinage (BAD-ə-NAHZH) *noun*
banter, humorous ridicule.

bagatelle (BAG-ə-TEL) *noun*
1. a trifle, something of little value; formerly a game resembling pinball.
2. in music, a brief, unpretentious composition, usually for piano.

bagnio (BAN-yoh) *noun, plural* **bagnios**
1. a brothel.
2. in some European countries, a bath house.

baksheesh (BAK-sheesh) *noun*
in the Near East and Middle East, a tip or gratuity; alms.

baleful (BAYL-fəl) *adjective*
1. destructive, malignant.
2. full of menacing influences.

Related words: **balefully** *adverb*, **balefulness** *noun*.

banal (bə-NAL) *adjective*
devoid of freshness, commonplace, trite.

Related words: **banality** (bə-NAL-i-tee) *noun*, **banally** (bə-NAL-ee) *adverb*.

baneful (BAYN-fəl) *adjective*
poisonous, deadly; pernicious.

Related words: **banefully** *adverb*, **banefulness** *noun*.

barbarism (BAHR-bə-RIZ-əm) *noun*

    1. a word or phrase not in accordance with normal standards; the use of such a word.

    2. an uncivilized state or condition.

    3. an instance of this.

    4. a barbarous act.

barratry (BAR-ə-tree) *noun*

    1. in law, the offense of frequently stirring up lawsuits and quarrels.

    2. in maritime law, fraud or gross criminal negligence by a captain or crew at the expense of a shipowner or of the owner of a ship's cargo.

    Related words: **barratrous** (BAR-ə-trəs) *adjective*, **barratrously** *adverb*.

basilisk (BAS-ə-lisk) *noun*

    1. in mythology, a reptile with lethal breath or look.

    2. a small tropical American lizard.

    Related words: **basiliscine** (BAS-ə-LIS-in) and **basiliscan** (BAS-ə-LIS-kən) *both adjectives*.

bastille (ba-STEEL) *noun*

    1. a fortress or prison, especially one that mistreats its convicts.

    2. a fortified tower, as of a castle.

bastinado (BAS-tə-NAH-doh) *noun, plural* **bastinadoes**

    punishment or torture by beating on the soles of the feet.

bathos (BAY-thos) *noun*

    1. in speech or writing, a ludicrous descent from the sublime to the commonplace; an anticlimax.

    2. sentimentality, mawkishness.

    Related word: **bathetic** (bə-THET-ik) *adjective*.

bawd (bawd) *noun*

    1. a procuress.

    2. a prostitute.

beau monde (boh mawnd)

    fashionable society.

behest (bi-HEST) *noun*
1. a command.
2. a strongly worded request.

belfry (BEL-free) *noun, plural* **belfries**
a bell tower, attached to a church or other structure or standing alone.

belvedere (BEL-vi-DEER) *noun*
a building designed to afford a fine view.

bemuse (bi-MYOOZ) *verb*
bewilder or befuddle (someone); stupefy.
Related word: **bemusement** *noun.*

beneficent (bə-NEF-ə-sənt) *adjective*
1. doing good, showing kindness.
2. charitable.
Related words: **beneficently** *adverb,* **beneficence** *noun.*

benighted (bi-NĪ-tid) *adjective*
unenlightened, ignorant.
Related words: **benightedly** *adverb,* **benightedness** *noun.*

benignant (bi-NIG-nənt) *adjective*
1. kind, especially to subordinates or inferiors.
2. beneficial, salutary.
Related words: **benignancy** *noun,* **benignantly** *adverb.*

besom (BEE-zəm) *noun*
a broom, especially one made of twigs or brush.

besot (bi-SOT) *verb*
1. stupefy or intoxicate, usually with drink.
2. obsess, infatuate.

bête noire (BAYT NWAHR), *plural* **bêtes noires** (BAYT NWAHRZ)
a person or thing strongly disliked or dreaded; a bane.

betide (bi-TĪD) *verb*
1. happen to (someone); befall.
2. come to pass; happen.

bhang (bang) *noun*
a narcotic and intoxicant prepared from the leaves of the Indian
hemp plant.

bibelot (BIB-loh) *noun, plural* **bibelots** (BIB-lohz)
a small curio or artistic trinket.

bibulous (BIB-yə-ləs) *adjective*
addicted to *or* fond of drink.

Related words: **bibulously** *adverb*, **bibulousness** and **bibulosity** (BIB-yə-LOS-i-tee) *both nouns*.

bifurcate (BĪ-fər-KAYT) *verb*
fork, divide into two branches.

Related words: **bifurcate** (BĪ-fər-kit) *adjective*, **bifurcately** (BĪ-fər-KAYT-lee) *adverb*, **bifurcation** (BĪ-fər-KAY-shən) *noun*.

billingsgate (BIL-ingz-GAYT) *noun*
coarsely abusive language.

biota (bī-OH-tə) *noun*
the plant and animal life of a region.

blandish (BLAN-dish) *verb*
coax or influence by gentle flattery; cajole.

Related words: **blandisher** and **blandishment** *both nouns*, **blandishingly** *adverb*.

blatant (BLAYT-ənt) *adjective*
1. brazenly obvious; flagrant.
2. obtrusive, tastelessly conspicuous.

Related words: **blatantly** *adjective*, **blatancy** *noun*.

blather (BLATH-ər) *noun*
foolish loquacious talk.

Related words: **blather** *verb*, **blatherer** *noun*.

blatherskite (BLATH-ər-SKĪT) *noun*
1. a person given to blathering.
2. blather; nonsense.

blench (blench) *verb*
1. draw back or flinch from; quail.
2. turn pale.

Related words: **blencher** *noun*, **blenchingly** *adverb*.

blithe (blīth) *adjective*
1. merry, joyous, cheerful.
2. carefree, heedless; without thought or regard.

Related words: **blitheful** *adjective*, **blithefully** and **blithely** *both adverbs*, **blitheness** *noun*.

blithesome (BLĪTH-səm) *adjective*
cheery.

Related words: **blithesomely** *adverb*, **blithesomeness** *noun*.

bloc (blok) *noun*
a group of persons, legislators, nations etc. united for a purpose.

Do not confuse **bloc** with **block**, which has many meanings, but not that of **bloc**.

bolus (BOH-ləs) *noun, plural* **boluses**
1. a large medicinal pill.
2. a roundish mass, especially a mass of chewed food.

boniface (BON-ə-FAYS) *noun*
an innkeeper or hotelkeeper.

bootless (BOOT-lis) *adjective*
1. unavailing, useless.
2. without result or gain.

Related words: **bootlessly** *adverb*, **bootlessness** *noun*.

boscage (BOS-kij) *noun*, also given as **boskage**
1. a mass of trees or shrubs.
2. sylvan scenery.

bosomy (BUUZ-ə-mee) *adjective*
of a woman, having a prominent bosom.

bourse (boors) *noun*
a stock exchange, especially one located in France and certain other European countries.

bowdlerize (BOHD-lə-RĪZ) *verb*
remove passages considered objectionable or vulgar from (a book etc.); expurgate.

Related words: **bowdlerism** (BOHD-lər-iz-əm), **bowdlerization** (BOHD-lər-i-ZAY-shən), and **bowdlerizer** (BOHD-lər-ĪZ-ər) *all nouns*.

brachylogy (brə-KIL-ə-jee) *noun, plural* **brachylogies**
1. conciseness or overconciseness of expression.
2. a concise or succinct expression.

braggadocio (BRAG-ə-DOH-shee-oh) *noun, plural* **braggadocios**
1. bragging, empty boasting.
2. a braggart, a boasting person.

Related word: **braggadocian** (BRAG-ə-DOH-shee-ən) *adjective*.

bravura (brə-VYUUR-ə) *noun, plural* **bravuras**
1. a brilliant performance.
2. a display of daring, especially in music.
3. a florid passage or piece requiring great skill to perform.

Related word: **bravura** *adjective*.

brigand (BRIG-ənd) *noun*
1. a member of a band of robbers living in forest or mountain regions.
2. a bandit.

Related words: **brigandage** (BRIG-ən-dij) *noun*, **brigandish** *adjective*, **brigandishly** *adverb*.

broach (brohch) *verb*
1. mention or suggest (a topic) for the first time.
2. begin drawing (beer, whiskey, etc.) as by tapping a keg or cask.

Related word: **broacher** *noun*.

bromide (BROH-mīd) *noun*
1. a platitude or trite remark.
2. a person who is unfailingly boring.

Related word: **bromidic** (broh-MID-ik) *adjective*.

brummagem (BRUM-ə-jəm) *adjective*
1. cheap and showy but inferior and worthless.
2. *(noun)* a showy but inferior thing.

brusque (brusk) *adjective*
1. blunt, offhand.
2. abrupt in manner.

Related words: **brusquely** *adverb*, **brusqueness** *noun*.

buccal (BUK-əl) *adjective*
of or pertaining to the cheek; of or in the mouth.

Related word: **buccally** *adverb*.

bucolic (byoo-KOL-ik) *adjective*, also given as **bucolical**
1. rustic, rural.
2. of or pertaining to shepherds, pastoral.

Related word: **bucolically** *adverb*.

bugaboo (BUG-ə-BOO) and **bugbear** (BUG-BAIR) *both nouns*
1. something that causes baseless fear or worry.
2. a false belief used to intimidate or dissuade.

bulimia (byoo-LIM-ee-ə) *noun*
an unnaturally persistent hunger or voracious appetite.

See **anorexia nervosa**.

Related word: **bulimic** (byoo-LIM-ik) *adjective*.

bulwark (BUUL-wərk) *noun*
1. a wall of earth or other material built for defense, rampart, fortification.
2. a protection against external danger or injury.
3. a person or principle that acts as a defense.

Related word: **bulwark** *verb*.

bumptious (BUMP-shəs) *adjective*
offensively conceited or self-assertive; pushy.

Related words: **bumptiously** *adverb*, **bumptiousness** *noun*.

burble (BUR-bəl) *verb*
1. speak at length; babble.
2. make a bubbling sound.

Related word: **burbler** *noun*.

burgeon (BUR-jən) *verb*
grow or develop rapidly; flourish.

burnish (BUR-nish) *verb*
1. polish by rubbing
2. brighten; cause to glow.

bushido (BOO-shee-DAW) *noun*
  in feudal Japan, the ethical code of the samurai.

Byzantine (BIZ-ən-TEEN) *adjective*
  1. complex or intricate.
  2. underhanded.
  3. characterized by complicated scheming and intrigue.

C

cabotage (KAB-ə-TAHZH) *noun*
  1. coastal trade or navigation.
  2. legal restriction of air traffic within a country's borders.

cachet (ka-SHAY) *noun, plural* **cachets** (ka-SHAYZ)
  1. prestige, superior status.
  2. a sign of approval, especially one given by a person who is highly regarded.
  3. an official seal, as on a document.

cachexia (kə-KEK-see-ə) *noun*
  general ill health causing chronic debility.

Related word: **cachectic** (kə-KEK-tik), **cachectical**, and **cachexic** (kə-KEK-sik) *all adjectives.*

cachinnate (KAK-ə-NAYT) *verb*
  laugh loudly or immoderately.

Related words: **cachinnation** and **cachinnator** *both nouns,* **cachinnatory** (KAK-ə-nə-TOR-ee) *adjective.*

cacodemon (KAK-ə-DEE-mən) *noun*
  an evil spirit or person.

Related words: **cacodemonic** (KAK-ə-di-MON-ik) and **cacodemoniac** (KAK-ə-di-MOH-nee-AK) *both adjectives.*

cacography (kə-KOG-rə-fee) *noun*
  1. bad handwriting.
  2. incorrect spelling.

Related words: **cacographer** *noun*, **cacographic** (KAK-ə-GRAF-ik) and **cacographical** *both adjectives.*

cacology (kə-KOL-ə-jee) *noun*
  1. bad choice of words.
  2. poor pronunciation.

cairn (kairn) *noun*
  a heap of stones arranged as a memorial or as a landmark.

Related words: **cairned** and **cairny** *both adjectives.*

callipygian (KAL-i-PIJ-ee-ən) *adjective,* also given as **callipygous** (KAL-i-PĪ-gəs)
  having shapely buttocks.

callosity (kə-LOS-i-tee) *noun, plural* **callosities**
  an abnormal hardness and thickness of the skin; a callus.

callous (KAL-əs) *adjective*
  1. insensitive, unsympathetic, indifferent.
  2. hardened, hard.

In rigorous adherence to the principle of descriptiveness, most conventional dictionaries have become guilty of attempted verbicide by indicating that **callus** (which see) is a noun meaning of **callous,** an adjective. In time, therefore, we can expect that most writers will be ignorant of the clear distinction between the two words that is maintained today by careful writers. Consider that until recently dictionaries identified this noun use of **callous** as a mistake in spelling, and that is how editors and writers should continue to regard it. Avoid **calluses** by learning how to type properly, not by **callous** disregard of good typing techniques.

Related words: **callously** *adverb,* **callousness** *noun.*

callus (KAL-əs) *noun, plural* **calluses**
  1. a thickened part of the skin; a callosity.
  2. *(verb)* form or produce a callus.

See the discussion at **callous** for guidance in differentiating the noun **callus** and the adjective **callous.**

calumniate (kə-LUM-nee-AYT) *verb*
  make false and malicious statements about; slander, traduce.

Related words: **calumniation** (kə-LUM-nee-AY-shən) and **calumniator** (kə-LUM-nee-AY-tər) *both nouns.*

calumny (KAL-əm-nee) *noun, plural* **calumnies**
1. a slander; a defamation.
2. the act of slandering.

Related words: **calumniate** (kə-LUM-nee-AYT) *verb,* **calumniation** (kə-LUM-nee-AY-shən) and **calumniator** (kə-LUM-nee-AY-tər) *both nouns,* **calumnious** (kə-LUM-nee-əs) and **calumniatory** (kə-LUM-nee-ə-TOR-ee) *both adjectives.*

canard (kə-NAHRD) *noun*
a false report; a hoax.

cant (kant) *noun*
1. insincere use of words, especially conventional expressions of piety.
2. hypocrisy.
3. *(derogatory)* the language peculiar to a party, class, profession, or the like; jargon.
4. the private language of the underworld.

capricious (kə-PRISH-əs) *adjective*
1. subject to or indicative of whim.
2. erratic.

Related words: **capriciously** *adverb,* **caprice** (kə-PREES) and **capriciousness** *both nouns.*

captious (KAP-shəs) *adjective*
1. apt to raise objections to trivial faults or defects.
2. difficult to please.

Related words: **captiously** *adverb,* **captiousness** *noun.*

carabao (KAR-ə-BAH-oh) *noun, plural* **carabaos**
in the Philippines, the water buffalo.

The noun **carabao** is often mispronounced by people who confuse it with the more familiar noun **caribou**, the magnificent North American deer, which is pronounced KAR-ə-BOO.

careen (kə-REEN) *verb*
said of a vehicle in motion: lean, sway, or tip to one side.

Many speakers and writers confuse the verb **career**, meaning *proceed at full speed*, with the verb **careen**. So prevalent is this confusion that modern dictionaries commonly identify the two verbs as synonyms, thus shrinking the scope of the American language and inviting ambiguity. Fully trained editors do not encourage this confusion. Nor should you.

Related word: **careener** *verb.*

career (kə-REER) *verb*

See **careen**.

caribou (KAR-ə-BOO) *noun*

See **carabao**.

carminative (kahr-MIN-ə-tiv) *noun*
a drug curing flatulence.

Related word: **carminative** *adjective,* as in "Some **carminative** compounds may be purchased over the counter."

caseous (KAY-see-əs) *adjective*
of or like cheese.

Cassandra (kə-SAN-drə) *noun*
a person who prophesies or warns of approaching evil and is usually disregarded. In classical mythology a prophet cursed by Apollo so her prophecies, though true, were fated never to be believed.

castigate (KAS-ti-GAYT) *verb*
reprimand severely, chastise, punish.

Related words: **castigation** (KAS-ti-GAY-shən) and **castigator** (KAS-ti-GAY-tər) *both nouns,* **castigative** (KAS-ti-GAY-tiv) and **castigatory** (KAS-ti-gə-TOR-ee) *both adjectives.*

casuistry (KAZH-oo-ə-stree)
1. the application of ethical principles to cases of conscience or conduct.
2. oversubtle reasoning, quibbling, or teaching, especially in questions of morality; sophistry.

Related words: **casuist** (KAZH-oo-ist) *noun,* **casuistic** (KAZH-oo-IS-tik) and **casuistical** *both adjectives,* **casuistically** *adverb.*

catachresis (KAT-ə-KREE-sis) *noun, plural* **catachreses** (KAT-ə-KREE-seez)

incorrect use of words, as in a mistaken metaphor.

Related words: **catachrestic** (KAT-ə-KRES-tik) and **catachrestical** *both adjectives,* **catachrestically** *adverb.*

catafalque (KAT-ə-FAWK) *noun*

a raised platform on which the body of a deceased person lies or is carried in state.

catamite (KAT-ə-MĪT) *noun*

a boy or youth kept by a man for homosexual practices.

catechumen (KAT-i-KYOO-mən) *noun*

a person under instruction in the rudiments of Christianity.

Related words: **catechumenal** and **catechumenical** (KAT-i-kyoo-MEN-i-kəl) *both adjectives,* **catechumenically** *adverb,* **catechumenate** (KAT-i-KYOO-mə-NAYT) and **catechumenism** (KAT-i-KYOO-mə-niz-əm) *both nouns.*

caterwaul (KAT-ər-WAWL) *verb*

make a long wailing cry, as of a cat in rut.

Related words: **caterwaul** and **caterwauling** *both nouns.*

cavil (KAV-əl) *verb*

raise petty and irritating objections.

Related words: **cavil** and **caviler** *both nouns,* **cavilingly** *adverb.*

censer (SEN-sər) *noun*

a container in which incense is burned during a religious service.

Do not confuse **censer** with **censor**, which see.

censor (SEN-sər) *noun*

any person who exercises supervision of manners or morality.

Do not confuse **censor** with **censer**, which means *incense burner.* This confusion would appear to be merely an end product of poor spelling.

Related words: **censor** *verb;* **censorable, censorial** (sen-SOR-ee-əl), and **censorian** (sen-SOR-ee-ən) *all adjectives.*

cerumen (si-ROO-mən) *noun*

earwax.

Related word: **ceruminous** *adjective.*

chafe (chayf) *verb*
1. make sore by rubbing.
2. irritate or annoy.
3. become annoyed, fret.

Do not confuse **chafe** with **chaff**, which see.

chaff (chaf) *verb*
1. tease or mock good-naturedly.
2. banter.

Do not confuse **chaff** with **chafe**. While one of the meanings of **chafe** is *irritate*, and most people show irritation when they are **chaffed**, there is no reason to confuse the two verbs beyond their closeness of spelling. In short, when we **chaff**, meaning *tease or mock good-naturedly*, we may also **chafe**, meaning *become annoyed*, but that's the whole story.

Related word: **chaffingly** *adverb*.

charisma (kə-RIZ-mə) *noun, plural* **charismata** (kə-RIZ-mə-tə)
a personal quality that inspires followers with devotion and enthusiasm.

Related words: **charismatic** (KAR-iz-MAT-ik) *adjective*, **charismatize** (kə-RIZ-mə-TĪZ) *verb*.

chary (CHAIR-ee) *adjective*
1. cautious, timid, wary.
2. ungenerous; sparing of.

Related words: **charily** *adverb*, **chariness** *noun*.

childish (CHĬL-dish) *adjective*
1. of, like, or befitting a child.
2. puerile, weak, unsuitable for an adult.

Do not confuse **childish** with **childlike**, which see.

Related words: **childishly** *adverb*, **childishness** *noun*.

childlike (CHILD-LĪK) *adjective*
like or befitting a child, as in innocence, meekness, or frankness.

Be careful to maintain the distinction between **childlike** and **childish** when applying these adjectives to adults. **Childlike** is entirely complimentary, but **childish** in the sense of *unsuitable* *for an adult* is pejorative. While we may be charmed by **child-like** innocence in a woman, we surely are repelled by **childish** behavior in the same woman or in any other adult. In short, we admire **childlike** innocence and we abhor temper tantrums and other **childish** behavior in a grown man or woman.

Related word: **childlikeness** *noun.*

chrestomathy (kres-TOM-ə-thee) *noun, plural* **chrestomathies**
a collection of choice literary passages, especially to help in learning a language.

Related word: **chrestomathic** (KRES-tə-MATH-ik) *adjective.*

chthonic (THON-ik) *adjective*, also given as **chthonian** (THOH-nee-ən)
dwelling in the underworld.

cicerone (SIS-ə-ROH-nee) *noun, plural* **cicerones** (SIS-ə-ROH-neez) and **ciceroni** (SIS-ə-ROH-nee)
a guide, especially for sightseers.

cicisbeo (CHEE-chiz-BAY-oh) *noun, plural* **cicisbei** (CHEE-chiz-BAY-ee)
a male escort or lover of a married woman.

Related word: **cicisbeism** (CHEE-chiz-BAY-iz-əm) *noun.*

climactic (klī-MAK-tik) *adjective*, also given as **climactical** (klī-MAK-ti-kəl)
pertaining to a climax.

Do not confuse **climactic** with **climatic**, which see.

Related word: **climactically** *adverb.*

climatic (klī-MAT-ik) *adjective*, also given as **climatical** (klī-MAT-i-kəl) and **climatal** (KLĪ-mi-təl)
pertaining to climate.

The confusion of the words **climatic** and **climactic** is usually a problem of pronunciation rather than usage. As you probably have noticed, **climatic** is frequently used mistakenly in substandard speech when **climactic**, a less commonly used adjective, conveys the intended meaning. Rarely, however, is **climactic** used when **climatic** is intended. While in published writing the confusion of **climatic**, *pertaining to climate*, and **climactic**, *per-*

taining to a climax, is seldom seen, over time the confusion will probably begin to appear in books and newspapers and should be guarded against. What we say eventually influences what we write, as any teacher of writing knows.

Related words: **climatically** *adverb*.

coeval (koh-EE-vəl) *adjective*
1. of the same age, date, or duration; equally old.
2. coincident.

Related words: **coevality** (KOH-i-VAL-i-tee) *noun*, **coevally** (koh-EE-və-lee) *adverb*.

cognizable (KOG-nə-zə-bəl) *adjective*
1. perceptible.
2. recognizable.

Related word: **cognizably** (KOG-nə-zə-blee) *adverb*.

cognizant (KOG-nə-zənt) *adjective*
aware.

collation (kə-LAY-shən) *noun*
a light meal.

colloquium (kə-LOH-kwee-əm) *noun*, *plural* **colloquiums** and **colloquia** (kə-LOH-kwee-ə)
an academic seminar or conference.

colloquy (KOL-ə-kwee) *noun*, *plural* **colloquies**
a dialogue or conversation.

Related word: **colloquist** *noun*.

colporteur (KOL-POR-tər) *noun*
a door-to-door book peddler, especially of Bibles.

comedo (KOM-i-DOH) *noun*, *plural* **comedos** and **comedones** (KOM-i-DOH-neez)
a blackhead.

comestibles (kə-MES-tə-bəlz) *plural noun*
articles of food; edibles.

Related word: **comestible** *adjective*.

commensurate (kə-MEN-sər-it) *adjective*
corresponding in amount, extent, or magnitude; proportionate.

Related words: **commensurately** *adverb,* **commensurateness** and **commensuration** (kə-MEN-sə-RAY-shən) *both nouns.*

commination (KOM-ə-NAY-shən) *adjective*
a threat of vengeance, especially divine vengeance.

Related words: **comminate** (KOM-ə-NAYT) *verb,* **comminator** *noun,* **comminatory** (kə-MIN-ə-TOR-ee) and **comminative** (KOM-mi-NAY-tiv) *both adjectives.*

complement (KOM-plə-mənt) *noun*
1. something that completes or makes perfect.
2. the amount or quantity required to complete something.
3. in grammar, a word or group of words added to a verb to complete the predicate.
4. *(verb)* complete; form a complement to.

Careless writers sometimes use the noun and verb **compliment** to express the meanings of the noun and verb **complement,** giving editors one more error to correct. We welcome **compliments** and are quick to **compliment** anyone who deserves such courtesies, but **compliments** and **compliment** have nothing to do with **complements. Complements** may be essential, but they have nothing to do with **complimenting** or paying **compliments.** Clear enough?

Related words: **complementarity** (KOM-plə-men-TAR-i-tee) *noun,* **complementary** (KOM-plə-MEN-tə-ree) *adjective.*

compliment (KOM-plə-mənt) *noun*
1. a polite expression of praise.
2. an act implying praise.
3. *(verb)* pay a compliment to.

See **complement.**

Related words: **complimentable** (KOM-plə-MEN-tə-bəl) *adjective,* **complimenter** (KOM-pli-MENT-ər) *noun.*

comprise (kəm-PRĪZ) *verb*
1. include, comprehend, consist of.
2. constitute, compose, make up.

The first definition of **comprise** given above, *include, consist of,* is considered by skilled writers and editors to be the only acceptable one. It follows the hallowed dictum "The whole *comprises* the parts." In fact, the second definition, suggesting "The parts *comprise* the whole," is widely used and has been accepted for a long time. Nevertheless, there is a strong inclination among trained editors to make the first definition the one that a careful writer should follow, and the second definition one that a careful writer should avoid. Thus, instead of writing "Players *comprise* a small army," you ought to write "Players *constitute* a small army" or "Players *make up* a small army." Following the same practice, instead of saying "A team *comprised of* dozens of specialists," you ought to write "A team *composed of* dozens of specialists."

Related words: **comprisable** *adjective*, **comprisal** *noun*.

compulsive (kəm-PUL-siv) *adjective*
1. acting as if from compulsion.
2. irresistible.

Do not confuse **compulsive** with **compulsory**, which see.

Related words: **compulsively** *adverb*, **compulsiveness** and **compulsivity** (KOM-pul-SIV-i-tee) *both nouns*.

compulsory (kəm-PUL-sə-ree) *adjective*
1. that must be done, required by the rules etc.
2. enforced.

The adjective **compulsory** has long been understood to mean *enforced*, as in **compulsory** education. It was clearly distinct in meaning from the adjective **compulsive**, which in psychological parlance means *irresistible*. With the growing influence of popular psychology, however, **compulsive** has drifted into everyday language and become confused with **compulsory**. The distinction between the two words should be maintained. Thus, **compulsory** education is required by the laws of our country, while **compulsive** gambling stems from a compulsion, an irresistible urge, to gamble. You must continue to keep these adjectives separate in your own writing, remembering that **compulsive** behavior is not mandated by law, but results from an inner urge entirely personal in nature.

Related words: **compulsorily** (kəm-PUL-sə-ri-lee) *adverb*, **compulsoriness** *noun*.

concatenate (kon-KAT-ən-AYT) *verb*
1. link together.
2. unite in a series or chain.

> Related word: **concatenated** *adjective*, **concatenation** (kon-KAT-ən-AY-shən) *noun*

concinnity (kən-SIN-i-tee) *noun, plural* **concinnities**
elegance of literary structure or style.

concupiscent (kon-KYOO-pi-sənt) *adjective*
lustful or sensual; eagerly desirous.

> Related words: **concupiscence** *noun*, **concupiscently** *adverb*.

condign (kən-DĪN) *adjective*
severe and well-deserved.

> Related word: **condignly** *adverb*.

confabulate (kən-FAB-yə-LAYT) *verb*
converse, chat.

> Related words: **confabulation** (kən-FAB-yə-LAY-shən) and **confabulator** (kən-FAB-yə-LAY-tər) *both nouns*, **confabulatory** (kən-FAB-yə-lə-TOR-ee) *adjective*.

congelation (KON-jə-LAY-shən) *noun*
1. congealing; the state of being congealed.
2. a congealed substance; a coagulation or concretion.

congenital (kən-JEN-i-təl) *adjective*
1. of a disease or physical defect, existing at birth.
2. having by nature a specified characteristic.

> See also **innate**.

> Related words: **congenitally** *adverb*, **congenitalness** *noun*.

congeries (KON-jə-reez) *singular or plural noun*
1. a mass or heap.
2. a disorderly collection.

connote (kə-NOHT) *verb*
1. of words, imply meanings or ideas beyond the explicit meaning.
2. of facts, involve as a condition or accompaniment.

> See **denote**.

Related words: **connotation** (KON-ə-TAY-shən) *noun*, **connotative** (KON-ə-TAY-tiv) and **connotive** (kə-NOH-tiv) *both adjectives*, **connotatively** and **connotively** *both adverbs.*

conspectus (kən-SPEK-təs) *noun, plural* **conspectuses**
a summary, digest, or synopsis.

constitute (KON-sti-TOOT) *verb*

See **comprise.**

contemporaneous (kən-TEM-pə-RAY-nee-əs) *adjective*
existing or occurring at the same time; contemporary.

Related words: **contemporaneity** (kən-TEM-pər-ə-NEE-i-tee) and **contemporaneousness** *both nouns*, **contemporaneously** *adverb.*

continual (kən-TIN-yoo-əl) *adjective*
1. continuing over a long time without stopping or with only short breaks; intermittent.
2. always happening.

Do not confuse **continual** with **continuous**, which see.

Related word: **continually** *adverb.*

continuous (kən-TIN-yoo-əs) *adjective*
1. uninterrupted in time or sequence; continuing without a break.
2. of things, connected; unbroken.

Valid distinctions can be drawn between **continuous** and **continual** in characterizing attitudes and actions. Consider the definitions given for **continual**: 1. *continuing over a long time without stopping or with only short breaks; intermittent.* 2. *always happening.* Thus, one might correctly say, "Jack's **continual** drinking finally had taken its toll." Jack's drinking surely has been *continuing over a long time*, and just as surely as it was *always happening*, it has been *intermittent.* No one drinks anything all the time. Now consider the first definition given for **continuous**: *uninterrupted in time; continuing without a break.* Thus, one might correctly say, "The minister's **continuous** interest in his congregants' welfare is never questioned." Surely this interest was *uninterrupted in time* and *continuing without a break.* You would do well, therefore, to make **continuous** your adjective of choice for unending attitudes or actions; **continual** your adjective of choice for attitudes or actions that are interrupted from time to time.

Related word: **continuously** *adverb*.

contumacious (KON-tuu-MAY-shəs) *adjective*
1. insubordinate.
2. disobedient, especially to an order of a court.

Related words: **contumaciously** *adverb*; **contumaciousness**, **contumacity** (KON-tuu-MAS-i-tee), and **contumacy** (KON-tuu-mə-see) *all nouns*.

contumelious (KON-tuu-MEE-lee-əs) *adjective*
insolent, reproachful.

Related words: **contumeliously** *adverb*, **contumeliousness** and **contumely** (KON-tuu-mə-lee) *both nouns*.

coquette (koh-KET) *noun*
a woman who flirts with men lightheartedly.

Related words: **coquettish** *adjective*, **coquettishly** *adverb*, **coquettishness** *noun*.

corrigendum (KOR-i-JEN-dəm) *noun, plural* **corrigenda** (KOR-i-JEN-də)
a mistake to be corrected, especially an error in a printed book.

corrigible (KOR-i-jə-bəl) *adjective*
1. of faults or weaknesses, capable of being corrected or reformed; rectifiable.
2. of persons, open to correction.

Do not confuse **corrigible** with its antonym **incorrigible**, which means *unrectifiable; not open to correction*.

Related words: **corrigibility** (KOR-i-jə-BIL-ə-tee) and **corrigibleness** (KOR-i-jə-bəl-nis) *both nouns*, **corrigibly** *adverb*.

corybantic (KOR-ə-BAN-tik) *adjective*
1. frenzied.
2. agitated.

cosset (KOS-it) *verb*
1. treat as a pet.
2. coddle, pamper.

costive (KOS-tiv) *adjective*
1. constipated.
2. slow to act.
3. uncommunicative.

Related words: **costively** *adverb*, **costiveness** *noun*.

coup de grâce (koo də GRAHS) *plural*, **coups de grâce**, same pronunciation
a death blow, especially one administered as an act of mercy to a dying person.

cozen (KUZ-ən) *verb*
cheat, defraud, trick.

Related words: **cozener** *noun*, **cozeningly** *adverb*.

crapulous (KRAP-yə-ləs) *adjective*
given to, characterized by, or suffering from gross excess in eating and drinking.

Related words: **crapulously** *adverb*, **crapulousness** and **crapulosity** (KRAP-yə-LOS-i-tee) *both nouns*.

credible (KRED-ə-bəl) *adjective*
1. of a person, believable or trustworthy.
2. of a threat or warning, convincing.

Related words: **credibility** and **credibleness** *both nouns*, **credibly** *adverb*.

creditable (KRED-i-tə-bəl) *adjective*
deserving or bringing credit, reputation, esteem, etc.

Do not confuse **creditable** with **credible**, *believable*, or **credulous**, *gullible*, both of which see.

Related words: **creditableness** and **creditability** (KRED-it-ə-BIL-i-tee) *both nouns*, **creditably** *adverb*.

credulous (KREJ-ə-ləs) *adjective*
too ready to believe things, gullible.

Do not confuse **credulous** with **credible** or **creditable**, both of which see.

Related words: **credulity** (krə-DOO-li-tee) and **credulousness** (KREJ-ə-ləs-nis) *both nouns*, **credulously** *adverb*.

crevasse (krə-VAS) *noun*
    a deep open crack, especially in the ice of a glacier.

    Do not confuse **crevasse** with **crevice**, which means *a narrow opening or crack.*

criterion (krī-TEER-ee-ən) *noun, plural* **criteria** (krī-TEER-ee-ə) and **criterions**
    1. a standard of judgment.
    2. a principle for evaluating something.

    When speakers or writers use **criteria** as a singular noun, they run counter to the practices of even the most permissive of lexicographers and the practices of all editors. *The criteria was considered . . .* STOP! A mistake has already been made. How did this error become so widespread in the speech and writing of the unskilled? Possibly because Latin plurals, for example, **criteria** and **errata**, lack the final letter *s* we are accustomed to in English plurals. But there may be more to it: Too many of us eagerly seize upon unfamiliar words and phrases, which somehow are thought to invest our thoughts with the appearance of learnedness. The result too often is that in doing so we make laughable errors and we appear unlearned. Remember that **criterion** is singular, and **criteria** is plural.

    Related word: **criterial** (kri-TEER-ee-əl) *adjective.*

cunctation (kungk-TAY-shən) *noun*
    1. delay.
    2. tardiness.

    Related words: **cunctatious** (kungk-TAY-shəs) and **cunctatory** (KUNGK-tə-TOR-ee) *both nouns,* **cunctative** (KUNGK-tə-tiv) *adjective.*

cupidity (kyoo-PID-i-tee) *noun*
    1. excessive desire to possess something.
    2. greed; avarice.

    Related word: **cupidinous** (kyoo-PID-i-nəs) *adjective.*

curmudgeon (kər-MUJ-ən) *noun*
    a bad-tempered, difficult person.

    Related word: **curmudgeonly** *adverb.*

cynosure (SIN-ə-SHUUR) *noun*
    a center of attraction or admiration.
        Related word: **cynosural** (SI-nə-SHUUR-əl) *adjective*.

D

dander (DAN-dər) *noun*

1. fighting spirit.
2. loose scales formed on the skin of certain animals and shed.

dandle (DAN-dəl) *verb*

dance (a child) in one's arms or on one's knees.

Related word: **dandler** (DAN-dlər) *noun*.

dastard (DAS-tərd) *noun*

a despicable coward.

Related words: **dastard** *adjective*, **dastardliness** *noun*, **dastardly** *adjective*.

decant (di-KANT) *verb*

pour (wine etc.) gently from one container into another without disturbing the sediment.

Related words: **decanter** and **decantation** (DEE-kan-TAY-shən) *both nouns*.

decedent (di-SEE-dənt) *noun*

a dead person.

décolletage (DAY-kol-TAHZH) *noun*, also given as **decolletage**, with the same pronunciation

a low-cut neck of a dress, exposing the neck and shoulders of the wearer.

decorum (di-KOR-əm) *noun*

correctness and dignity of behavior.

decrescent (di-KRES-ənt) *adjective*
1. decreasing gradually.
2. waning, as the moon.

Related word: **decrescence** *noun*.

defalcation (DEE-fal-KAY-shən) *noun*
misappropriation of funds; the sum misappropriated.

Related word: **defalcate** (di-FAL-kayt) *verb*.

defenestration (dee-FEN-ə-STRAY-shən) *noun*
the act of throwing a thing or person out of a window.

definite (DEF-ə-nit) *adjective*
clear and unmistakable; unambiguous.

Do not confuse **definite** with **definitive**, which see.

Related words: **definitely** *adverb*, **definiteness** *noun*.

definitive (di-FIN-i-tiv) *adjective*
1. of a book, report, author, etc., most authoritative.
2. finally fixing or settling something; conclusive.

Do not confuse **definitive** with **definite**, meaning *clear and unmistakable, unambiguous*. A **definitive** edition of a work is one that has authoritative status—it is considered the last word on a topic. The adjective **definite** cannot be used to modify "edition." A **definitive** offer is one that is in final form and must be accepted or rejected without alteration of its terms. By contrast, a **definite** offer is one that is clearly stated. The mistaken use of **definitive**, meaning *most authoritative, conclusive*, instead of **definite** when the intended meaning is *unambiguous* may reflect a mind-set that leads some speakers and writers to employ words they regard as glamorous instead of staying with more common words they fully understand. Don't fall into this trap.

Related words: **definitively** *adverb*, **definitiveness** *noun*.

deflagrate (DEF-lə-GRAYT) *verb*
burn, especially suddenly and violently.

Related words: **deflagrable** (DEF-lə-grə-bəl) *adjective*, **deflagrability** (DEF-lə-grə-BIL-i-tee) and **deflagration** (DEF-lə-GRAY-shən) *both nouns*.

déjà vu (DAY-zhah VOO)

    1. a mistaken feeling of having experienced something that actually is encountered for the first time.

    2. something tediously familiar.

deleterious (DEL-i-TEER-ee-əs) *adjective*

harmful to the body or mind; injurious.

    Related words: **deleteriously** *adverb*, **deleteriousness** *noun*.

Delilah (di-LĪ-lə) *noun*

    1. a seductive and treacherous woman; a wily temptress.

    2. in the Old Testament, Samson's mistress, who betrayed him to the Philistines.

delusive (di-LOO-siv) *adjective*

deceptive, misleading, raising vain hopes.

    Related words: **delusively** *adverb*, **delusiveness** *noun*.

demoniac (di-MOH-nee-ak) *adjective*, also given as **demoniacal** (DEE-mə-NĪ-ə-kəl)

    1. of or like a demon.

    2. possessed, as by an evil spirit.

    3. frenzied, fiercely energetic.

    4. **demoniac** *(noun)* a person possessed by an evil spirit.

    Related word: **demoniacally** (DEE-mə-NĪ-ik-lee) *adverb*.

demotic (di-MOT-ik) *adjective*

    1. of ordinary people.

    2. popular.

demulcent (di-MUL-sənt) *noun*

a soothing medicine.

    Related word: **demulcent** *adjective*.

denote (di-NOHT) *verb*

    1. be the sign or symbol or name of.

    2. indicate.

    See **connote**.

    Related words: **denotative** (DEE-noh-TAY-tiv) and **denotive** (di-NOH-tiv) *both adjectives*, **denotation** (DEE-noh-TAY-shən) *noun*, meaning *the explicit meaning of a word*, as distinct from its connotation.

denouement (DAY-noo-MAHN) *noun*, also given as **dénouement**, with the same pronunciation
1. the clearing up at the end of a play or story of the complications of the plot.
2. the outcome of a tangled sequence of events.

deprecate (DEP-ri-KAYT) *verb*
1. feel and express disapproval of.
2. try to turn aside (praise or blame) politely.

Do not confuse **deprecate** with **depreciate**, which see.

Related words: **deprecatingly** *adverb*, **deprecation** (DEP-ri-KAY-shən) and **deprecator** (DEP-ri-KAY-tər) *both nouns*, **deprecative** (DEP-ri-KAY-tiv) and **deprecatory** (DEP-ri-kə-TOR-ee) *both adjectives*.

depreciate (di-PREE-shee-AYT) *verb*
1. make or become lower in value.
2. disparage, belittle.

Careful writers do not use **depreciate** in its second sense, *disparage, belittle.* The confusion of **depreciate** with **deprecate** by many speakers and writers appears to reflect their familiarity with **depreciate** and their unfamiliarity with **deprecate**, which means *express disapproval of.* The two verbs are similar in spelling and fairly close in meaning—*belittle* may appear to be but one step removed from *express disapproval of*—and the more familiar word, **depreciate**, appears to be winning out. Indeed, descriptive dictionaries now treat the two words as synonyms. Careful speakers and writers, however, use both words appropriately. Prices **depreciate**; hostile critics **deprecate**. Modest people **deprecate** praise directed at them; nothing can **depreciate** deserved praise.

Related words: **depreciation** (di-PREE-shee-AY-shən) *noun*, **depreciatory** (di-PREE-shee-ə-TOR-ee) *adjective*.

deracinate (di-RAS-ə-NAYT) *verb*
uproot; isolate (someone) from his home or environment.

Related word: **deracination** (di-RAS-ə-NAY-shən) *noun*.

derision (di-RIZH-ən) *noun*
scorn, ridicule.

Related word: **derisible** (di-RIZ-ə-bəl) *adjective*.

derisive (di-RĪ-siv) *adjective*
expressing or causing derision; scornful, mocking.

See **derisory**.

Related words: **derisiveness** *noun*, **derisively** *adverb*.

derisory (di-RĪ-sə-ree) *adjective*
worthy of ridicule; too insignificant for serious consideration.

Derisory and **derisive** are close in meaning, but careful writers use the two adjectives differently. For example, something *worthy of ridicule* may be described as **derisory**, as in "Entry-level wages in our firm are **derisory**." Again, a remark *expressing derision* may be characterized as **derisive**, as in "His **derisive** comments were intended to destroy his opponent's candidacy."

derogate (DER-ə-GAYT) *verb*
detract from; disparage, belittle.

"They were known for their inclination to destroy reputations of people they worked with, but they could truthfully say they never intended to **derogate** their immediate supervisor's authority."

Related word: **derogation** (DER-ə-GAY-shən) *noun*.

derogatory (di-ROG-ə-TOR-ee) *adjective*
disparaging; contemptuous.

Related words: **derogatorily** (di-ROG-ə-TOR-ə-lee) *adverb*, **derogatoriness** (di-ROG-ə-TOR-ee-nis) *noun*.

deserts (di-ZURTS) *plural noun*
what one deserves (whether good or bad).

Do not confuse **deserts** with **desserts**, a word whose meaning we all understand. Hint: we look forward to a choice of **desserts** at the end of a good meal, but if we overeat to the point of suffering gastric pain, we are getting our just **deserts**.

desideratum (di-SID-ə-RAH-təm) *noun, plural* **desiderata** (di-SID-ə-RAH-tə)
something that is lacking but is needed or desired.

despoil (di-SPOYL) *verb*
strip of possessions; rob, pillage, plunder (a place or person).

Related words: **despoiler** and **despoilment** *both nouns*.

desuetude (DES-wi-TOOD) *noun*
a state of disuse.

detritus (di-TRĪ-təs) *noun*
1. fragments (of gravel, silt, etc.) caused by the rubbing away of a larger mass.
2. any waste; debris.

Related word: **detrital** (di-TRĪ-təl) *adjective.*

detumescence (DEE-too-MES-əns) *noun*
reduction or subsidence from a swollen state.

Related word: **detumescent** *adjective.*

devolve (di-VOLV) *verb*
pass or be passed on to a deputy or successor.

Related word: **devolvement** *noun.*

diadem (DĪ-ə-DEM) *noun*
a crown or headband worn as a sign of sovereignty.

dialectic (DĪ-ə-LEK-tik) *noun*
the investigation of the truth of opinions in philosophy, economics, etc. by systematic reasoning and logical disputation.

Related words: **dialectic, dialectal,** and **dialectical** *all adjectives,* **dialectician** (DĪ-ə-lek-TISH-ən) *noun.*

Diaspora (dī-AS-pər-ə) *noun,* also given as **diaspora,** especially in sense 2 below
1. the dispersion of the Jews to countries outside of Palestine after the end of the Babylonian captivity.
2. the dispersion of any minority religious or ethnic group among people of a prevailing religion or ethnicity.

dichotomy (dī-KOT-ə-mee) *noun, plural* **dichotomies**
division into two parts or kinds.

Related words: **dichotomic** (DĪ-kə-TOM-ik) and **dichotomous** (dī-KOT-ə-məs) *both adjectives,* **dichotomically** (DĪ-kə-TOM-i-klee) *adverb,* **dichotomize** (dī-KOT-ə-MĪZ) *verb.*

dictum (DIK-təm) *noun, plural* **dicta** (DIK-tə) or **dictums**
1. a formal expression of opinion, especially a judicial assertion.
2. a maxim, a saying.

diffident (DIF-i-dənt) *adjective*
lacking self-confidence; hesitating to put oneself or one's ideas forward.
Related words: **diffidence** *noun*, **diffidently** *adverb*.

dilatory (DIL-ə-TOR-ee) *adjective*
slow in doing something; not prompt; tending to procrastinate.
Related words: **dilatorily** *adverb*, **dilatoriness** *noun*.

dipsomania (DIP-sə-MAY-nee-ə) *noun*
an uncontrollable craving for alcoholic drink.
Related words: **dipsomaniac** (DIP-sə-MAY-nee-AK) *noun*, **dipsomaniacal** (DIP-sə-mə-NĪ-ə-kəl) *adjective*.

disaffected (DIS-ə-FEK-tid) *adjective*
discontented and disloyal, as toward authority.
Related words: **disaffectedly** *adverb*, **disaffectedness** *noun*.

disaffection (DIS-ə-FEK-shən) *noun*
estrangement; disloyalty; political discontent.

discomfit (dis-KUM-fit) *verb*
1. disconcert; confuse and deject.
2. thwart, foil; frustrate the plans of.

Do not confuse **discomfit** with **discomfort**, which see.

Related word: **discomfiter** *noun*.

discomfiture (dis-KUM-fi-chər) *noun*
embarrassment, confusion; frustration.

discomfort (dis-KUM-fərt) *noun*
1. uneasiness, hardship, or mild pain.
2. *(verb)* make uncomfortable or uneasy.

Do not confuse the verb **discomfort** with the verb **discomfit**. Many of today's speakers and writers are not aware at all of the word **discomfit**, and when they occasionally meet the word in a book think it is a misprint. The most assiduous of such readers may turn to a dictionary for help, but the next time they meet the word they must go back to the dictionary. Rest assured that **discomfit**, meaning *disconcert*, is still in use and serves a good purpose, as does **discomfort**, a word that gives readers and writers no trouble.

Related words: **discomfortable** *adjective*, **discomfortingly** *adverb*.

disconsolate (dis-KON-sə-lit) *adjective*
1. disappointed; unhappy at the loss of something.
2. hopelessly unhappy; gloomy; inconsolable.

Related words: **disconsolately** *adverb*, **disconsolation** (dis-KON-sə-LAY-shən) and **disconsolateness** *both nouns*.

discreet (di-SKREET) *adjective*
1. showing caution and good judgment in what one does; judicious; not giving away secrets.
2. unostentatious, not showy or obtrusive.

Do not confuse **discreet** with **discrete**, which see.

Related words: **discreetly** *adverb*, **discreetness** and **discretion** (dis-KRESH-ən) both *nouns*.

discrete (di-SKREET) *adjective*
~~discontinuous; detached from others; individually distinct.~~

Seldom can the transposition of two letters in a word create as much misunderstanding as in the mistaken use of **discrete**, *individually distinct*, in place of **discreet**, *judicious, unostentatious*, when the latter word is clearly intended. This error appears to stem from the tendency of unskilled writers to want to appear learned by using relatively uncommon words in place of common words. (Or could it merely be a keyboarding error that goes undiscovered by word processing features that check one's spelling?) Whatever the reason, **discrete** in place of **discreet** is an error that can hold a writer up to ridicule as well as to misunderstanding. Take care to avoid this confusion.

Related words: **discretely** *adverb*, **discreteness** *noun*.

disingenuous (DIS-in-JEN-yoo-əs) *adjective*
insincere, not frank; hypocritically ingenuous.

Related words: **disingenuously** *adverb*, **disingenuousness** *noun*.

disinterested (dis-IN-tə-RES-tid) *adjective*
impartial; not influenced by self-interest.

The adjective **disinterested** increasingly is misconstrued as a synonym for **uninterested**. So prevalent has this misuse become that descriptive dictionaries give *uninterested* as a second meaning of **disinterested**, although some supply the label *colloquial* for this sense, implicitly suggesting that this is the way ordinary people use the word and, perhaps, that the best speakers and writers do not accept this definition. An argument is made by descriptivists that **disinterested** historically was defined as *indifferent; not interested*, and that many people still use the word in this sense. Most careful 20th-century writers, however, choose not to accept this attitude. They find satisfaction in promoting the sense of *impartial* for **disinterested**, and you should cast your lot with them and indicate by the way you frame your sentences that you mean **disinterested** to be taken in the sense of *impartial*.

Related words: **disinterestedly** *adverb*, **disinterestedness** *noun*.

disparage (di-SPAR-ij) *verb*
belittle; speak of in a slighting way.

Related words: **disparager** and **disparagement** *both nouns*, **disparaging** *adjective*, **disparagingly** *adverb*.

disparate (DIS-pər-it) *adjective*
different in kind; without relation or comparison.

Related words: **disparately** *adverb*, **disparateness** *noun*.

dispassionate (dis-PASH-ə-nit) *adjective*
calm, impartial; free from emotion.

Related words: **dispassion** and **dispassionateness** *both nouns*, **dispassionately** *adverb*.

disquisition (DIS-kwə-ZISH-ən) *noun*
a long elaborate spoken or written account of something.

Related word: **disquisitional** *adjective*.

dissemble (di-SEM-bəl) *verb*
conceal (one's true motives or feelings); pretend.

Related words: **dissembler** *noun*, **dissemblingly** *adverb*.

dissentient (di-SEN-shənt) *adjective*.
1. dissenting, especially from the views of the majority.
2. *(noun)* a person who dissents, especially from the views of the majority.

Related words: **dissentience** and **dissentiency** *both nouns*, **dissentiently** *adverb*.

dissentious (di-SEN-shəs) *adjective*
quarrelsome; contentious.

dither (DITH-ər) *verb*
1. tremble or quiver.
2. hesitate indecisively.

    Related words: **ditherer** *noun*, **dithery** *adjective*.

divagate (DĪ-və-GAYT) *verb*
1. stray, wander.
2. digress.

    Related word: **divagation** (DĪ-və-GAY-shən) *noun*.

doctrinaire (DOK-trə-NAIR) *adjective*
1. applying theories or principles without regard for practical considerations.
2. *(noun)* a pedantic theorist.

    Related word: **doctrinairism** (DOK-trə-NAIR-iz-əm) *noun*.

dolmen (DOHL-mən) *noun*
a prehistoric structure, considered to be a tomb, with a large, relatively flat stone laid atop large upright stones.

    Related word: **dolmenic** (dohl-MEN-ik) *adjective*.

dottle (DOT-əl) *noun*, also given as **dottel**
the plug of unburned tobacco left in a pipe after smoking.

dour (duur) *adjective*
gloomy; stern; obstinate.

    Related words: **dourly** *adverb*, **dourness** *noun*.

doyen (dwah-YAN), **doyenne** (dwah-YEN), *both nouns, plurals* **doyens** and **doyennes**
the senior member (male **doyen**, female **doyenne**) of a body of colleagues.

dross (draws) *noun*
1. impurities; rubbish.
2. scum on molten metal.

    Related words: **drossy** *adjective*, **drossiness** *noun*.

dubiety (doo-BĪ-i-tee) *noun, plural* **dubieties**; also given as **dubiosity** (DOO-bee-OS-i-tee), *plural* **dubiosities**
   a feeling of doubt; a doubtful matter.

   Related words: **dubious** (DOO-bee-əs) *adjective,* **dubiously** *adverb,* **dubiousness** *noun.*

dudgeon (DUJ-ən) *noun*
   resentment, indignation.

dutiful (DOO-tə-fəl) *adjective*
   1. showing due obedience.
   2. expressive of a sense of duty.

   Related words: **dutifully** *adverb,* **dutifulness** *noun.*

dysphemism (DIS-fə-MIZ-əm) *noun*
   an unpleasant or derogatory word or phrase substituted for a more pleasant or less offensive one; such a substitution.

   See **euphemism.**

   Related word: **dysphemistic** (DIS-fə-MIS-tik) *adjective.*

dysphoria (dis-FOR-ee-ə) *noun*
   a state of anxiety, unease, or mental discomfort.

   Related word: **dysphoric** *adjective.*

dystopia (dis-TOH-pee-ə) *noun*
   a place real or imaginary where living conditions are considered to be as bad as possible.

   Related words: **dystopian** *adjective,* **dystopianism** *noun.*

E

---

eager (EE-gər) *adjective*
See **anxious**.

ebullient (i-BUUL-yənt) *adjective*
bubbling over with excitement or high spirits; exuberant.

> Related words: **ebullience** and **ebulliency** *both nouns*, **ebulliently** *adverb*.

éclat (ay-KLAH) *noun*
brilliant success, general applause; elaborate display.

eclectic (i-KLEK-tik) *adjective*
choosing or accepting from various sources.

> Related words: **eclectically** *adverb*, **eclecticism** (i-KLEK-tə-SIZ-əm) and **eclecticist** (i-KLEK-tə-sist) *both nouns*.

ecology (i-KOL-ə-jee) *noun*
1. the scientific study of living things in relation to each other and their environment.
2. this relationship.

> Do not confuse **ecology** with **environment**, which means *surroundings, especially those affecting people's lives.* Misuse of **ecology**—a rapidly growing phenomenon—occurs in writing as well as speech, for example, in such locutions as "Pollution is contaminating our **ecology**." Substitution of **environment** makes this sentence understandable as well as correct.

> Related words: **ecologic** (EE-kə-LOJ-ik) and **ecological** *both adjectives*, **ecologically** *adverb*.

economic (EK-ə-NOM-ik) *adjective*
  1. of economics.
  2. pertaining to one's own finances.
    Do not confuse **economic** with **economical**, which see.

economical (EK-ə-NOM-i-kəl) *adjective*
  thrifty, avoiding waste.

> To set aright most succinctly the frequent confusion between **economic** and **economical**, consider the following: An **economical** person is not an **economic** person. And an **economic** historian is not an **economical** historian. Thus, **economical** has nothing to with *economics*, while **economic** has everything to do with *economics*. To conclude, writers may be **economical**, *sparing*, in their use of words, and scholars usually write **economic** tomes that may well be **uneconomical**, *unsparing*, in their use of words. So use both adjectives correctly in your own speech and writing. You will make your audience and your editors happy.

    Related word: **economically** *adverb*.

edacious (i-DAY-shəs)
  devouring, consuming; voracious.
    Related word: **edacity** (i-DAS-i-tee) *noun*.

educe (i-DOOS) *verb*
  1. bring out or develop; elicit (from a person).
  2. infer (from information).
    Related word: **educible** *adjective*.

effect (i-FEKT) *noun* and *verb*
    See **affect**.

effective (i-FEK-tiv) *adjective*
  1. powerful in its effect; producing an effect.
  2. making a striking impression.
  3. actual, existing; real.
  4. operative, in effect.
    Do not confuse **effective** with **effectual**, which see.
    Related words: **effectively** *adverb*, **effectiveness** and **effectivity** (i-fek-TIV-i-tee) *both nouns*.

effectual (i-FEK-choo-əl) *adjective*
answering its purpose; sufficient to produce a desired effect.

The difference between the meanings of **effective** and **effectual** is rather subtle, but careful speakers and writers perceive this difference and choose between the two adjectives carefully. The best way to illustrate the difference is to point out that a law that is **effective**—*operative, in effect*—becomes **effectual**—*answers its purpose*—only when the law is enforced.

Related words: **effectually** *adverb*, **effectualness** and **effectuality** (i-FEK-choo-AL-i-tee) *both nouns.*

effectuate (i-FEK-choo-AYT) *verb*
cause to happen; accomplish.

Related word: **effectuation** *noun.*

effete (i-FEET) *adjective*
lacking in vitality; worn out; sterile.

Related words: **effetely** *adverb*, **effeteness** *noun.*

efficacious (EF-i-KAY-shəs) *adjective*
producing the desired result; effective as a remedy or means.

Related words: **efficaciously** *adverb*, **efficaciousness** and **efficacity** (EF-i-KAS-i-tee) *noun.*

effulgent (i-FUL-jənt) *adjective*
radiant; splendid; shining forth brilliantly.

Related words: **effulgence** *noun*, **effulgently** *adverb.*

egregious (i-GREE-jəs) *adjective*
outstandingly bad; flagrant; glaring.

Related words: **egregiously** *adverb*, **egregiousness** *noun.*

eleemosynary (EL-ə-MOS-ə-NER-ee) *adjective*
charitable; supported by charity; gratuitous.

elegy (EL-i-jee) *noun, plural* **elegies**
a sorrowful or serious poem or piece of music, especially one written as a lament for a dead person.

Do not confuse **elegy** with **eulogy**, which see.

Related words: **elegiac** (EL-i-JĪ-ək) *adjective*, **elegist** (EL-i-jist) *noun*, **elegize** (EL-i-JĪZ) *verb*

elenchus (i-LENG-kəs) *noun, plural* **elenchi** (i-LENG-kī)
a logical argument that refutes another argument by proving the
contrary of its conclusion.

elixir (i-LIK-sər) *noun*
an aromatic remedy believed to cure all ills.

emanate (EM-ə-NAYT) *verb*
issue or originate from a source.

> Related words: **emanative** (EM-ə-nə-TIV) and **emanatory** (EM-ə-
> nə-TOR-ee) *both adjectives,* **emanation** (EM-ə-NAY-shən) and
> **emanator** (EM-ə-NAY-tər) *both nouns.*

emasculate (i-MAS-kyə-LAYT) *verb*
1. deprive of force, especially said of writing style.
2. castrate; geld.

> Related words: **emasculate** (i-MAS-kyə-lit), **emasculative** (i-
> MAS-kyə-LAY-tiv), and **emasculatory** (i-MAS-kyə-lə-TOR-ee) *all
> adjectives;* **emasculation** (i-MAS-kyə-LAY-shən) and **emasculator**
> (i-MAS-kyə-LAY-tər) *both nouns.*

embrocation (EM-broh-KAY-shən) *noun*
a liquid used for rubbing on the body to relieve muscular pain, etc.

> Related word: **embrocate** (EM-broh-KAYT) *verb*

emetic (ə-MET-ik) *noun*
a medicine or other agent used to induce vomiting.

> Related words: **emetic** *adjective,* **emetically** *adverb.*

éminence grise (ay-mee-nahns GREEZ)
French: in English translated as "gray eminence," a close adviser,
especially one who exercises power behind the scenes.

emollient (i-MOL-yənt) *adjective*
softening or soothing the skin.

> Related words: **emollience** and **emollient** *both nouns.*

emolument (i-MOL-yə-mənt) *noun*
a fee received; a salary.

empathy (EM-pə-thee) *noun*
the ability to identify oneself mentally with a person or thing and
so understand his feelings or its meaning.

Do not confuse **empathy** with the well-known word **sympathy**, with several meanings, especially *a feeling of pity or tenderness toward one suffering pain, grief, or trouble.*

Related words: **empathetic** (EM-pǝ-THET-ik) and **empathic** (em-PATH-ik) *both adjectives,* **empathetically** and **empathically** *both adverbs,* **empathize** (EM-pǝ-THĪZ) *verb.*

encomiast (en-KOH-mee-AST) *noun*
1. a person who writes or utters an **encomium,** which see.
2. a eulogist.

Related words: **encomiastic** (en-KOH-mee-AS-tik) *adjective,* **encomiastically** *adverb.*

encomium (en-KOH-mee-ǝm) *noun, plural* **encomiums** and **encomia** (en-KOH-mee-ǝ)
high praise given in speech or writing.

endemic (en-DEM-ik) *adjective,* also given as **endemical**
1. of a disease, commonly found in a particular country or district or group of people.
2. *(noun)* such a disease.

Do not confuse **endemic** with **epidemic,** which see.

Related words: **endemically** *adverb,* **endemism** (EN-dǝ-MIZ-ǝm) and **endemicity** (EN-dǝ-MIS-i-tee) *both nouns.*

energize (EN-ǝr-JĪZ) *verb*

See **enervate.**

enervate (EN-ǝr-VAYT) *verb*
cause to lose vitality.

In poor writing and speech, the verb **enervate** often appears mistakenly in place of **energize,** a well understood verb that means *invigorate* or *give energy to.* Writers and speakers may be misled perhaps by the similarity in spelling, perhaps by the dangerous impulse to choose an uncommon word wherever a common word will do. In this case, such writers substitute an antonym for the correct word, and thus end up saying exactly the opposite of what they want to say. In your own writing, stay away from unfamiliar words unless you first check them in a dictionary. Stressing elegance in word choice can lead you down the garden path.

Related words: **enervation** (EN-ər-VAY-shən) and **enervator** (EN-ər-VAY-tər) *both nouns,* **enervative** (EN-ər-VAY-tiv) *adjective.*

engender (en-JEN-dər) *verb*
give rise to; beget.

Related words: **engenderer** and **engenderment** *both nouns.*

ennui (ahn-WEE) *noun*
a feeling of mental weariness from lack of interest; boredom.

enormity (i-NOR-mi-tee) *noun, plural* **enormities**
1. great wickedness.
2. a serious crime or error.

The noun **enormity** is used frequently with the meaning of *enormous size* or *immensity.* Whatever the historical justification for this definition, the use of **enormity** in this sense starts the other meanings of this valuable word down the path to extinction. While it easy to see the confusion of **enormousness** with **enormity**, careful writers and speakers do not fall into this trap. Nor should you. Use **enormity** in discussing heinous crimes, **immensity** in discussing great size.

enormousness (i-NOR-məs-nis) *noun*

See **enormity**.

entreat (en-TREET) *verb*
request earnestly or emotionally; beseech.

Related words: **entreatingly** *adverb,* **entreatment** and **entreaty** *both nouns.*

enviable (EN-vee-ə-bəl) *adjective*
desirable enough to arouse envy.

Do not confuse **enviable** with the more common adjective **envious,** meaning *full of envy.* Thus, we write "She has an **enviable** reputation," not an **envious** reputation. Writers who mistakenly use these words interchangeably—a definite no-no—are held in low regard by editors and intelligent readers.

Related words: **enviableness** *noun,* **enviably** *adverb.*

envious (EN-vee-əs) *adjective*

See **enviable**.

environment (en-VĪ-rən-mənt) *noun*
    See **ecology**.

ephemeral (i-FEM-ər-əl) *adjective*
    lasting only a very short time; transitory.
    Related words: **ephemerally** *adverb*, **ephemerality** (i-FEM-ə-RAL-i-tee) and **ephemeralness** (i-FEM-ər-əl-nis) *both nouns*.

epicene (EP-i-SEEN) *adjective*
    1. belonging to, or sharing the characteristics of, both sexes; of no definite sex or kind.
    2. effeminate; unmasculine.
    Related word: **epicenism** (EP-i-SEEN-iz-əm) *noun*.

epicure (EP-i-KYUUR) *noun*
    See **gourmet**.

epidemic (EP-i-DEM-ik) *adjective*
    1. of a disease, spreading rapidly through a community where the disease is not always prevalent, infecting many persons at the same time.
    2. *(noun)* such a disease.
    Do not confuse **epidemic** with **endemic**. The word **epidemic** is in common use and well known, but **endemic**, as an adjective meaning *commonly found in a particular country or district or group of people*, is less frequently used and is most likely to be used correctly by knowledgable epidemiologists. Try to remember.
    Related words: **epidemically** *adverb*, **epidemicity** (EP-i-də-MIS-i-tee) *noun*.

epigone (EP-i-GOHN) *noun*, *plural* **epigones** and **epigoni** (e-PI-goh-nī); the singular form is also given as **epigon** (EP-i-GON), *plural* **epigons**
    an undistinguished imitator or descendant of an illustrious person or family.
    Related words: **epigonic** (EP-i-GON-ik) *adjective*, **epigonism** (i-PIG-ə-NIZ-əm) *noun*.

epiphany (i-PIF-ə-nee) *noun*, *plural* **epiphanies**
    1. a manifestation, as of God; usually, a manifestation of Christ as divine.

2. a sudden, intuitive insight into the essential meaning of something.

Related words: **epiphanic** (EP-ə-FAN-ik) and **epiphanous** (i-PIF-ə-nəs) *both adjectives.*

epistolary (i-PIS-tə-LER-ee) *adjective*
contained in or carried on by letters; of or pertaining to letters.

epitaph (EP-i-TAF) *noun*
See **epithet**.

epithet (EP-ə-THET) *noun*
1. a descriptive word or phrase.
2. a contemptuous word or phrase.

Do not confuse **epithet** with the well-understood **epitaph**, meaning *words inscribed on a tomb or describing a dead person.* While **epitaph** is almost never used incorrectly, **epithet** frequently appears incorrectly in student themes.

Related words: **epithetic** (EP-i-THET-ik) and **epithetical** (EP-i-THET-i-kəl) *both adjectives.*

epitome (i-PIT-ə-mee) *noun*
1. something that shows on a small scale the qualities of something larger.
2. a person who embodies a quality.

Epitome does not mean *the best,* even though many people think this is one of the word's meanings. Use the word only as defined above, for example, "She is the **epitome** of grace."

Related words: **epitomic** (EP-i-TOM-ik) and **epitomical** (EP-i-TOM-i-kəl) *both adjectives,* **epitomize** (i-PIT-ə-MĪZ) *verb.*

eponym (EP-ə-nim) *noun*
a person whose name is taken for a people, place, institution, etc.

Related words: **eponymic** (EP-ə-NIM-ik) and **eponymous** (ə-PON-ə-məs) *both adjectives,* **eponymy** (ə-PON-ə-mee) *noun.*

equable (EK-wə-bəl) *adjective*
1. uniform, unvarying.
2. even-tempered.

Do not confuse **equable** with **equitable**, which see.

Related words: **equability** (EK-wə-BIL-i-tee) and **equableness** (EK-wə-bəl-nis) *both nouns,* **equably** *adverb.*

equitable (EK-wi-tə-bəl) *adjective*
fair and just.

Do not confuse **equitable** with **equable,** meaning *uniform, unvarying; even-tempered.* A legal claim may be **equitable;** a region's weather conditions and a person's temperament may be **equable.**

Related words: **equitableness** *noun,* **equitably** *adverb.*

equivocal (i-KWIV-ə-kəl) *adjective*
1. able to be interpreted in two ways; ambiguous.
2. of doubtful nature or character; questionable; suspicious.

Related words: **equivocacy** (i-KWIV-ə-kə-see), **equivocality** (i-KWIV-ə-KAL-i-tee), and **equivocalness** (i-KWIV-ə-kəl-nis) *all nouns;* **equivocally** *adverb.*

equivocate (i-KWIV-ə-KAYT) *verb*
1. use ambiguous words in order to conceal the truth.
2. tell lies.

Related words: **equivocatingly** (i-KWIV-ə-KAYT-ing-lee) *adverb,* **equivocation** (i-KWIV-ə-KAY-shən) and **equivocator** (i-KWIV-ə-KAY-tər) *both nouns.*

equivoque (EK-wə-VOHK) *noun,* also given as **equivoke**
1. a play on words; a pun.
2. ambiguity.

eremite (ER-ə-MĪT) *noun*
a hermit or recluse, especially one who has taken religious vows.

Related words: **eremitic** (ER-ə-MIT-ik), **eremitical** (ER-ə-MIT-i-kəl), and **eremitish** (ER-ə-MĪ-tish) *all adjectives;* **eremitism** (ER-ə-MIT-iz-əm) *noun.*

eructation (i-ruk-TAY-shən) *noun*
1. belching.
2. discharge of a volcano.

Related words: **eruct** (i-RUKT) and **eructate** (i-RUK-tayt) *both verbs,* **eructative** (i-RUK-tə-tiv) *adjective.*

eschew (es-CHOO) *verb*
avoid; abstain from.

> Related words: **eschewal** and **eschewer** *both nouns.*

escritoire (ES-kri-TWAHR) *noun*
a writing desk with drawers.

esoteric (ES-ə-TER-ik) *adjective*
intended only for people with special knowledge or interest; not generally intelligible.

> Do not confuse **esoteric** with **exoteric**, which see.

> Related words: **esoterica** (ES-ə-TER-i-kə) *noun,* **esoterically** *adverb.*

esurient (i-SUUR-ee-ənt) *adjective*
1. hungry.
2. greedy.

> Related words: **esurience** and **esuriency** *both nouns,* **esuriently** *adverb.*

ethos (EE-thos) *noun*
the characteristic spirit and beliefs of a community, person, or literary work.

etiology (EE-tee-OL-ə-jee), *plural* **etiologies**
1. the study of causes, as in philosophy, physics, etc.
2. the assignment of cause, especially in disease.

> Related word: **etiologist** *noun.*

eulogy (YOO-lə-jee) *noun, plural* **eulogies**; also given as **eulogium** (yoo-LOH-jee-əm), *plural* **eulogiums** and **eulogia** (yoo-LOH-jee-ə)
a speech or piece of writing in praise of a person, especially a funeral oration; praise.

> Do not confuse **eulogy** with **elegy**, meaning *sorrowful music or poetry, especially a piece written as a lament for a dead person.* The distinction is that a **eulogy**—not an **elegy**—is given at a funeral or memorial service and, particularly in modern times, may be cast as a message of general hope or of genial good humor.

> Related words: **eulogist** *noun,* **eulogize** (YOO-lə-JĪZ) *verb.*

euphemism (YOO-fə-MIZ-əm) *noun*
a mild or roundabout expression substituted for one considered offensive, too harsh, or too blunt.

Do not confuse **euphemism** with **euphuism**, which see.

Related words: **euphemist** *noun*; **euphemistic** (YOO-fə-MIS-tik), **euphemistical**, and **euphemious** (yoo-FEE-mee-əs) *all adjectives*; **euphemistically** and **euphemiously** *both adverbs*.

euphuism (YOO-fyoo-IZ-əm) *noun*
1. an artificial or affected style of writing.
2. high-flown language.

Do not confuse **euphuism**, *an affected style*, with **euphemism**, *a roundabout expression*. The former is considered excessively ornate, the latter inappropriately indirect, in contrast with modern writing, which values calling a spade a spade.

Related words: **euphuist** *noun*, **euphuistic** (YOO-fyoo-IS-tik) and **euphuistical** (YOO-fyoo-IS-ti-kəl) *both adjectives,* **euphuistically** (YOO-fyoo-IS-ti-klee) *adverb.*

exacerbate (ig-ZAS-ər-BAYT) *verb*
make (pain, disease, anger, etc.) worse; aggravate.

Related words: **exacerbatingly** (ig-ZAS-ər-BAYT-eeng-lee) *adverb,* **exacerbation** (ig-ZAS-ər-BAY-shən) *noun.*

excoriate (ik-SKOR-ee-AYT) *verb*
1. denounce, reproach harshly.
2. remove part of the skin by abrasion; strip or peel off (skin).

Related word: **excoriation** (ik-SKOR-ee-AY-shən) *noun.*

exculpate (EK-skul-PAYT) *verb*
free (a person) from blame; clear of a charge of wrongdoing; exonerate.

Related words: **exculpable** (ik-SKUL-pə-bəl) and **exculpatory** (ik-SKUL-pə-TOR-ee) *both adjectives,* **exculpation** (EK-skul-PAY-shən) *noun.*

execrable (EK-si-krə-bəl) *adjective*
very bad; abhorrent, detestable, abominable.

Related words: **execrableness** *noun,* **execrably** *adverb.*

execrate (EK-si-KRAYT) *verb*
detest greatly; denounce; utter curses upon.

Related words: **execration** (EK-si-KRAY-shən) and **execrator** (EK-si-KRAY-tər) *both nouns;* **execrative** (EK-si-KRAY-tiv) and **execratory** (EK-si-krə-TOR-ee) *both adjectives.*

exegesis (EK-si-JEE-sis) *noun, plural* **exegeses** (EK-si-JEE-seez)
critical exposition or interpretation of a text, especially of Scripture.

Related words: **exegetic** (EK-si-JET-ik) and **exegetical** *both adjectives.*

exegete (EK-si-JEET) *noun,* also given as **exegetist** (EK-si-JET-ist)
a person skilled in exegesis.

exemplar (ig-ZEM-plahr) *noun*
1. a worthy model or pattern.
2. a typical example.

exemplary (ig-ZEM-plə-ree) *adjective*
1. very good, an example to others.
2. serving as an example.

Related words: **exemplarily** (ig-ZEM-plə-rə-lee) *adverb,* **exemplariness** and **exemplarity** (IG-zem-PLAR-i-tee) *both nouns.*

exemplify (ig-ZEM-plə-FLĪ) *verb*
serve as an example of.

Related words: **exemplifiable** (ig-ZEM-plə-FĪ-ə-bəl) and **exemplificative** (ig-ZEM-plə-fi-KAY-tiv) *both adjectives,* **exemplification** (ig-ZEM-plə-fi-KAY-shən) and **exemplifier** (ig-ZEM-plə-FĪ-ər) *both nouns.*

exequies (EK-si-kweez) *noun plural; singular* **exequy**
funeral rites; obsequies.

exhaustive (ig-ZAWS-tiv) *adjective*
trying all possibilities; thorough.

Do not confuse **exhaustive** with **exhausted** or **exhausting,** which are used primarily to mean *fatigued* and *fatiguing* respectively. An **exhaustive** search means a *thorough search,* not a *tiring search.*

Related words: **exhaustively** *adverb,* **exhaustiveness** *noun.*

existentialism (EG-zi-STEN-shə-LIZ-əm) *noun*

a philosophical theory emphasizing that a person is responsible for his own actions and free to choose his development and destiny.

Related words: **existential** *adjective*, **existentialist** *adjective* and *noun*, **existentially** *adverb*.

exoteric (EK-sə-TER-ik) *adjective*

1. understandable by outsiders.
2. commonplace, popular.

Do not confuse **exoteric** with **esoteric**, which means *intended only for people with special knowledge or interest*. Thus, **esoteric** is used to characterize knowledge or information that may be possessed by persons on the inside, **exoteric** to characterize knowledge or information that is widely available.

Related words: **exoterically** *adverb*, **exotericism** (EK-sə-TER-i-siz-əm) *noun*.

expatiate (ik-SPAY-shee-AYT) *verb*

speak or write about (a subject) at great length or in detail.

Related words: **expatiation** (ik-SPAY-shee-AY-shən) and **expatiator** (ik-SPAY-shee-AY-tər) *both nouns*.

expiate (EK-spee-AYT) *verb*

make amends for (wrongdoing); atone.

Related words: **expiable** (EK-spee-ə-bəl) and **expiatory** (EK-spee-ə-TOR-ee) *both adjectives*, **expiation** (EK-spee-AY-shən) and **expiator** (EK-spee-AY-tər) *both nouns*.

explicate (EK-spli-KAYT) *verb*

1. make clear.
2. explain (a literary work etc.); interpret.

Related words: **explicable** (EK-spli-kə-bəl), **explicative** (EK-spli-kə-tiv), and **explicatory** (EK-spli-kə-TOR-ee) *all adjectives*; **explication** (EK-spli-KAY-shən) and **explicator** (EK-spli-KAY-tər) *both nouns*.

expostulate (ik-SPOS-chə-LAYT) *verb*

1. make a friendly protest.
2. reason or argue with a person.

Related words: **expostulatingly** (ik-SPOS-chə-LAYT-ing-lee) *adverb*, **expostulation** (ik-SPOS-chə-LAY-shən) and **expostulator** (ik-SPOS-chə-LAY-tər) *both nouns*, **expostulatory** (ik-SPOS-chə-lə-TOR-ee) *adjective*.

expunge (ik-SPUNJ) *verb*
wipe or rub out; erase; delete.

Related word: **expunger** *noun*.

expurgate (EK-spər-GAYT) *verb*
1. purify (a book etc.) by removing objectionable matter.
2. remove (such matter).

Related works: **expurgation** (EK-spər-GAY-shən) and **expurgator** (EK-spər-GAY-tər) *both nouns*.

extenuate (ik-STEN-yoo-AYT) *verb*
make (a person's guilt or offense) seem less by providing a partial excuse.

Related words: **extenuating** and **extenuative** (ik-STEN-yoo-AY-tiv) *both adjectives*, **extenuatingly** *adverb*, **extenuator** *noun*.

extirpate (EK-stər-PAYT) *verb*
root out and destroy completely.

Related words: **extirpation** (EK-stər-PAY-shən) and **extirpator** (EK-stər-PAY-tər) *both nouns*, **extirpative** (EK-stər-PAY-tiv) *adjective*.

extrinsic (ek-STRIN-sik) *adjective*
1. originating from outside.
2. not essential or inherent; extraneous.
Related word: **extrinsically** *adverb*.

F

factious (FAK-shəs) *adjective*
1. having factions.
2. creating dissension; turbulent.

Do not confuse **factious** with **factitious**, which see.

Related words: **factiously** *adverb*, **factiousness** *noun*.

factitious (fak-TISH-əs) *adjective*
1. made for a special purpose.
2. not genuine, contrived, artificial.

Do not confuse **factitious** with its look-alike, **factious**. **Factious** has meanings related to *factions*. **Factitious** suggests *manufacture; contrivance* and *artificiality*.

Related words: **factitiously** *adverb*, **factitiousness** *noun*.

fainéant (FAY-nay-ahn) *noun*, also given as **faineant** (FAY-nee-ənt)
1. an idler.
2. *(adjective)* idle, indolent.

Related words: **fainéance** *noun*, also given as **faineance** (FAY-nee-əns).

fakir (fə-KEER) *noun*, also given as **fakeer**
a Muslim or Hindu religious beggar regarded as a holy man.

Do not confuse **fakir** with **faker**, *someone who tries to deceive people.*

famous (FAY-məs) *adjective*
See **notorious**.

farrago (fə-RAH-goh) *noun, plural* **farragos** or **farragoes**
a confused mixture; a medley, a hodgepodge.

> Related word: **farraginous** (fə-RAJ-ə-nəs) *adjective*.

fascicle (FAS-i-kəl) *noun*
1. one section of a book that is published in installments.
2. in botany, a small bundle or tight cluster.

> Related words: **fascicular** (fə-SIK-yə-lər) and **fasciculate** (fə-SIK-yə-lit) *both adjectives*, **fasciculation** (fə-SIK-yə-LAY-shən) *noun*.

fatidic (fay-TID-ik) *adjective*, also given as **fatidical** (fay-TID-i-kəl)
1. prophetic.
2. possessing prophetic power.

> Related word: **fatidically** *adverb*.

fatuous (FACH-oo-əs) *adjective*
1. foolish, silly; purposeless.
2. unreal.

> Related words: **fatuitous** (fə-TOO-i-təs) *adjective*; **fatuity** (fə-TOO-i-tee), **fatuitousness**, and **fatuousness** (FACH-oo-əs-nis) *all nouns*; **fatuously** (FACH-oo-əs-lee) *adverb*.

fealty (FEE-əl-tee) *noun, plural* **fealties**
loyalty; fidelity.

febrifuge (FEB-rə-FYOOJ) *noun*
a cooling drink or medicine to reduce fever.

> Related word: **febrifugal** (FEB-rə-FYOO-gəl) *adjective*.

febrile (FEB-rəl) *adjective*
feverish.

> Related word: **febrility** (fi-BRIL-i-tee) *noun*.

feckless (FEK-lis) *adjective*
feeble and incompetent; irresponsible.

> Related words: **fecklessly** *adverb*, **fecklessness** *noun*.

feculent (FEK-yə-lənt) *adjective*
full of dregs or fecal matter; turbid; foul; stinking.

> Related word: **feculence** *noun*.

fecund (FEE-kənd) *adjective*
fertile; prolific.

Related word: **fecundity** (fi-KUN-di-tee) *noun.*

feisty (FĪ-stee) *adjective*
1. exuberant; spirited; spunky.
2. pugnacious; aggressive; ill-tempered.
3. troublesome; difficult.

Related words: **feistily** (FĪST-i-lee) *adverb,* **feistiness** *noun.*

fell (fel) *adjective*
1. ruthless, cruel, savage.
2. destructive.

Related word: **fellness** *noun.*

feral (FER-əl) *adjective*
1. wild, untamed.
2. in a wild state after escape from captivity.

fervid (FUR-vid) *adjective*
ardent, intense; fervent.

Related words: **fervidity** (fur-VID-i-tee) *noun,* **fervidly** (FUR-vid-lee) *adverb.*

fetid (FET-id) *adjective*
stinking.

Related words: **fetidly** *adverb,* **fetidness** and **fetidity** (fe-TID-i-tee) *both nouns.*

fictive (FIK-tiv) *adjective*
1. imaginary; fictitious.
2. related to the creation of fiction.

Related word: **fictively** *adverb.*

flagitious (flə-JISH-əs) *adjective*
deeply criminal; utterly villainous.

Related words: **flagitiously** *adverb,* **flagitiousness** *noun.*

flatulent (FLACH-ə-lənt) *adjective*
1. causing or suffering from the formation of gas in the intestinal tract.

2. pretentious; windy, puffed up.

Related words: **flatulence** and **flatulency** *both nouns*, **flatulently** *adverb*.

flaunt (flawnt) *verb*

display oneself or one's possessions ostentatiously.

Do not confuse **flaunt** with **flout**, which see.

Related words: **flaunter** *noun*, **flauntingly** *adverb*.

fledged (flejd) *adjective*

1. of young birds, with fully grown wing feathers; able to fly.
2. mature, trained, and experienced.

fleer (fleer) *verb*

laugh impudently or mockingly; jeer, deride.

Related words: **fleer** *noun*, **fleeringly** (FLEER-ing-lee) *adverb*.

flotsam (FLOT-səm) *noun*

1. debris or wreckage found floating on the water.
2. **flotsam and jetsam**, tramps, vagrants, etc.; odds and ends.

See **jetsam**.

flounder (flown-dər) *verb*

1. move clumsily and with difficulty, as in mud.
2. make mistakes or become confused when trying to do something.

Do not confuse **flounder** with **founder**, which see.

Related word: **flounderingly** *adverb*.

flout (flowt) *verb*

1. disobey openly and scornfully.
2. mock; express scorn for.

Careless writers and speakers, encouraged by the siren call of permissive dictionaries, may use **flaunt**, meaning *display ostentatiously*, when **flout**, meaning *express scorn for*, is the meaning intended. While this misuse is often seen, perhaps because the two verbs are close in pronunciation, it should be avoided. Here is a sentence that will help you remember the principal meanings of the two verbs: "People **flaunt** their ignorance when they **flout** established principles of good writing and speech."

Related words: **flouter** *noun,* **floutingly** *adverb.*

forceful (FORS-fəl) *adjective*
powerful and vigorous; effective; impressive

Do not confuse **forceful** with **forcible,** which see.

Related words: **forcefully** *adverb,* **forcefulness** *noun.*

forcible (FOR-sə-bəl) *adjective*
accomplished by force.

Some dictionaries treat **forceful** as one of the meanings of **forcible,** since people more and more use **forcible** in this sense. Notwithstanding, it is worthwhile to maintain the distinction between the two words. Careful writers and speakers use **force-ful** in the sense of *powerful and vigorous,* **forcible** in the sense of *accomplished by force.* When inspired, most of us can deliver a **forceful** speech, but only a felon or an authorized person—for example, a police officer or a firefighter—can ever make a **forcible** entry.

Related words: **forcibleness** and **forcibility** (FOR-sə-BIL-ə-tee) *both nouns,* **forcibly** *adverb.*

forswear (for-SWAIR) *verb*
1. give up.
2. renounce, especially under oath.
3. **forswear oneself,** swear falsely, commit perjury.

Related word: **forswearer** *noun.*

forte (fort) *noun*
a person's strong point.

The pronunciation of **forte** as FOR-tay is frequently heard but must be considered incorrect except when **forte** is intended as a term in music, with the meaning of *loud* or *loudly.*

forthcoming (FORTH-KUM-ing) *adjective*
1. about to appear; approaching.
2. made available or produced when needed.
3. willing to give information; responsive.

Related word: **forthcomingness** *noun.*

forthwith (FORTH-WITH) *adverb*
without delay; immediately.

fortuitous (for-TOO-i-təs) *adjective*
happening by chance; accidental.

> **Fortuitous** is rapidly losing the meanings given above, with most writers and speakers preferring to use this adjective to mean *lucky*. The adjective they appear to have in mind—if indeed they think about what they are saying—is **fortunate**. So widespread is this rape of **fortuitous** that *lucky* or its equivalent is now given by many dictionaries as a second meaning of this otherwise excellent, unambiguous adjective. Careful writers and speakers resist this misguided use of **fortuitous**, but maybe they are fighting a losing battle. In your own work, fight the good fight to preserve **fortuitous** and keep editors happy.

> Related words: **fortuitously** *adverb*, **fortuitousness** and **fortuity** (for-TOO-i-tee) *both nouns*.

fortunate (FOR-chə-nit) *adjective*

See **fortuitous**.

founder (FOWN-dər) *verb*
1. of a ship, fill with water and sink.
2. fail completely.

> **Flounder**, meaning *move clumsily and with difficulty*, is sometimes confused with **founder**, meaning *fail completely* and *fill with water and sink*. Undoubtedly, the similarity in spelling of the two verbs does not make life easy for careless writers and speakers, but the distinction between **founder** and **flounder** should be retained. Remember that you and I can **flounder** helplessly until we get our bearings, and while ships, political parties, organizations, and the like can also **flounder** as they try to make their way through difficult situations, when they are going down for the count, they are **foundering**. And that's as final as things can get.

fractious (FRAK-shəs) *adjective*
irritable, peevish; unruly.

> Do not confuse **fractious** with **factious**, which has the meaning *creating tension*. The two words are so nearly identical in

spelling that this confusion is understandable. But who ever said good writing is easy? Above all, don't become **fractious** when you must deal with **factious** people.

Related words: **fractiously** *adverb*, **fractiousness** *noun*.

frangible (FRAN-jə-bəl) *adjective*
breakable, fragile.

Related words: **frangibility** (FRAN-jə-BIL-i-tee) and **frangibleness** (FRAN-jə-bəl-nis) *both nouns*.

fratricide (FRA-tri-SĪD) *noun*
1. the act of killing one's brother or sister.
2. a person who commits this crime.

Related word: **fratricidal** (FRA-tri-SĪD-əl) *adjective*.

frenetic (frə-NET-ik) *adjective*
frantic; frenzied.

Related word: **frenetically** *adverb*.

friable (FRĪ-ə-bəl) *adjective*
easily crumbled, crumbly.

Related words: **friability** (FRĪ-ə-BIL-i-tee) and **friableness** (FRĪ-ə-bəl-nis) *both nouns*.

frisson (free-SAWN) *noun, plural* **frissons** (free-SAWNZ)
1. an emotional thrill.
2. a shudder of emotion.

frowzy (FROW-zee) *adjective*, also given as **frowsy** (FROW-zee)
1. ill-smelling or musty.
2. unkempt; slovenly.

Related words: **frowzily** (FROW-zi-lee) *adverb*, **frowziness** *noun*.

fugacious (fyoo-GAY-shəs) *adjective*
1. fleeting, transitory.
2. difficult to capture.

Related words: **fugaciousness** and **fugacity** (fyoo-GAS-i-tee) *both nouns*, **fugaciously** *adverb*.

fulsome (FUUL-səm) *adjective*
cloying, excessive, disgusting.

Fulsome is an example of a word with a well-defined and useful meaning that is in danger of being lost because many writers use the word loosely, and permissive lexicographers write their definitions based on how writers use words rather than how writers should use words. Thus, because many uninformed writers, who may view **fulsome** as a synonym for **full**, use **fulsome** to convey the meaning of *copious* or *abundant*, modern dictionaries often include this sense in writing their definitions. While there is controversy over this use of **fulsome**, there is little doubt today that informed writers and their editors wish to preserve the meaning of **fulsome** as *cloying*, *excessive*, and *disgusting*. At the same time, because of the need to avoid ambiguity in your writing, you ought to use **fulsome** only to convey the meanings given above, and make it clear you do not mean *copious* or *abundant*.

Related words: **fulsomely** *adverb*, **fulsomeness** *noun*.

G

---

galimatias (GAL-ə-MAY-shee-əs) *noun*
confused or unintelligible talk.

gallimaufry (GAL-ə-MAW-free) *noun, plural* **gallimaufries**
a jumble or medley; a hodgepodge.

gambit (GAM-bit) *noun*
1. an opening move in chess in which a player intentionally sacrifices a pawn or other piece in order to gain an advantage.
2. a maneuver, especially in conversation, that is intended to secure an advantage.

gastronome (GAS-trə-NOHM) *noun*
a connoisseur of good eating and drinking.

> Related words: **gastronomic** (GAS-trə-NOM-ik) and **gastronomical** *both adjectives,* **gastronomically** *adverb,* **gastronomist** (ga-STRON-ə-mist) and **gastronomy** (ga-STRON-ə-mee) *both nouns.*

gauche (gohsh) *adjective*
1. lacking in ease and grace of manner; awkward.
2. tactless.

> Related words: **gauchely** *adverb,* **gaucheness** *noun.*

gaucherie (GOH-shə-REE) *noun, plural* **gaucheries** (GOH-shə-REEZ)
1. a gauche action.
2. gauche manners.

gelid (JEL-id) *adjective*
icy, ice-cold; chilly.

Related words: **gelidity** (jə-LID-i-tee) and **gelidness** (JEL-id-nis) *both nouns*, **gelidly** (JEL-id-lee) *adverb*.

genuflect (JEN-yuu-FLEKT) *verb*

1. bend the knee and lower the body, especially in reverence.
2. show servility.

Related words: **genuflection** (JEN-yuu-FLEK-shən) and **genu-flector** (JEN-yuu-FLEK-tər) *both nouns*.

gibbet (JIB-it) *noun*

a gallows; an upright post with an arm from which the bodies of executed criminals were formerly suspended.

gloaming (GLOH-ming) *noun*

the evening twilight; dusk.

glossolalia (GLAW-sə-LAY-lee-ə) *noun*

the power of speaking in unknown languages as claimed by religious groups in ecstatic worship; the gift of tongues.

Related word: **glossolalist** (glaw-SOL-ə-list) *noun*

gnosis (NOH-sis) *noun*

1. knowledge of spiritual mysteries.
2. mystical knowledge.

Related words: **gnostic** (NOS-tik) *adjective* and *noun*, **gnostical** (NOS-ti-kəl) *adjective*, **gnostically** *adverb*.

gourmand (guur-MAHND) *noun*

1. a lover of food.
2. a glutton.

Do not confuse **gourmand** with **gourmet**, which see.

Related words: **gourmandize** (GUUR-mən-DĪZ) *verb*, **gourmandise** (GUUR-mən-DEEZ) and **gourmandism** (GUUR-mən-diz-əm) *both nouns*.

gourmet (guur-MAY) *noun*

a connoisseur of good food and drink; an epicure; a gastronome.

Good writers and speakers do not use **gourmet** and **gourmand** as synonyms, even though many dictionaries bow to those who do not observe this distinction by supplying **gourmet** as one meaning of **gourmand**. It is important to be able to differentiate these two words, as even these same dictionaries implicitly do, since they stop short of supplying **gourmand** as one meaning of **gourmet**. Of course, their reason for doing so surely reflects the much less common use of **gourmand**, making it unlikely that writers will use **gourmand** mistakenly, if at all. As a careful writer, you ought to reserve **gourmand** for a person who can best be described as a *glutton*, **gourmet** for a person who can best be described as a *connoisseur of good food and drink* or *epicure*.

grabble (GRAB-əl) *verb*
1. feel or search with the hands; grope about.
2. sprawl on all fours; scramble for.

Related word: **grabbler** *noun*.

gracile (GRAS-il) *adjective*
slender, thin; gracefully slender.

Related words: **gracility** (gra-SIL-i-tee) and **gracileness** (GRAS-il-nis) *both nouns*.

grandiloquent (gran-DIL-ə-kwənt) *adjective*
1. using pompous language.
2. given to boastful talk.

Related words: **grandiloquence** *noun*, **grandiloquently** *adverb*.

gratuitous (grə-TOO-i-təs) *adjective*
1. given or done without good reason.
2. given or done without payment; free, unearned.

Related words: **gratuitously** *adverb*, **gratuitousness** *noun*.

grisette (gri-ZET) *noun*
a young French workingwoman, especially a seamstress or shop assistant.

Related word: **grisettish** *adjective*.

Grundyism (GRUN-dee-IZ-əm) *noun*
1. a narrow-minded adherence to conventionality, combining propriety and prudery in matters of personal behavior.
2. **grundyism**, an instance of such conventionalism.

Mrs. Grundy, a character created by English playwright Thomas Morton in his play *Speed the Plough* (1798), personifies the tyrannical constraints of conventional opinion in matters of propriety. Although Mrs. Grundy does not appear in the play, her presence is strongly felt when her name repeatedly comes up in the question "What will Mrs. Grundy say?" The modern counterpart of this question is our own "What will the neighbors say?"

Related words: **Grundyist** and **Grundyite** (GRUN-dee-ĪT) *both nouns.*

gudgeon (GUJ-ən) *noun*

1. a small freshwater fish used as bait.
2. a credulous person.
3. a dupe.

H

habitué (hə-BICH-oo-AY) *noun, plural* **habitués**
   one who visits a place regularly.

hagiography (HAG-ee-OG-rə-fee) *noun, plural* **hagiographies**
   the writing and study of the lives of saints.

   Related words: **hagiographer** (HAG-ee-OG-rə-fər) *noun,* **hagiographic** (HAG-ee-ə-GRAF-ik) and **hagiographical** *both adjectives.*

halcyon (HAL-see-ən) *adjective,* less frequently given as **halcyonian** (HAL-see-OH-nee-ən) and **halcyonic** (HAL-see-ON-ik)
   1. calm and peaceful.
   2. happy and prosperous.

harbinger (HAHR-bin-jər) *noun*
   a person, event, or thing that announces the approach of another; a forerunner; an omen.

harridan (HAR-i-dən) *noun*
   a bad-tempered old woman; a shrew.

haruspex (hə-RUS-peks) *noun, plural* **haruspices** (hə-RUS-pə-SEEZ)
   in ancient Rome, a priest who practiced divination, especially by examining the entrails of dead animals; a soothsayer.

   Related words: **haruspicy** (hə-RUS-pə-see) and **haruspication** (hə-RUS-pi-KAY-shən) *both nouns,* **haruspical** (hə-RUS-pi-kəl) *adjective.*

hauteur (hoh-TUR) *noun*
   1. haughtiness of manner.
   2. arrogance.

healthful (HELTH-fəl) *adjective*
1. conducive to good health.
2. beneficial; salutary.

Do not confuse **healthful** with **healthy**, which see.

Related words: **healthfully** *adverb*, **healthfulness** *noun*.

healthy (HEL-thee) *adjective*
1. having or showing good health.
2. prosperous or sound.

In discussing climate, diet, and other factors affecting health, our best writers and speakers employ **healthful** in the sense of *conducive to good health*. In describing a person, situation, business etc. showing health, our best writers employ **healthy** in the sense of *having or showing good health* or, as appropriate, *prosperous or sound*. So widespread is the confusion of **healthy** with **healthful** that—you guessed it—permissive lexicographers sprinkle holy water on this example of poor usage by treating the two words as synonyms. There is little hope of reversing this trend, but you will do yourself no harm by continuing to maintain the separate meanings of **healthful** and **healthy**. In doing so, you will mark yourself as a careful writer by continuing to have a **healthy** respect for the English language and do yourself a lot of good by following **healthful** practices in your daily life.

Related words: **healthily** *adverb*, **healthiness** *noun*.

hebdomedal (heb-DOM-ə-dəl) *adjective*
weekly.

Related word: **hebdomadally** *adverb*.

hebetude (HEB-i-TOOD) *noun*
dullness, obtuseness; lethargy.

Related words: **hebetate** (HEB-i-TAYT) *verb*, **hebetudinous** (HEB-i-TOO-də-nəs) *adjective*.

hector (HEK-tər) *verb*
1. intimidate by bullying; bully.
2. treat with insolence.

hegemony (hi-JEM-ə-nee) *noun, plural* **hegemonies**
1. dominance of leadership, especially by one nation over another.

2. leadership, predominance.

Related words: **hegemonic** (HEJ-ə-MON-ik) and **hegemonical** *both adjectives*, **hegemonism** (hi-JEM-ə-NIZ-əm) and **hegemonist** (hi-JEM-ə-nist) *both nouns*.

hegira (hi-JĪ-rə) *noun*, also given as **hejira**, with the same pronunciation, and as **hijra** (HIJ-rə)
1. a journey undertaken to escape danger or to enjoy a more congenial place.
2. **Hijra**, the flight of Muhammad to Medina in A.D. 622.

heinous (HAY-nəs) *adjective*
very wicked, odious; outrageous; totally reprehensible.

Related words: **heinously** *adverb*, **heinousness** *noun*.

henotheism (HEN-ə-thee-IZ-əm) *noun*
the belief in one god as the deity of one's family or tribe without disbelieving in the existence of other gods.

Related words: **henotheist** (HEN-ə-THEE-ist) *noun*, **henotheistic** (HEN-ə-thee-IS-tik) *adjective*.

hermeneutics (HUR-mə-NOO-tiks) *noun*
the art or science of interpretation, especially of Scripture.

Related words: **hermeneutic** and **hermeneutical** *both adjectives*.

heteroclite (HET-ər-ə-KLĪT) *adjective*, also given as **heteroclitic** (HET-ər-ə-KLIT-ik) and **heteroclitical**
1. abnormal or irregular.
2. *(noun)* a person or thing that deviates from what is considered normal.

heterodox (HET-ər-ə-DOKS) *adjective*
not in accordance with accepted doctrines or opinions; unorthodox.

Related words: **heterodoxly** *adverb*, **heterodoxy** *noun*.

heuristic (hyuu-RIS-tik) *adjective*
1. serving to discover.
2. pertaining to a trial-and-error method of computer problem solving.

Related word: **heuristically** *adverb*.

hircine (HUR-sīn) *adjective*
1. goatlike.
2. lustful.

historic (hi-STOR-ik) *adjective*
1. well-known or important in history.
2. making history, momentous.

Do not confuse **historic** with **historical**, which see.

historical (hi-STOR-i-kəl) *adjective*
1. belonging to or dealing with history or past events.
2. concerned with history.

Despite the willingness of some lexicographers to accept **historic** as a synonym for **historical**, the two words carry separate and useful meanings worth preserving. Consider that publication of a **historical** novel—*one that deals with past events, whether factual or not*—can intrigue us or leave us flat, but it seldom can achieve celebrity worthy of a place in history. On the other hand, a **historic** event—*one that has made history*—finds a place in history regardless of whether a novel is published that is based on the event. Again, a **historical** novel can achieve widespread readership even though it may not be based on a **historic** event, indeed even if it is based on an event that is actually the product of a novelist's imagination. Thus, you are advised to use this pair of adjectives as suggested here. **Historic** events may or may not become subjects of **historical** fiction.

Related word: **historically** *adverb*, **historicalness** *noun*.

histrionic (HIS-tree-ON-ik) *adjective*
1. of actors or acting.
2. dramatic or theatrical in manner.

Related word: **histrionically** *adverb*.

histrionics (HIS-tree-ON-iks) *noun, plural* or *singular*
dramatic behavior intended to impress people.

homunculus (hə-MUNG-kyə-ləs) *noun, plural* **homunculi** (hə-MUNG-kyə-lī)
1. a little man.
2. a manikin, a dwarf.

Related word: **homuncular** *adjective.*

honorific (ON-ə-RIF-ik) *noun*
1. an expression implying respect.
2. a mark of esteem.

Related words: **honorific** and **honorifical** *both adjectives,* **honorifically** *adverb.*

hortative (HOR-tə-tiv) and **hortatory** (HOR-tə-TOR-ee) *both adjectives*
1. serving or tending to exhort.
2. encouraging.

Related words: **hortation** (hor-TAY-shən) *noun,* **hortatively** (HOR-tə-tiv-lee) and **hortatorily** (HOR-tə-TOR-i-lee) *both adverbs.*

hotelier (OH-tel-YAY) *noun*
a hotelkeeper.

houri (HUUR-ee) *noun, plural* **houris**
1. a beautiful and voluptuous woman.
2. a beautiful virgin provided in paradise for each faithful Muslim.

hoyden (HOYD-ən) *noun,* also given as **hoiden**
1. a boisterous, carefree girl.
2. a tomboy.

Related words: **hoydenish** *adjective,* **hoydenism** *noun.*

hubris (HYOO-bris) *noun,* also given as **hybris** (HĪ-bris)
insolent pride or self-confidence; arrogance.

Related words: **hubristic** (hyoo-BRIS-tik) and **hybristic** (hī-BRIS-tik) *both adjectives.*

hyperbole (hī-PUR-bə-lee) *noun*
an exaggerated statement that is not meant to be taken literally.

Do not confuse **hyperbole** with **hyperbola** (hī-PUR-bə-lə), in geometry a plane curve of two equal infinite branches.

Related words: **hyperbolic** (HĪ-pər-BOL-ik) and **hyperbolical** *both adjectives,* **hyperbolically** *adverb.*

hypothecate (hī-POTH-ə-KAYT) *verb*
pledge or mortgage.

Related words: **hypothecation** (hī-POTH-ə-KAY-shən) and **hypothecator** (hī-POTH-ə-KAY-tər) *both nouns.*

I

iatrogenic (Ī-A-trə-JEN-ik) *adjective*
of a disease or medical condition, caused by diagnosis or treatment by a physician.
>Related word: **iatrogenicity** (Ī-A-trə-jə-NIS-i-tee) *noun.*

iconoclast (Ī-KON-ə-KLAST) *noun*
1. a person who attacks cherished beliefs.
2. a person who opposes the use of religious images in worship.
>Related words: **iconoclasm** (Ī-KON-ə-KLAZ-əm) *noun,* **iconoclastic** (Ī-KON-ə-KLAS-tik) *adjective,* **iconoclastically** (Ī-KON-ə-KLAS-ti-kə-lee) *adverb.*

idiosyncrasy (ID-ee-ə-SING-krə-see) *noun, plural* **idiosyncrasies**
a person's own attitude or way of thinking, behaving, etc. that is unlike that of any other.
>Related words: **idiosyncratic** (ID-ee-oh-sin-KRAT-ik) *adjective,* **idiosyncratically** (ID-ee-oh-sin-KRAT-i-kə-lee) *adverb.*

ignominious (IG-nə-MIN-ee-əs) *adjective*
bringing contempt or disgrace; humiliating.
>Related words: **ignominiously** *adverb,* **ignominiousness** and **ignominy** (IG-nə-MIN-ee) *both nouns.*

illusory (i-LOO-sə-ree) *adjective*
based on illusion; not real.
>Related words: **illusorily** (i-LOO-sə-rə-lee) *adverb,* **illusoriness** (i-LOO-sə-ree-nis) *noun.*

immure (i-MYUUR) *verb*
1. imprison.
2. shut in; seclude.

Related words: **immurement** and **immuration** (IM-yə-RAY-shən) *both nouns.*

impalpable (im-PAL-pə-bəl) *adjective*
1. unable to be touched, intangible.
2. not easily grasped by the mind.

Related words: **impalpability** (im-PAL-pə-BIL-i-tee) *noun*, **impalpably** (im-PAL-pə-blee) *adverb.*

impassioned (im-PASH-ənd) *adjective*
full of deep feeling, passionate; ardent.

Related words: **impassionedly** *adverb*, **impassionedness** *noun.*

impassive (im-PAS-iv) *adjective*
not feeling or showing emotion; apathetic.

Related words: **impassively** *adverb*, **impassiveness** and **impassivity** (IM-pa-SIV-i-tee) *both nouns.*

impeach (im-PEECH) *verb*
1. call in question, discredit.
2. charge a public official before an appropriate tribunal with misconduct in office.

Do not use **impeach** to mean *convict a public official.* First one is **impeached,** meaning *charged,* then one may or may not be convicted.

Related words: **impeachable** (im-PEE-chə-bəl) *adjective*, **impeacher** and **impeachment** *both nouns.*

impecunious (IM-pi-KYOO-nee-əs) *adjective*
having little or no money; penniless, needy.

Related words: **impecuniously** *adverb*, **impecuniousness** and **impecuniosity** (IM-pi-KYOO-nee-OS-i-tee) *both nouns.*

imply (im-PLĪ) *verb*
1. suggest without stating directly; hint.
2. mean; signify.
3. involve necessarily.

Do not confuse **imply** with **infer**, which see.

importunate (im-POR-chə-nit) *adjective*
1. making persistent requests.
2. troublesome, annoying.

Related words: **importunacy** (im-POR-chə-nə-see) and **importunateness** *both nouns*, **importunately** *adverb*, **importune** (IM-por-TOON) *verb*.

impracticable (im-PRAK-ti-kə-bəl) *adjective*
incapable of being put into practice.

Do not confuse **impractable** with **impractical**, which means *unwise* or *not practical* and is used most often to denote unrealistic behavior in the management of one's finances. This distinction does not reflect the practice of permissive lexicographers, who bow to uninformed writers and speakers by treating **impracticable** and **impractical** as synonyms. A careful writer, however, preserves the differences in meaning of these two adjectives. You may find it helpful to realize that *unwise management of one's resources* may be termed **impractical**, while a foolish plan may be termed **impractable** because it *will never be put into practice*.

Related words: **impracticability** (im-PRAK-ti-kə-BIL-i-tee) and **impracticableness** (im-PRAK-ti-kə-bəl-nis) *both nouns*, **impracticably** *adverb*.

imprecate (IM-prə-KAYT) *verb*
call down or invoke (a curse or evil) upon a person.

Related words: **imprecation** (IM-pri-KAY-shən) and **imprecator** (IM-pri-KAY-tər) *both nouns*, **imprecatory** (IM-pri-kə-TOR-ee) *adjective*.

imprimatur (IM-pri-MAH-tər) *noun*
1. sanction or approval.
2. an official license to print, especially works sanctioned by the Catholic Church.

impudicity (IM-pyuu-DIS-i-tee) *noun*
shamelessness; immodesty.

impugn (im-PYOON) *verb*
1. express doubts about the truth or honesty of.

2. try to discredit (motives, etc.).

Related words: **impugnable** (im-PYOON-ə-bəl) *adjective*; **impugnability, impugner,** and **impugnment** *all nouns.*

inamorata (in-AM-ə-RAH-tə), **inamorato** (in-AM-ə-RAH-toh) *both nouns, plural* **inamoratas, inamoratos**
a lover; a sweetheart (*female* **inamorata,** *male* **inamorato**).

inanition (IN-ə-NISH-ən) *noun*
lack of vigor, especially exhaustion from lack of nourishment.

Do not confuse **inanition** with **inanity,** which see.

inanity (i-NAN-i-tee) *noun, plural* **inanities**
silliness; shallowness, superficiality.

When two words are similar in spelling, careless writers may think they share a meaning. So it is with **inanity,** which means *silliness,* and **inanition,** which means *lack of vigor.* These words are related in etymology, which accounts for their similarity in spelling, but have totally different meanings. Do not fall into the trap of confusing them. Try not to slip into **inanity** when you are exhausted or so hungry that you risk **inanition.**

Related words: **inane** (i-NAYN) *adjective,* **inanely** *adverb.*

inauspicious (IN-aw-SPISH-əs) *adjective*
1. not auspicious, ill-omened.
2. unlucky; unfavorable.

Related words: **inauspiciously** *adverb,* **inauspiciousness** *noun.*

inchoate (in-KOH-it) *adjective*
just begun; undeveloped.

Related words: **inchoately** *adverb,* **inchoateness** *noun.*

incredible (in-KRED-ə-bəl) *adjective*
unbelievable; hard to believe.

Do not confuse **incredible** with **incredulous,** which see.

Related words: **incredibility** (in-KRED-ə-BIL-i-tee) and **incredibleness** (in-KRED-ə-bəl-nis) *both nouns,* **incredibly** *adverb.*

incredulous (in-KREJ-ə-ləs) *adjective*
unbelieving; showing disbelief; skeptical.

When careless writers or speakers use **incredulous**, meaning *unbelieving*, in place of **incredible**, meaning *unbelievable*, they are guilty of an error that is becoming more and more common, particularly among ill-educated persons. No editor will let this boner pass, nor should you. Remember that you may appear **incredulous** when a high official of our national government shows **incredible** ignorance of how simple words are spelled.

Related words: **incredulity** (IN-kri-DOO-li-tee) and **incredulousness** (in-KREJ-ə-ləs-nis) *both nouns,* **incredulously** (in-KREJ-ə-ləs-lee) *adverb.*

incubus (IN-kyə-bəs) *noun, plural* **incubuses** and **incubi** (IN-kyə-BĪ)

1. a nightmare.
2. a person or thing that oppresses like a nightmare.
3. a spirit said to haunt or trouble sleeping people, especially by having sexual intercourse with sleeping women.

indefatigable (IN-di-FAT-i-gə-bəl) *adjective*

1. that cannot be tired out.
2. untiring, unwearying.

Related words: **indefatigability** (IN-di-FAT-i-gə-BIL-i-tee) and **indefatigableness** (IN-di-FAT-i-gə-bəl-nis) *both nouns,* **indefatigably** *adverb.*

indigenous (in-DIJ-ə-nəs) *adjective*

born or produced naturally in a country or region.

Related words: **indigenity** (IN-di-JEN-i-tee) and **indigenousness** (in-DIJ-ə-nəs-nis) *both nouns,* **indigenously** *adverb.*

indomitable (in-DOM-i-tə-bəl) *adjective*

1. having an unyielding spirit, unconquerable.
2. stubbornly persistent when faced with difficulty or opposition.

Related words: **indomitability** (in-DOM-i-tə-BIL-i-tee) and **indomitableness** (in-DOM-i-tə-bəl-nis) *both nouns,* **indomitably** *adverb.*

indurate (IN-duu-RAYT) *verb*

1. make or become hard.
2. make callous or unfeeling.
3. accustom or become accustomed.

Related words: **induration** (IN-duu-RAY-shən) *noun,* **indurative** (IN-duu-RAY-tiv) *adjective.*

inebriety (IN-i-BRĪ-i-tee) *noun*
drunkenness; the habit of drunkenness.

Related words: **inebriant** (in-EE-bree-ənt) and **inebriation** (in-EE-bree-AY-shən) *both nouns,* **inebriate** (in-EE-bree-it) and **inebriated** (in-EE-bree-AYT-id) *both adjectives,* **inebriate** (in-EE-bree-AYT) *verb.*

ineffable (in-EF-ə-bəl) *adjective*
too great to be described; inexpressible.

Related words: **ineffability** (in-EF-ə-BIL-i-tee) and **ineffableness** *both nouns,* **ineffably** *adverb.*

ineluctable (IN-i-LUK-tə-bəl) *adjective*
that cannot be avoided or overcome.

Related words: **ineluctability** (IN-i-LUK-tə-BIL-i-tee) *noun,* **ineluctably** *adverb.*

inexorable (in-EK-sər-ə-bəl) *adjective*
unable to be persuaded by request or entreaty; relentless.

Related words: **inexorability** (in-EK-sər-ə-BIL-i-tee) and **inexorableness** *both nouns,* **inexorably** *adverb.*

infamous (IN-fə-məs) *adjective*
See **notorious.**

infelicitous (IN-fə-LIS-i-təs) *adjective*
inappropriate; unfortunate; unhappy.

Related words: **infelicitously** *adverb,* **infelicity** *noun.*

infer (in-FUR) *verb*
reach an opinion from facts or reasoning.

Even though many people use **infer** and **imply** interchangeably, you should not fall into this practice, which obscures an important difference in meaning. **Imply** has as one of its meanings *hint or suggest without stating directly,* and the person performing such an action is actively hinting or suggesting. With **infer,** the person who is *reaching an opinion from facts or reasoning* is an interpreter of one's voice, facial expression, demeanor, etc.

An easy way to keep these two verbs distinct from one another is to remember that the sender of an unstated message is **implying**, and the receiver of the message is **inferring**.

Related words: **inference** (IN-fər-əns) *noun*, **inferential** (IN-fə-REN-shəl) *adjective*, **inferentially** *adverb*.

infrangible (in-FRAN-jə-bəl) *adjective*
1. unbreakable.
2. inviolable.

Related words: **infrangibility** (in-FRAN-jə-BIL-i-tee) and **infrangibleness** *both nouns*, **infrangibly** *adverb*.

ingenious (in-JEEN-yəs) *adjective*
1. clever at inventing new things or methods.
2. cleverly contrived.

Do not confuse **ingenious** with **ingenuous**, which see.

Related words: **ingeniously** *adverb*, **ingeniousness** and **ingenuity** (IN-jə-NOO-i-tee) *both nouns*.

ingenuous (in-JEN-yoo-əs) *adjective*
1. open, frank, sincere.
2. unsophisticated, naive.

The adjective **ingenuous** seems to have an attraction for ill-educated writers and speakers who are beguiled by the word's relative rareness compared with **ingenious**, a more common adjective they understand well. While **ingenuous** and **ingenious** a long time ago were synonyms, they now have entirely different meanings despite their similar spellings. Whatever the reason for the confusion of the two words, you must use them correctly. **Ingenuous** means *unsophisticated*, and **ingenious** means *clever at inventing*. **Ingenious** inventers who are **ingenuous**, therefore, will do well to hire a lawyer to protect their interests, lest they fail to protect themselves when dealing with possibly unscrupulous manufacturers interested in putting attractive inventions on the market.

Related words: **ingenuously** *adverb*, **ingenuousness** *noun*.

ingratiate (in-GRAY-shee-AYT) *verb*
bring (oneself) into a person's favor, especially in order to gain an advantage.

Related words: **ingratiating** and **ingratiatory** (in-GRAY-shee-ə-TOR-ee) *both adjectives*, **ingratiation** (in-GRAY-shee-AY-shən) *noun.*

innocuous (i-NOK-yoo-əs) *adjective*
1. not injurious, harmless.
2. insignificant and dull.

Related words: **innocuously** *adverb*, **innocuousness** and **innocuity** (IN-ə-KYOO-i-tee) *both nouns.*

inordinate (in-OR-də-nit) *adjective*
excessive; immoderate, intemperate.

Related words: **inordinately** *adverb*, **inordinateness** *noun.*

insatiate (in-SAY-shee-it) *adjective*
never satisfied.

Related words: **insatiately** *adverb*, **insatiateness** and **insatiety** (IN-sə-TĪ-ə-tee) *both nouns.*

inscrutable (in-SKROO-tə-bəl) *adjective*
1. impossible to understand or interpret.
2. mysterious, baffling.

Related words: **inscrutability** (in-SKROO-tə-BIL-i-tee) and **inscrutableness** (in-SKROO-tə-bəl-nis) *both nouns*, **inscrutably** *adverb.*

insensate (in-SEN-sayt) *adjective*
1. without physical sensation, unfeeling.
2. without good sense, foolish.

Related words: **insensately** *adverb*, **insensateness** *noun.*

instauration (IN-staw-RAY-shən) *noun*
restoration, renewal, renovation.

Related word: **instaurator** (IN-staw-RAY-tər) *noun.*

internecine (IN-tər-NEE-seen) *adjective*, also given as **internecive** (IN-tər-NEE-siv)
1. mutually destructive; deadly.
2. of a struggle within a nation, organization, or the like.

Sense 2 of **internecine** has given thoughtful writers and some lexicographers much to argue about. They prefer not to use this adjective in any sense but *mutually destructive or deadly,* as in

"The **internecine** war we waged in Europe in World War II," which clearly was not *a struggle within a nation*. But anyone who holds to this puristic view is bound to lose out. You are well advised to use the term in either of the senses given above and not argue against either sense. Notwithstanding, when you wish to use **internecine**, make sure the context indicates clearly which sense you intend.

intestate (in-TES-tayt) *adjective*
not having made a valid will before death occurs.

Related word: **intestacy** (in-TES-tə-see) *noun*.

intumesce (IN-tuu-MES) *verb*
swell up, become swollen.

Related words: **intumescence** (IN-tuu-MES-əns) *noun*, **intumescent** *adjective*.

inure (in-YUUR) *verb*
accustom, especially to something unpleasant; habituate.

Related word: **inuredness** (in-YUUR-id-nis) and **inurement**, *both nouns*.

inveigh (in-VAY) *verb*
attack violently or bitterly in words; revile.

Related word: **inveigher** *noun*.

inveterate (in-VET-ər-it) *adjective*
1. habitual.
2. firmly established.

Related words: **inveteracy** and **inveterateness** *both nouns*, **inveterately** *adverb*.

invidious (in-VID-ee-əs) *adjective*
1. likely to cause resentment because of real or imagined injustice.
2. hateful.

Related words: **invidiously** *adverb*, **invidiousness** *noun*.

irascible (i-RAS-ə-bəl) *adjective*
irritable, hot-tempered.

Related words: **irascibility** (i-RAS-ə-BIL-i-tee) and **irascibleness** *both nouns*, **irascibly** *adverb*.

irrefragable (i-REF-rə-gə-bəl) *adjective*
indisputable, incontestable; unanswerable.

> Related words: **irrefragability** (i-REF-rə-gə-BIL-i-tee) and **irrefragableness** (i-REF-rə-gə-bəl-nis) *both nouns,* **irrefragably** (i-REF-rə-gə-blee) *adverb.*

isocracy (ī-SOK-rə-see) *noun, plural* **isocracies**
a government in which all individuals have equal political power.

> Related words: **isocrat** (ī-sə-KRAT) *noun,* **isocratic** (ī-sə-KRAT-ik) *adjective.*

iterate (IT-ə-RAYT) *verb*
utter again; repeat or perform again.

> Related words: **iteration** (IT-ə-RAY-shən) *noun,* **iterative** (IT-ər-ə-tiv) *adjective,* **iteratively** *adverb.*

J

jactation (jak-TAY-shən) *noun*
boasting; bragging.

janissary (JAN-ə-SER-ee) *noun, plural* **janissaries**; also given as **janizary**
(JAN-ə-ZER-ee), *plural* **janizaries**
1. a devoted follower or supporter.
2. a Turkish soldier.
3. from the 14th to the 19th century, a member of the Turkish Sultan's guard.

jaundiced (JAWN-dist) *adjective*
1. discolored as if by jaundice (a disease marked by yellowness of the skin, of the whites of the eyes, etc.).
2. filled with resentment, envy, or jealousy.

jejune (ji-JOON) *adjective*
1. scanty.
2. meager, not nourishing.
3. unsatisfying to the mind; without significance; insipid.
4. puerile, childish; immature.
    Related words: **jejunely** *adverb*, **jejuneness** and **jejunity** (ji-JOON-ə-tee) *both nouns*.

jeremiad (JER-ə-MĪ-əd) *noun*
1. a prolonged mournful complaint about one's troubles.
2. a lamentation.

jerkin (JUR-kin) *noun*
a sleeveless jacket or vest.

jetsam (JET-səm) *noun*
goods thrown overboard from a ship in distress to lighten it, especially such goods that are washed ashore.

See **flotsam**.

jettison (JET-ə-sən) *verb*
1. throw (goods) overboard, especially to lighten a ship in distress.
2. discard (something that is no longer wanted); abandon.

Related word: **jettisonable** (JET-ə-sən-ə-bəl) *adjective*.

jocular (JOK-yə-lər) *adjective*
1. given to joking or jesting.
2. humorous; waggish.

Related words: **jocularity** (JOK-yə-LAR-i-tee) *noun*, **jocularly** (JOK-yə-lər-lee) *adverb*.

jocund (JOK-ənd) *adjective*
merry; cheerful; sprightly.

Related words: **jocundity** (joh-KUN-di-tee) *noun*, **jocundly** (JOK-ənd-lee) *adverb*.

jodhpurs (JOD-pərz) *noun*
riding breeches cut full about the hips and fitting closely from the knees to the ankles.

The aspect of **jodhpurs** that demands attention is its pronunciation, which is mistakenly and often heard as JOD-fərz. Take note of the correct pronunciation, JOD-pərz, and remember to pronounce **jodhpurs** correctly.

joust (jowst *or* joost, *also pronounced* just) *verb*
1. compete or struggle.
2. contend in a jousting tournament.

Related word: **jouster** *noun*.

justiciable (ju-STISH-ə-bəl) *adjective*
capable of being settled by the action of a court.

Related word: **justiciability** (ju-STISH-ə-BIL-i-tee) *noun*.

juxtapose (JUK-stə-POHZ) *verb*
place side by side or close together, especially for purposes of comparison or contrast.

Related word: **juxtaposition** (JUK-stə-pə-ZISH-ən) *noun*.

K

Kafkaesque (KAHF-kə-ESK) *adjective*

resembling, especially in nightmare quality, a state of affairs or a state of mind described by the writer Franz Kafka (1883–1924).

Related word: **Kafkaesquely** (KAHF-kə-ESK-lee) *adverb*.

kakemono (KAH-ke-MOH-noh) *noun, plural* **kakemonos** and **kakemono**

a Japanese wall-hanging, usually painted on paper or silk and mounted on rollers.

karma (KAHR-mə) *noun*

1. fate, destiny.
2. in Buddhism and Hinduism, the sum of a person's actions in one of his successive states of existence, seen as affecting the person's present life or his fate in the next incarnation.

Related word: **karmic** (KAHR-mik) *adjective*.

kedgeree (KEJ-ə-REE) *noun*

an East Indian dish made of rice, lentils, onions, eggs, etc.

kepi (KAY-pee) *noun, plural* **kepis**

a French military cap with a flat circular top and a visor.

kermis (KUR-mis) *noun*, also given as **kermess** and **kirmiss**, with the same pronunciations

1. in Holland and other Low Countries, an annual outdoor fair with much merrymaking.
2. a charity fair.

ketch (kech) *noun*
> a small sailing vessel with foremast and mizzenmast.

kiosk (KEE-osk) *noun*
> a light structure in a public place for use as a newsstand, refreshment stand, etc.

kismet (KIZ-mit) *noun*, also given as **kismat** (KIZ-mət)
> fate; destiny.

kitsch (kich) *noun*
> 1. pretentiousness and lack of good taste in art.
> 2. an object of tawdry design.
>
> Related word: **kitschy** *adjective*.

knout (nowt) *noun*
> a flogging whip with a lash of leather thongs formerly used in Russia as an instrument of punishment.
>
> Related word: **knout** *verb, punish with a knout*.

kyphosis (kī-FOH-sis) *noun*
> an abnormal convex curvature of the spine.
>
> Related word: **kyphotic** (kī-FOT-ik) *adjective*.

L

lachrymose (LAK-rə-MOHS) *adjective*
1. given to weeping.
2. tearful.

Related words: **lachrymosely** *adverb*, **lachrymosity** (LAK-rə-MOS-i-tee) *noun*.

laconic (lə-KON-ik) *adjective*
1. not talkative; terse;
2. concise.

Related words: **laconically** *adverb*, **laconicism** (lə-KON-ə-SIZ-əm) and **laconism** (LAK-ə-NIZ-əm) *both nouns*.

lacuna (lə-KYOO-nə) *noun, plural* **lacunae** (lə-KYOO-nee) and **lacunas**
1. a gap.
2. something missing from a book or argument etc.
3. a hiatus.

Related words: **lacunal** (lə-KYOON-əl), **lacunar** (lə-KYOO-nər), **lacunary** (lə-KYOON-ər-ee), and **lacunose** (lə-KYOO-nohs) *all adjectives*.

lambent (LAM-bənt) *adjective*
1. of light or flame, playing on a surface without burning it; with soft radiance.
2. of eyes, sky, etc., softly radiant.
3. of wit etc., dealing lightly and gracefully with a subject, lightly brilliant.

Related words: **lambency** (LAM-bən-see) *noun*, **lambently** *adverb*.

languid (LANG-gwid) *adjective*
lacking vigor or vitality; feeble, apathetic.

> Related words: **languidly** *adverb*, **languidness** *noun*.

languorous (LANG-gər-əs) *adjective*
1. fatigued, lacking alertness; languid.
2. dull, listless, drooping.
3. of air, oppressively still.

> Related words: **languorously** *adverb*, **languor** and **languorousness** *both nouns*.

lecher (LECH-ər) *noun*
1. a man given to unrestrained indulgence of sexual lust.
2. a lascivious man.

> Related words: **lecherous** *adjective*, **lecherously** *adverb*, **lecherousness** and **lechery** (LECH-ə-ree) *both nouns*.

lectern (LEK-tərn) *noun*
a stand with a sloping top to hold a book or notes for a speaker or reader.

legerdemain (LEJ-ər-də-MAYN) *noun*
1. sleight of hand, magic tricks.
2. sophistry; trickery.

> Related word: **legerdemainist** (LEJ-ər-də-MAYN-ist) *noun*.

lenity (LEN-i-tee) *noun, plural* **lenities**
1. gentleness; mercifulness.
2. an act of mercy.

> Related word: **lenitive** *adjective*.

lese majesty (LEEZ MAJ-ə-stee), also given as **lèse-majesté** (les-mah-zhəs-TAY), as in French
1. an insult to a sovereign or ruler.
2. treason.
3. presumptuous behavior.

leviathan (lə-VĪ-ə-thən) *noun*
1. something of enormous size and power.
2. any huge sea creature.

libido (li-BEE-doh) *noun, plural* **libidos**
emotional energy or urge, especially that associated with sexual desire.

Related words: **libidinal** (li-BID-ə-nəl) and **libidinous** (li-BID-ən-əs) *both adjectives,* **libidinally** *adverb.*

limpid (LIM-pid) *adjective*
of a liquid, the atmosphere, or literary style, clear; lucid; transparent.

Related words: **limpidity** (lim-PID-i-tee) and **limpidness** (LIM-pid-nis) *both nouns,* **limpidly** *adverb.*

linchpin (LINCH-PIN) *noun,* also given as **lynchpin**
1. a person or thing that is vital to an organization, plan, etc.
2. a pin passed through the end of an axle to keep the wheel in position.

lissome (LIS-əm) *adjective,* also given as **lissom**
1. supple, flexible.
2. lithe, agile.

Related words: **lissomely** *adverb,* **lissomeness** *noun.*

littoral (LIT-ər-əl) *adjective*
1. of or pertaining to the shore.
2. *(noun)* the region lying along the shore.

loath (lohth) *adjective*
1. unwilling.
2. reluctant, disinclined.

Do not confuse **loath** with **loathe**, which see.

Related words: **loathly** *adverb,* **loathness** *noun.*

loathe (loh*th*) *verb*
feel great hatred and disgust for (a person or thing).

Loathe, meaning *feel great hatred,* and **loath**, meaning *reluctant,* are easily confused, first because of their similar spellings, secondly because many speakers pronounce both words as loh*th.* To avoid this confusion, you are well advised to pronounce **loath** as lohth. Save loh*th* for **loathe**, and remember that one should be eager to love and **loath** to **loathe**.

Related words: **loather** (LOHTH-ər) *noun*, **loathsome** (LOHTH-səm) *adjective*, **loathsomely** (LOHTH-səm-lee) *adverb*.

locum tenens (LOH-kəm TEN-inz), *plural* **locum tenentes** (LOH-kəm tə-NEN-teez)

a temporary substitute, especially for a physician or a member of the clergy.

Related word: **locum-tenency** (LOH-kəm-TEN-ən-see) *noun*.

logomachy (loh-GOM-ə-kee) *noun, plural* **logomachies**
1. a dispute about words.
2. a meaningless battle of words.

Related words: **logomachic** (LOH-gə-MAK-ik) and **logomachical** *both adjectives*, **logomachist** (loh-GOM-ə-kist) and **logomach** (LOH-gə-MAK) *both nouns*.

lordosis (lor-DOH-sis) *noun*

an abnormal forward curvature of the spine.

Related word: **lordotic** (lor-DOT-ik) *adjective*.

louche (loosh) *adjective*
1. shifty; shady.
2. disreputable.

lour (lowr) and **lower** (LOW-ər) *both verbs*
1. frown or scowl.
2. of the sky or clouds etc., look dark and threatening.

Related words: **lour** and **lower** *both nouns*, **loury** (LOW-ree) and **lowery** (LOW-ər-ee) *both adjectives*.

lubricious (loo-BRISH-əs) *adjective*
1. slippery; smooth.
2. oily.
3. lewd, salacious.

Related words: **lubricity** (loo-BRIS-i-tee) *noun*, **lubriciously** (loo-BRISH-əs-lee) *adverb*.

lucent (LOO-sənt) *adjective*
1. shining, luminous.
2. clear, translucent.

Related words: **lucency** *noun*, **lucently** *adverb*.

lucubration (LOO-kyuu-BRAY-shən) *noun*
1. laborious work, especially late at night.
2. a literary work, especially one of pedantic or elaborate character.

Related words: **lucubrate** (LOO-kyuu-BRAYT) *verb*, **lucubrator** (LOO-kyuu-BRAY-tər) *noun*, **lucubratory** (loo-KYOO-brə-TOR-ee) *adjective*.

Lucullan (loo-KUL-ən) *adjective*, also given as **Lucullean** and **Lucullian**, both pronounced LOO-kə-LEE-ən
marked by lavishness, especially said of feasting; sumptuous.

lugubrious (luu-GOO-bree-əs) *adjective*
dismal, mournful, gloomy, especially in an exaggerated manner.

Related words: **lugubriously** *adverb*, **lugubriousness** and **lugubriosity** (lə-GOO-bree-OS-i-tee) *both nouns*.

luxuriant (lug-ZHUUR-ee-ənt) *adjective*
growing profusely.

Do not confuse **luxuriant** with **luxurious**, which see.

Related words: **luxuriance** *noun*, **luxuriantly** *adverb*.

luxurious (lug-ZHUUR-ee-əs) *adjective*
1. supplied with luxuries.
2. very comfortable.

What a difference a change of suffixes makes! Many writers hesitate when having to make a choice between **luxurious** and **luxuriant**. While there is some argument over whether to accept these two adjectives as synonyms, you are best advised to take a hard line. Use **luxurious** in the sense of *supplied with luxuries* or *very comfortable*, and **luxuriant** in the sense of *growing profusely*, and you will be in excellent company, admired by editors and readers who appreciate careful usage. In short, you will be able to **luxuriate**, *enjoy yourself*, in the knowledge that your unimpeachable and carefully crafted prose style meets the highest standards.

Related words: **luxuriate** (lug-ZHUUR-ee-AYT) *verb*, **luxuriously** (lug-ZHUUR-ee-əs-lee) *adverb*, **luxuriousness** and **luxury** (LUG-zhə-ree) *both nouns*.

lycanthropy (lī-KAN-thrə-pee) *noun*

a delusion in which one imagines oneself to be a wild animal, especially a wolf, and exhibits depraved appetites.

Related words: **lycanthrope** (LĪ-kən-THROHP) *noun*, **lycanthropic** (LĪ-kən-THROP-ik) *adjective*.

M

macerate (MAS-ə-RAYT) *verb*
1. make or become soft by steeping in a liquid.
2. waste away by fasting.

> Related words: **macerater** (MAS-ə-RAYT-ər), **macerator** and **maceration** (MAS-ə-RAY-shən) *all nouns*; **macerative** (MAS-ə-RAY-tiv) *adjective*.

maenad (MEE-nad) *noun*
1. a riotous or frenzied woman.
2. a Bacchante—a priestess of Bacchus—in classical mythology the god of wine.

magniloquent (mag-NIL-ə-kwənt) *adjective*
1. lofty in expression.
2. boastful; bombastic.
3. pompous.

> Related words: **magniloquence** *noun*, **magniloquently** *adverb*.

maladroit (MAL-ə-DROYT) *adjective*
1. awkward, bungling.
2. tactless.

> Related words: **maladroitly** *adverb*, **maladroitness** *noun*.

malediction (MAL-i-DIK-shən) *noun*
a curse.

> Related words: **maledictive** (MAL-i-DIK-tiv) and **maledictory** (MAL-i-DIK-tə-ree) *both adjectives*.

malefic (mə-LEF-ik) *adjective*
of magical arts, harmful, malign, baneful.

> Related words: **maleficent** (mə-LEF-ə-sənt) *adjective*, **maleficence** *noun*.

malevolent (mə-LEV-ə-lənt) *adjective*
1. wishing harm to others.
2. evil, injurious.

> Related words: **malevolence** *noun*, **malevolently** *adverb*.

malinger (mə-LING-gər) *verb*
pretend to be ill in order to avoid work or shirk duty.

> Related word: **malingerer** *noun*.

Mammon (MAM-ən) *noun*
wealth personified, regarded as an evil influence.

> Related words: **mammonish** *adjective*, **mammonism** (MAM-ə-NIZ-əm) *noun*.

mansuetude (MAN-swi-TOOD) *noun*
meekness; gentleness.

marmoreal (mahr-MOR-ee-əl) *adjective*, also given as **marmorean** (mahr-MOR-ee-ən)
of or resembling marble.

> Related word: **marmoreally** *adverb*.

martinet (MAHR-tə-NET) *noun*
1. a person who demands strict obedience.
2. a disciplinarian.

> Related words: **martinetish** *adjective*, **martinetism** *noun*.

masticate (MAS-ti-KAYT) *verb*
chew (food).

> Related words: **masticable** (MAS-ti-kə-bəl) and **masticatory** (MAS-ti-kə-TOR-ee) *both adjectives*, **mastication** (MAS-ti-KAY-shən) and **masticator** (MAS-ti-KAY-tər) *both nouns*.

matricide (MA-tri-SĪD) *noun*
1. a person who kills his mother.
2. the crime itself.

> Related word: **matricidal** (MA-tri-SĪD-əl) *adjective*.

maudlin (MAWD-lin) *adjective*
sentimental in a silly or tearful way, especially from drunkenness.

Related words: **maudlinism** and **maudlinness** *both nouns*, **maudlinly** *adverb*.

mawkish (MAW-kish) *adjective*
feebly or falsely sentimental.

Related words: **mawkishly** *adverb*, **mawkishness** *noun*.

media (MEE-dee-ə) *plural noun, singular* **medium** (MEE-dee-əm)
the means of modern communication, especially the press, journals, radio, and television.

Many words are mistreated in everyday speech, perhaps none more than **media** in the sense given above. **Media** is clearly a plural form of **medium** (which also has the plural **mediums** when used in some other senses, for example, in speaking of *persons who claim to be able to communicate with the spirits of dead persons*). So pervasive is the misuse of **media** as a singular noun—consider "The media is biased"—that it is regularly seen even in publications of high quality. Further, if you ever hear "The media are unbiased" in a news broadcast, you can bet that the item in which it appeared was written, edited, or spoken by a well-educated person, for example, an honors graduate of a leading university. In short, **media** as a singular noun is on the verge of winning the battle. At the same time, however, if you have the good fortune to write for learned readers, you will avoid criticism if you consistently use **media** as a plural noun, **medium** as a singular noun.

menarche (mə-NAHR-kee) *noun*
the onset of first menstruation.

Related words: **menarcheal** (mə-NAHR-kee-əl) and **menarchial**, pronounced the same way, *both adjectives*.

mendacious (men-DAY-shəs) *adjective*
1. untruthful, telling lies, especially habitually.
2. false, untrue.

Related words: **mendacity** (men-DAS-i-tee) and **mendaciousness** (men-DAY-shəs-nis) *both nouns*, **mendaciously** *adverb*.

menhir (MEN-heer) *noun*
a tall upright stone set in place in prehistoric times.

mephitic (mə-FIT-ik) *adjective*
1. of gases etc., smelling unpleasant.
2. poisonous.

Related words: **mephitically** *adverb*, **mephitis** (mə-FĪ-tis) *noun*.

mercurial (mər-KYUUR-ee-əl) *adjective*
1. liable to sudden changes of mood; flighty, fickle.
2. having a lively temperament; animated.

Related words: **mercuriality** (mər-KYUU-ree-AL-i-tee) and **mercurialness** (mər-KYUU-ree-əl-nis) *both nouns*, **mercurially** *adverb*.

meretricious (MER-i-TRISH-əs) *adjective*
showily attractive but cheap or insincere; tawdry.

Related words: **meretriciously** *adverb*, **meretriciousness** *noun*.

métier (MAY-tyay) *noun*
1. a person's trade, profession, or field of work.
2. a specialty, a forte.

mettle (MET-əl) *noun*
courage or strength of character.

Related word: **mettlesome** (MET-əl-səm) *adjective*.

miasma (mī-AZ-mə) *noun, plural* **miasmas** and **miasmata** (mī-AZ-mə-tə)
unpleasant or unwholesome air.

Related words: **miasmal, miasmatic** (MĪ-az-MAT-ik), **miasmatical** (MĪ-az-MAT-i-kəl), and **miasmic** (mī-AZ-mik) *all adjectives*.

micturition (MIK-chə-RISH-ən) *noun*
urination.

Related word: **micturate** (MIK-chə-RAYT) *verb*.

militate (MIL-i-TAYT) *verb*
1. have a substantial effect.
2. weigh heavily (in one's consideration).

Do not confuse **militate** with **mitigate**, which see.

Related word: **militation** (MIL-i-TAY-shən) *noun*.

mimesis (mi-MEE-sis) *noun*
imitation, mimicry.

Related words: **mimetic** (mi-MET-ik) *adjective,* **mimetically** *adverb.*

minatory (MIN-ə-TOR-ee) *adjective*
threatening, menacing.

Related word: **minatorily** (MIN-ə-TOR-i-lee) *adverb.*

misanthrope (MIS-ən-THROHP) *noun*
a person who dislikes people in general.

Related words: **misanthropic** (MIS-ən-THROP-ik) and **misanthropical** *both adjectives,* **misanthropically** *adverb,* **misanthropy** (mis-AN-thrə-pee) *noun.*

miscegenation (mi-SEJ-ə-NAY-shən) *noun*
marriage or interbreeding of races, formerly said especially in the United States of whites with non-whites.

Related word: **miscegenetic** (MIS-i-jə-NET-ik) *adjective.*

miscreant (MIS-kree-ənt) *noun*
1. a wrongdoer, a villain.
2. *(adjective)* depraved, villainous.

Related word: **miscreancy** (MIS-kree-ən-see) *noun.*

misogamy (mi-SOG-ə-mee) *noun*
hatred of marriage.

Related words: **misogamic** (MIS-ə-GAM-ik) *adjective,* **misogamist** (mi-SOG-ə-mist) *noun.*

misogyny (mi-SOJ-ə-nee) *noun,* also given as **misogynism** (mi-SOJ-ə-NIZ-əm)
hatred or mistrust of all women.

Related word: **misogynist** *noun.*

misprision (mis-PRIZH-ən) *noun*
a wrong action or neglect by a public official.

mitigate (MIT-i-GAYT) *verb*
make less intense or serious or severe; appease.

In recent years **mitigate** has been appearing incorrectly when **militate** is intended. **Militate** means *weigh heavily* and is used correctly, for example, in "Only one factor **militated** against the success of our proposal." Remember that it is never correct to **mitigate** *against* anything; it is correct to **mitigate** anything if it is thought to be deserving of **mitigation**, as in "His contrite behavior *mitigated* our anger." Editors reject as incorrect the use of **mitigate** in place of **militate**, and you should too.

Related words: **mitigable** (MIT-i-gə-bəl), **mitigative** (MIT-i-GAY-tiv), and **mitigatory** (MIT-i-gə-TOR-ee) *all adjectives*; **mitigation** (MIT-i-GAY-shən) and **mitigator** (MIT-i-GAY-tər) *both nouns*.

moiety (MOY-i-tee) *noun, plural* **moieties**
1. approximately half of something.
2. a half.

monomania (MON-ə-MAY-nee-ə) *noun*
an obsession with one idea or interest.

Related words: **monomaniac** (MON-ə-MAY-nee-AK) *noun,* **mono-maniacal** (MON-ə-mə-NI-ə-kəl) *adjective*

moot (moot) *adjective*
1. debatable, undecided.
2. doubtful.

Related word: **mootness** *noun*.

morass (mə-RAS) *noun*
1. something that confuses or impedes people; an entanglement.
2. a marsh, a bog.

mordant (MOR-dənt) *adjective*
characterized by a biting sarcasm.

Related words: **mordantly** *adverb*, **mordancy** (MOR-dən-see) *noun*.

morganatic (MOR-gə-NAT-ik) *adjective*
pertaining to a form of marriage between a man of high rank and a woman of lower rank who, along with their children, has no claim to the man's possessions or title.

Related word: **morganatically** *adverb*.

moribund (MOR-ə-BUND) *adjective*
1. in a dying state.

2. no longer effective.

Related words: **moribundity** (MOR-ə-BUN-di-tee) *noun*, **moribundly** (MOR-ə-BUND-lee) *adverb*.

motif (moh-TEEF) *noun*
1. a recurring design or feature in a literary or artistic work.
2. a short melody or theme that recurs and is developed in a piece of music.

mountebank (MOWN-tə-BANGK) *noun*
1. a swindler.
2. a charlatan.

Related word: **mountebankery** (MOWN-tə-BANGK-ə-ree) *noun*.

mucous (MYOO-kəs) *adjective*
1. of or like mucus.
2. secreting mucus.
3. covered with mucus.

Do not confuse **mucous** with **mucus**, which see.

Related word: **mucosity** (myoo-KOS-i-tee) *noun*.

mucus (MYOO-kəs) *noun*
the moist sticky substance that lubricates and forms a protective covering on the inner surfaces of the body's hollow organs.

The confusion of **mucus** and **mucous** can be understood readily. Not only are the two words spelled almost identically, but they are pronounced identically. Yet, no editors or writers worth their salt would fail to agree that **mucus** is a noun, and **mucous** is an adjective. So when they miss a confusion of the two words in a text they are working on, they are guilty of carelessness, not ignorance. Stay alert and avoid this boner.

mulct (mulkt) *verb*
take money away from (a person), as by a fine or taxation, or by dubious means.

muliebrity (MYOO-lee-EB-ri-tee) *noun*
1. womanhood.
2. normal characteristics of a woman.

Related word: **muliebral** (MYOO-lee-EB-rəl) *adjective*.

mutable (MYOO-tə-bəl) *adjective*
　1. liable to change.
　2. fickle, inconstant.
　　Related words: **mutability** (MYOO-tə-BIL-i-tee) and **mutableness** (MYOO-tə-bəl-nis) *both nouns*, **mutably** *adverb*.

myrmidon (MUR-mi-DON) *noun*
　an unscrupulously faithful follower; a henchman.

N

nadir (NAY-dər) *noun*
1. the lowest point.
2. the time of greatest adversity.

Related word: **nadiral** (NAY-dər-əl) *adjective*.

narcissism (NAHR-sə-SIZ-əm) *noun*
1. a tendency to self-worship.
2. excessive or erotic interest in one's own personal features; vanity.

Related words: **narcissist** (NAHR-sə-sist) *noun*, **narcissistic** (NAHR-sə-SIS-tik) *adjective*.

nascent (NAY-sənt) *adjective*
1. in the act of being born.
2. just beginning to exist; immature.

Related word: **nascency** (NAY-sən-see) *noun*.

natter (NAT-ər) *verb*
1. chatter idly.
2. grumble.

Related word: **natter** *noun*.

nausea (NAW-zee-ə) *noun*
a feeling of sickness or extreme disgust.

See **nauseous**.

nauseate (NAW-zee-AYT) *verb*
cause to feel nausea.

See **nauseous**.

Related words: **nauseating** (NAW-zee-AY-ting) *adjective*, **nauseatingly** *adverb*.

nauseous (NAW-shəs) *adjective*
1. causing nausea.
2. experiencing nausea.

Some writers and editors insist stubbornly that **nauseous** should not be used in the second sense, *experiencing nausea*. Instead of "I feel nauseous," they prefer to write "I feel nauseated." Unfortunately for writers and editors so inclined, **nauseous** has been used in senses 1 and 2 for at least four centuries. Moreover, most people today use **nauseous** exclusively in sense 2, never thinking for a moment of speaking about **nauseous** medicines or **nauseous** anything else. So, whenever you feel sick to your stomach, ignore the advice of **nauseating**, self-proclaimed experts and express your feeling of **nausea** any way you wish. But first take something to restore you to good health.

Related words: **nauseously** *adverb*, **nauseousness** *noun*.

nebulous (NEB-yə-ləs) *adjective*
1. having no definite form.
2. indistinct.

Related words: **nebulously** *adverb*, **nebulousness** *noun*.

necrology (nə-KROL-ə-jee) *noun, plural* **necrologies**
1. a list of persons recently dead.
2. an obituary.

Related words: **necrological** (NEK-rə-LOJ-i-kəl) and **necrologic** (NEK-rə-LOJ-ik) *both adjectives*, **necrologically** (NEK-rə-LOJ-ə-klee) *adverb*, **necrologist** (nə-KROL-ə-jist) *noun*.

necropolis (nə-KROP-ə-lis) *noun, plural* **necropolises**
a cemetery, especially a cemetery of an ancient city.

Related word: **necropolitan** (NEK-rə-POL-i-tən) *adjective*.

nefarious (ni-FAIR-ee-əs) *adjective*
wicked.

Related words: **nefariously** *adverb*, **nefariousness** *noun*.

nemesis (NEM-ə-sis) *noun, plural* **nemeses** (NEM-ə-SEEZ)
1. retributive justice.
2. a downfall.
3. the agent of downfall.
4. a rival who is seen as inevitably victorious.

neologism (nee-OL-ə-JIZ-əm) *noun,* also given as **neology** (nee-OL-ə-jee)
1. a newly coined word or phrase.
2. the coining or using of new words.

> Related words: **neologist** (nee-OL-ə-jist) *noun,* **neologistic** (nee-OL-ə-JIS-tik) and **neologistical** (nee-OL-ə-JIS-ti-kəl) *both adjectives,* **neologize** (nee-OL-ə-JĪZ) *verb.*

neonatal (NEE-oh-NAYT-əl) *adjective*
of or relating to a newborn child.

> Related word: **neonatally** *adverb.*

neonate (NEE-ə-NAYT) *noun*
1. a newborn child.
2. a child in its first 28 days.

neoteric (NEE-ə-TER-ik) *adjective*
1. modern, recent.
2. newfangled.

> Related word: **neoterically** *adverb.*

nepotism (NEP-ə-TIZ-əm) *noun*
favoritism shown to relatives in appointing them to jobs.

> Related words: **nepotist** (NEP-ə-tist) *noun,* **nepotistic** (NEP-ə-TIS-tik) and **nepotistical** *both adjectives.*

nescience (NESH-əns) *noun*
1. absence of knowledge.
2. ignorance.

> Related word: **nescient** *adjective.*

nevus (NEE-vəs) *noun, plural* **nevi** (NEE-vī)
a birthmark consisting of a mole or a red patch on the skin.

> Related word: **nevoid** (NEE-void) *adjective.*

nexus (NEK-səs) *noun, plural* **nexuses** or **nexus**
a bond, link, or connection.

nirvana (nir-VAH-nə) *noun*
in Buddhist and Hindu teaching, the state of perfect bliss attained when the soul is freed from all suffering and absorbed into the supreme spirit.
Related word: **nirvanic** *adjective*.

noctambulist (nok-TAM-byə-list) *noun,* also given as **noctambule** (nok-TAM-byool)
a sleepwalker; a somnambulist.

Related words: **noctambulant** (nok-TAM-byə-lənt), **noctambulistic** (nok-TAM-byə-LIS-tik), and **noctambulous** (nok-TAM-byə-ləs) *all adjectives;* **noctambulism** (nok-TAM-byə-LIZ-əm) and **noctambulation** (nok-TAM-byə-LAY-shən) *both nouns*.

nocuous (NOK-yoo-əs) *adjective*
1. harmful, likely to cause damage.
2. noxious.
Related words: **nocuously** *adverb,* **nocuousness** *noun*.

noisome (NOY-səm) *adjective*
1. harmful.
2. offensive, disgusting.
3. noxious.

Obviously, **noisome** shares no meaning with **noise** or **noisy**, yet careless writers mistakenly use this adjective as a synonym for **noisy**. Remember that while **noisy** environments may be thought of as **noisome**, it is because they are often considered to be *harmful* or *offensive*. The two adjectives are not even remotely synonymous.
Related words: **noisomely** *adverb,* **noisomeness** *noun*.

nonpareil (NON-pə-REEL) *adjective*
1. without equal; peerless.
2. *(noun)* a person having no equal.
3. *(noun)* a chocolate candy decorated with sugar pellets.

nostrum (NOS-trəm) *noun*
1. a quack remedy.

2. a patent medicine.

3. a panacea.

notorious (noh-TOR-ee-əs) *adjective*
well known, especially in an unfavorable way.

Many writers and speakers mistakenly use **famous** as an exact synonym for **notorious**, which is better thought of as a close synonym for **infamous**. Save **famous** for persons of enviable achievements and good reputations. **Infamous** persons are those having or deserving very bad reputations.

Related words: **notoriously** *adverb*, **notoriousness** and **notoriety** (NOH-tə-RĪ-i-tee) *both nouns.*

noxious (NOK-shəs) *adjective*

1. unpleasant; injurious to health.

2. corrupting, morally harmful; pernicious.

3. nocuous.

Related words: **noxiously** *adverb*, **noxiousness** *noun.*

nugatory (NOO-gə-TOR-ee) *adjective*

1. trifling, worthless; futile.

2. inoperative, ineffective, not valid.

nyctalopia (NIK-təl-OH-pee-ə) *noun*
night blindness.

Related word: **nyctalopic** (NIK-təl-OP-ik) *adjective.*

0

obdurate (OB-duu-rit) *adjective*
1. stubborn, unyielding.
2. impenitent.

    Related words: **obduracy** (OB-duu-rə-see) and **obdurateness** (OB-duu-rit-nis) *both nouns,* **obdurately** *adverb.*

obeisance (oh-BAY-səns) *noun*
1. deference or homage.
2. a deep bow or curtsy.

    Related words: **obeisant** *adjective,* **obeisantly** *adverb.*

objurgate (OB-jər-GAYT) *verb*
denounce, upbraid harshly; revile.

    Related words: **objurgation** (OB-jər-GAY-shən) and **objurgator** (OB-jər-GAY-tər) *both nouns,* **objurgative** (əb-JUR-gə-tiv) and **objurgatory** (əb-JUR-gə-TOR-ee) *both adjectives,* **objurgatively** (əb-JUR-gə-tiv-lee) and **objurgatorily** (əb-JUR-gə-TOR-ə-lee) *both adverbs.*

obloquy (OB-lə-kwee) *noun, plural* **obloquies**
1. verbal censure or abuse; detraction.
2. discredit, disgrace, or bad reputation as a result of being badly spoken of.

obnubilate (ob-NOO-bə-LAYT) *verb*
cloud over; darken; obscure.

    Related word: **obnubilation** (ob-NOO-bə-LAY-shən) *noun.*

obsecrate (OB-si-KRAYT) *verb*
1. plead, beseech.
2. supplicate in the name of something sacred.

> Related word: **obsecration** (OB-si-KRAY-shən) *noun*.

obsequies (OB-si-kweez) *plural noun, singular* **obsequy**
funeral rites; a funeral.

obsequious (əb-SEE-kwee-əs) *adjective*
obsessively or sickeningly respectful.

> Related words: **obsequiously** *adverb*, **obsequiousness** *noun*.

obtrude (əb-TROOD) *verb*
1. force (oneself or one's ideas) on others.
2. thrust forth; push out.

> Related words: **obtruder** and **obtrusion** (əb-TROO-zhən) *both
> nouns*, **obtrusive** (əb-TROO-siv) *adjective*, **obtrusively** *adverb*.

obviate (OB-vee-AYT) *verb*
1. make unnecessary.
2. neutralize (inconvenience, danger, etc.).

occlude (ə-KLOOD) *verb*
1. close, obstruct, stop up.
2. shut in.

> Related words: **occludent** *adjective*, **occluder** and **occlusion** (ə-
> KLOO-zhən) *both nouns*.

ochlocracy (ok-LOK-rə-see) *noun*
mob rule.

> Related words: **ochlocrat** (OK-lə-KRAT) *noun*, **ochlocratic** (OK-lə-
> KRAT-ik) and **ochlocratical** (OK-lə-KRAT-ə-kəl) *both adjectives*,
> **ochlocratically** *adverb*.

odalisque (OHD-əl-isk) *noun*, also given as **odalisk**
a female slave or concubine, especially in a harem.

odious (OH-dee-əs) *adjective*
hateful, detestable; disgusting, offensive, repugnant.

> **Odious**, influenced by its superficial resemblance to **odorous**, is
> frequently used mistakenly with the meaning of *ill-smelling*.

Speakers and writers who make this mistake open themselves to ridicule. Take care.

Related words: **odiously** *adverb*, **odiousness** *noun*.

oenophile (EE-nə-FĪL) *noun*

a lover of wine, especially a wine connoisseur.

Related words: **oenophilia** (EE-nə-FĪL-ee-ə) *noun*, **oenophilic** (EE-nə-FĪL-ik) *adjective*.

offal (AW-fəl) *noun*

1. the parts cut off as waste from a butchered animal.
2. carrion.
3. refuse or waste in general; dregs.

officious (ə-FISH-əs) *adjective*

aggressively asserting one's authority; bossy.

Do not confuse **officious** with the well-known word **official**, even though some **officials** may be **officious**.

Related words: **officiously** *adverb*, **officiousness** *noun*.

oligarchy (OL-i-GAHR-kee) *noun, plural* **oligarchies**

1. a form of government in which power is in the hands of a few people.
2. the group that holds this power.
3. a country governed this way.

Related words: **oligarch** (OL-i-GAHRK) *noun*, **oligarchic** (OL-i-GAHR-kik) and **oligarchical** *both adjectives*, **oligarchically** *adverb*.

operose (OP-ə-ROHS) *adjective*

1. of work, requiring much effort; tedious, laborious.
2. of a person, industrious.

Related words: **operosely** *adverb*, **operoseness** *noun*.

opprobrious (ə-PROH-bree-əs) *adjective*

1. of words etc., showing scorn or reproach.
2. abusive, vituperative.

Related words: **opprobriously** *adverb*, **opprobriousness** and **opprobrium** (ə-PROH-bree-əm) *both nouns*.

ordure (OR-jər) *noun*
manure, dung, excrement.

Related word: **ordurous** (OR-jər-əs) *adjective*.

orison (OR-ə-zən) *noun*
a prayer.

orotund (OR-ə-TUND) *adjective*
1. with full voice, imposing, dignified.
2. pompous, pretentious.

Do not confuse **orotund** with **rotund**, which see.

Related word: **orotundity** (OR-ə-TUN-di-tee) *noun*.

orthoepy (or-THOH-ə-pee) *noun*
the study of correct pronunciation.

Related words: **orthoepic** (OR-thoh-EP-ik), **orthoepical**, and **orthoepistic** (OR-thoh-ə-PIS-tik) *all adjectives*; **orthoepist** (or-THOH-ə-pist) *noun*.

orthography (or-THOG-rə-fee) *noun, plural* **orthographies**
1. correct or conventional spelling.
2. a perspective projection used in maps or elevations.

Related words: **orthographer** (or-THOG-rə-fər) *noun*, **orthographic** (OR-thə-GRAF-ik) and **orthographical** *both adjectives*, **orthographically** *adverb*.

oscitation (os-i-TAY-shən) *noun*
1. yawning.
2. drowsiness.

Related words: **oscitant** (OS-i-tənt) *adjective*, **oscitance** and **oscitancy** *both nouns*.

ostensible (o-STEN-sə-bəl) *adjective*
1. pretended.
2. professed.
3. put forward as actual or genuine to conceal the real.

Related word: **ostensibly** (o-STEN-sə-blee) *adverb*.

otiose (OH-shee-OHS) *adjective*
not required, serving no practical purpose; superfluous.

Related words: **otiosely** *adverb*, **otioseness** and **otiosity** (OH-shee-OS-i-tee) *both nouns*.

outré (oo-TRAY) *adjective*
outside the bounds of what is considered correct or proper.

overweening (OH-vər-WEE-ning) *adjective*
1. arrogant, conceited, presumptuous.
2. overconfident.
3. excessive.

Related words: **overweeningly** *adverb*, **overweeningness** *noun*.

oviparous (oh-VIP-ər-əs) *adjective*
producing young by means of eggs expelled from the body before they are hatched.

Related words: **oviparity** (oh-və-PAR-i-tee) and **oviparousness** (oh-VIP-ər-əs-nis) *both nouns*, **oviparously** *adverb*.

oxymoron (OK-si-MOR-on) *noun*
a figure of speech combining seemingly contradictory expressions.
Related word: **oxymoronic** (OK-see-mə-RON-ik) *adjective*.

P

palindrome (PAL-in-DROHM) *noun*
a word or phrase that reads the same backward as forward.

Related words: **palindromic** (PAL-in-DROM-ik) and **palindromical** *both adjectives*, **palindromically** *adverb*, **palindromist** (pə-LIN-droh-mist) *noun*.

palliative (PAL-ee-ə-tiv) *adjective*
1. reducing the bad effects of something.
2. *(noun)* something that does this.

Related word: **palliatively** *adverb*.

pallid (PAL-id) *adjective*
pale, especially from illness.

Related words: **pallidly** *adverb*, **pallidness** *noun*.

palmy (PAH-mee) *adjective*
1. flourishing, prosperous.
2. triumphant.

palpable (PAL-pə-bəl) *adjective*
1. able to be touched or felt.
2. easily perceived; obvious.

Related words: **palpability** (PAL-pə-BIL-i-tee) and **palpableness** (PAL-pə-bəl-nis) *both nouns*, **palpably** (PAL-pə-blee) *adverb*.

panacea (PAN-ə-SEE-ə) *noun*
a remedy for all kinds of diseases or troubles.

Related word: **panacean** (PAN-ə-SEE-ən) *adjective*.

panache (pə-NASH) *noun*
1. a grand or flamboyant manner.
2. swagger, verve.

pandemic (pan-DEM-ik) *adjective*
1. of a disease, occurring over a whole country or the whole world.
2. *(noun)* such a disease.

Related word: **pandemicity** (PAN-də-MIS-i-tee) *noun.*

panegyric (PAN-i-JĪR-ik) *noun*
a speech or piece of writing praising a person or thing; a tribute.

Related words: **panegyrical** *adjective,* **panegyrically** *adverb,* **panegyrist** (PAN-i-JĪR-ist) *noun,* **panegyrize** (PAN-i-jə-RĪZ) *verb.*

panjandrum (pan-JAN-drəm) *noun*
1. a mock title of a self-important personage.
2. a pompous official or pretender.

paraclete (PAR-ə-KLEET) *noun*
an advocate, especially a person who intercedes on behalf of someone.

paradigm (PAR-ə-DĪM) *noun*
1. something serving as an example or model of how things should be done.
2. in grammar, a set of forms of the inflection of a noun, a verb, etc.

Related words: **paradigmatic** (PAR-ə-dig-MAT-ik) and **paradigmatical** *both adjectives,* **paradigmatically** *adverb.*

parameter (pə-RAM-i-tər) *noun*
1. a variable quantity or quality that restricts or gives a particular form to the thing it characterizes.
2. a boundary, a limit.

Whereas **parameter** formerly was primarily a scholarly word, used only in sense 1 above, recent years have seen its meaning extended in popular use to sense 2. Perhaps because **parameter** has a cachet lacking in *boundary* or *limit,* this once-rare word has rapidly become the word of choice for many speakers and writers, who use it only in sense 2 and appear entirely unaware of **parameter** in sense 1. Even educated persons use it in sense 2, but as a careful writer you will do well to use **parameter** exclusively in sense 1, for example, "Height and weight were the parameters of immediate interest to us." When writing of boundaries or limits, use *boundary* or *limit*, two straightforward and simple words that everyone will readily understand.

Related words: **parametric** (PAR-ə-MET-rik) and **parametrical** *both adjectives*.

paronomasia (PAR-ə-noh-MAY-zhə) *noun*
1. word play; punning.
2. a pun.

Related words: **paronomastic** (PAR-ə-noh-MAS-tik) *adjective*, **paronomastically** *adverb*.

parricide (PAR-ə-SĪD) *noun*
1. the act of killing one's father, mother, or other close relative.
2. a person who commits parricide.

Do not confuse **parricide** with **patricide**, which see.

Related word: **parricidal** (PAR-ə-SĪD-əl) *adjective*.

parsimony (PAHR-sə-MOH-nee) *noun*
carefulness in use of money etc., especially excessive carefulness with money; stinginess.

Related words: **parsimonious** (PAHR-sə-MOH-nee-əs) *adjective*, **parsimoniously** *adverb*, **parsimoniousness** *noun*.

parturition (PAHR-tuu-RISH-ən) *noun*
1. the process of giving birth.
2. childbirth.

pastiche (pa-STEESH) *noun*
a musical or other composition made up of selections from various sources; a medley.

pathos (PAY-thos) *noun*
in literature, speech, etc., a quality that arouses pity or sadness.

patricide (PA-trə-SĪD) *noun*
1. the act of killing one's father.
2. a person who commits patricide.

Do not confuse **patricide** with **parricide**. A **parricide** is taken to mean a person who may kill close relatives, not just his father.

Related word: **patricidal** (PA-trə-SĪD-əl) *adjective.*

patronize (PAY-trə-nīz) *verb*
1. be a regular customer at (a store etc.).
2. treat (someone) in a condescending manner.

Related words: **patronizable** (PAY-trə-NĪ-zə-bəl) and **patronizing** (PAY-trə-NĪ-zing) *both adjectives,* **patronization** (PAY-trən-i-ZAY-shən) and **patronizer** (PAY-trə-NĪZ-ər) *both nouns.*

patronymic (PA-trə-NIM-ik) *noun,* also given as **patronym** (PA-trə-nim)
1. a name derived from the name of a father or ancestor.
2. a family name.

patulous (PACH-ə-ləs) *adjective*
1. open; gaping.
2. expanded.
3. of a tree or tree limbs, spreading.

Related words: **patulously** *adverb,* **patulousness** *noun.*

peccable (PEK-ə-bəl) *adjective*
1. liable to sin or error.
2. capable of sinning.

Do not confuse **peccable** with **peccant**, which see.

Related word: **peccability** (PEK-ə-BIL-i-tee) *noun.*

peccadillo (PEK-ə-DIL-oh) *noun, plural* **peccadilloes** and **peccadillos**
a trivial sin or offense.

peccant (PEK-ənt) *adjective*
1. guilty of a moral offense.
2. sinning; offending.

Keep the distinction between **peccable**, meaning *capable of sinning,* and **peccant**, meaning *guilty of a moral offense.* While one may argue that everyone is **peccable**, we hope that not everyone is **peccant**.

Related words: **peccancy** and **peccantness** *both nouns,* **peccantly** *adverb.*

peculation (PEK-yə-LAY-shən) *noun*
embezzlement.

Related words: **peculate** (PEK-yə-LAYT) *verb*, **peculator** (PEK-yə-LAY-tər) *noun*.

pederasty (PED-ə-RAS-tee) *noun*
an act of sodomy committed by men, especially by men with boys.

Related words: **pederast** (PED-ə-RAST) *noun*, **pederastic** (PED-ə-RAS-tik) *adjective*, **pederastically** *adverb*.

pejorative (pi-JOR-ə-tiv) *adjective*
disparaging; derogatory.

Related words: **pejorative** *noun*, **pejoratively** *adverb*.

pellucid (pə-LOO-sid) *adjective*
1. very clear in expression.
2. transparent; translucent.

Related words: **pellucidity** (PEL-uu-SID-i-tee) and **pellucidness** (pə-LOO-sid-nis) *both nouns*, **pellucidly** (pə-LOO-sid-lee) *adverb*.

penchant (PEN-chənt *or* pahn-SHAHN) *noun*
a liking or inclination.

penultimate (pi-NUL-tə-mit) *adjective*
next to last.

percipient (pər-SIP-ee-ənt) *adjective*
1. capable of perceiving.
2. showing keenness of insight; discerning.

Related words: **percipience** and **percipiency** *both nouns*.

perdurable (pər-DUUR-ə-bəl) *adjective*
1. very durable.
2. permanent, eternal.

Related words: **perdurability** (pər-DUUR-ə-BIL-i-tee) and **perdurableness** (pər-DUUR-ə-bəl-nis) *both nouns*, **perdurably** (pər-DUUR-ə-blee) *adverb*, **perdure** (pər-DUUR) *verb*.

peregrination (PER-i-grə-NAY-shən) *noun*
1. traveling.
2. a journey.

Related words: **peregrinate** (PER-i-grə-NAYT) *verb*, **peregrinator** (PER-i-grə-NAY-tər) *noun*.

perfidious (pər-FID-ee-əs) *adjective*
1. treacherous, disloyal.
2. deceitful.

Related words: **perfidiously** *adverb*, **perfidiousness** and **perfidy** (PUR-fi-dee) *both nouns.*

peripatetic (PER-ə-pə-TET-ik) *adjective*
going from place to place; itinerant.

Related words: **peripatetically** *adverb*, **peripateticism** (PER-ə-pə-TET-ə-SIZ-əm) *noun.*

periphrasis (pə-RIF-rə-sis) *noun, plural* **periphrases** (pə-RIF-rə-SEEZ)
a roundabout phrase or way of speaking; a circumlocution.

Related word: **periphrastic** (PER-ə-FRAS-tik) *adjective*, **periphrastically** *adverb.*

pernicious (pər-NISH-əs) *adjective*
having a very harmful effect; ruinous.

Related words: **perniciously** *adverb*, **perniciousness** *noun.*

perquisite (PUR-kwə-zit) *noun*
a profit, allowance, privilege, etc. given or looked upon as one's right in addition to wages or salary.

perseverate (pər-SEV-ə-RAYT) *verb*
repeat something insistently or over and over again.

Related words: **perseveration** (pər-SEV-ə-RAY-shən) *noun*, **perseverative** (pər-SEV-ə-RAY-tiv) *adjective.*

persiflage (PUR-sə-FLAHZH) *noun*
1. banter.
2. a flippant way of treating a subject.

personify (pər-SON-ə-FĪ) *verb*
1. represent (an idea) in human form or (a thing) as having human characteristics.
2. embody (a quality) in one's life or behavior.

Related words: **personifiable** (pər-SON-i-FĪ-ə-bəl) *adjective*, **personification** (pər-SON-ə-fi-KAY-shən) and **personifier** (pər-SON-ə-FĪ-ər) *both nouns.*

perspicacious (PUR-spi-KAY-shəs) *adjective*
 having or showing great insight; discerning.

 Do not confuse **perspicacious** with **perspicuous**, which see.

 Related words: **perspicacity** (PUR-spi-KAS-i-tee) and **perspicaciousness** *both nouns*, **perspicaciously** *adverb*.

perspicuous (pər-SPIK-yoo-əs) *adjective*
 1. clearly expressed; easily understood, lucid.
 2. of a person, expressing things clearly.

 Permissive lexicographers, always eager to reflect common usage, may show **perspicuous** as a synonym for **perspicacious**, thereby encouraging writers to misuse the two words. While these adjectives have long been confused by the unwary, perhaps because their spellings are so similar, **perspicuous** and **perspicacious** have different meanings, and careful writers and editors are able to keep them apart. If you wish to use one of these adjectives to describe a person *who expresses things clearly*, choose **perspicuous**. Again, if you wish to characterize a piece of writing or an explanation as *lucid*, choose **perspicuous**. On the other hand, if you wish to characterize a person, a person's thoughts, or a piece of writing or an explanation as *having or showing great insight*, choose **perspicacious**. Show your **perspicacity** by thinking and writing **perspicuously**.

 Related words: **perspicuity** (PUR-spi-KYOO-i-tee) and **perspicuousness** (pər-SPIK-yoo-əs-nis) *both nouns*, **perspicuously** *adverb*.

pertinacious (PUR-tə-NAY-shəs) *adjective*
 1. holding firmly to an opinion or course of action.
 2. persistent and determined; resolute.
 3. obstinate.

 Related words: **pertinacity** (PUR-tə-NAS-i-tee) and **pertinaciousness** (PUR-tə-NAY-shəs-nis) *both nouns*, **pertinaciously** *adverb*.

petard (pi-TAHRD) *noun*
 a small bombshell formerly used to blow in a castle door, breach a wall, etc.

pettifog (PET-ee-FOG) *verb*
 1. quibble.

2. engage in legal trickery.

Related words: **pettifogger** and **pettifoggery** *both nouns*, **petti-fogging** *adjective*.

petulance (PECH-ə-ləns) *noun*
unreasonable impatience; peevishness.

Related words: **petulant** (PECH-ə-lənt) *adjective*, **petulantly** *adverb*.

piacular (pī-AK-yə-lər) *adjective*
1. sinful, wicked.
2. culpable; requiring atonement.
3. atoning, expiatory.

Related words: **piacularly** *adverb*, **piacularness** *noun*.

picaresque (PIK-ə-RESK) *adjective*
of fiction, dealing with the adventures of a rogue.

picayune (PIK-ə-YOON) *adjective*, also given as **picayunish** (PIK-ə-YOON-ish)
1. trifling, petty.
2. mean, contemptible.

Related words: **picayunishly** *adverb*, **picayunishness** *noun*.

pilose (PĪ-lohs) *adjective*, also given as **pilous** (PĪ-ləs)
covered with hair, especially soft hair; hairy.

Related word: **pilosity** (pī-LOS-i-tee) *noun*.

pinguid (PING-gwid) *adjective*
1. fat.
2. oily; greasy.

Related word: **pinguidity** (ping-GWID-i-tee) *noun*.

piscivorous (pi-SIV-ər-əs) *adjective*
fish-eating.

placebo (plə-SEE-boh) *noun, plural* **placebos** or **placeboes** (plə-SEE-bohz)
a harmless substance given as if it were medicine, to humor a patient or as a dummy pill etc. in a controlled experiment.

plangent (PLAN-jənt) *adjective*
1. of sounds, loud and reverberating.

2. of sounds, mournful.

Related words: **plangency** *noun,* **plangently** *adverb.*

platitude (PLAT-i-TOOD) *noun*
a commonplace remark, especially one uttered solemnly as if it were new.

Related words: **platitudinal** (PLAT-i-TOOD-ən-əl) and **platitudinous** *both adjectives,* **platitudinarian** (PLAT-i-TOOD-ən-AIR-ee-ən) *noun,* **platitudinize** (PLAT-i-TOOD-ən-īz) *verb.*

plenitude (PLEN-i-TOOD) *noun*
abundance; profusion.

A common error in speech is to pronounce this word as though it were written *plentitude.* An understandable error, but strictly a no-no. Like saying *irregardless* rather than *regardless.*

Related word: **plenitudinous** (PLEN-i-TOOD-ə-nəs) *adjective.*

pleonasm (PLEE-ə-NAZ-əm) *noun*
an expression in which a word or words are redundant.

Related words: **pleonastic** (PLEE-ə-NAS-tik) *adjective,* **pleonastically** (PLEE-ə-NAS-ti-kə-lee) *adverb.*

plethora (PLETH-ər-ə) *noun*
an overabundance; an excess amount.

Related words: **plethoric** (ple-THOR-ik) *adjective,* **plethorically** (ple-THOR-i-kə-lee) *adverb.*

poetaster (POH-it-AS-tər) *noun*
an inferior poet.

Related words: **poetastering, poetasterism,** and **poetastry** *all nouns;* **poetastric** (POH-it-AS-trik) and **poetastrical** (POH-it-AS-tri-kəl) *both adjectives.*

polyhistor (POL-ee-HIS-tər) and **polymath** (POL-ee-MATH) *both nouns*
1. a person with knowledge of many subjects.
2. a great scholar.

Related words: **polyhistoric** (POL-ee-hi-STOR-ik) *adjective,* **polyhistorian** (POL-ee-hi-STOR-ee-ən) and **polyhistory** *both nouns;* **polymath** and **polymathic** (POL-ee-MATH-ik) *both adjectives,* **polymathy** (pə-LIM-ə-thee) *noun.*

popinjay (POP-in-JAY) *noun*
a conceited and talkative person.

posit (POZ-it) *verb*
state or assume as fact.

postprandial (pohst-PRAN-dee-əl) *adjective*
after a meal, especially dinner.

Related word: **postprandially** *adverb*.

practicable (PRAK-ti-kə-bəl) *adjective*
1. able to be put into practice.
2. usable; feasible.

Do not confuse **practicable** with **practical**, which see.

Related words: **practicability** (PRAK-ti-kə-BIL-i-tee) and **practicableness** (PRAK-ti-kə-bəl-nis) *both nouns*, **practicably** (PRAK-ti-kə-blee) *adverb*.

practical (PRAK-ti-kəl) *adjective*
1. involving activity as distinct from study or theory.
2. capable of being put to use; useful.
3. of people, clever at doing and making things.
4. virtual.

Writers and speakers, perhaps seduced by the fatal charm of an adjective less common compared with the perceived banality of an adjective encountered more often, slip into the trap of using **practicable** when they would be well advised to use **practical**. By doing so, they blur the important distinction between that which is *usable*, **practicable**, and that which is *useful*, **practical**. This happens particularly when writers and speakers are discussing plans, ideas, or the like. Thus, when they wish to say something is *useful*, the adjective of choice should be **practical**, perhaps ignoring the question of whether it can be accomplished. When, however, writers and speakers wish to say something is *feasible* or *usable*, that is, *able to be put into practice*, the adjective of choice should be **practicable**. Many things, many improvements, and the like may be said to be useful—**practical**—but how many useful ideas are also feasible—**practicable**? In trying to use the two adjectives correctly in your own writing and speech, it may be helpful to remember that many

practical, *useful,* inventions may never see the light of day because they are not **practicable,** *feasible* or *usable.* In addition, many people may be characterized as **practical,** *clever at doing or making things,* but never as **practicable.**

Related words: **practicality** (PRAK-ti-KAL-i-tee) and **practicalness** (PRAK-ti-kəl-nis) *both nouns,* **practically** (PRAK-ti-kə-lee) *adverb.*

pragmatic (prag-MAT-ik) *adjective,* also given as **pragmatical** treating things or making decisions from a practical point of view.

Related words: **pragmatism** (PRAG-mə-TIZ-əm), **pragmaticality** (prag-MAT-i-KAL-i-tee) and **pragmaticalness** (prag-MAT-i-kəl-nis) *all nouns,* **pragmatically** *adverb.*

prate (prayt) and **prattle** (PRAT-əl) *both verbs*
1. talk too much; chatter.
2. **prattle,** chatter in a childish way.

Related words: **prater** (PRAY-tər) *noun,* **pratingly** *adverb*; **prattler** (PRAT-lər) *noun,* **prattlingly** *adverb.*

prattle (PRAT-əl) *verb*

See **prate.**

precipitate (pri-SIP-i-tit) *adjective*
1. headlong, violently hurried.
2. of a person or action, hasty, rash; sudden.
3. *(verb)* (pri-SIP-i-TAYT) cause to happen suddenly or soon.

Do not confuse the adjective **precipitate** with **precipitous,** which see.

Related words: **precipitately** (pri-SIP-i-tit-lee) *adverb,* **precipitateness** (pri-SIP-i-tit-nis) and **precipitator** (pri-SIP-i-TAY-tər) *both nouns,* **precipitative** (pri-SIP-i-TAY-tiv) *adjective.*

precipitous (pri-SIP-i-təs) *adjective*
1. dangerously steep.
2. like a precipice.

The adjectives **precipitous** and **precipitate**—along with the corresponding adverbs **precipitously** and **precipitately**—are used interchangeably by writers and speakers who should know better. So prevalent is this confusion that permissive lexicographers, as one might expect, label the adjectives as synonyms in at least one sense. Well educated writers and their editors reject this practice, as should you. Reserve **precipitous** and **precipitously** for sentences in which the desired meaning is *dangerously steep* or *steeply*. Reserve **precipitate** and **precipitately** for sentences intended to convey the meaning of *sudden* and *suddenly*. Thus, you might write "They stopped just short of going over the rim of the **precipitous** cliff," and "They voted against making any **precipitate** decisions." Your editors will love you.

Related words: **precipitously** *adverb*, **precipitousness** *noun*.

preclude (pri-KLOOD) *verb*
1. exclude the possibility of.
2. prevent, forestall; debar.

Related words: **precludable** and **preclusive** (pri-KLOO-siv) *both adjectives*, **preclusion** (pri-KLOO-zhən) *noun*, **preclusively** *adverb*.

preponderate (pri-PON-də-RAYT) *verb*
surpass others in numbers, intensity, force, etc.

Related words: **preponderance** (pri-PON-dər-əns), **preponderation** (pri-PON-də-RAY-shən), and **preponderancy** (pri-PON-də-rən-see) *all nouns*; **preponderant** (pri-PON-dər-ənt) *adjective*, **preponderantly** *adverb*.

presage (PRES-ij) *noun*
1. an omen, a portent, a foreboding.
2. *(verb)* portend, foreshadow, also pronounced pri-SAYJ.

Related words: **presageful** *adjective*, **presagefully** *adverb*, **presager** *noun*.

prescience (PRESH-əns) *noun*
1. foreknowledge.
2. foresight.

Related words: **prescient** *adjective*, **presciently** *adverb*.

presentiment (pri-ZEN-tə-mənt) *noun*
a feeling that something is about to happen, especially something evil; a foreboding.

Related word: **presentimental** (pri-ZEN-tə-MEN-təl) *adjective*.

primer (PRIM-ər) *noun*
1. an elementary textbook.
2. (PRĪ-mər) a substance to prepare a surface for painting.
3. (PRĪ-mər) a detonator for explosives.

This entry is supplied primarily (no pun intended) to call attention to the correct pronunciations for the noun **primer** in its three meanings.

primeval (prī-MEE-vəl) *adjective*
1. of the earliest times of the world.
2. ancient.
3. primitive.

Related word: **primevally** *adverb*.

probative (PROH-bə-tiv) and **probatory** (PROH-bə-TOR-ee) *both adjectives*
1. providing proof.
2. designed to test or try something.

probatory (PROH-bə-TOR-ee) *adjective*

See **probative**.

probity (PROH-bi-tee) *noun*
1. honesty; integrity.
2. moral excellence.

proclivity (proh-KLIV-i-tee) *noun, plural* **proclivities**
1. a natural or habitual tendency.
2. an inclination.

profligate (PROF-li-git) *adjective*
1. recklessly wasteful or extravagant.
2. dissolute; immoral.

Related words: **profligacy** (PROF-li-gə-see) and **proligateness** (PROF-li-git-nis) *both nouns*, **profligately** *adverb*.

prolegomenon (PROH-lə-GOM-ə-NON) *noun, plural* **prolegomena** (PROH-lə-GOM-ə-nə)
1. preliminary matter in a book.
2. an introductory essay in a book.

Related word: **prolegomenous** (PROH-lə-GOM-ə-nəs) *adjective*.

prolix (proh-LIKS *or* PROH-liks) *adjective*
1. lengthy.
2. tediously wordy.

Related words: **prolixity** (proh-LIK-si-tee) and **prolixness** (proh-LIKS-nis) *both nouns,* **prolixly** (proh-LIKS-lee) *adverb.*

propinquity (proh-PING-kwi-tee) *noun*
nearness in place, kinship, disposition, or time.

propitiate (prə-PISH-ee-AYT) *verb*
1. win the favor or forgiveness of.
2. placate.

Related words: **propitiable** (prə-PISH-ee-ə-bəl), **propitiative** (prə-PISH-ee-AY-tiv), and **propitiatory** (prə-PISH-ee-ə-TOR-ee) *all adjectives;* **propitiation** (prə-PISH-ee-AY-shən) and **propitiator** (prə-PISH-ee-AY-tər) *both nouns.*

propitious (prə-PISH-əs) *adjective*
1. favorably inclined.
2. giving a good omen or a suitable opportunity.

Related words: **propitiously** *adverb,* **propitiousness** *noun.*

prostrate (PROS-trayt) *adjective*
1. lying face downward, especially as a sign of submission or humility.
2. lying in horizontal position.
3. helpless; overcome; physically exhausted.
4. *(verb)* cause to be prostrate; cast oneself face downward on the ground in humility or adoration.
5. *(verb)* reduce to physical exhaustion or helplessness.

The confusion of the adjective **prostrate**, *lying horizontal, helpless,* with the noun **prostate** (PROS-tayt), *a gland around the neck of the bladder in males,* is a boner we hear too often on radio talk shows. Remember to join in the laughter when you hear "He was **prostate** with grief." While **prostate** trouble may lead to grief, we all hope it does not leave the victim **prostrate**.

Related words: **prostration** (pros-TRAY-shən) and **prostrator** (PROS-tray-tər) *both nouns,* **prostrative** (PROS-trə-tiv) *adjective.*

protagonist (proh-TAG-ə-nist) *noun*
1. one of the chief contenders in a contest.

2. an advocate or champion of a cause etc.

3. the leading character in a literary work.

Related word: **protagonism** *noun.*

protean (PROH-tee-ən) *adjective*

1. taking many forms.

2. variable.

3. versatile.

Related word: **proteanism** (PROH-tee-ən-iz-əm) *noun.*

provenance (PROV-ə-nəns) *noun*
of a work of art etc., a place of origin.

proximate (PROK-sə-mit) *adjective*

1. nearest.

2. next before or after.

Related words: **proximately** *adverb*, **proximateness** and **proximation** (PROK-sə-MAY-shən) *both nouns.*

prurient (PRUUR-ee-ənt) *adjective*
having or arising from lewd thoughts.

Related words: **prurience** and **pruriency** *both nouns*, **pruriently** *adverb.*

puissant (PYOO-ə-sənt) *adjective*
having great power or strength; potent.

Related words: **puissance** *noun*, **puissantly** *adverb.*

punctilious (pungk-TIL-ee-əs) *adjective*
very careful to carry out duties or details of ceremony etc. correctly; conscientious.

Related words: **punctiliously** *adverb*, **punctiliousness** *noun.*

purulent (PYUUR-yə-lənt) *adjective*

1. containing or consisting of pus.

2. discharging pus.

Related words: **purulence** *noun*, **purulently** *adverb.*

pusillanimous (PYOO-sə-LAN-ə-məs) *adjective*

1. timid, faint-hearted.

2. cowardly.

Related words: **pusillanimity** (PYOO-sə-lə-NIM-i-tee) *noun*, **pusillanimously** (PYOO-sə-LAN-ə-məs-lee) *adverb*.

putative (PYOO-tə-tiv) *adjective*
reputed, supposed.

Related word: **putatively** *adverb*.

putrescent (pyoo-TRES-ənt) *adjective*
1. in process of decaying.
2. rotting.

Related words: **putrescence** and **putrescency** *both nouns*.

Pyrrhic (PIR-ik) **victory**
a victory gained at too great a cost.

Q

---

quash (kwosh) *verb*
1. annul; by legal authority, reject as not valid.
2. suppress or crush.

> Do not confuse **quash** with **squash**. Uprisings and indictments are **quashed**; hats and ripe grapes are **squashed**. But see **squelch**, which in one of its meanings is synonymous with **quash**.

querulous (KWER-ə-ləs) *adjective*
complaining, peevish

> Related words: **querulously** *adverb*, **querulousness** *noun*.

quidnunc (KWID-NUNGK) *noun*
1. a busybody.
2. a gossip.

quid pro quo (KWID proh KWOH), *plural* **quid pro quos** or **quids pro quo**
a thing given or taken in return for something.

quietus (kwī-EE-təs) *noun, plural* **quietuses**
1. final release from life, death.
2. a receipt given on payment of a debt.

quintessence (kwin-TES-əns) *noun*
1. an essence of a substance.
2. the essence or essential part of a theory, speech, condition, etc.
3. a perfect example of a quality.

Related words: **quintessential** (KWIN-tə-SEN-shəl) *adjective*, **quint-essentially** (KWIN-tə-SEN-shee-əl-ee) *adverb*.

quisling (KWIZ-ling) *noun*
a traitor, especially one who collaborates with an enemy occupying his country.

quixotic (kwik-SOT-ik) *adjective*, also given as **quixotical** (kwik-SOT-i-kəl)
1. chivalrous and unselfish to an exaggerated degree.
2. impracticable, visionary.

Related word: **quixotically** *adverb*.

quondam (KWON-dəm) *adjective*
former; sometime; onetime.

quotidian (kwoh-TID-ee-ən) *adjective*
1. daily.
2. usual, everyday.
3. ordinary, commonplace; trivial.

Related words: **quotidianly** *adverb*, **quotidianness** *noun*.

R

rabid (RAB-id) *adjective*
1. fanatical.
2. raging, violently intense.
3. affected with rabies.
   Related words: **rabidity** (rə-BID-i-tee) and **rabidness** (RAB-id-nis) *both nouns,* **rabidly** *adverb.*

raconteur (RAK-ən-TUR) *noun*
a person skilled in telling stories and anecdotes.
   Related word: **raconteuse** (RAK-ən-TUZ) *noun,* a woman thus skilled.

raffish (RAF-ish) *adjective*
1. gaudily vulgar or cheap, tawdry.
2. engagingly nonconformist.
3. flashy, rakish.
   Related words: **raffishly** *adverb,* **raffishness** *noun.*

raillery (RAY-lə-ree) *noun, plural* **railleries**
good-humored joking or teasing; banter.

rakish (RAY-kish) *adjective*
1. immoral or debauched.
2. debonair and jaunty in appearance or manner.

rale (rahl) *noun*
an abnormal sound perceived in the chest, indicating disease or congestion of the lungs.

rancor (RANG-kər) *noun*
1. bitter resentment, ill will.
2. hatred, malice.

> Related words: **rancorous** (RANG-kər-əs) *adjective*, **rancorously** *adverb*, **rancorousness** *noun*.

randy (RAN-dee) *adjective*
lustful; eager for sexual gratification; lecherous.

> Related word: **randiness** *noun*.

rankle (RANG-kəl) *verb*
cause lasting and bitter annoyance or resentment.

> Related word: **ranklingly** *adverb*.

rapacious (rə-PAY-shəs) *adjective*
1. greedy and grasping, especially for money.
2. given to plundering and robbing others.

> Related words: **rapaciously** *adverb*, **rapacity** (rə-PAS-i-tee) and **rapaciousness** (rə-PAY-shəs-nis) *both nouns*.

rapine (RAP-in) *noun*
1. plunder; pillage.
2. robbery.

rapprochement (RA-prohsh-MAHN) *noun*
the reestablishment of harmonious relations.

rara avis (RAIR-ə AY-vis)
a person or thing rarely encountered; a rarity.

ratiocination (RASH-ee-OS-ə-NAY-shən) *noun*
the use of logical processes and formal reasoning.

> Related words: **ratiocinate** (RASH-ee-OS-ə-NAYT) *verb*, **ratiocinative** (RASH-ee-OS-i-NAY-tiv) *adjective*, **ratiocinator** (RASH-ee-OS-i-NAY-tər) *noun*.

rationale (RASH-ə-NAL) *noun*
1. a fundamental reason.
2. the logical basis of something.
3. a reasoned explanation of something.

raze (rayz) *verb*
1. destroy completely.
2. tear down to the ground.

Related word: **razer** *noun*.

rebarbative (ree-BAHR-bə-tiv) *adjective*
causing aversion or irritation; repellent.

recension (ri-SEN-shən) *noun*
1. an editorial revision of a literary work.
2. a work that has been editorially revised.

Related word: **recensionist** *noun*.

recherché (rə-shair-SHAY) *adjective*
1. devised or selected with great care.
2. very rare.
3. choice, precious; pretentious.

recidivist (ri-SID-ə-vist) *noun*
a person who continually commits crime and seems unable to be cured of criminal tendencies; a persistent offender.

Related words: **recidivism** (ri-SID-ə-VIZ-əm) *noun*, **recidivistic** (ri-SID-ə-VIS-tik) and **recidivous** (ri-SID-ə-vəs) *both adjectives*.

réclame (ray-KLAHM) *noun*
1. publicity.
2. notoriety.
3. public acclaim.

recondite (REK-ən-DĪT) *adjective*
1. of a subject, obscure.
2. of an author, writing about an obscure subject.

Related words: **reconditely** *adverb*, **reconditeness** *noun*.

recreant (REK-ree-ənt) *noun*
1. a coward.
2. a traitor.

Related words: **recreant** *adjective*, **recreantly** *adverb*, **recreance** and **recreancy** *both nouns*.

recriminate (ri-KRIM-ə-NAYT) *verb*

1. indulge in countercharges.
2. accuse in return.

Related words: **recrimination** (ri-KRIM-ə-NAY-shən) and **recriminator** (ri-KRIM-ə-NAY-tər) *both nouns*, **recriminative** (ri-KRIM-ə-NAY-tiv) and **recriminatory** (ri-KRIM-ə-nə-TOR-ee) *both adjectives*.

recrudesce (REE-kroo-DES) *verb*

of a disease or sore or hostile feeling, break out again.

Related words: **recrudescence** (REE-kroo-DES-əns) and **recrudescency** *both nouns*, **recrudescent** *adjective*.

recumbent (ri-KUM-bənt) *adjective*

1. lying down.
2. reclining.

Related words: **recumbence** and **recumbency** *both nouns*, **recumbently** *adverb*.

redact (ri-DAKT) *verb*

put into suitable literary form; edit.

Related words: **redaction** and **redactor** *both nouns*, **redactional** (ri-DAK-shən-əl) *adjective*.

redintegrate (red-IN-tə-GRAYT) *verb*

1. make whole again.
2. reestablish in a perfect state; renew.

Related words: **redintegration** (red-IN-tə-GRAY-shən) *noun*, **redintegrative** (red-IN-tə-GRAY-tiv) *adjective*.

redolent (RED-ə-lənt) *adjective*

1. having a strong smell, odorous.
2. having a pleasing smell, fragrant.
3. strongly suggestive, reminiscent.

Related works: **redolence** and **redolency** *both nouns*, **redolently** *adverb*.

redundant (ri-DUN-dənt) *adjective*

1. no longer needed; superfluous.
2. verbose, unnecessarily repetitive.

3. of equipment in a system, having more than the minimum needed for safe operation; back-up.

Related words: **redundancy** *noun*, **redundantly** *adverb*.

refectory (ri-FEK-tə-ree) *noun, plural* **refectories**
the dining hall of a monastery, college, or similar institution.

refractory (ri-FRAK-tə-ree) *adjective*
1. resisting control or discipline.
2. of a disease or other abnormal condition, not yielding to treatment.
3. of a substance, resistant to heat; hard to fuse or work.

Related words: **refractories** *plural noun* meaning *bricks used to line kilns*, **refractorily** *adverb*, **refractoriness** *noun*.

refulgent (ri-FUL-jənt) *adjective*
1. shining brightly, gleaming.
2. radiant.

Related words: **refulgence, refulgency,** and **refulgentness** *all nouns*; **refulgently** *adverb*.

regimen (REJ-ə-mən) *noun*
1. a prescribed course of exercise or way of life, especially a diet.
2. a government; a regime.

regretful (ri-GRET-fəl) *adjective*
full of regret, especially for something lost, done, gone, etc.

Do not confuse **regretful** with **regrettable**, which see.

Related words: **regretfully** *adverb*, **regretfulness** *noun*.

regrettable (ri-GRET-ə-bəl) *adjective*
1. causing or deserving regret.
2. unfortunate.

Do not confuse **regrettable** with **regretful**. Actions, accidents, errors, and the like may be **regrettable**. People may feel **regretful**. So while you will surely make **regrettable** mistakes from time to time and feel properly **regretful** about your lapses, choose correctly when you are considering whether to use **regretful** or **regrettable**.

Related words: **regrettableness** *noun*, **regrettably** *adverb*.

reify (REE-ə-FĪ) *verb*
1. convert mentally into a thing.
2. materialize.

Related word: **reification** (REE-ə-fi-KAY-shən) *noun.*

religiose (ri-LIJ-ee-OHS) *adjective*
unduly occupied with religion, excessively religious.

Do not confuse **religiose** with **religious**, with a meaning easily understood. People who are **religious** are not necessarily **religiose**.

religious (ri-LIJ-əs) *adjective*

See **religiose**.

reliquary (REL-i-KWER-ee) *noun, plural* **reliquaries**
a receptacle or a shrine for relics.

remanent (REM-ə-nənt) *adjective*
of a substance or electrical activity, remaining; residual.

Related word: **remanence** *noun.*

remonstrate (ri-MON-strayt) *verb*
1. make a protest.
2. plead in protest.

Related words: **remonstrance** (ri-MON-strəns), **remonstration** (REE-mon-STRAY-shən), and **remonstrator** (ri-MON-stray-tər) *all nouns;* **remonstrative** (ri-MON-strə-tiv) *adjective;* **remonstratively** (ri-MON-strə-tiv-lee) and **remonstratingly** (ri-MON-strayt-ing-lee) *both adverbs.*

renitent (REN-i-tənt) *adjective*
1. resistant to pressure.
2. persistently opposing; recalcitrant.

Related words: **renitence** and **renitency,** *both nouns.*

repine (ri-PĪN) *verb*
1. be discontented.
2. fret.

Related word: **repiner** *noun.*

retroussé (RE-troo-SAY) *adjective*
especially of the nose, turned up at the tip.

revenant (REV-ə-nənt) *noun*
one who returns from the dead or from exile etc.

revile (ri-VĪL) *verb*
criticize angrily in abusive language.

Related words: **revilement** and **reviler** *both nouns,* **revilingly** *adverb.*

rhabdomantist (RAB-də-MAN-tist) *noun*
a person who practices divination by means of a rod or wand to locate underground ore etc.; a dowser.

Related word: **rhabdomancy** (RAB-də-MAN-see) *noun.*

riparian (ri-PAIR-ee-ən) *adjective*
of or on a riverbank.

risible (RIZ-ə-bəl) *adjective*
1. of or relating to laughter.
2. causing laughter.
3. laughable, ludicrous, comical.

Related word: **risibility** (RIZ-ə-BIL-i-tee) *noun.*

rodomontade (ROD-ə-mon-TAYD) *noun*
1. boastful talk.
2. *(adjective)* boastful, bragging.
3. *(verb)* boast, brag.
4. *(verb)* rant.

roister (ROY-stər) *verb*
1. revel noisily.
2. act boisterously.

Related words: **roisterous** *adjective,* **roisterously** *adverb.*

rotund (roh-TUND) *adjective*
1. rounded, plump.
2. of the mouth, rounded in speaking or singing.
3. of speech etc., sonorous, full-toned.

Do not confuse **rotund** in sense 3 with **orotund**, which see.

While the two adjectives are similar in spelling and both are used to characterize sounds made by the human voice, they carry different meanings. **Orotund** is defined as *with full voice, imposing, dignified; pompous, pretentious.* **Rotund** in sense 3 means *sonorous, full-toned.* Close, but no cigar. Notice particularly the final words of the definition of **orotund**: *pompous, pretentious.* In this sense **orotund** is far from complimentary, while **rotund** in sense 3 indicates nothing but praise for the characteristic thus described. So take care when using these troublesome adjectives.

Related words: **rotundity** (roh-TUN-di-tee) and **rotundness** *both nouns,* **rotundly** *adverb.*

roustabout (ROWST-ə-BOWT) *noun*
an unskilled worker employed in an oil field, on the docks or, especially, in a circus.

rubicund (ROO-bə-KUND) *adjective*
of the complexion, red; ruddy.

Related word: **rubicundity** (ROO-bə-KUN-di-tee) *noun.*

rubric (ROO-brik) *noun*
1. a heading of a chapter, section, etc.
2. an explanatory note.
3. a direction indicating how something must be done.

Related words: **rubrician** (roo-BRISH-ən) and **rubrist** (ROO-brist) *both nouns.*

ruminant (ROO-mə-nənt) *noun*
1. an animal that chews the cud.
2. *(adjective)* chewing the cud, ruminative.
3. *(adjective)* contemplative, meditative.

Related word: **ruminantly** *adverb.*

ruminate (ROO-mə-NAYT) *verb*
1. chew the cud.
2. meditate, muse; ponder.

Related words: **rumination** (ROO-mə-NAY-shən) and **ruminator** (ROO-mə-NAY-tər) *both nouns,* **ruminative** (ROO-mə-NAY-tiv) *adjective,* **ruminatively** (ROO-mə-NAY-tiv-lee) *adverb.*

rusticate (RUS-ti-KAYT) *verb*
1. settle or vacation in the country.
2. live a rural life.

Related words: **rustication** (RUS-ti-KAY-shən) and **rusticator** (RUS-ti-KAY-tər) *both nouns.*

S

sacerdotal (SAS-ər-DOHT-əl) *adjective*
1. of priests or the priesthood.
2. priestly.

>Related words: **sacerdotalism** (SAS-ər-DOHT-əl-IZ-əm) and **sacerdotalist** (SAS-ər-DOHT-əl-ist) *both nouns,* **sacerdotally** *adverb.*

sagacious (sə-GAY-shəs) *adjective*
showing wisdom in one's understanding and judgment of things; wise.

>Related words: **sagacity** (sə-GAS-i-tee) and **sagaciousness** (sə-GAY-shəs-nis) *both nouns,* **sagaciously** *adverb.*

salacious (sə-LAY-shəs) *adjective*
1. erotic.
2. lewd, grossly indecent, obscene.

>Related words: **salaciously** *adverb,* **salaciousness** *noun.*

salubrious (sə-LOO-bree-əs) *adjective*
health-promoting; health-giving; healthful.

>Related words: **salubriously** *adverb,* **salubriousness** and **salubrity** (sə-LOO-bri-tee) *both nouns.*

salutary (SAL-yə-TER-ee) *adjective*
producing a beneficial or wholesome effect.

>Related words: **salutarily** (SAL-yə-TER-ə-lee) *adverb,* **salutariness** (SAL-yə-TER-ee-nis) *noun.*

sanctimonious (SANGK-tə-MOH-nee-əs) *adjective*
making a hypocritical show of righteousness or piety.

Related words: **sanctimoniously** *adverb*, **sanctimoniousness** and **sanctimony** (SANGK-tə-MOH-nee) *both nouns*.

sang-froid (sah*n*-FRWAH) *noun*
1. calmness in the face of danger or difficulty.
2. composure; self-possession.

sanguinary (SANG-gwə-NER-ee) *adjective*
1. full of bloodshed.
2. bloodthirsty; savage.

Do not confuse **sanguinary** with **sanguine**, which see.

Related words: **sanguinarily** (SANG-gwə-NER-i-lee) *adverb*, **sanguinariness** *noun*.

sanguine (SANG-gwin) *adjective*
1. hopeful, optimistic.
2. confident.

Do not confuse **sanguine**, *optimistic, hopeful*, with **sanguinary**, *bloodthirsty*. The resemblance of the two words sets a trap for the unwary. Remember that it never hurts to be **sanguine**, but **sanguinary** is a horse of a different color — red, for blood.

Related words: **sanguinely** *adverb*, **sanguinness** and **sanguinity** (sang-GWIN-i-tee) *both nouns*.

sapid (SAP-id) *adjective*
1. having flavor, especially agreeable flavor.
2. palatable, savory.
3. of speech or writing, agreeable; interesting.

Related words: **sapidity** (sə-PID-i-tee), **sapidness** (SAP-id-nis) *both nouns*.

sapient (SAY-pee-ənt) *adjective*, also given as **sapiential** (SAY-pee-EN-shəl)
having or pretending to have great wisdom.

Related words: **sapience** and **sapiency** *both nouns*, **sapiently** *adverb*.

sarcophagus (sahr-KOF-ə-gəs) *noun, plural* **sarcophagi** (sahr-KOF-ə-JĪ) or **sarcophaguses**

a stone coffin, especially one bearing sculpture, inscriptions, etc.

Do not confuse the noun **sarcophagus** with the adjective **sarcophagous** (sahr-KOF-ə-gəs), which means *carnivorous, flesh-eating.*

sardonic (sahr-DON-ik) *adjective*

1. humorous in a grim or sarcastic way.
2. cynical.

Related words: **sardonically** *adverb*, **sardonicism** (sahr-DON-i-siz-əm) *noun.*

satiate (SAY-shee-AYT) *verb*

1. satisfy an appetite fully.
2. glut or cloy with an excess of something.

Related words: **satiation** (SAY-shee-AY-shən) and **satiety** (sə-TĪ-i-tee) *both nouns.*

saturnine (SAT-ər-NĪN) *adjective*

of a person or his looks, having a gloomy and forbidding appearance.

Related words: **saturninely** *adverb*, **saturninity** (SAT-ər-NIN-i-tee) and **saturnineness** (SAT-ər-NĪN-nis) *both nouns.*

scabrous (SKAB-rəs) *adjective*

1. indecent, salacious.
2. behaving indecently or immorally.
3. having a rough surface.
4. of a subject or situation, hard to handle with decency; requiring tactful treatment.

Related words: **scabrously** *adverb*, **scabrousness** *noun.*

scapegoat (SKAYP-GOHT) *noun*

a person who is made to bear blame or punishment that should rightly fall on others.

Do not confuse **scapegoat** with **scapegrace**, which see.

Related words: **scapegoat** *verb*, **scapegoating** and **scapegoatism** (SKAYP-goh-TIZ-əm) *both nouns.*

scapegrace (SKAYP-GRAYS) *noun*
1. a rascal.
2. a person who is constantly getting into trouble.

> Do not confuse **scapegrace** with **scapegoat**. The former is a relatively uncommon word, the latter an all too common word. A **scapegrace** is a *rascal, constantly in trouble,* and deserving of blame; a **scapegoat** is the *undeserving recipient of blame.* Thus, it would appear that anyone who must be called one thing or another may prefer to become a **scapegoat** rather than a **scapegrace**, since **scapegoats** are the victims of people of evil intent, and **scapegraces** earn their pejorative characterizations by virtue of their undesirable proclivities. So you must take care when using either of these words to choose the one that is correct for the meaning you intend to convey. And understand that **scapegraces** are often unjustifiably made **scapegoats** when wagging tongues are seeking to fix blame on someone.

scarify (SKAR-ə-FĪ) *verb*
1. make slight surgical cuts in skin or tissue.
2. of a person, pain by merciless criticism.
3. of garden soil etc., loosen the surface.

> Related words: **scarifier** and **scarification** (SKAR-ə-fi-KAY-shən) *both nouns.*

schadenfreude (SHAHD-ən-FROY-də) *noun*
malicious satisfaction felt at the misfortunes of someone else.

sciamachy (sī-AM-ə-kee) *noun, plural* **sciamachies**
an act of fighting with shadows or an imaginary enemy.

sciolist (SĪ-ə-list) *noun*
a superficial pretender to knowledge.

> Related words: **sciolism** (SĪ-ə-LIZ-əm) *noun,* **sciolistic** (SĪ-ə-LIS-tik) *adjective.*

scoliosis (SKOH-lee-OH-sis) *noun*
an abnormal lateral curvature of the spine.

> Related word: **scoliotic** (SKOH-lee-OT-ik) *adjective.*

scourge (skurj) *noun*
1. a person or thing regarded as a great affliction.

2. a whip for flogging people.
3. *(verb)* flog with a whip.
4. *(verb)* afflict greatly.

Related words: **scourger** *noun*, **scourgingly** *adverb*.

scurrilous (SKUR-ə-ləs) *adjective*
1. abusive and insulting.
2. coarsely humorous or derisive.

Related words: **scurrility** (skə-RIL-i-tee) and **scurrilousness** (SKUR-ə-ləs-nis) *both nouns*, **scurrilously** *adverb*.

sedulous (SEJ-ə-ləs) *adjective*
diligent and persevering; assiduous.

Related words: **sedulously** *adverb*, **sedulousness** *noun*.

self-abnegation (SELF-AB-ni-GAY-shən) *noun*

See **abnegate**.

semiology (SEE-mee-OL-ə-jee) *noun*
the branch of linguistics concerned with signs and symbols.

Related words: **semiologic** (SEE-mee-ə-LOJ-ik) and **semiological** *both adjectives*, **semiologist** (SEE-mee-OL-ə-jist) *noun*.

sempiternal (SEM-pi-TUR-nəl) *adjective*
everlasting; eternal.

Related word: **sempiternally** *adverb*.

senescent (si-NES-ənt) *adjective*
growing old; aging.

Related word: **senescence** *noun*.

sensual (SEN-shoo-əl) *adjective*
1. physical.
2. gratifying to the body.
3. indulging oneself with physical pleasures.
4. worldly, materialistic, irreligious.

Do not confuse **sensual** with **sensuous**, which see.

Related words: **sensually** *adverb*, **sensualism** (SEN-shoo-ə-LIZ-əm), **sensualist**, and **sensuality** (SEN-shoo-AL-i-tee) *all nouns*.

sensuous (SEN-shoo-əs) *adjective*
affecting or appealing to the senses, especially by beauty or delicacy.

Do not confuse **sensuous** with **sensual**. While both adjectives refer to experience gained through the senses, they differ markedly in interpretation. **Sensual** often carries an unfavorable connotation, for example, in such phrases as *sensual excesses* and *sensual sunbathing in which one's curves are displayed*. By way of contrast, **sensuous** offers such phrases as *sensuous music* and *sensuous poetry*, and no one ever came to a sordid end by indulging in the enjoyment of music or poetry that appeals to the senses.

Related words: **sensuously** *adverb*, **sensuosity** (SEN-shoo-OS-i-tee) and **sensuousness** *both nouns*.

sententious (sen-TEN-shəs) *adjective*
1. putting on an air of wisdom.
2. dull and moralizing.

Related words: **sententiously** *adverb*, **sententiousness** and **sententiosity** (sen-TEN-shee-OS-i-tee) *both nouns*.

sepulcher (SEP-əl-kər) *noun*
a tomb.

Related words: **sepulchral** (sə-PUL-krəl) *adjective*, **sepulchrally** (sə-PUL-krə-lee) *adverb*.

sepulture (SEP-əl-chər) *noun*
burial, interment.

Related word: **sepultural** (sə-PUL-chər-əl) *adjective*.

serendipity (SER-ən-DIP-i-tee) *noun*
1. the making of pleasant discoveries by accident.
2. the knack of doing this.

Related words: **serendipiter**, **serendipitist**, and **serendipper** *all nouns*; **serendipitous** *adjective*.

sesquipedalian (SES-kwi-pi-DAYL-yən) *adjective*
1. of a word, having many syllables.
2. of a writer, tending to use long words.

Related words: **sesquipedalianism** (SES-kwi-pi-DAYL-yən-iz-əm) and **sesquipedality** (SES-kwi-pi-DAL-i-tee) *both nouns.*

shibboleth (SHIB-ə-lith) *noun*
1. an old slogan or principle that is still considered essential by some members of a party or group.
2. a test word, principle, behavior, or opinion whose use reveals one's party, nationality, orthodoxy, etc.

sibyl (SIB-əl) *noun*
1. a fortune-teller; a prophetess.
2. a witch.
3. one of the women of classical legend who were supposed to prophesy under the influence of a god.

Related word: **sibylline** (SIB-ə-LĪN) *adjective.*

simplistic (sim-PLIS-tik) *adjective*
tending to simplify something unjustifiably.

Anyone who listens to talk radio or reads letters written to newspaper editors knows there is an army of poor speakers and writers for whom the elegant adjective **simplistic** holds a fatal fascination—fatal because these speakers and writers mistakenly use **simplistic** as a synonym for **simple**. And one thing **simplistic** is not is a synonym for **simple**. Anyone who uses **simplistic** must be certain he or she intends to convey the meaning of *tending to simplify something unjustifiably.* The adverb *unjustifiably* is the red flag alerting us to the negative connotation of **simplistic**. For example, telling Americans that by eliminating the Internal Revenue Service we will solve all our economic problems is usually taken by rational people to be an example of a **simplistic** proposal. And there are, of course, many other examples of **simplistic** reasoning. So remember that when you describe some idea or proposal as **simplistic**, you are criticizing it as you characterize it.

Related words: **simplistically** *adverb*, **simplism** (SIM-pliz-əm) *noun.*

Sisyphean (SIS-ə-FEE-ən) *adjective*
1. everlastingly laborious and unavailing.
2. of or pertaining to Sisyphus who, in Greek legend, was con-

demned to roll a huge boulder to the top of a hill in Hades, but every time he reached the summit, the boulder slipped out of his grasp and rolled down again.

sluggard (SLUG-ərd) *noun*
a slow or lazy person.

Related words: **sluggard** and **sluggardly** *both adjectives*, **sluggardliness** *noun*.

smegma (SMEG-mə) *noun*
a thick, cheeselike secretion in the folds of the skin, especially in the foreskin.

Related word: **smegmatic** (smeg-MA-tik) *adjective*.

sobriquet (SOH-brə-KAY) *noun*
a nickname.

Related word: **sobriquetical** (SOH-brə-KET-i-kəl) *adjective*

sodomy (SOD-ə-mee) *noun*
a copulation-like act between male persons or with a member of the opposite sex or between a person and an animal.

Related words: **sodomite** (SOD-ə-MĪT) **sodomist** (SOD-ə-mist) *both nouns*, **sodomitical** (SOD-ə-MIT-i-kəl) *adjective*, **sodomitically** *adverb*.

soi-disant (swah-dee-ZAHN) *adjective*, French
1. self-styled.
2. so-called.
3. pretended.

soigné (swahn-YAY) *adjective*, *feminine* **soignée**
1. well-groomed and sophisticated.
2. carefully designed and prepared.

solecism (SOL-ə-SIZ-əm) *noun*
1. a mistake in the use of language.
2. an offense against good manners or etiquette.

Do not confuse **solecism** with **solipsism**, which see.

Related words: **solecist** (SOL-ə-sist) *noun*, **solecistic** (SOL-ə-SIS-tik) and **solecistical** *both adjectives*, **solecistically** *adverb*.

solicitous (sə-LIS-i-təs) *adjective*
anxious and concerned about a person's welfare or comfort.

> Related words: **solicitously** *adverb*, **solicitousness** and **solicitude** (sə-LIS-i-TOOD) *both nouns.*

solipsism (SOL-ip-SIZ-əm) *noun*
1. the philosophical theory that the self is the only knowable, or the only existent, thing.
2. egoistic self-absorption.

> The nouns **solecism** and **solipsism** are relatively uncommon words, sharing nothing but similarity of spelling and pronunciation, yet careless writers and speakers confuse the words. One meaning of **solecism** is *a mistake in the use of language,* and one meaning of **solipsism** is *egoistic self-absorption.* If you intend to use either of these words, keep their meanings firmly in mind so you will not be misled by superficial similarities. And while you avoid **solecisms** in your writing, beware of falling prey to **solipsism.**

> Related words: **solipsist** (SOL-ip-sist) and **solipsistic** (SOL-ip-SIS-tik) *both adjectives,* **solipsist** *noun.*

somnambulism (som-NAM-byə-LIZ-əm) *noun*
sleepwalking.

> Related words: **somnambulant** (som-NAM-byə-lənt) and **somnambulistic** (som-NAM-byə-LIS-tik) *both adjectives,* **somnambulate** (som-NAM-byə-LAYT) *verb,* **somnambulation** (som-NAM-byə-LAY-shən) and **somnambulist** (som-NAM-byə-list) *both nouns.*

somnolent (SOM-nə-lənt) *adjective*
sleepy, drowsy; asleep.

> Related words: **somnolence** and **somnolency** *both nouns,* **somnolently** *adverb.*

sonorous (sə-NOR-əs) *adjective*
1. giving a deep powerful sound; resonant.
2. of language or diction, high-flown, grandiloquent.

> Related words: **sonority** and **sonorousness** *nouns,* **sonorously** *adverb.*

sophism (SOF-iz-əm) *noun*
a false argument, especially one intended to deceive.

Related words: **sophist** (SOF-ist) *noun,* **sophistic** (sə-FIS-tik) and **sophistical** *both adjectives,* **sophistically** *adverb.*

sophistry (SOF-ə-stree) *noun, plural* **sophistries**
  clever and subtle but perhaps misleading reasoning.

soporific (SOP-ə-RIF-ik) *adjective*
  1. tending to produce sleep.
  2. *(noun)* a medicinal substance that produces sleep.

  Related word: **soporifically** *adverb.*

sororicide (sə-ROR-ə-SĪD) *noun*
  1. the act of killing one's sister.
  2. a person who commits sororicide.

  Related word: **sororicidal** (sə-ROR-ə-SĪD-əl) *adjective.*

soubrette (soo-BRET) *noun*
  1. an actress or opera singer playing a maidservant or similar character, especially with the implication of pertness or coquetry.
  2. the role itself.
  3. any lively or pert young woman.

  Related word: **soubrettish** *adjective.*

soupçon (soop-SAWN) *noun*
  a very small quantity; a trace; a dash.

specious (SPEE-shəs) *adjective*
  seeming good or sound at first sight but lacking real merit.

  Related words: **speciously** *adverb,* **speciousness** *noun.*

splenetic (spli-NET-ik) *adjective*
  1. of a person, ill-tempered; peevish, irascible.
  2. of the spleen.

  Related word: **splenetically** *adverb.*

spoonerism (SPOO-nə-RIZ-əm) *noun*
  the interchange of the initial letters of two words, usually as a slip of the tongue.

squash (skwosh) *verb*
  This verb is well understood and is supplied merely to call attention to the difference between **squash** and **quash**, which see.

squelch (skwelch) *verb*

1. silence, as with a crushing reply.
2. suppress, quell; quash.

Notice that **squelch** in its second sense is synonymous with **quash**, which see.

Related words: **squelcher** *noun*, **squelchingly** *adverb*, **squelchingness** *noun*.

stanch (stawnch) *verb*

1. restrain the flow of (blood etc.).
2. restrain the flow of blood from (a wound etc.).

Do not confuse **stanch** with **staunch**, which see.

Related words: **stanchable** *adjective*, **stancher** *noun*.

stationary (STAY-shə-NER-ee) *adjective*

1. not moving, not movable.
2. unchanging in condition or quantity etc.

Do not confuse the adjective **stationary** with the noun **stationery**. Both are pronounced identically, but there the similarity ends. **Stationery** is defined as *writing materials, such as paper, envelopes, and the like*.

staunch (stawnch) *adjective*

firm in attitude, opinion, or loyalty.

The adjective **staunch** and the verb **stanch** are frequently confused. As you can see, the two words are pronounced identically, but listeners alert to the context in which they hear the words have no trouble. It is when encountering the words in a piece of writing that trouble may arise for readers. Beginning far back in the history of the language, the two words were merely spelling variants, used interchangeably, so writers had nothing to worry about. In the 20th century, however, **staunch** and **stanch** began to be treated as different words, the first meaning *firm in attitude etc.*, the second meaning *restrain a flow*. Thus, even though some permissive dictionaries still may treat the two words as spelling variants, one of the things you must do as a careful writer is use **staunch** and **stanch** correctly. Remember to be **staunch** in your most cherished beliefs, and to **stanch** the flow of blood whenever you cut yourself badly. Also remember that **staunch** is an adjective, and **stanch** is a verb.

Related words: **staunchly** *adverb*, **staunchness** *noun*.

steatopygia (stee-AT-ə-PĪ-jee-ə) *noun*
excessive development of fat on the buttocks, especially of women.

Related words: **steatopygic** (stee-AT-ə-PIJ-ik) and **steatopygous** (stee-AT-ə-PĪ-gəs) *both adjectives.*

stratagem (STRAT-ə-jəm) *noun*
1. a cunning method of achieving something.
2. a piece of trickery.

Related words: **stratagemical** (STRAT-ə-JEM-i-kəl) *adjective*, **stratagemically** *adverb.*

stratum (STRAT-əm) *noun, plural* **strata** (STRAT-ə) and **stratums**
1. a social level or class.
2. one of a series of layers, especially of rock in Earth's crust.

Many students of English style have remarked on the increasing use of **strata** as a singular, but editors and careful writers use it only as a plural. Until poor usage overwhelms the conventional use of **strata** as a plural, you would do well to use **stratum** consistently as a singular, and **strata** or **stratums** as plurals.

Related word: **stratous** *adjective.*

stricture (STRIK-chər) *noun*
1. a remark or comment expressing criticism or condemnation.
2. an abnormal constriction of a tubelike part of the body.

Related words: **striction** (STRIK-shən) *noun*, **strictured** (STRIK-chərd) *adjective.*

stridulate (STRIJ-ə-LAYT) *verb*
of a cricket or cicada etc., make a shrill and grating sound by rubbing parts of the body together.

Related words: **stridulation** (STRIJ-ə-LAY-shən) *noun*, **stridulatory** (STRIJ-ə-lə-TOR-ee) and **stridulous** (STRIJ-ə-ləs) *both adjectives.*

stultify (STUL-tə-FĪ) *verb*
impair or make ineffective.

Related words: **stultification** (STUL-ti-fi-KAY-shən) and **stultifier** (STUL-ti-FĪ-ər) *both* *nouns,* **stultifyingly** (STUL-ti-FĪ-ing-lee) *adverb.*

sublimate (SUB-lə-MAYT) *verb*
divert the energy of (a primitive impulse) into a culturally higher activity.

Related words: **sublimable** (SUB-lə-mə-bəl) and **sublimational** (SUB-lə-MAY-shə-nəl) *both adjectives,* **sublimableness** (SUB-lə-mə-bəl-nis) and **sublimation** (SUB-lə-MAY-shən) *both nouns.*

subliminal (sub-LIM-ə-nəl) *adjective*
below the threshold of consciousness.

Related word: **subliminally** *adverb.*

succubus (SUK-yə-bəs) *noun, plural* **succubi** (SUK-yə-bī); also given as **succuba** (SUK-yə-bə), *plural* **succubae** (SUK-yə-bee)
1. a female demon said to have sexual intercourse with sleeping men.
2. any evil spirit.

sudorific (SOO-də-RIF-ik) *adjective*
1. causing sweating.
2. *(noun)* a drug that induces sweating.

suggestible (səg-JES-tə-bəl) *adjective*
1. easily influenced by people's suggestions.
2. that may be suggested.

Do not confuse **suggestible** with **suggestive**, which see.

Related words: **suggestibility** (səg-JES-tə-BIL-i-tee) and **suggestibleness** (səg-JES-tə-bəl-nis) *both nouns,* **suggestibly** (səg-JES-tə-blee) *adverb.*

suggestive (səg-JES-tiv) *adjective*
1. tending to convey an indecent or improper meaning; risqué.
2. conveying a suggestion.

Do not confuse **suggestive** with **suggestible**. The confusion that can result from careless use of these two adjectives gives us a wonderful example of the difference a suffix can make. The adjective **suggestive** is most often used in the sense of *tending to convey an indecent or improper meaning,* while **suggestible** is most often used in the sense of *easily influenced by people's suggestions*. Facial expressions and activities may be **suggestive**, while people, their ideas, their thoughts, and the like may be **suggestible**. Be careful in your use of these adjectives.

Related words: **suggestively** *adverb*, **suggestiveness** *noun*.

sui generis (SOO-ee JEN-ə-ris), Latin
1. of its, his, her, their own kind.
2. one of a kind; unique.

superannuate (SOO-pər-AN-yoo-AYT) *verb*
1. retire (an employee) with a pension because of age or infirmity.
2. discard (something) as too old for further use.

Related words: **superannuated** *adjective*, **superannuation** (SOO-pər-AN-yoo-AY-shən) *noun*.

supercilious (SOO-pər-SIL-ee-əs) *adjective*
1. with an air of superiority.
2. haughty and scornful.

Related words: **superciliously** *adverb*, **superciliousness** *noun*.

supererogation (SOO-pər-ER-ə-GAY-shən) *noun*
the doing of more than is required by duty.

Related words: **supererogate** (SOO-pər-ER-ə-GAYT) *verb*, **supererogatory** (SOO-pər-ə-ROG-ə-TOR-ee) *adjective*, **supererogatorily** *adverb*, **supererogator** (SOO-pər-ER-ə-GAY-tər) *noun*.

supernal (suu-PUR-nəl) *adjective*
1. heavenly, divine.
2. lofty.

Related word: **supernally** *adverb*.

supervene (SOO-pər-VEEN) *verb*
occur as an interruption or change from some condition or process.

Related words: **supervenience** (SOO-pər-VEEN-yəns) and **supervention** (SOO-pər-VEN-shən) *both nouns*, **supervenient** (SOO-pər-VEEN-yənt) *adjective*.

supine (soo-PĪN) *adjective*
1. lying face upward.
2. not inclined to take action.
3. indolent.

> Related words: **supinely** *adverb*, **supineness** *noun*.

suppliant (SUP-lee-ənt) *noun*
a person asking humbly for something; a supplicant.

> Related words: **suppliant** *adjective*, **suppliantly** *adverb*, **suppliantness** *noun*.

suppurate (SUP-yə-RAYT) *verb*
form pus; fester.

> Related words: **suppuration** (SUP-yə-RAY-shən) *noun*, **suppurative** (SUP-yə-RAY-tiv) *adjective*.

surcease (sur-SEES) *noun*
end, cessation.

susurration (SOO-sə-RAY-shən) *noun*
1. whispering; murmuring.
2. rustling.

> Related words: **susurrant** (suu-SUR-ənt) and **susurrous** (suu-SUR-əs) *both adjectives*, **susurrus** (suu-SUR-əs) *noun*.

svelte (svelt) *adjective*
1. of a person or figure, slender and graceful; lissome, lithe.
2. suave, urbane.

sybarite (SIB-ə-RĪT) *noun*
a person who is excessively fond of comfort and luxury.

> Related words: **sybaritic** (SIB-ə-RIT-ik) and **sybaritical** *both adjectives*, **sybaritically** *adverb*, **sybaritism** (SIB-ə-ri-TIZ-əm) *noun*.

sycophant (SIK-ə-fənt) *noun*
1. a person who tries to win people's favor by flattering them.
2. a parasite.

> Related words: **sycophancy** (SIK-ə-fən-see) and **sycophantism** *both nouns*; **sycophantic** (SIK-ə-FAN-tik), **sycophantical**, and **sycophantish** *all adjectives*; **sycophantically** (SIK-ə-FAN-tik-ə-lee) and **sycophantishly** (SIK-ə-FAN-tish-lee) *both adverbs*.

symbiosis (SIM-bee-OH-sis) *noun, plural* **symbioses** (SIM-bee-OH-seez)
the association of two different organisms living attached to each
other or one within the other to their mutual advantage.

Related words: **symbiotic** (SIM-bee-OT-ik) and **symbiotical** *both
adjectives*, **symbiotically** *adverb*.

sympathy (SIM-pə-thee) *noun*

See **empathy**.

synecdoche (si-NEK-də-kee) *noun*
a figure of speech in which a part is used for the whole, or vice
versa; or the less comprehensive is used for the more comprehensive, or vice versa.

Related words: **synecdochic** (SIN-ik-DOK-ik) and **synecdochical**
(SIN-ik-DOK-i-kəl) *both adjectives*, **synecdochically** (SIN-ik-
DOK-ik-ə-lee) *adverb*.

synergism (SIN-ər-JIZ-əm) *noun,* also given as **synergy** (SIN-ər-jee),
plural **synergies** (SIN-ər-jeez)
the combined effect of drugs, contributions, efforts, etc. that
exceeds the sum of their individual effects.

Related words: **synergist** (SIN-ər-jist) *noun;* **synergetic** (SIN-ər-
JET-ik), **synergistic** (SIN-ər-JIS-tik), and **synergic** (si-NUR-jik) *all
adjectives;* **synergistically** (SIN-ər-JIS-ti-kə-lee) *adverb*.

T

tabula rasa (TAB-yə-lə RAH-sə)
1. a blank tablet, especially the human mind at birth viewed as
   having no innate ideas.
2. anything existing undisturbed in its original state.
3. anything restored to its original state; a clean slate.

taciturn (TAS-i-TURN) *adjective*
1. habitually saying very little, uncommunicative.
2. reserved in speech.

Related words: **taciturnity** (TAS-i-TUR-ni-tee) *noun*, **taciturnly**
(TAS-i-TURN-lee) *adverb*.

talisman (TAL-is-mən) *noun, plural* **talismans**
an object supposed to work wonders or to bring its possessor good
luck.

Related words: **talismanic** (TAL-is-MAN-ik) and **talismanical**
both adjectives, **talismanically** *adverb*.

tarantism (TA-rən-TIZ-əm) *noun*
a mania characterized by an irresistible urge to dance, popularly
and incorrectly supposed to result from the bite of a tarantula.

Related word: **tarantist** (TA-rən-tist) *noun*.

tartuffe (tahr-TUUF) *noun*
a religious hypocrite, from the name of the central character in
Tartuffe, a 17th-century comedy by the French playwright
Molière.

Related word: **tartuffery** (tahr-TUUF-ə-ree) *noun*, **tartuffian** (tahr-TUUF-ee-ən) *adjective.*

tauromachy (taw-ROM-ə-kee) *noun*
the art of bullfighting.

Related word: **tauromachian** (TOR-ə-MAY-kee-ən) *adjective.*

tautology (taw-TOL-ə-jee) *noun, plural* **tautologies**
saying of the same thing twice over in different words, especially as a fault of style.

Related words: **tautological** (TAW-tə-LOJ-i-kəl), **tautologic**, and **tautologous** (taw-TOL-ə-gəs) *all adjectives*; **tautologically** and **tautologously** *both adverbs*; **tautologist** (taw-TOL-ə-jist) *noun.*

taxonomy (tak-SON-ə-mee) *noun*
the principles or science of classification, especially in biology.

Related words: **taxonomic** (TAK-sə-NOM-ik) and **taxonomical** *both adjectives*, **taxonomically** *adverb*, **taxonomist** (tak-SON-ə-mist) and **taxonomer** *both nouns.*

temerarious (TEM-ə-RAIR-ee-əs) *adjective*
reckless; rash.

Related words: **temerariously** *adjective*, **temerariousness** and **temerity** (tə-MER-i-tee) *both nouns.*

tendentious (ten-DEN-shəs) *adjective*, also given as **tendential** (ten-DEN-shəl)
1. of a speech or piece of writing etc., aimed at helping a cause.
2. exhibiting partiality.

Related words: **tendentially** *adverb*, **tendentiousness** *noun.*

tenebrific (TEN-ə-BRIF-ik) *adjective*
1. producing darkness.
2. obscuring.

tenuous (TEN-yoo-əs) *adjective*
1. having little substance or validity.
2. of slight significance.
3. very thin in form or consistency.

Related words: **tenuously** *adverb*, **tenuousness** and **tenuity** (tə-NOO-i-tee) *both nouns.*

tergiversate (TUR-ji-vər-SAYT) *verb*
1. turn one's back on one's party, cause, etc.
2. make evasive or conflicting statements; equivocate.

Related words: **tergiversation** (TUR-ji-vər-SAY-shən) **tergiversator** (TUR-ji-vər-SAY-tər), and **tergiversant** (TUR-ji-VUR-sənt) *all nouns*; **tergiversatory** (TUR-ji-VUR-sə-TOR-ee) *adjective.*

termagant (TUR-mə-gənt) *noun*
a shrewish bullying woman, a virago.

Related word: **termagant** *adjective*, meaning *shrewish*; *bullying*; **termagantly** *adverb.*

tessera (TES-ər-ə) *noun, plural* **tesserae** (TES-ə-ree)
a small cubical block of marble, glass, etc. used in mosaic.

thaumaturge (THAW-mə-TURJ) *noun*
1. a worker of miracles.
2. a wonder-worker.
3. a magician.

Related words: **thaumaturgic** (THAW-mə-TUR-jik) and **thaumaturgical** *both adjectives*, **thaumaturgy** (THAW-mə-TUR-jee) *noun.*

thrall (thrawl) *noun*
1. bondage, servitude.
2. captivity.
3. a slave of or to a person or thing.

Related word: **thralldom** (THRAWL-dəm) *noun.*

threnody (THREN-ə-dee) *noun, plural* **threnodies**
1. a song of lamentation, especially on a person's death; a dirge.
2. an elegy.

Related words: **threnodial** (thri-NOH-dee-əl) and **threnodic** (thri-NOD-ik) *both adjectives*, **threnodist** (THREN-ə-dist).

tinnitus (ti-NĪ-təs) *noun*
an abnormal condition of ringing or similar sensation in the ears.

titillate (TIT-əl-AYT) *verb*
1. excite or stimulate pleasantly.
2. tickle.

Do not confuse **titillate** with **titivate**, which see.

Related words: **titillatingly** (TIT-əl-AYT-ing-lee) *adverb*, **titillation** (TIT-əl-AY-shən) *noun*, **titillative** (TIT-əl-AY-tiv) *adjective*.

titivate (TIT-ə-VAYT) *verb*, also given as **tittivate**

1. spruce up.
2. adorn.
3. put the finishing touches to.

The temptation to treat **titivate** and **titillate** as synonyms is apparently so strong that some dictionaries list **titivate** as a synonym for the much older word **titillate**, when the only connection between the two verbs is their similarity of spelling. **Titillate** means *tickle*, and **titivate** means *spruce up*. In your own writing and speech, you should retain the distinction between the words, always keeping in mind that mistaken use of **titivate** will **titillate** educated readers and listeners.

Related words: **titivation** (TIT-ə-VAY-shən) and **titivator** (TIT-ə-VAY-tər) *both nouns*.

titubation (TICH-uu-BAY-shən) *noun*

1. unsteadiness, especially as caused by a nervous disease.
2. staggering.

Related word: **titubant** (TICH-uu-bənt) *adjective*.

tocsin (TOK-sin) *noun*

1. a signal of disaster.
2. a bell rung as an alarm.

tonsure (TON-shər) *noun*

1. the shaving of the top or all of the head of a person entering certain priesthoods or monastic orders.
2. the part of the head left bare after being shaved in this way.

Related word: **tonsure** *verb*, meaning *subject to tonsure*.

toothsome (TOOTH-səm) *adjective*

1. pleasant to eat; palatable.
2. attractive.
3. voluptuous.

Related words: **toothsomely** *adverb*, **toothsomeness** *noun*.

torpid (TOR-pid) *adjective*
sluggish and inactive; lethargic.

Related words: **torpidity** (tor-PID-i-tee), **torpidness** (TOR-pid-nis), and **torpor** (TOR-pər) *all nouns*; **torpidly** *adverb*.

tortuous (TOR-choo-əs) *adjective*
1. full of twists and turns.
2. of policy etc., not straightforward; devious; circuitous.

Do not confuse **tortuous** with **torturous**, which see.

Related words: **tortuosity** (TOR-choo-OS-i-tee) and **tortuousness** (TOR-choo-əs-nis) *both nouns,* **tortuously** *adverb.*

torturous (TOR-chər-əs) *adjective*
involving or causing torture or suffering; excruciating.

It is doubtful whether **tortuous** will ever recover from the ever-growing misuse of **torturous,** meaning *excruciating,* when a context calls for **tortuous,** meaning *full of twists and turns.* So painful is this misuse to anyone who values clear expression that not even permissive lexicographers are willing to bless this corruption. The message is clear: Be good to your editor and hold fast on the distinction between **tortuous** and **torturous.** No matter how **tortuous** your path through life, remember that *twists and turns* cannot break your bones, but **torturous** treatment by an alert and sadistic editor can be *excruciating.*

Related word: **torturously** *adverb.*

tractable (TRAK-tə-bəl) *adjective*
easy to manage or deal with; docile; manageable.

Related words: **tractability** (TRAK-tə-BIL-i-tee) and **tractableness** (TRAK-tə-bəl-nis) *both nouns,* **tractably** *adverb.*

traduce (trə-DOOS) *verb*
1. misrepresent.
2. slander; vilify.

Related words: **traducement** and **traducer** *both nouns,* **traducingly** *adverb.*

transcend (tran-SEND) *verb*
1. exceed in extent, degree, etc.; surpass.
2. excel.

3. go or be beyond the range of (human experience or belief or powers of description etc.).

Related words: **transcendence** (tran-SEN-dəns) and **transcendency** *both nouns,* **transcendingly** *adverb.*

translucent (trans-LOO-sənt) *adjective*
allowing light to pass through but not transparent.

Related words: **translucence** and **translucency** *both nouns,* **translucently** *adverb.*

transmute (trans-MYOOT) *verb*
cause to change in form or nature or substance; transform.

Related words: **transmutable** *adjective;* **transmutability** (trans-MYOOT-ə-BIL-i-tee), **transmutableness** (trans-MYOOT-ə-bəl-nis), and **transmuter** *all nouns;* **transmutably** *adverb.*

transpire (tran-SPĪR) *verb*
1. of information etc., be revealed, leak out, become known.
2. occur, take place, happen.
3. of plants, give off watery vapor from the surface of leaves etc.

Some writers do not use **transpire** in sense 2, *occur, happen,* given above. For example, they prefer to write "Something awful was about to happen" rather than "Something awful was about to transpire." Surely there is something to be said in favor of using the simpler word *happen* in such sentences, but there is nothing wrong with using **transpire** in this sense, as it has been for at least two centuries. And your readers will readily understand **transpire** used this way. So this is a case of you pays your money and you takes your choice.

Related words: **transpirable** (tran-SPĪR-ə-bəl) and **transpiratory** (tran-SPĪR-ə-TOR-ee) *both adjectives.*

trencherman (TREN-chər-mən) *noun, plural* **trenchermen**
1. a person who eats heartily.
2. a heavy eater.

triage (tree-AHZH) *noun*
1. the assignment of degrees of urgency to decide the order of treatment of people injured in a battle or disaster etc.
2. a selection system.

Related word: **triage** *adjective*, meaning *performing triage.*

troglodyte (TROG-lə-DĪT) *noun*
1. a cave dweller in prehistoric times; a caveman.
2. a person living in seclusion.
3. a hermit.

Related words: **troglodytic** (TROG-lə-DIT-ik) and **troglodytical** *both adjectives,* **troglodytism** (TROG-lə-dĭ-TIZ-əm) *noun.*

trollop (TROL-əp) *noun*
1. a promiscuous woman.
2. a prostitute; a slut.

Related word: **trollopy** *adjective.*

trope (trohp) *noun*
the use of a word in other than its literal sense; a figure of speech.

truculent (TRUK-yə-lənt) *adjective*
1. defiant and aggressive.
2. fierce, cruel.
3. pugnacious.

Related words: **truculence** and **truculency** *both nouns,* **truculently** *adverb.*

truism (TROO-iz-əm) *noun*
a self-evident, obvious truth; platitude.

Uninformed speakers and writers mistakenly use **truism** as a synonym for **truth**. As the definition above indicates, a **truism**, unlike **truth**, is seen as *self-evident, obvious.* Thus, **truism** is uncomplimentary, while **truth** surely is complimentary. So take care in keeping the two nouns distinct.

Related words: **truistic** (troo-IS-tik) and **truistical** *both adjectives.*

tsunami (tsuu-NAH-mee) *noun*
1. a series of huge sea waves caused by disturbance of the ocean floor or by seismic movement.
2. any comparably devastating force.

Related word: **tsunamic** (tsuu-NAH-mik) *adjective.*

turbid (TUR-bid) *adjective*
1. of liquids, muddy; thick; not clear.

2. unclear, obscure; confused; disordered.

Do not confuse **turbid** with **turgid**, which see.

Related words: **turbidity** (tur-BID-i-tee) and **turbidness** (TUR-bid-nis) *both nouns,* **turbidly** *adverb.*

turgid (TUR-jid) *adjective*

1. of language or style, pompous; overblown, grandiloquent; not flowing easily.
2. enlarged; swollen and not flexible.

In characterizing someone's literary style, do not confuse **turgid** in sense 1, *overblown, grandiloquent,* with **turbid** in sense 2, *unclear, obscure.* The spellings of these two adjectives invite confusion, and even knowledgable writers and editors fall into error. Again, **turgid** is somewhat more common than **turbid** and thus is likely to be used mistakenly when the sense of *unclear, obscure* is intended. To review the bidding: Remember that while **turgid** writing is properly thought of as *overblown* or *grandiloquent,* such writing may at the same time also be considered **turbid,** *unclear* or *obscure.* Yet, these two adjectives are clearly distinguishable from one another, and in your writing you must take care in using them, showing readers by your context which of the two derogatory meanings you intend. In fact, **turgid** writing is so often **turbid** that your task is not simple. Good luck.

Related words: **turgidity** (tur-JID-i-tee) and **turgidness** (TUR-jid-nis) *both nouns,* **turgidly** (TUR-jid-lee) *adverb.*

turpitude (TUR-pi-TOOD) *noun*

1. wickedness.
2. vileness; depravity.

tyrannicide (ti-RAN-ə-SĪD) *noun*

1. the act of killing a tyrant.
2. a person who commits tyrannicide.

Related word: **tyrannicidal** (ti-RAN-ə-SĪD-əl) *adjective.*

U

ubiquitous (yoo-BIK-wi-təs) *adjective*
being everywhere at the same time.

> Related words: **ubiquity** (yoo-BIK-wi-tee) and **ubiquitousness**
> *both nouns,* **ubiquitously** *adverb.*

ukase (yoo-KAYS) *noun*
1. an edict of the czarist Russian government.
2. an arbitrary order.

ultra vires (UL-trə VĪ-reez)
of a court or public official, beyond one's legal power or authority.

ululate (YOOL-yə-LAYT) *verb*
1. lament loudly and shrilly; wail.
2. howl; hoot.

> Related words: **ululant** (YOOL-yə-lənt) *adjective,* **ululation**
> (YOOL-yə-LAY-shən) *noun.*

umbrage (UM-brij) *noun*
a feeling of being offended.

> Related words: **umbrageous** (um-BRAY-jəs) *adjective,* **umbra-
> geously** (um-BRAY-jəs-lee) *adverb.*

unbosom (un-BUUZ-əm) *verb*
disclose (a secret, a feeling, etc.), especially disclose one's opinions
or thoughts in confidence.

> Related word: **unbosomer** (un-BUUZ-ə-mər) *noun.*

unconscionable (un-KON-shə-nə-bəl) *adjective*
1. unscrupulous.
2. contrary to what one's conscience feels is right.
3. outrageous.

Related words: **unconscionableness** *noun*, **unconscionably** *adverb*.

unction (UNGK-shən) *noun*
1. anointing with oil, especially as a religious rite.
2. pretended earnestness.
3. excessive politeness, especially in speaking.

unctuous (UNGK-choo-əs) *adjective*
1. having an oily manner.
2. smugly earnest or virtuous.

Related words: **unctuously** *adverb*, **unctuosity** (UNGK-choo-OS-i-tee) and **unctuousness** *both nouns*.

unequivocal (UN-i-KWIV-ə-kəl) *adjective*
clear and unmistakable; plain; unambiguous.

Related words: **unequivocally** *adverb*, **unequivocalness** *noun*.

unfledged (un-FLEJD) *adjective*
1. of a young bird, not yet able to fly; not fledged.
2. of a person, inexperienced.

uninterested (un-IN-tər-ə-stid) *adjective*
1. not interested.
2. showing or feeling no concern; indifferent.

See **disinterested** for guidance in the uses of **uninterested** and **disinterested**.

Related words: **uninterestedly** *adverb*, **uninterestedness** *noun*.

unjaundiced (un-JAWN-dist) *adjective*
free of distorted or prejudiced views.

unmitigated (un-MIT-i-GAY-tid) *adjective*
1. not modified.
2. unqualified; absolute.

Related word: **unmitigatedly** *adverb*.

unstudied (un-STUD-eed) *adjective*
1. natural in manner.
2. not affected; spontaneous.

untoward (un-TORD) *adjective*
1. inconvenient.
2. awkward.
3. refractory.
4. improper.

Related word: **untowardness** *noun*.

unwitting (un-WIT-ing) *adjective*
1. unaware.
2. unintentional.

Related words: **unwittingly** *adverb*, **unwittingness** *noun*.

urbane (ur-BAYN) *adjective*
having manners that are smooth and polite.

Related words: **urbanity** (ur-BAN-i-tee) and **urbaneness** (ur-BAYN-nis) *both nouns*, **urbanely** *adverb*.

ursine (UR-sīn) *adjective*
1. of or like a bear.
2. bearlike.

uxoricide (uk-SOR-ə-SĪD) *noun*
1. the act of killing one's wife.
2. a person who commits uxoricide.

Related word: **uxoricidal** (uk-SOR-ə-SĪD-əl) *adjective*.

uxorious (uk-SOR-ee-əs) *adjective*
1. foolishly fond of one's wife.
2. of an action, showing such fondness.

Related words: **uxoriously** *adverb*, **uxoriousness** *noun*.

V

vacuous (VAK-yoo-əs) *adjective*
1. empty-headed; inane.
2. expressionless.

Related words: **vacuity** (va-KYOO-i-tee) and **vacuousness** (VAK-yoo-əs-nis) *both nouns*, **vacuously** *adverb*.

vade mecum (VAY-dee MEE-kəm), *plural* **vade mecums**
1. a handbook or other small useful reference work a person carries with him.
2. a manual.

vagary (və-GAIR-ee *or* VAY-gə-ree) *noun, plural* **vagaries**
a capricious act, idea, or fluctuation.

vainglory (VAYN-GLOR-ee) *noun*
1. boastfulness.
2. extreme vanity.

Related words: **vainglorious** (vayn-GLOR-ee-əs) *adjective*, **vaingloriously** *adverb*, **vaingloriousness** *noun*.

valetudinarian (VAL-i-TOO-də-NAIR-ee-ən) *noun*, also given as **valetudinary** (VAL-i-TOO-də-NER-ee)
a person who pays excessive attention to preserving his health.

Related words: **valetudinary** *adjective*, **valetudinarianism** (VAL-i-TOO-də-NAIR-ee-ə-NIZ-əm) *noun*.

vapid (VAP-id) *adjective*
1. insipid; dull, uninteresting.

2. tedious.

Related words: **vapidity** (va-PID-i-tee) and **vapidness** (VAP-id-nis) *both nouns,* **vapidly** *adverb.*

variorum (VAIR-ee-OR-əm) *adjective*

with notes of various editors or commentators or with various versions of a text.

Related word: **variorum** *noun,* meaning *a variorum edition.*

venal (VEEN-əl) *adjective*

1. able to be bribed.
2. corruptible.
3. of conduct, influenced by bribery.

Do not confuse **venal** with **venial,** which see.

Related words: **venality** (vee-NAL-i-tee) *noun,* **venally** (VEEN-ə-lee) *adverb.*

venial (VEE-nee-əl) *adjective*

1. of a fault or sin, pardonable.
2. of misconduct, trifling, not serious.

Some writers and speakers confuse **venial,** meaning *trifling* or *pardonable,* with **venal,** meaning *corruptible.* Since these words are so far apart in meaning, this confusion seems to be caused solely by the closeness in spelling of the two words. Although this sin of confusion by writers and readers may be **venial,** or *pardonable,* most of us believe **venality,** or *corruptibility,* is never pardonable. Let us resolve, therefore, to do our best (1) to overcome even *trivial,* or **venial,** personal faults and (2) to avoid **venality,** or *corruptibility,* completely by eschewing any behavior that may be characterized as **venal.**

Related words: **veniality** (VEE-nee-AL-i-tee) and **venialness** (VEE-nee-əl-nis) *both nouns,* **venially** *adverb.*

veracious (və-RAY-shəs) *adjective*

1. truthful, honest.
2. true.

Related words: **veraciousness** and **veracity** (və-RAS-i-tee) *both nouns,* **veraciously** *adverb.*

verbiage (VUR-bee-ij) *noun*

an excessive number of words used to express an idea; verbosity.

verbicide (VUR-bə-sīD) *noun*
1. the destruction of the sense or value of a word.
2. one who willfully commits verbicide.

verbose (vər-BOHS) *adjective*
using more words than are needed; prolix; long-winded.

Related words: **verboseness** and **verbosity** (vər-BOS-i-tee) *both nouns*, **verbosely** *adverb*.

veridical (və-RID-i-kəl) *adjective*, also given as **veridic** (və-RID-ik)
1. truthful, veracious.
2. genuine.

Related words: **veridicality** (və-RID-i-KAL-i-tee) *noun*, **veridically** (və-RID-i-kə-lee) *adverb*.

verisimilitude (VER-ə-si-MIL-i-TOOD) *noun*
1. an appearance of being true.
2. likelihood, probability.

veritable (VER-i-tə-bəl) *adjective*
1. real.
2. rightly named.

Related words: **veritableness** *noun*, **veritably** *adverb*.

vernacular (vər-NAK-yə-lər) *noun*
1. the language or dialect of a country.
2. the everyday speech of ordinary people.

Related words: **vernacular** *adjective*, **vernacularly** *adverb*.

viable (VĪ-ə-bəl) *adjective*
1. practicable.
2. able to exist successfully.
3. of a fetus, sufficiently developed to be able to survive after birth.
4. of plants, able to live or grow.

Related words: **viability** (VĪ-ə-BIL-i-tee) *noun*, **viably** (VĪ-ə-blee) *adverb*.

vicarious (vī-KAR-ee-əs) *adjective*
of feelings or emotions, felt through sharing imaginatively in the feelings or emotions of another person.

Related words: **vicariously** *adverb*, **vicariousness** *noun*.

vicissitude (vi-SIS-i-TOOD) *noun*
a change of circumstances affecting one's life.

Related words: **vicissitudinary** (vi-SIS-i-TOO-də-NER-ee) and **vicissitudinous** (vi-SIS-i-TOO-də-nəs) *both adjectives.*

vincible (VIN-sə-bəl) *adjective*
that can be overcome or conquered.

Related words: **vincibility** (VIN-si-BIL-i-tee) and **vincibleness** (VIN-sə-bəl-nis) *both nouns.*

virago (vi-RAH-goh) *noun, plural* **viragoes** and **viragos**
a shrewish bullying woman; a scold; a termagant.

Related words: **viraginian** (VIR-ə-JIN-ee-ən) and **viraginous** (vi-RAJ-ə-nəs) *both adjectives,* **viraginity** (VIR-ə-JIN-i-tee) *noun.*

viscid (VIS-id) *adjective*
of liquid, thick and sticky; viscous.

Related words: **viscidity** (vi-SID-i-tee) and **viscidness** (VIS-id-nis) *both nouns,* **viscidly** *adverb.*

viscous (VIS-kəs) *adjective*
of liquid, not pouring easily; thick and sticky.

Related words: **viscosity** (vi-SKOS-i-tee) and **viscousness** *both nouns,* **viscously** *adverb.*

vitiate (VISH-ee-AYT) *verb*
1. impair the quality of; debase.
2. make ineffectual; weaken; invalidate.

Related words: **vitiable** (VISH-ee-ə-bəl) *adjective,* **vitiation** (VISH-ee-AY-shən) and **vitiator** (VISH-ee-AY-tər) *both nouns.*

vituperate (vī-TOO-pə-RAYT) *verb*
use abusive language; abuse; objurgate, revile.

Related words: **vituperation** (vī-TOO-pə-RAY-shən) and **vituperator** (vī-TOO-pər-AY-tər) *both nouns,* **vituperative** (vī-TOO-pər-ə-tiv) *adjective,* **vituperatively** *adverb.*

viva voce (VĪ-və VOH-see)
1. a university examination conducted orally.
2. the oral part of a university examination.

3. **viva-voce** (VĪ-və-VOH-see) *adjective*, of such an examination, conducted orally; spoken not written.

viviparous (vi-VIP-ər-əs) *adjective*
1. bringing forth young alive, not hatching by means of an egg.
2. producing bulbs or seeds that germinate while still attached to the parent plant.

Related words: **viviparism** (vi-VIP-ə-riz-əm), **viviparity** (VIV-ə-PAR-i-tee), **viviparousness** (vi-VIP-ər-əs-nis) *all nouns*; **viviparously** *adverb*.

vociferate (voh-SIF-ə-RAYT) *verb*
1. speak or say loudly or noisily.
2. shout.

Related words: **vociferant** (voh-SIF-ə-rənt) *adjective* and *noun*, **vociferation** (voh-SIF-ə-RAY-shən) *noun*, **vociferous** (voh-SIF-ə-rəs) *adjective*, **vociferousness** *noun*.

volatile (VOL-ə-til) *adjective*
1. of a person, lively.
2. of a person, changing quickly or easily from one mood or interest to another.
3. of a liquid, evaporating quickly.

Related words: **volatility** (VOL-ə-TIL-i-tee) and **volatileness** *both nouns*.

volition (voh-LISH-ən) *noun*
use of one's own will in choosing or making a decision etc.

Related words: **volitional** and **volitionary** (voh-LISH-ə-NER-ee) *both adjectives*, **volitionally** *adverb*.

volte-face (volt-FAHS) *noun, plural* **volte-face**
1. a complete change of one's attitude toward something.
2. a reversal of opinion; a turnabout.

voluble (VOL-yə-bəl) *adjective*
1. talking very much.
2. speaking or spoken with great fluency.

Related words: **volubility** (VOL-yə-BIL-i-tee) and **volubleness** (VOL-yə-bəl-nis) *both nouns*, **volubly** *adverb*.

voluptuary (və-LUP-choo-ER-ee) *noun, plural* **voluptuaries**
a person whose life is devoted to indulgence in luxury and sensual
pleasure; a sybarite.

voracious (vaw-RAY-shəs) *adjective*
1. greedy in eating; gluttonous.
2. ravenous.
3. insatiable.

Related words: **voracity** (vaw-RAS-i-tee) and **voraciousness** (vaw-
RAY-shəs-nis) *both nouns,* **voraciously** *adverb.*

vouchsafe (vowch-SAYF) *verb*
give or grant in a gracious or condescending manner.

Related word: **vouchsafement** (vowch-SAYF-mənt) *noun.*

voyeur (vwah-YUR) *noun*
a person who obtains sexual gratification from observing the sexual
actions or organs of others, especially secretively.

Related words: **voyeurism** (vwah-YUR-iz-əm) *noun,* **voyeuristic**
(VWAH-yə-RIS-tik) *adjective,* **voyeuristically** *adverb.*

vulpine (VUL-pīn) *adjective*
1. of or like a fox.
2. crafty, cunning.

W

wanton (WON-tən) *adjective*
1. lacking proper restraint or motives.
2. irresponsible.
   Related words: **wantonly** *adverb*, **wantonness** *noun*.

waspish (WOS-pish) *adjective*
1. sharp in retort.
2. ill-tempered, irascible.
   Related words: **waspishly** *adverb*, **waspishness** *noun*.

wastrel (WAY-strəl) *noun*
a wasteful person, especially one who wastes money; a spendthrift.

watershed (WAW-tər-SHED) *noun*
1. a turning point in the course of events.
2. a region drained by a river or river system.

weir (weer) *noun*
1. a small dam built across a river or stream so that water flows over it, serving to regulate the flow or to raise the level of water upstream.
2. a fence, as of brushwood or stakes with nets, built in a stream or channel to catch fish.

wheedle (HWEE-dəl) *verb*
1. coax.
2. persuade or obtain by coaxing.
   Related words: **wheedler** *noun*, **wheedlingly** *adverb*.

whet (hwet) *verb*
1. sharpen (a tool etc.) by rubbing against an abrasive stone etc.
2. stimulate; make keen or eager.

Related word: **whetter** *noun*.

willful (WIL-fəl) *adjective*
1. done with deliberate intention and not by accident.
2. self-willed; obstinate; headstrong.

Related words: **willfully** *adverb*, **willfulness** (WIL-fəl-nis) *noun*.

winnow (WIN-oh) *verb*
1. expose (grain) to a current of air by tossing or fanning (the grain) so that the loose dry outer part is blown away.
2. separate (chaff) in this way.
3. sift or separate (worthwhile material) from worthless or inferior material.

Related word: **winnower** *noun*.

wont (wawnt *or* wohnt) *noun*
1. a habit, practice, or custom.
2. *(adjective)* accustomed.

Related word: **wontless** *adjective*.

wreak (reek) *verb*
1. inflict.
2. cause.

Related word: **wreaker** *noun*.

wunderkind (VUUN-dər-KIND) *noun*, *plural* **wunderkinds**, *German plural* **Wunderkinder** (VUUN-dər-KIND-ər)
1. a child prodigy.
2. a person who achieves great success, especially in business, while relatively young.

XYZ

Xanthippe (zan-TIP-ee) *noun,* also given as **Xantippe**
a shrew, especially a shrewish wife; a scold.

yahoo (YAH-hoo) *noun, plural* **yahoos**
1. a coarse or brutish person; a lout.
2. a philistine; a yokel.

  Related word: **yahooism** (YAH-hoo-iz-əm) *noun.*

yarmulke (YAHR-məl-kə) *noun,* also given as **yarmelke** and **yarmulka,**
with the same pronunciation
  a skullcap worn by male Orthodox and Conservative Jews, especially in a synagogue and during prayers.

yclept (ee-KLEPT) *adjective*
called (by the name of).

yeasty (YEE-stee) *adjective*
1. tasting of yeast.
2. frothy, foamy.
3. light and superficial; frivolous.
4. very enthusiastic or joyful.

  Related words: **yeastily** (YEE-sti-lee) *adverb,* **yeastiness** *noun.*

zealot (ZEL-ət) *noun*
1. a zealous person.
2. a fanatic.

  Related word: **zealotry** (ZEL-ə-tree) *noun.*

zealous (ZEL-əs) *adjective*

    1. full of fervor for a person, a cause, or an object.

    2. devoted, diligent.

    Related words: **zealously** *adverb*, **zealousness** *noun*.

Zeitgeist (TSĪT-GĪST) *noun*, German

    the trend of thought and feeling in a period of time.

zucchetto (zoo-KET-oh) *noun*, *plural* **zucchettos** or **zucchetti** (zoo-KET-ee)

    in the Roman Catholic Church, an ecclesiastical skullcap, black for a priest, violet for a bishop, red for a cardinal, and white for the pope.